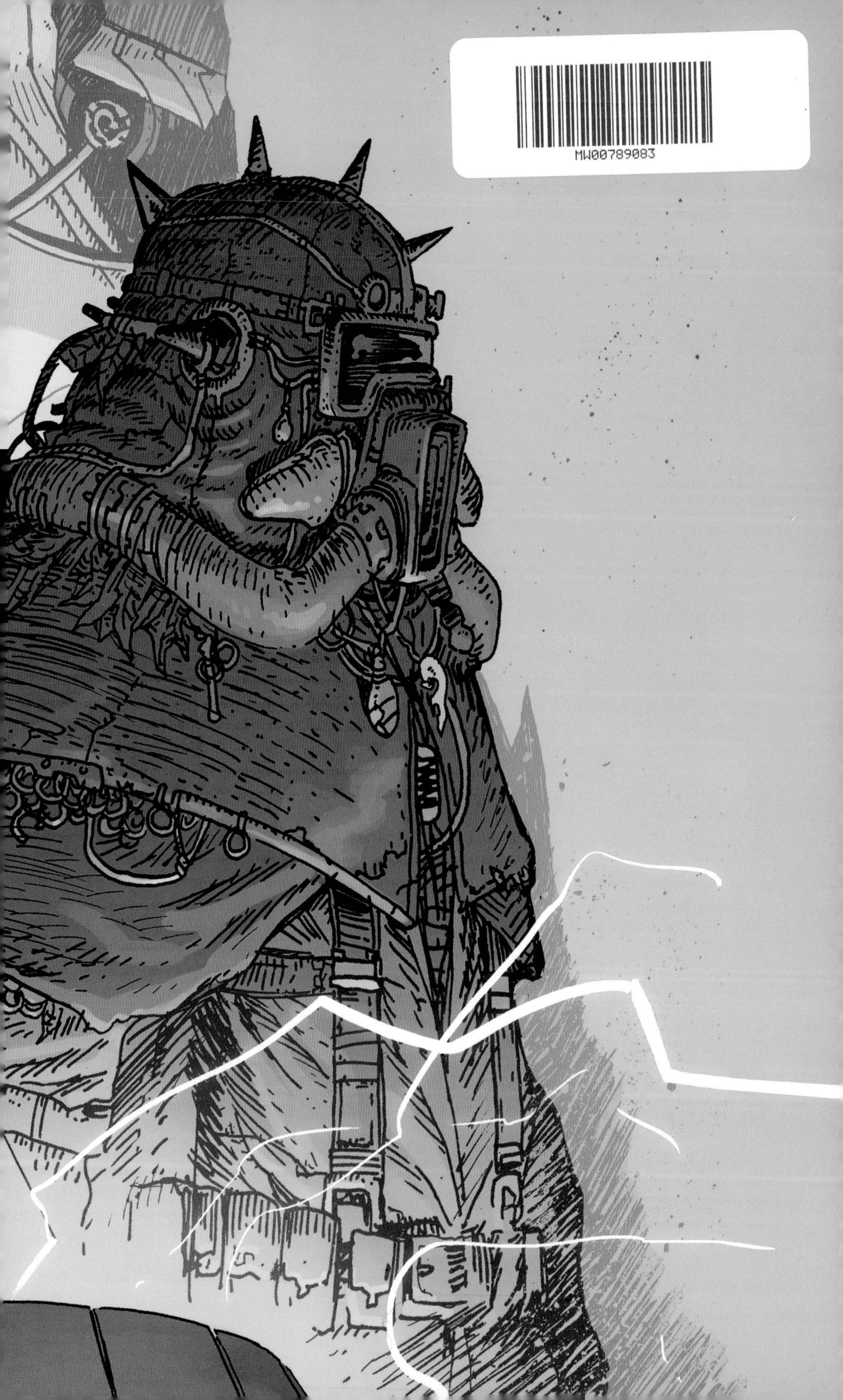

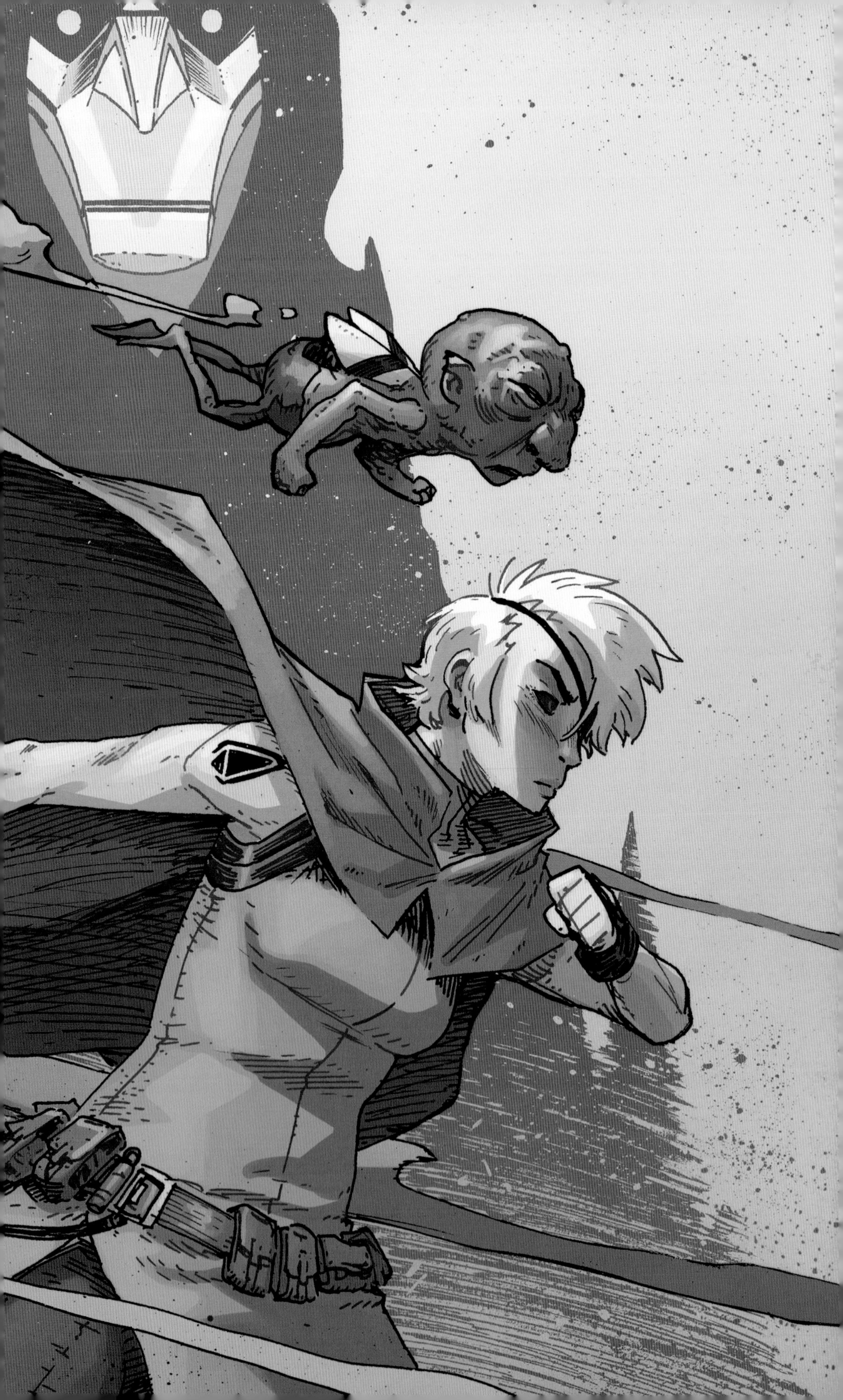

THE SPIRE ™

CREATED BY **SIMON SPURRIER & JEFF STOKELY**

WRITTEN BY
SIMON SPURRIER

ILLUSTRATED BY
JEFF STOKELY

COLORED BY
ANDRÉ MAY

LETTERED BY
STEVE WANDS

COVER BY
JEFF STOKELY

DESIGNER
KELSEY DIETERICH

ASSOCIATE EDITOR
CAMERON CHITTOCK

EDITOR
ERIC HARBURN

CHAPTER
ONE

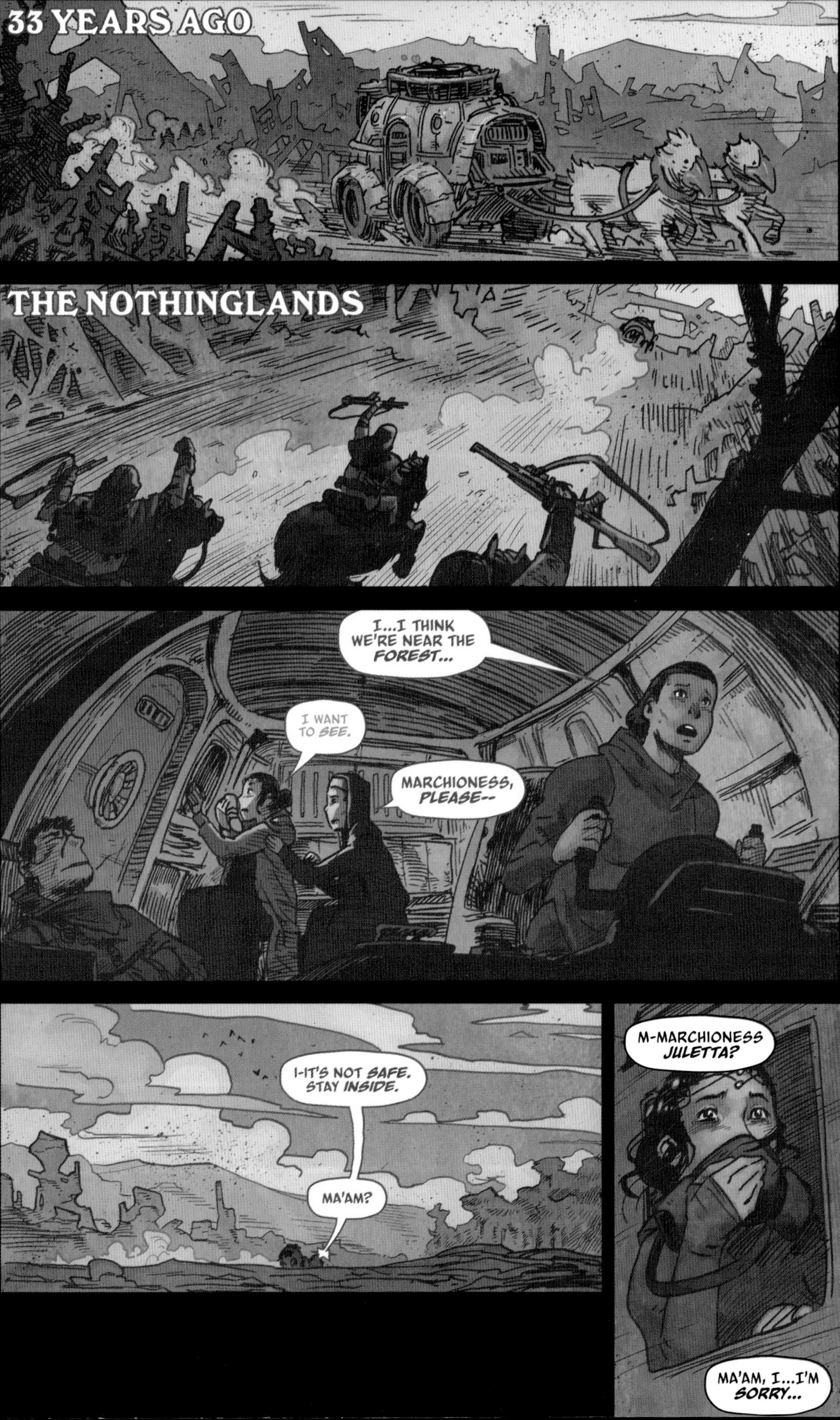
33 YEARS AGO
THE NOTHINGLANDS
I...I THINK WE'RE NEAR THE FOREST...
I WANT TO SEE.
MARCHIONESS, PLEASE--
I-IT'S NOT SAFE. STAY INSIDE.
MA'AM?
M-MARCHIONESS JULETTA?
MA'AM, I...I'M SORRY...

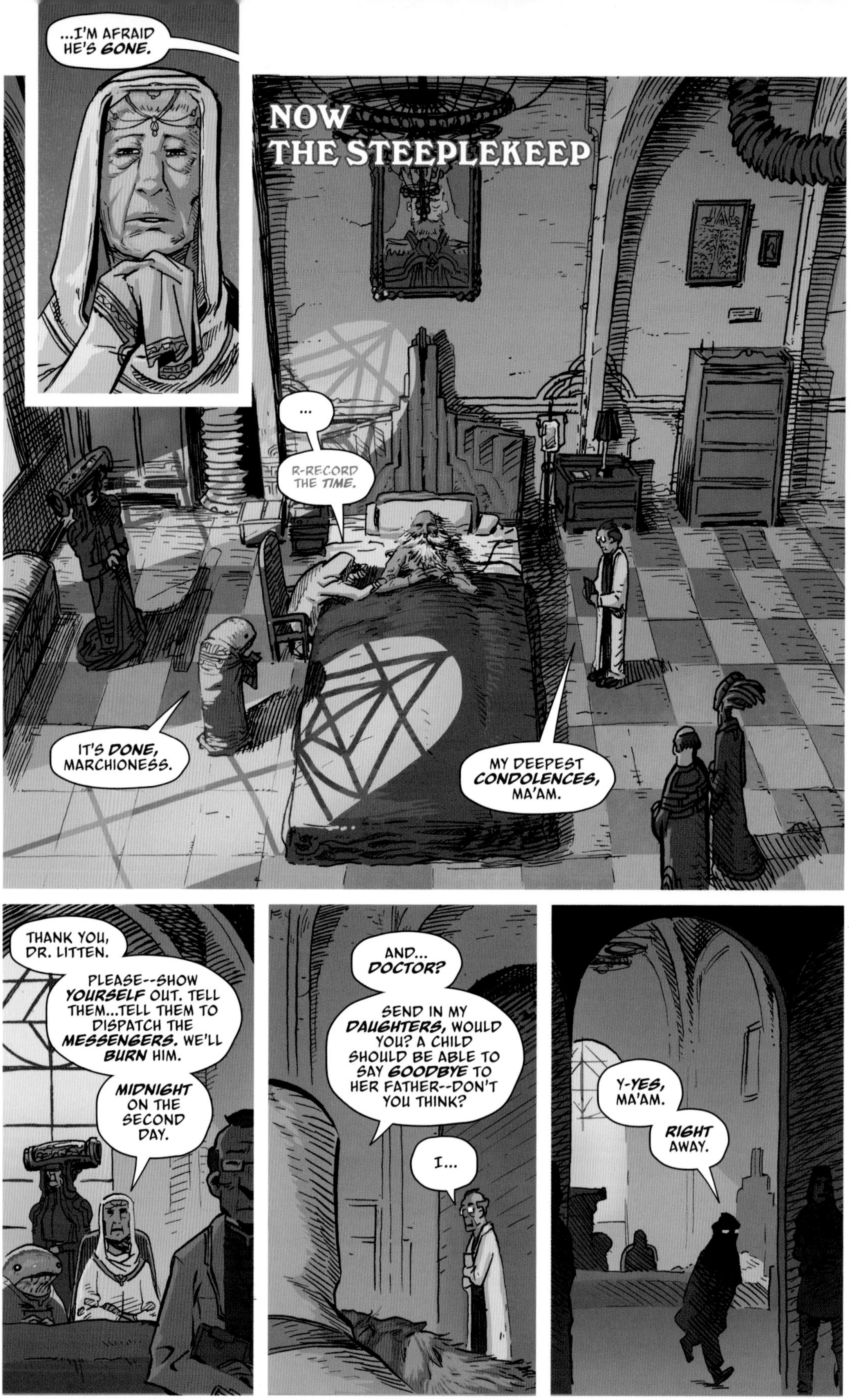
...I'M AFRAID HE'S GONE.
NOW THE STEEPLEKEEP
...
R-RECORD THE TIME.
IT'S DONE, MARCHIONESS.
MY DEEPEST CONDOLENCES, MA'AM.
THANK YOU, DR. LITTEN.
PLEASE--SHOW YOURSELF OUT. TELL THEM...TELL THEM TO DISPATCH THE MESSENGERS. WE'LL BURN HIM.
MIDNIGHT ON THE SECOND DAY.
AND... DOCTOR?
SEND IN MY DAUGHTERS, WOULD YOU? A CHILD SHOULD BE ABLE TO SAY GOODBYE TO HER FATHER--DON'T YOU THINK?
I...
Y-YES, MA'AM.
RIGHT AWAY.

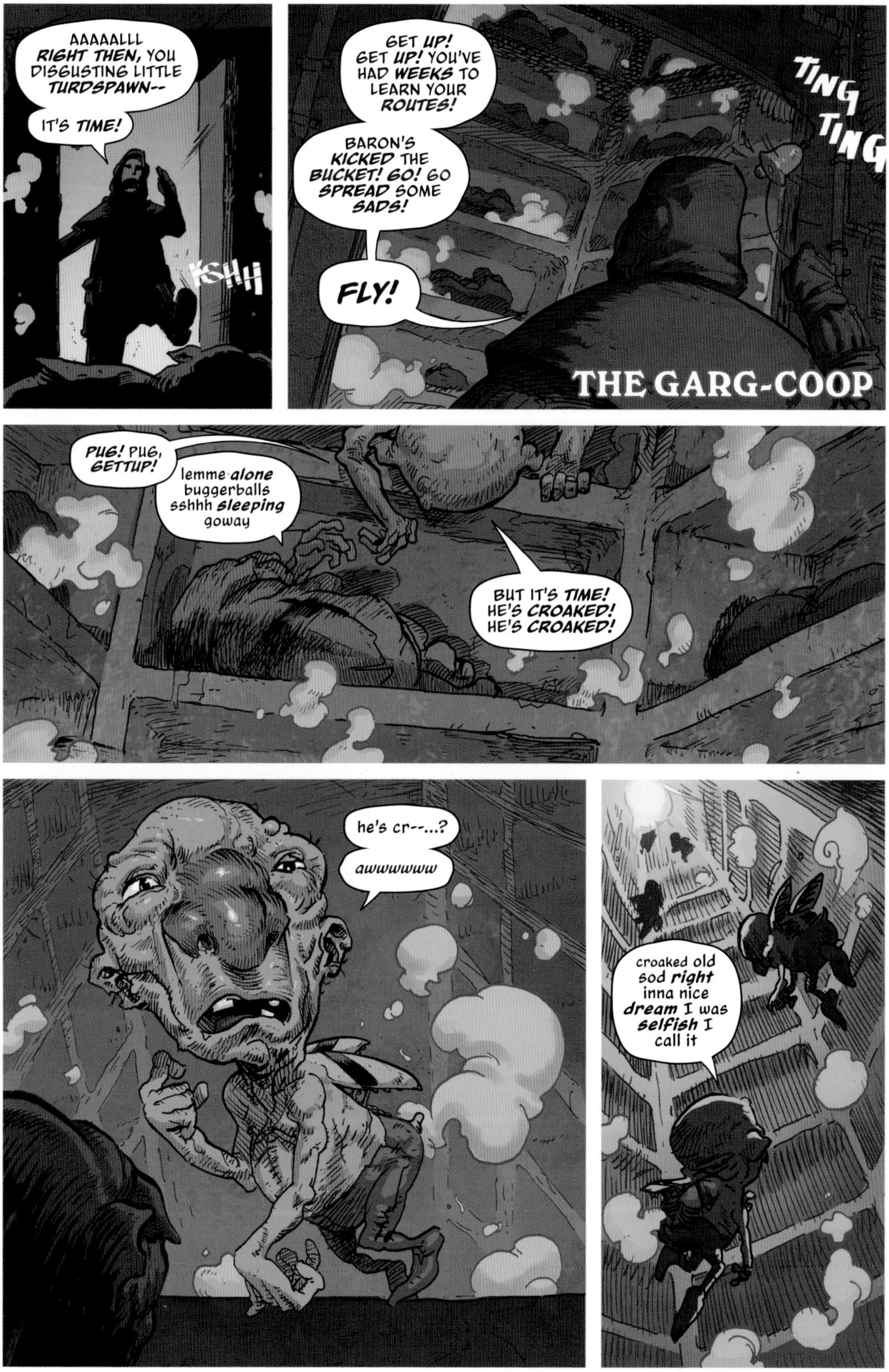
AAAAALLL RIGHT THEN, YOU DISGUSTING LITTLE TURDSPAWN--
IT'S TIME!
KSHH
GET UP! GET UP! YOU'VE HAD WEEKS TO LEARN YOUR ROUTES!
BARON'S KICKED THE BUCKET! GO! GO SPREAD SOME SADS!
FLY!
TING TING
THE GARG-COOP
PUG! PUG, GETTUP!
lemme alone buggerballs sshhh sleeping goway
BUT IT'S TIME! HE'S CROAKED! HE'S CROAKED!
he's cr--...?
awwwwww
croaked old sod right inna nice dream I was selfish I call it

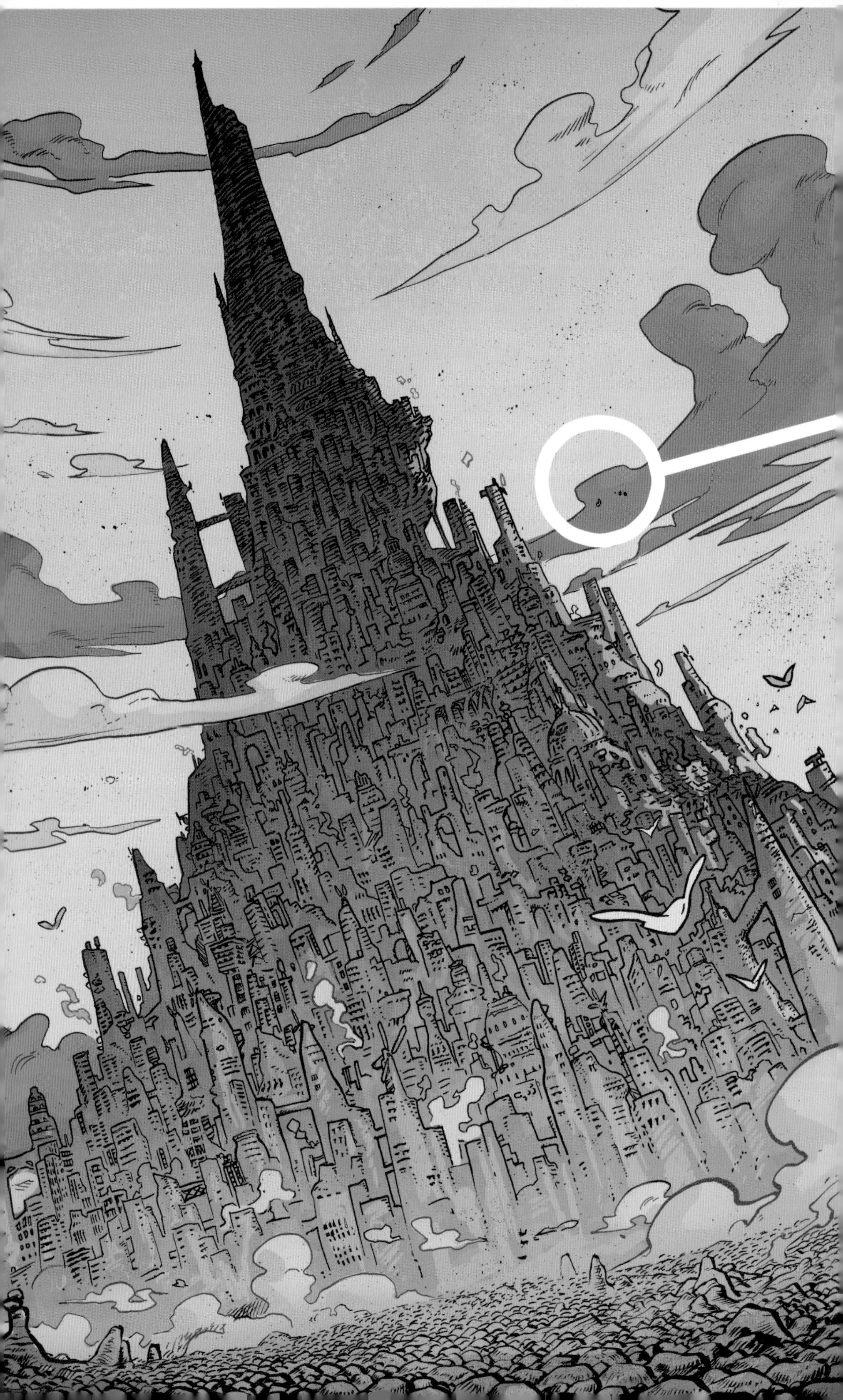

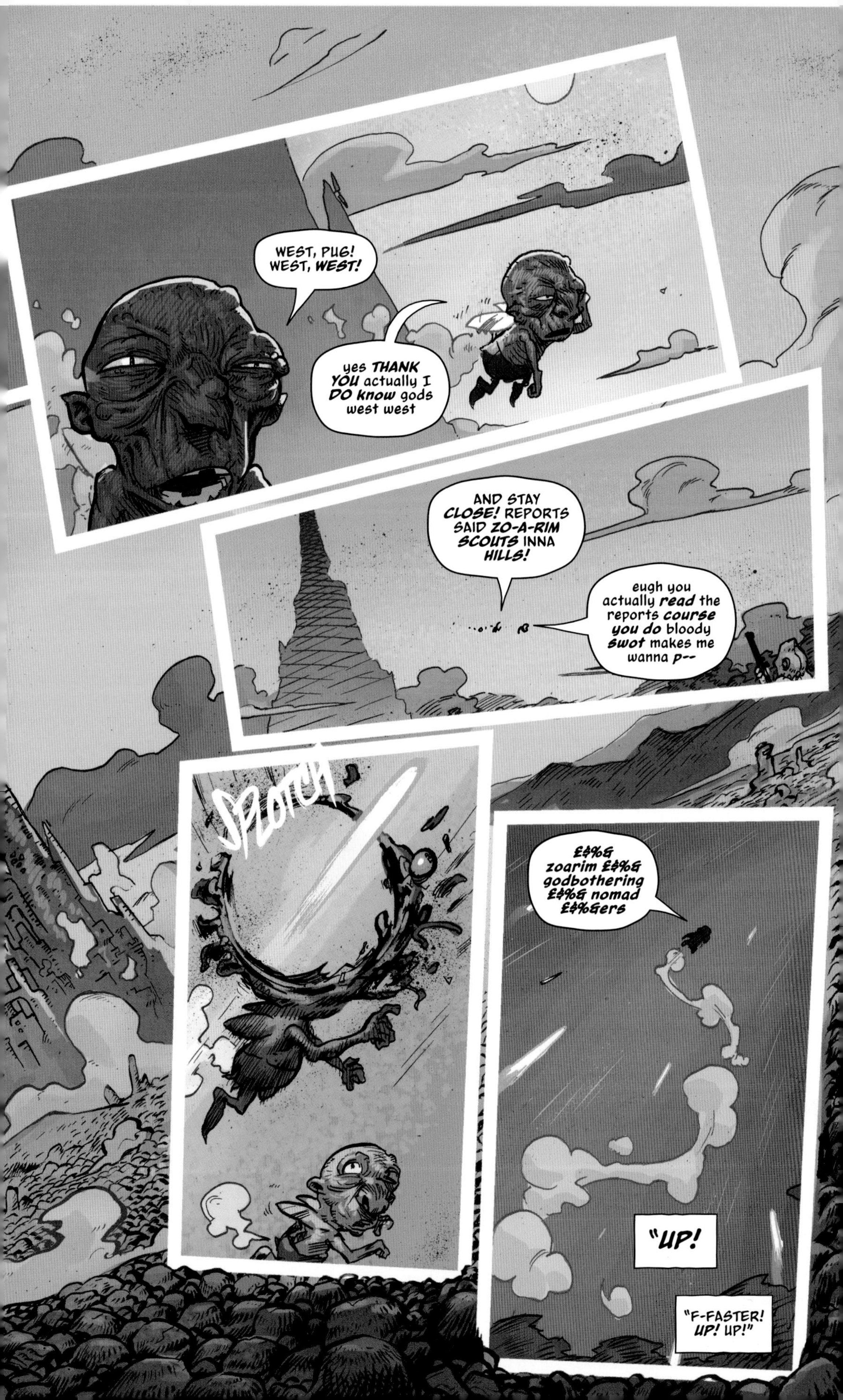

WEST, PUG! WEST, WEST!
yes THANK YOU actually I DO know gods west west
AND STAY CLOSE! REPORTS SAID ZO-A-RIM SCOUTS INNA HILLS!
eugh you actually read the reports course you do bloody swot makes me wanna p--
SPLOTCH
£$%& zoarim £$%& godbothering £$%& nomad £$%&ers
"UP!
"F-FASTER! UP! UP!"

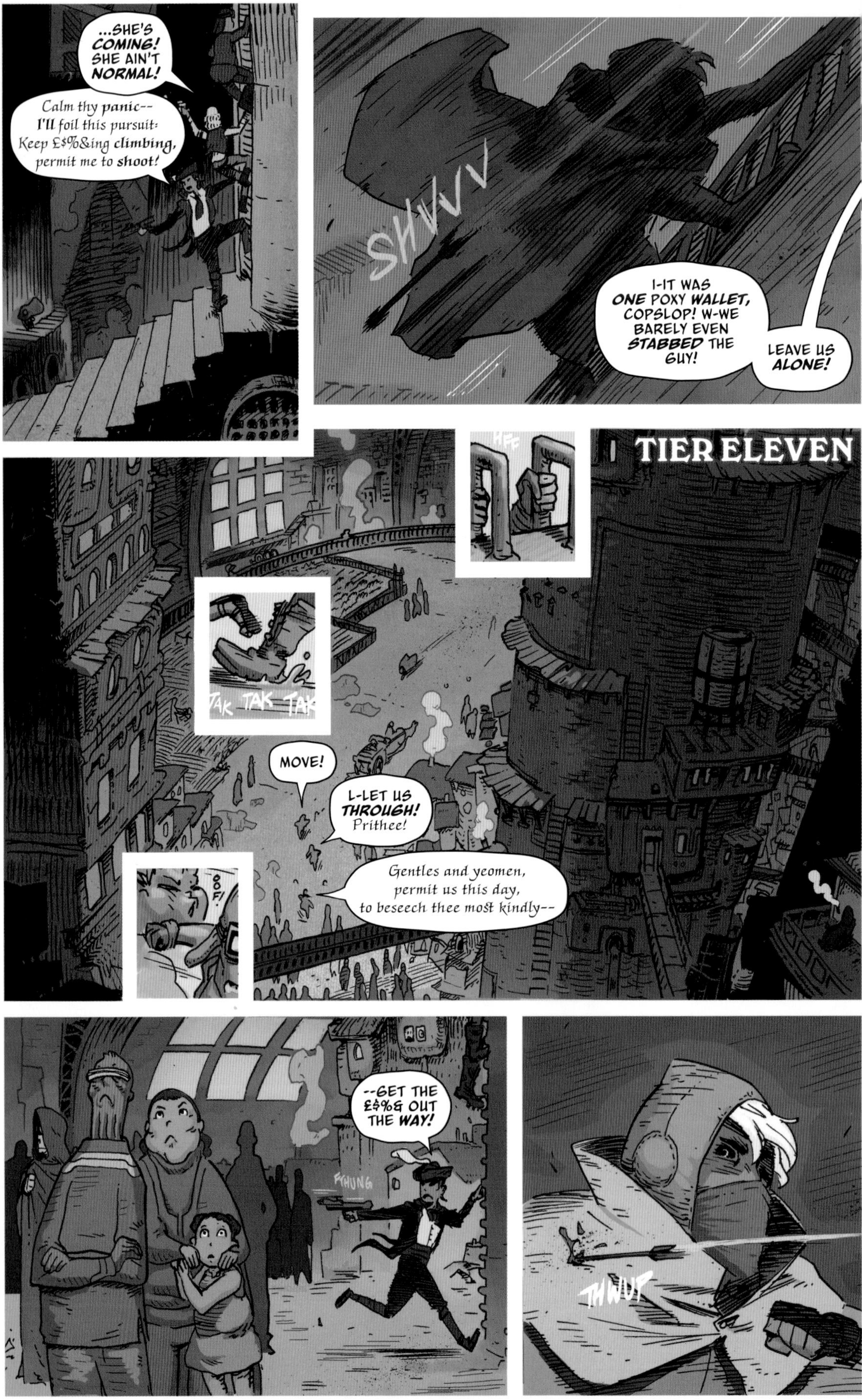
...SHE'S COMING! SHE AIN'T NORMAL!
Calm thy panic-- I'll foil this pursuit: Keep £$%&ing climbing, permit me to shoot!
SHVVV
I-IT WAS ONE POXY WALLET, COPSLOP! W-WE BARELY EVEN STABBED THE GUY!
LEAVE US ALONE!
TIER ELEVEN
TAK TAK TAK
MOVE!
L-LET US THROUGH! Prithee!
Gentles and yeomen, permit us this day, to beseech thee most kindly--
--GET THE £$%& OUT THE WAY!
THWUP

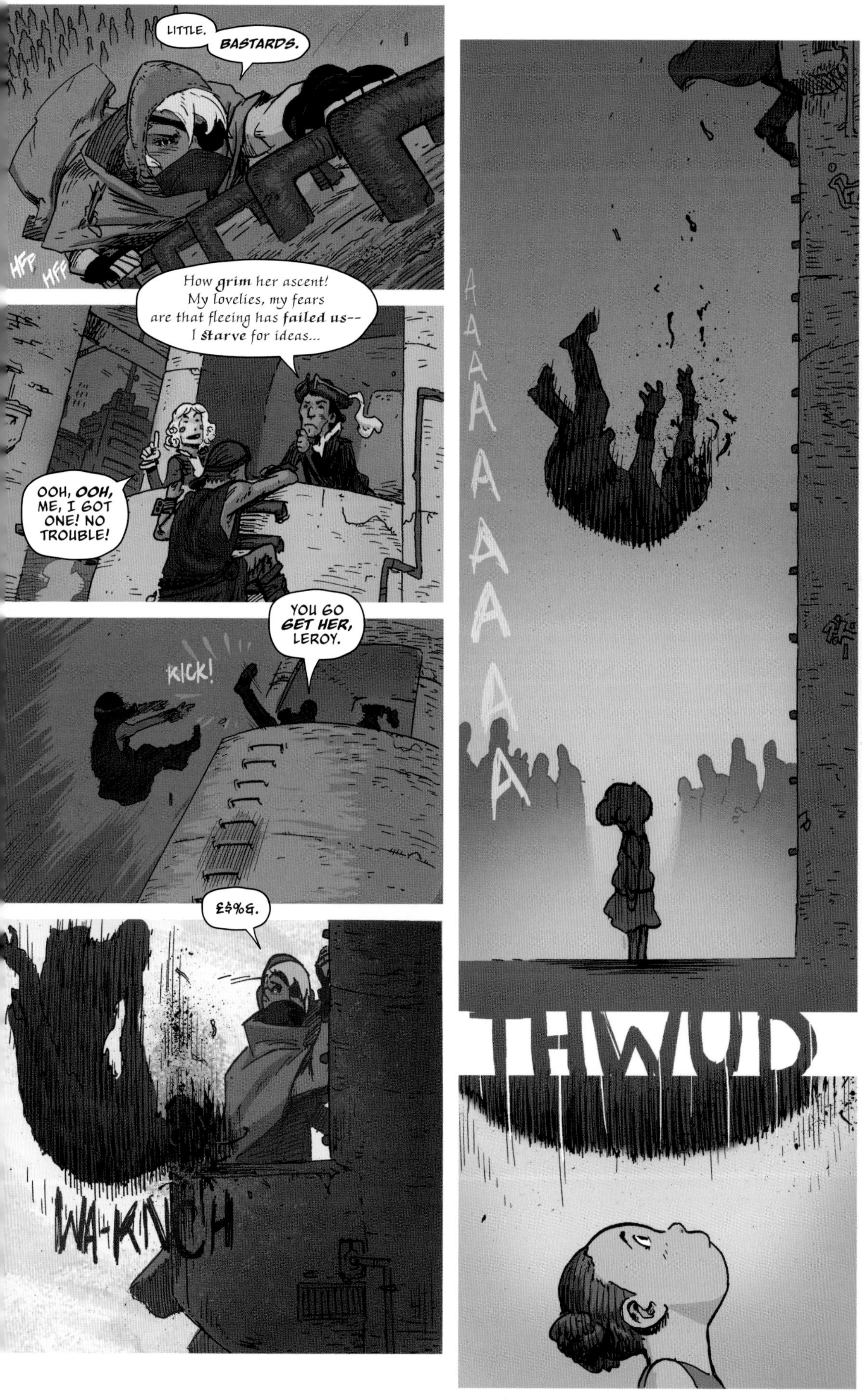
LITTLE. BASTARDS.
HFF HFF
How grim her ascent! My lovelies, my fears are that fleeing has failed us-- I starve for ideas...
OOH, OOH, ME, I GOT ONE! NO TROUBLE!
YOU GO GET HER, LEROY.
KICK!
£$%&.
WA-KNCH
AAAAAAAAA
THWUD

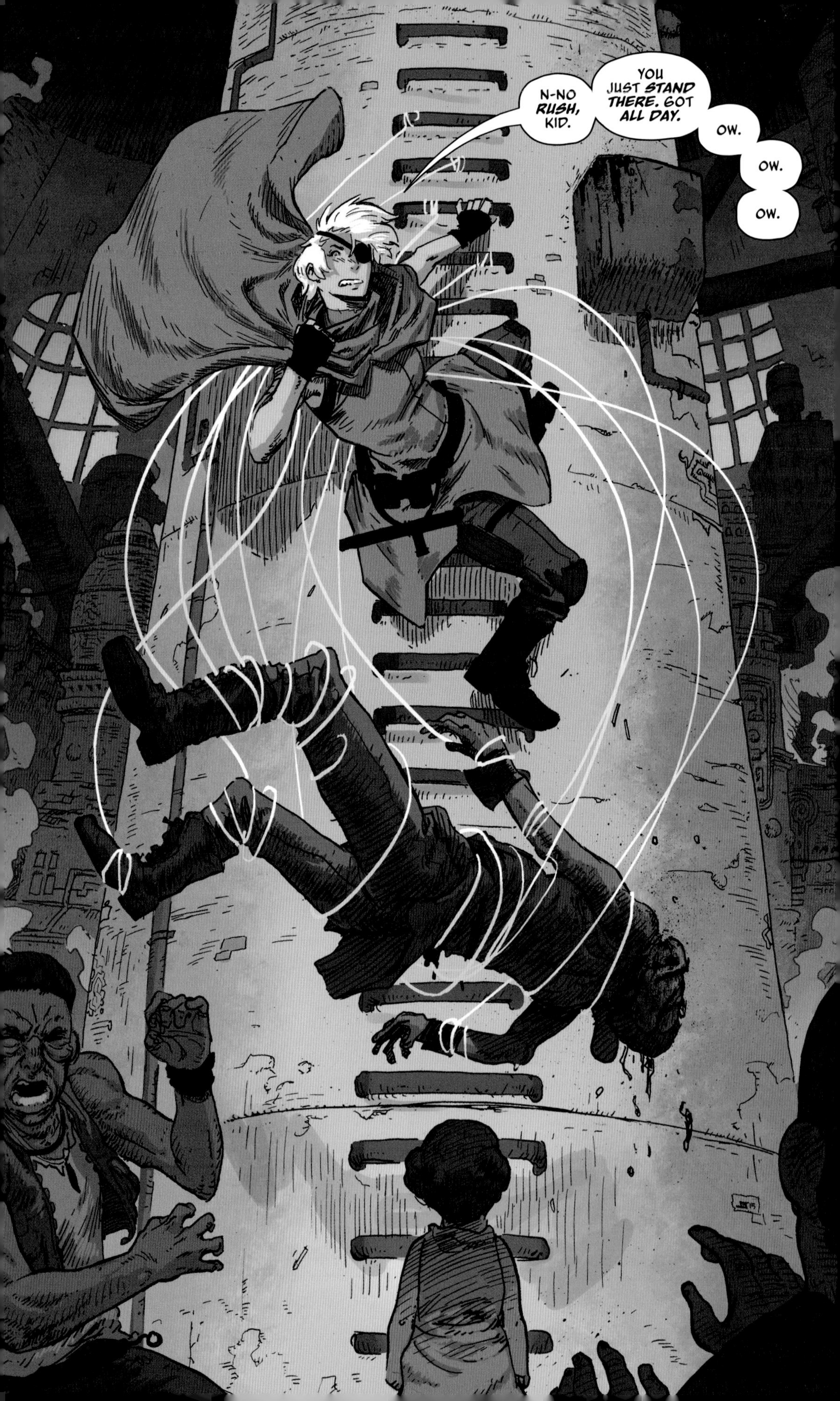
N-NO RUSH, KID.
YOU JUST STAND THERE. GOT ALL DAY.
OW.
OW.
OW.

OBSERVANT.

COMMANDER SHÄ, CITY WATCH. CLEAR THE **AREA**.

I ONLY GOT **TWO**, SEE?

J-J-J-JESMIN. C...COME **AWAY**...

YOU GOT LOTS'A **LEGS**, LADY.

SUPER OBSERVANT. IT'S **DIFFERENT**, KID--FORGET ABOUT IT. AND **SERIOUSLY**, SOD OFF.

DIFFERENT LIKE **MISTER YORBUL** THE SCUTTLEJACK? HIS **BUM** LEAKS.

...**SORT** OF LIKE THAT, YEAH.

MOM SAYS HE'S **GROSS**. BOMMY-NAY-SHUN, **SHE** SAYS.

AAAAAHAHAAAA TH-THAT'S NOT WHAT I SAID AT ALL, DARLING. **KIDS**, HUH? YOU KNOW WHAT THEY'RE L--

NOPE.

WHAT'S WITH THE BIG **GET-TOGETHER**, ANYWAY? WHY'S EVERYONE **CROWDED** 'ROUND UP H...

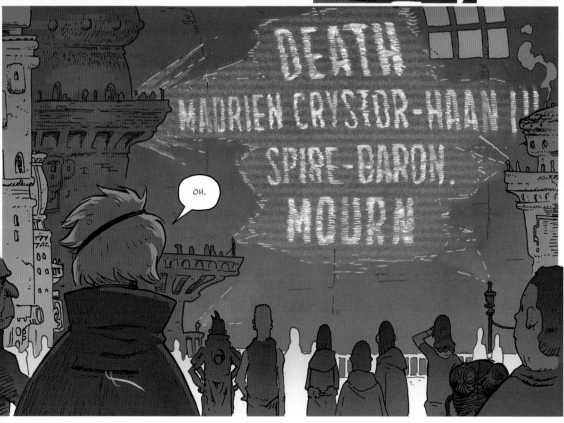

OH.

DEATH
MADRIEN CRYSTOR-HAAN III
SPIRE-BARON.
MOURN

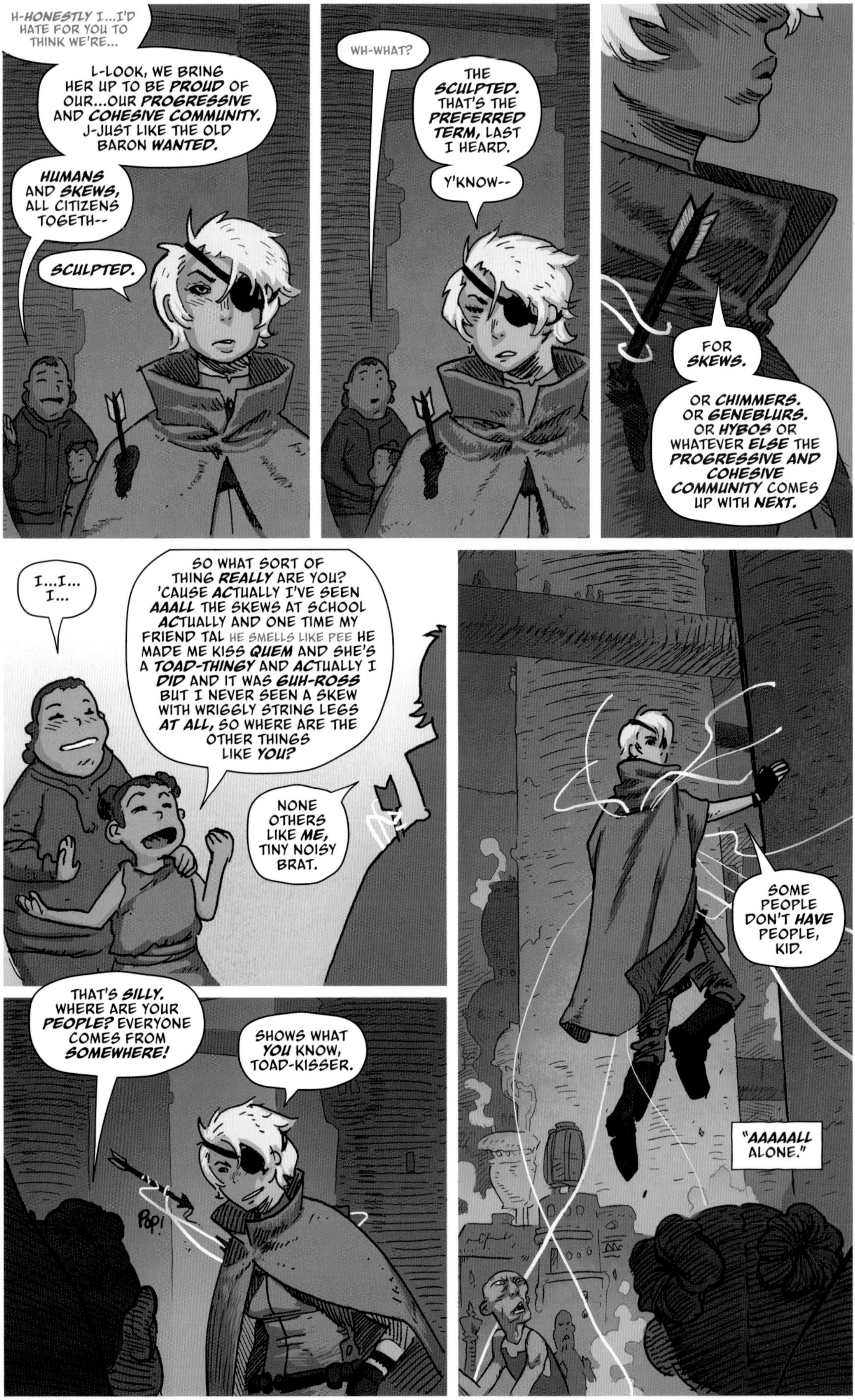
H-HONESTLY I...I'D HATE FOR YOU TO THINK WE'RE...
L-LOOK, WE BRING HER UP TO BE PROUD OF OUR...OUR PROGRESSIVE AND COHESIVE COMMUNITY. J-JUST LIKE THE OLD BARON WANTED.
HUMANS AND SKEWS, ALL CITIZENS TOGETH--
SCULPTED.
WH-WHAT?
THE SCULPTED. THAT'S THE PREFERRED TERM, LAST I HEARD.
Y'KNOW--
FOR SKEWS.
OR CHIMMERS. OR GENEBLURS. OR HYBOS OR WHATEVER ELSE THE PROGRESSIVE AND COHESIVE COMMUNITY COMES UP WITH NEXT.
I...I... I...
SO WHAT SORT OF THING REALLY ARE YOU? 'CAUSE ACTUALLY I'VE SEEN AAALL THE SKEWS AT SCHOOL ACTUALLY AND ONE TIME MY FRIEND TAL HE SMELLS LIKE PEE HE MADE ME KISS QUEM AND SHE'S A TOAD-THINGY AND ACTUALLY I DID AND IT WAS GUH-ROSS BUT I NEVER SEEN A SKEW WITH WRIGGLY STRING LEGS AT ALL, SO WHERE ARE THE OTHER THINGS LIKE YOU?
NONE OTHERS LIKE ME, TINY NOISY BRAT.
THAT'S SILLY. WHERE ARE YOUR PEOPLE? EVERYONE COMES FROM SOMEWHERE!
SHOWS WHAT YOU KNOW, TOAD-KISSER.
POP!
SOME PEOPLE DON'T HAVE PEOPLE, KID.
"AAAAALL ALONE."

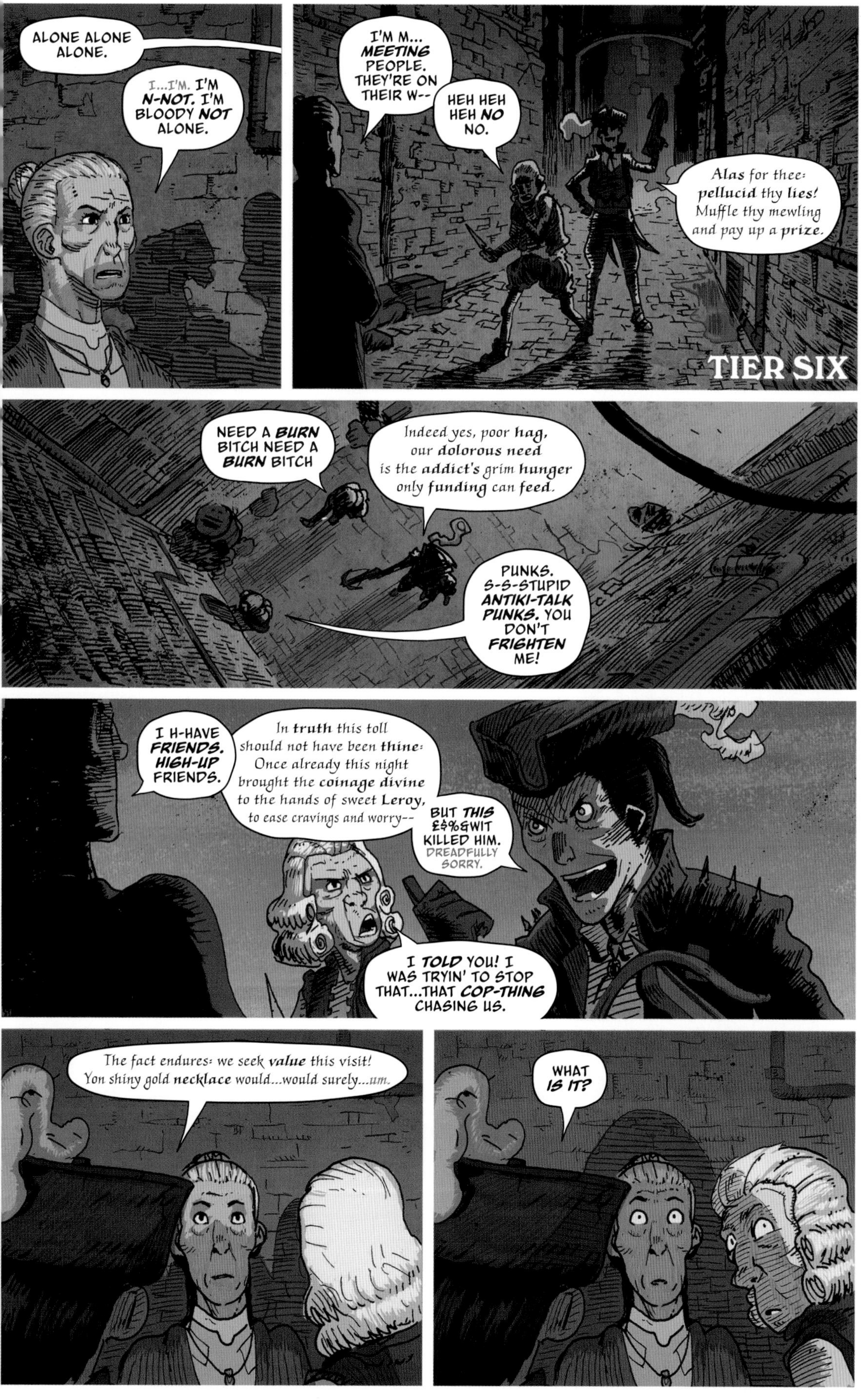
ALONE ALONE ALONE.
I...I'M. I'M N-NOT. I'M BLOODY NOT ALONE.
I'M M... MEETING PEOPLE. THEY'RE ON THEIR W--
HEH HEH HEH NO NO.
Alas for thee: pellucid thy lies! Muffle thy mewling and pay up a prize.
TIER SIX
NEED A BURN BITCH NEED A BURN BITCH
Indeed yes, poor hag, our dolorous need is the addict's grim hunger only funding can feed.
PUNKS. S-S-STUPID ANTIKI-TALK PUNKS. YOU DON'T FRIGHTEN ME!
I H-HAVE FRIENDS. HIGH-UP FRIENDS.
In truth this toll should not have been thine: Once already this night brought the coinage divine to the hands of sweet Leroy, to ease cravings and worry--
BUT THIS £$%&WIT KILLED HIM. DREADFULLY SORRY.
I TOLD YOU! I WAS TRYIN' TO STOP THAT...THAT COP-THING CHASING US.
The fact endures: we seek value this visit! Yon shiny gold necklace would...would surely...um.
WHAT IS IT?

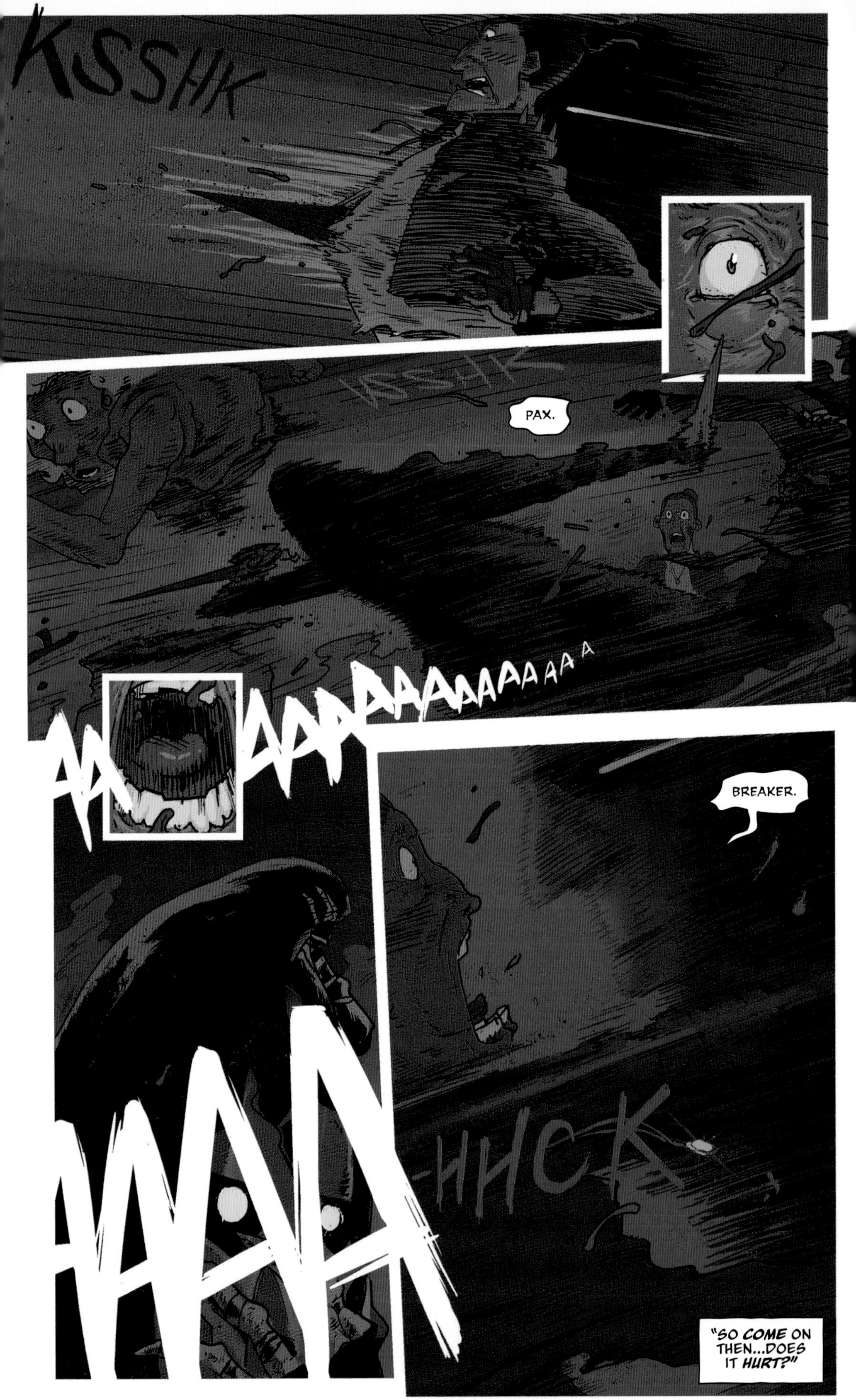
KSSHK
KSSHK
PAX.
AAAAAAAAAAAAAAA
BREAKER.
HHCK
"SO COME ON THEN...DOES IT HURT?"

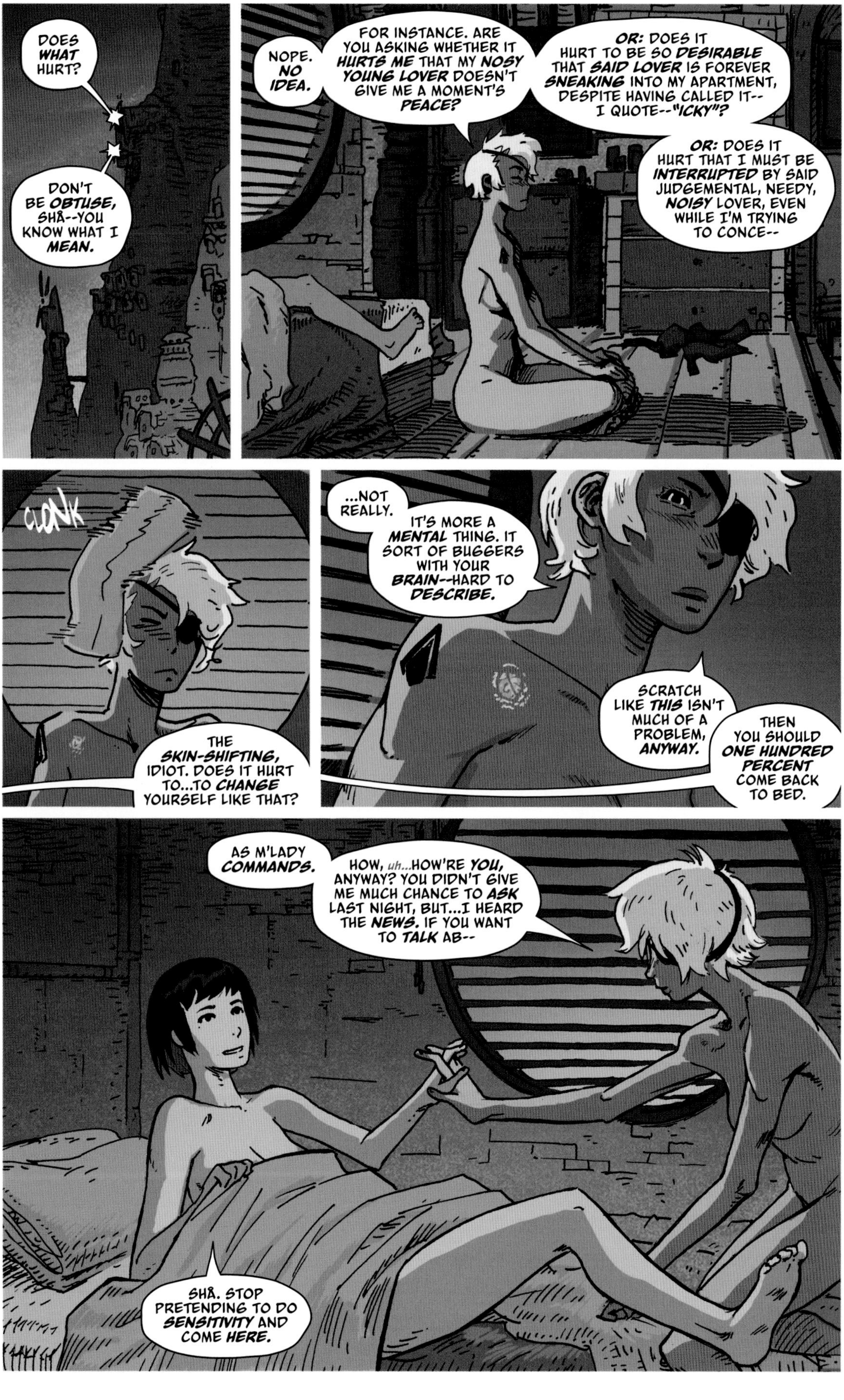

DOES WHAT HURT?
DON'T BE OBTUSE, SHÅ--YOU KNOW WHAT I MEAN.
NOPE. NO IDEA.
FOR INSTANCE. ARE YOU ASKING WHETHER IT HURTS ME THAT MY NOSY YOUNG LOVER DOESN'T GIVE ME A MOMENT'S PEACE?
OR: DOES IT HURT TO BE SO DESIRABLE THAT SAID LOVER IS FOREVER SNEAKING INTO MY APARTMENT, DESPITE HAVING CALLED IT-- I QUOTE--"ICKY"?
OR: DOES IT HURT THAT I MUST BE INTERRUPTED BY SAID JUDGEMENTAL, NEEDY, NOISY LOVER, EVEN WHILE I'M TRYING TO CONCE--
CLONK
THE SKIN-SHIFTING, IDIOT. DOES IT HURT TO...TO CHANGE YOURSELF LIKE THAT?
...NOT REALLY.
IT'S MORE A MENTAL THING. IT SORT OF BUGGERS WITH YOUR BRAIN--HARD TO DESCRIBE.
SCRATCH LIKE THIS ISN'T MUCH OF A PROBLEM, ANYWAY.
THEN YOU SHOULD ONE HUNDRED PERCENT COME BACK TO BED.
AS M'LADY COMMANDS.
HOW, uh...HOW'RE YOU, ANYWAY? YOU DIDN'T GIVE ME MUCH CHANCE TO ASK LAST NIGHT, BUT...I HEARD THE NEWS. IF YOU WANT TO TALK AB--
SHÅ. STOP PRETENDING TO DO SENSITIVITY AND COME HERE.

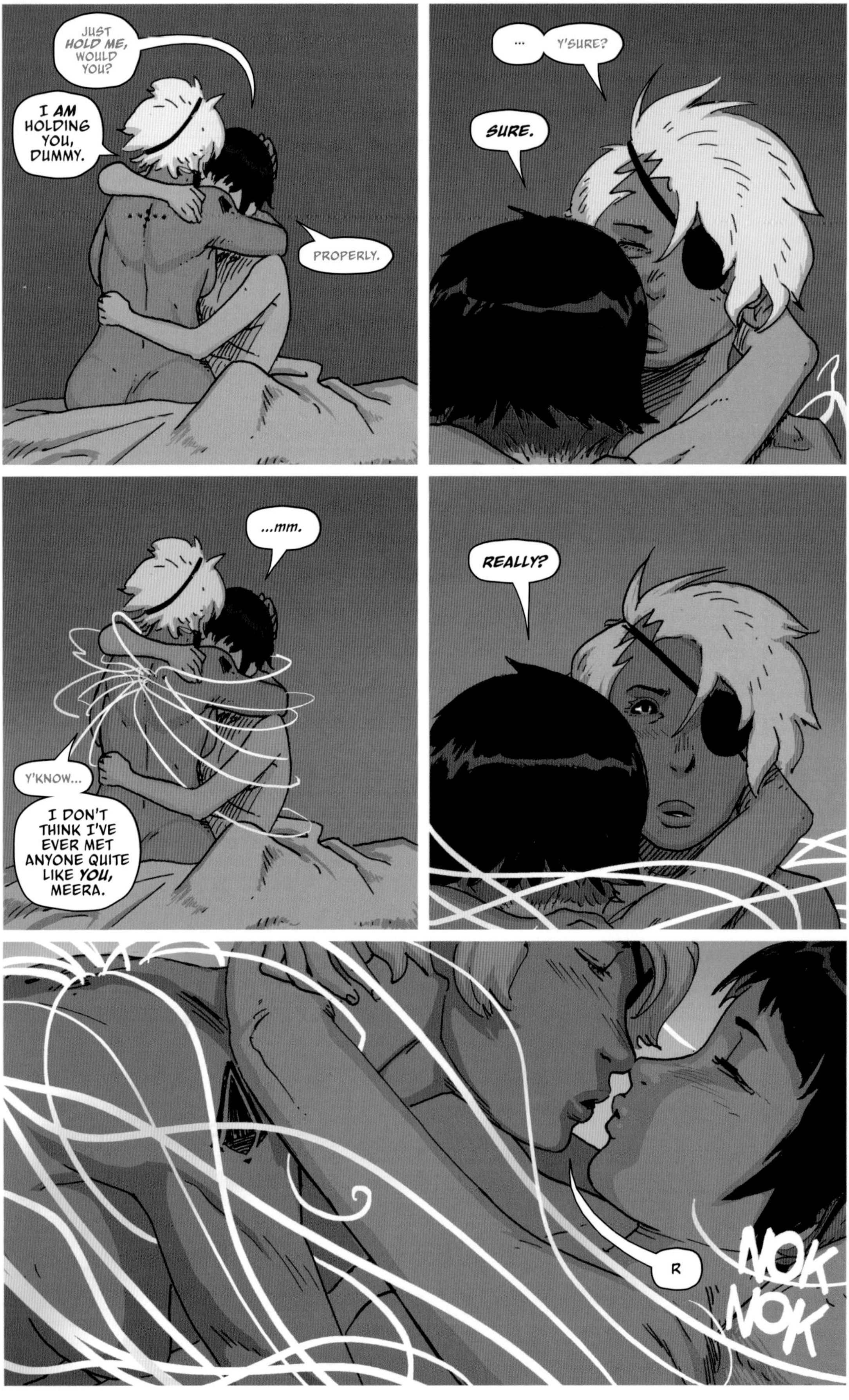
JUST HOLD ME, WOULD YOU?
I AM HOLDING YOU, DUMMY.
PROPERLY.
...
Y'SURE?
SURE.
...mm.
Y'KNOW...
I DON'T THINK I'VE EVER MET ANYONE QUITE LIKE YOU, MEERA.
REALLY?
R
NOK NOK

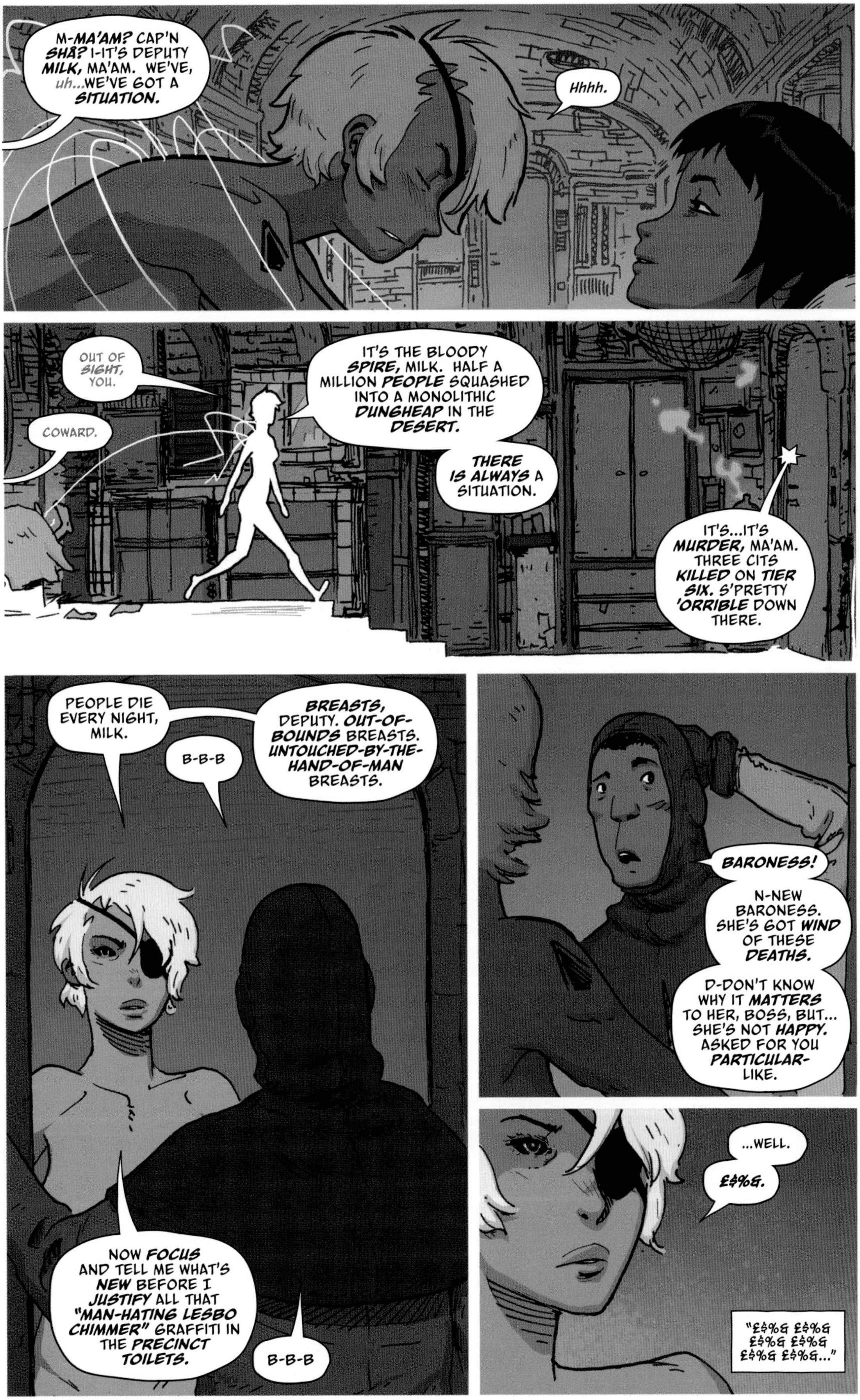
M-MA'AM? CAP'N SHĀ? I-IT'S DEPUTY MILK, MA'AM. WE'VE, uh...WE'VE GOT A SITUATION.
Hhhh.
OUT OF SIGHT, YOU.
COWARD.
IT'S THE BLOODY SPIRE, MILK. HALF A MILLION PEOPLE SQUASHED INTO A MONOLITHIC DUNGHEAP IN THE DESERT.
THERE IS ALWAYS A SITUATION.
IT'S...IT'S MURDER, MA'AM. THREE CITS KILLED ON TIER SIX. S'PRETTY 'ORRIBLE DOWN THERE.
PEOPLE DIE EVERY NIGHT, MILK.
B-B-B
BREASTS, DEPUTY. OUT-OF-BOUNDS BREASTS. UNTOUCHED-BY-THE-HAND-OF-MAN BREASTS.
NOW FOCUS AND TELL ME WHAT'S NEW BEFORE I JUSTIFY ALL THAT "MAN-HATING LESBO CHIMMER" GRAFFITI IN THE PRECINCT TOILETS.
B-B-B
BARONESS!
N-NEW BARONESS. SHE'S GOT WIND OF THESE DEATHS.
D-DON'T KNOW WHY IT MATTERS TO HER, BOSS, BUT... SHE'S NOT HAPPY. ASKED FOR YOU PARTICULAR-LIKE.
...WELL.
£$%&.
"£$%& £$%& £$%& £$%& £$%& £$%&..."

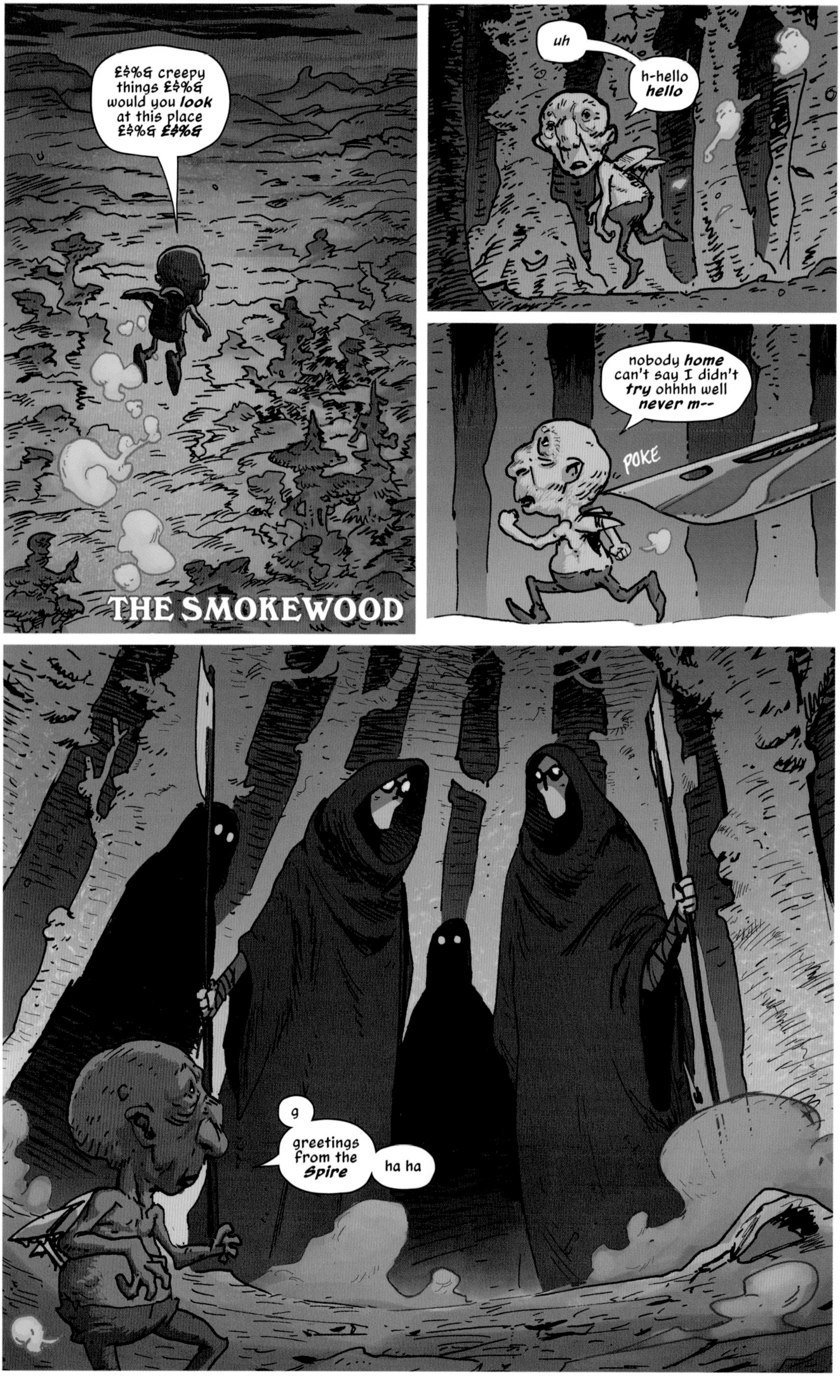
£$%& creepy things £$%& would you look at this place £$%& £$%&
THE SMOKEWOOD
uh
h-hello hello
nobody home can't say I didn't try ohhhh well never m--
POKE
g
greetings from the Spire
ha ha

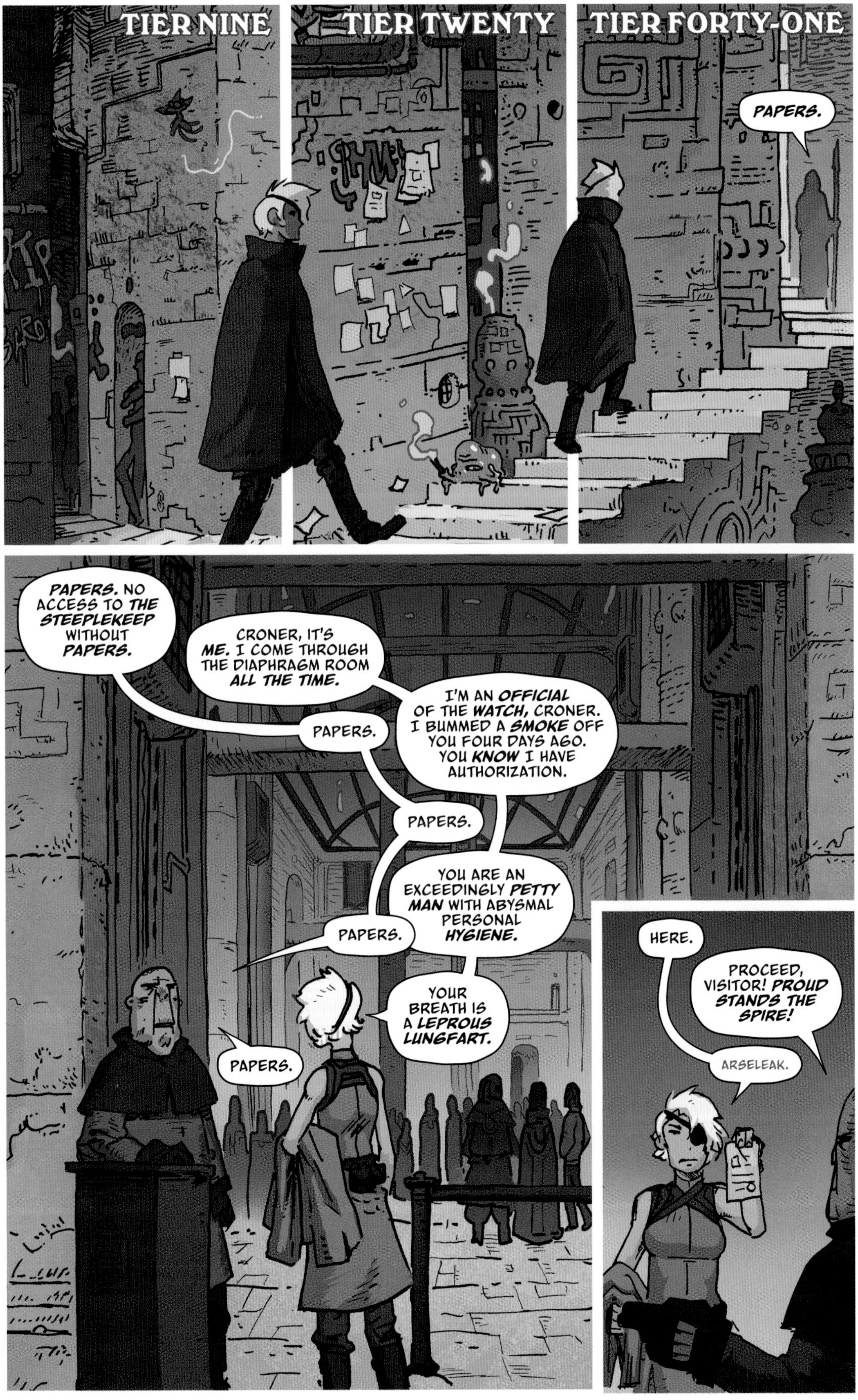
TIER NINE
TIER TWENTY
TIER FORTY-ONE
PAPERS.
PAPERS. NO ACCESS TO THE STEEPLEKEEP WITHOUT PAPERS.
CRONER, IT'S ME. I COME THROUGH THE DIAPHRAGM ROOM ALL THE TIME.
PAPERS.
I'M AN OFFICIAL OF THE WATCH, CRONER. I BUMMED A SMOKE OFF YOU FOUR DAYS AGO. YOU KNOW I HAVE AUTHORIZATION.
PAPERS.
YOU ARE AN EXCEEDINGLY PETTY MAN WITH ABYSMAL PERSONAL HYGIENE.
PAPERS.
YOUR BREATH IS A LEPROUS LUNGFART.
PAPERS.
HERE.
PROCEED, VISITOR! PROUD STANDS THE SPIRE!
ARSELEAK.

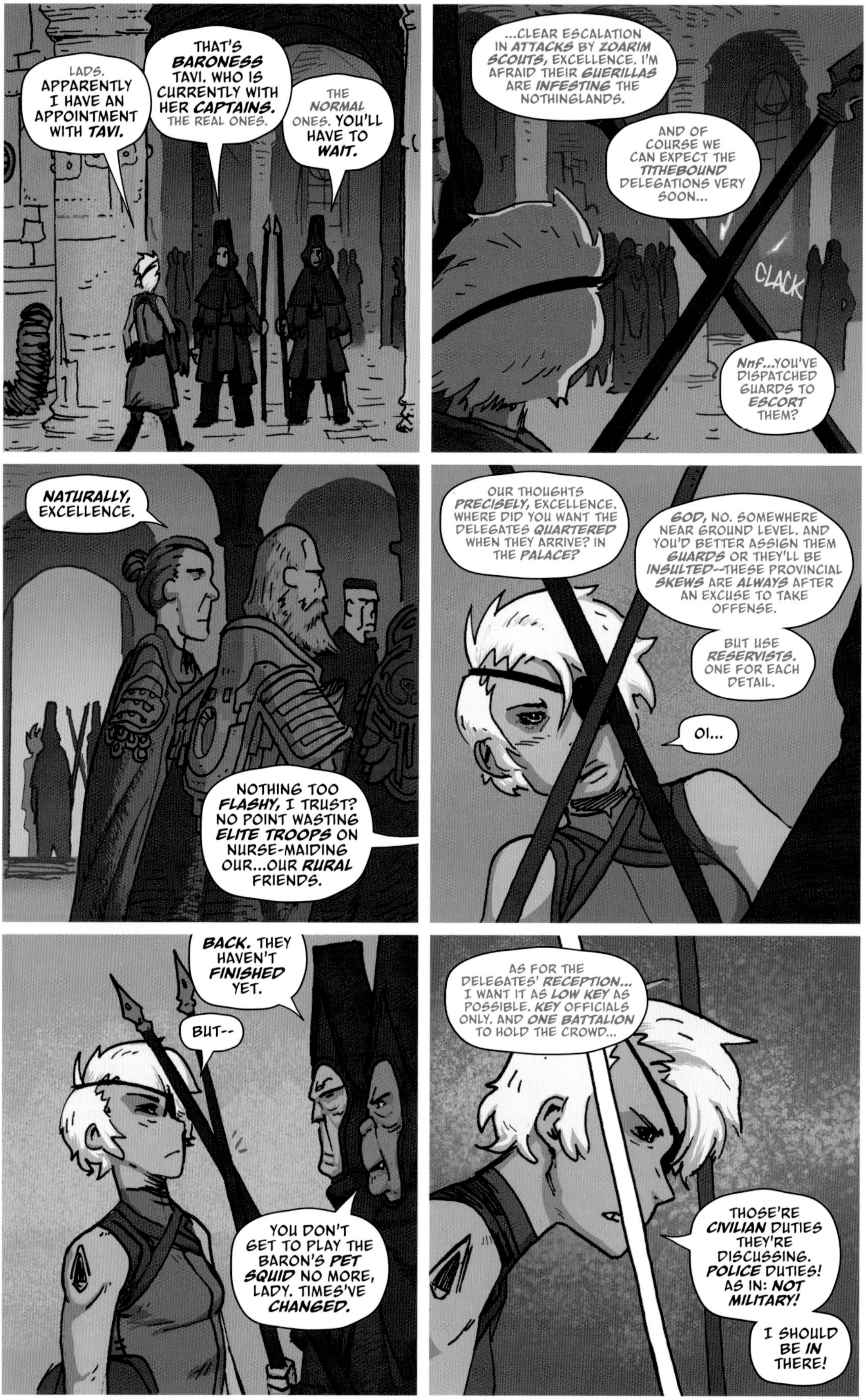
LADS. APPARENTLY I HAVE AN APPOINTMENT WITH TAVI.
THAT'S BARONESS TAVI. WHO IS CURRENTLY WITH HER CAPTAINS. THE REAL ONES.
THE NORMAL ONES. YOU'LL HAVE TO WAIT.
...CLEAR ESCALATION IN ATTACKS BY ZOARIM SCOUTS, EXCELLENCE. I'M AFRAID THEIR GUERILLAS ARE INFESTING THE NOTHINGLANDS.
AND OF COURSE WE CAN EXPECT THE TITHEBOUND DELEGATIONS VERY SOON...
CLACK
Nnf...YOU'VE DISPATCHED GUARDS TO ESCORT THEM?
NATURALLY, EXCELLENCE.
NOTHING TOO FLASHY, I TRUST? NO POINT WASTING ELITE TROOPS ON NURSE-MAIDING OUR...OUR RURAL FRIENDS.
OUR THOUGHTS PRECISELY, EXCELLENCE. WHERE DID YOU WANT THE DELEGATES QUARTERED WHEN THEY ARRIVE? IN THE PALACE?
GOD, NO. SOMEWHERE NEAR GROUND LEVEL. AND YOU'D BETTER ASSIGN THEM GUARDS OR THEY'LL BE INSULTED--THESE PROVINCIAL SKEWS ARE ALWAYS AFTER AN EXCUSE TO TAKE OFFENSE.
BUT USE RESERVISTS. ONE FOR EACH DETAIL.
OI...
BACK. THEY HAVEN'T FINISHED YET.
BUT--
YOU DON'T GET TO PLAY THE BARON'S PET SQUID NO MORE, LADY. TIMES'VE CHANGED.
AS FOR THE DELEGATES' RECEPTION... I WANT IT AS LOW KEY AS POSSIBLE. KEY OFFICIALS ONLY. AND ONE BATTALION TO HOLD THE CROWD...
THOSE'RE CIVILIAN DUTIES THEY'RE DISCUSSING. POLICE DUTIES! AS IN: NOT MILITARY!
I SHOULD BE IN THERE!

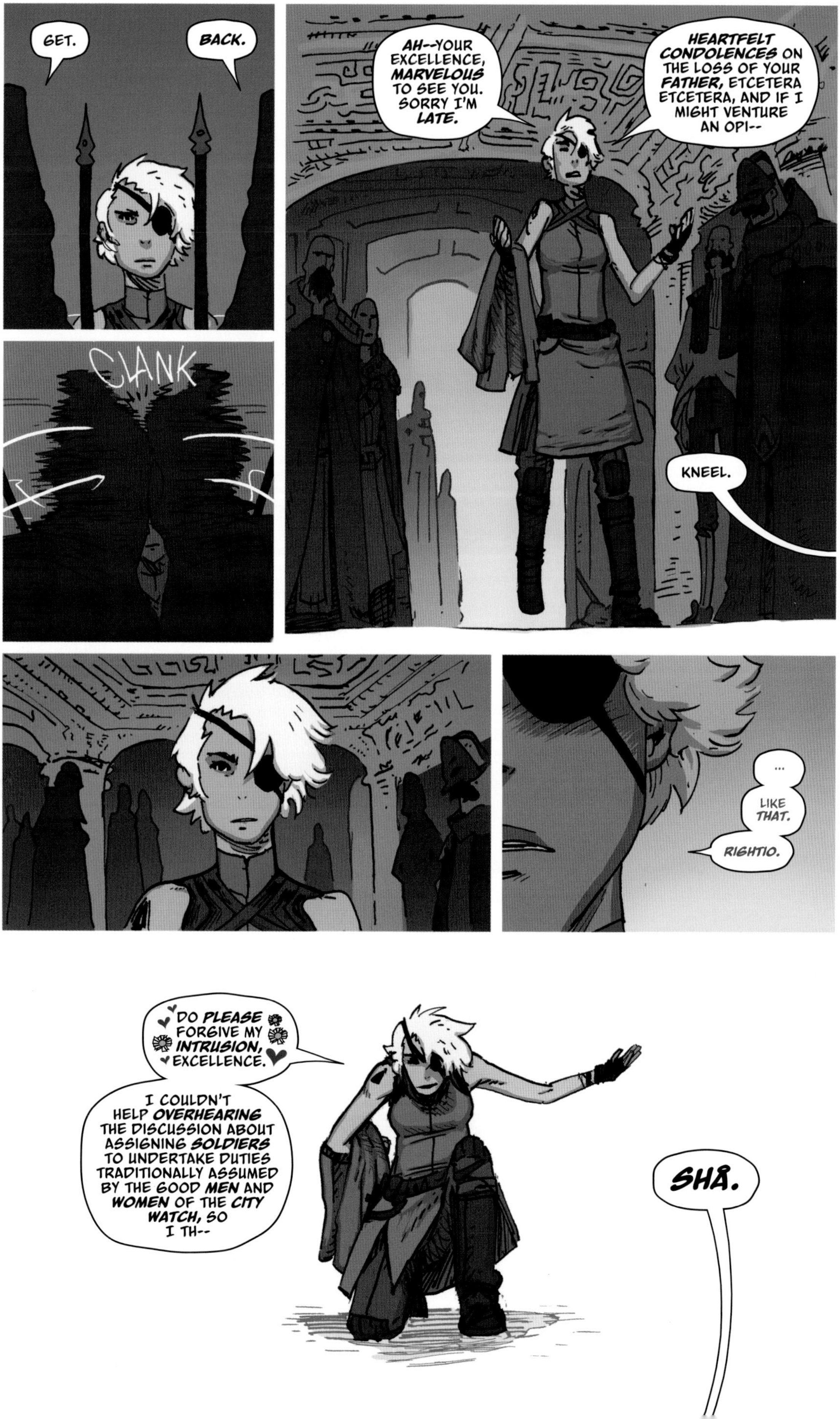
GET.
BACK.
CLANK
AH--YOUR EXCELLENCE, MARVELOUS TO SEE YOU. SORRY I'M LATE.
HEARTFELT CONDOLENCES ON THE LOSS OF YOUR FATHER, ETCETERA ETCETERA, AND IF I MIGHT VENTURE AN OPI--
KNEEL.
...
LIKE THAT.
RIGHTIO.
DO PLEASE FORGIVE MY INTRUSION, EXCELLENCE.
I COULDN'T HELP OVERHEARING THE DISCUSSION ABOUT ASSIGNING SOLDIERS TO UNDERTAKE DUTIES TRADITIONALLY ASSUMED BY THE GOOD MEN AND WOMEN OF THE CITY WATCH, SO I TH--
SHÂ.

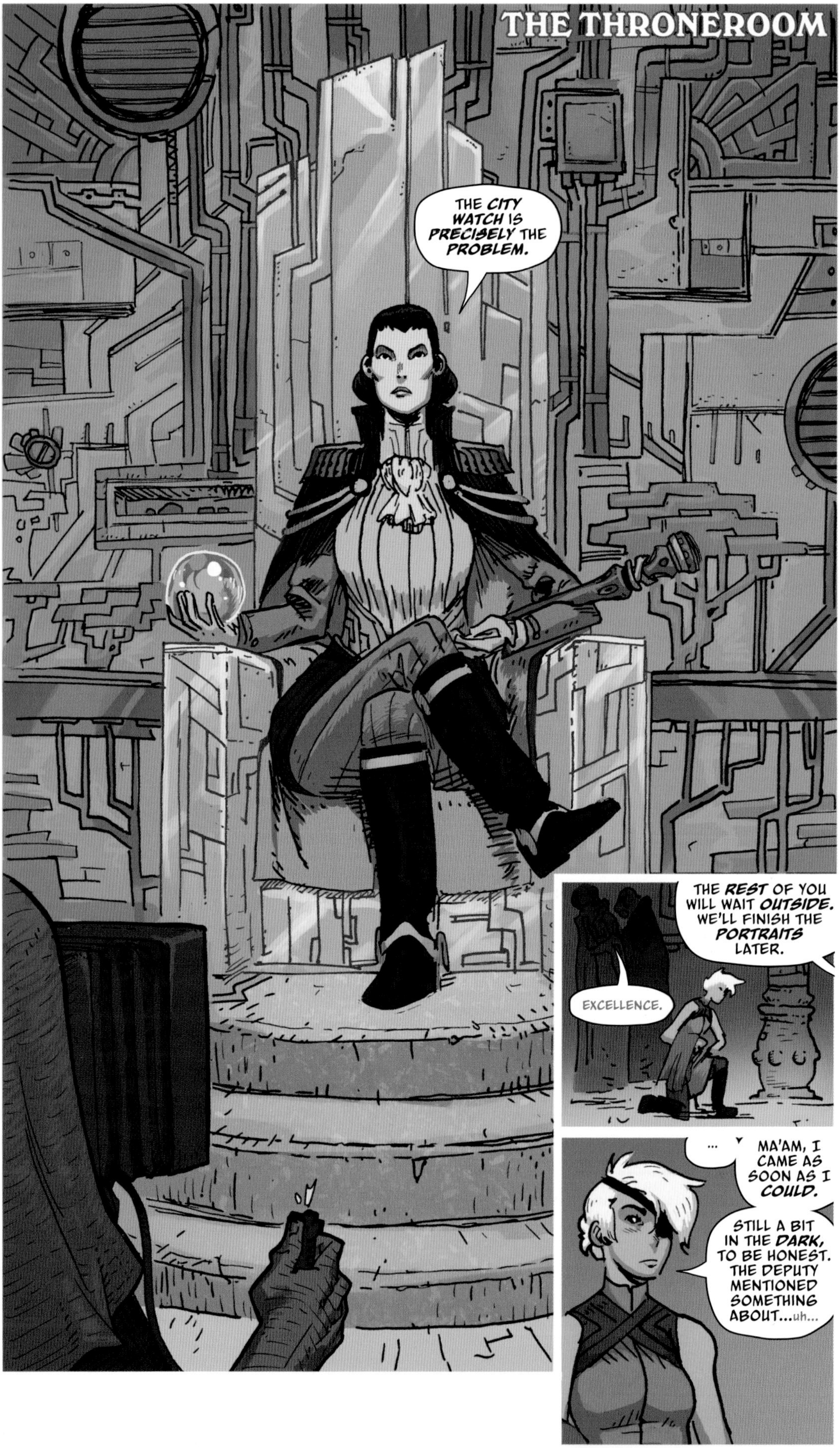
THE THRONEROOM
THE CITY WATCH IS PRECISELY THE PROBLEM.
THE REST OF YOU WILL WAIT OUTSIDE. WE'LL FINISH THE PORTRAITS LATER.
EXCELLENCE.
...
MA'AM, I CAME AS SOON AS I COULD.
STILL A BIT IN THE DARK, TO BE HONEST. THE DEPUTY MENTIONED SOMETHING ABOUT...uh...

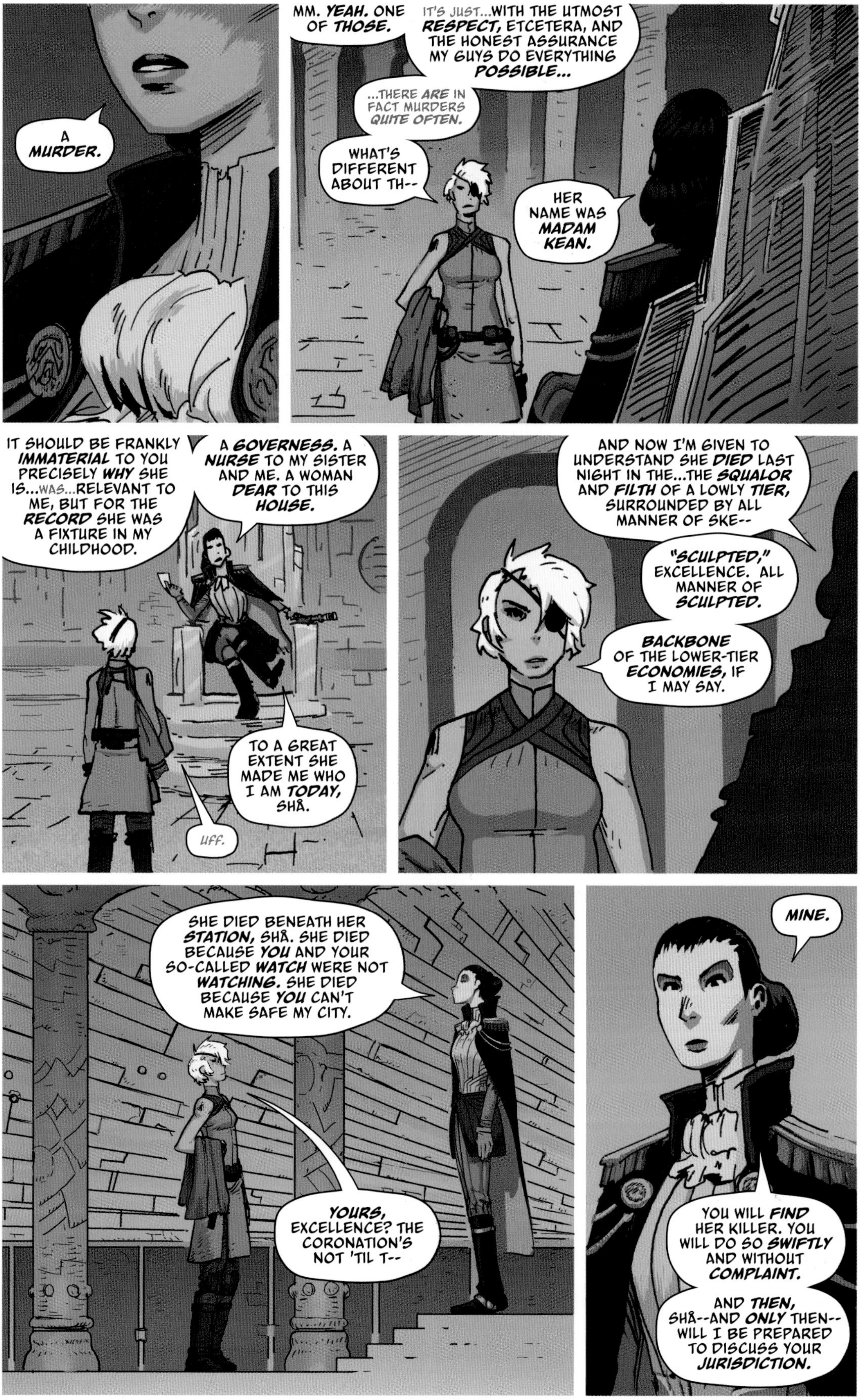
A MURDER.
MM. YEAH. ONE OF THOSE.
IT'S JUST...WITH THE UTMOST RESPECT, ETCETERA, AND THE HONEST ASSURANCE MY GUYS DO EVERYTHING POSSIBLE...
...THERE ARE IN FACT MURDERS QUITE OFTEN.
WHAT'S DIFFERENT ABOUT TH--
HER NAME WAS MADAM KEAN.
IT SHOULD BE FRANKLY IMMATERIAL TO YOU PRECISELY WHY SHE IS...WAS...RELEVANT TO ME, BUT FOR THE RECORD SHE WAS A FIXTURE IN MY CHILDHOOD.
A GOVERNESS. A NURSE TO MY SISTER AND ME. A WOMAN DEAR TO THIS HOUSE.
TO A GREAT EXTENT SHE MADE ME WHO I AM TODAY, SHÅ.
UFF.
AND NOW I'M GIVEN TO UNDERSTAND SHE DIED LAST NIGHT IN THE...THE SQUALOR AND FILTH OF A LOWLY TIER, SURROUNDED BY ALL MANNER OF SKE--
"SCULPTED," EXCELLENCE. ALL MANNER OF SCULPTED.
BACKBONE OF THE LOWER-TIER ECONOMIES, IF I MAY SAY.
SHE DIED BENEATH HER STATION, SHÅ. SHE DIED BECAUSE YOU AND YOUR SO-CALLED WATCH WERE NOT WATCHING. SHE DIED BECAUSE YOU CAN'T MAKE SAFE MY CITY.
YOURS, EXCELLENCE? THE CORONATION'S NOT 'TIL T--
MINE.
YOU WILL FIND HER KILLER. YOU WILL DO SO SWIFTLY AND WITHOUT COMPLAINT.
AND THEN, SHÅ--AND ONLY THEN--WILL I BE PREPARED TO DISCUSS YOUR JURISDICTION.

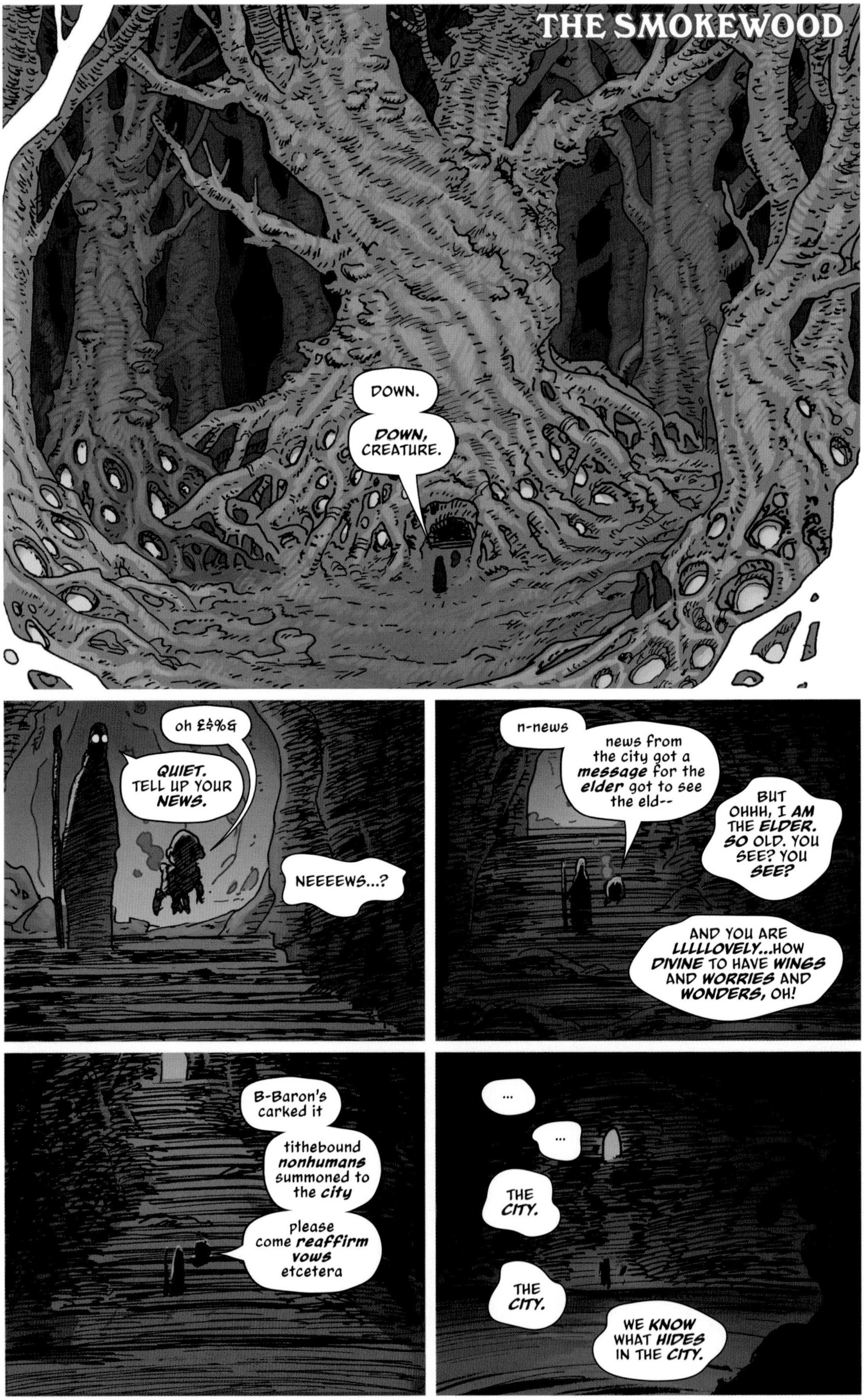
THE SMOKEWOOD
DOWN.
DOWN, CREATURE.
oh £$%&
QUIET. TELL UP YOUR NEWS.
NEEEEWS...?
n-news
news from the city got a message for the elder got to see the eld--
BUT OHHH, I AM THE ELDER. SO OLD. YOU SEE? YOU SEE?
AND YOU ARE LLLLLOVELY...HOW DIVINE TO HAVE WINGS AND WORRIES AND WONDERS, OH!
B-Baron's carked it
tithebound nonhumans summoned to the city
please come reaffirm vows etcetera
...
...
THE CITY.
THE CITY.
WE KNOW WHAT HIDES IN THE CITY.

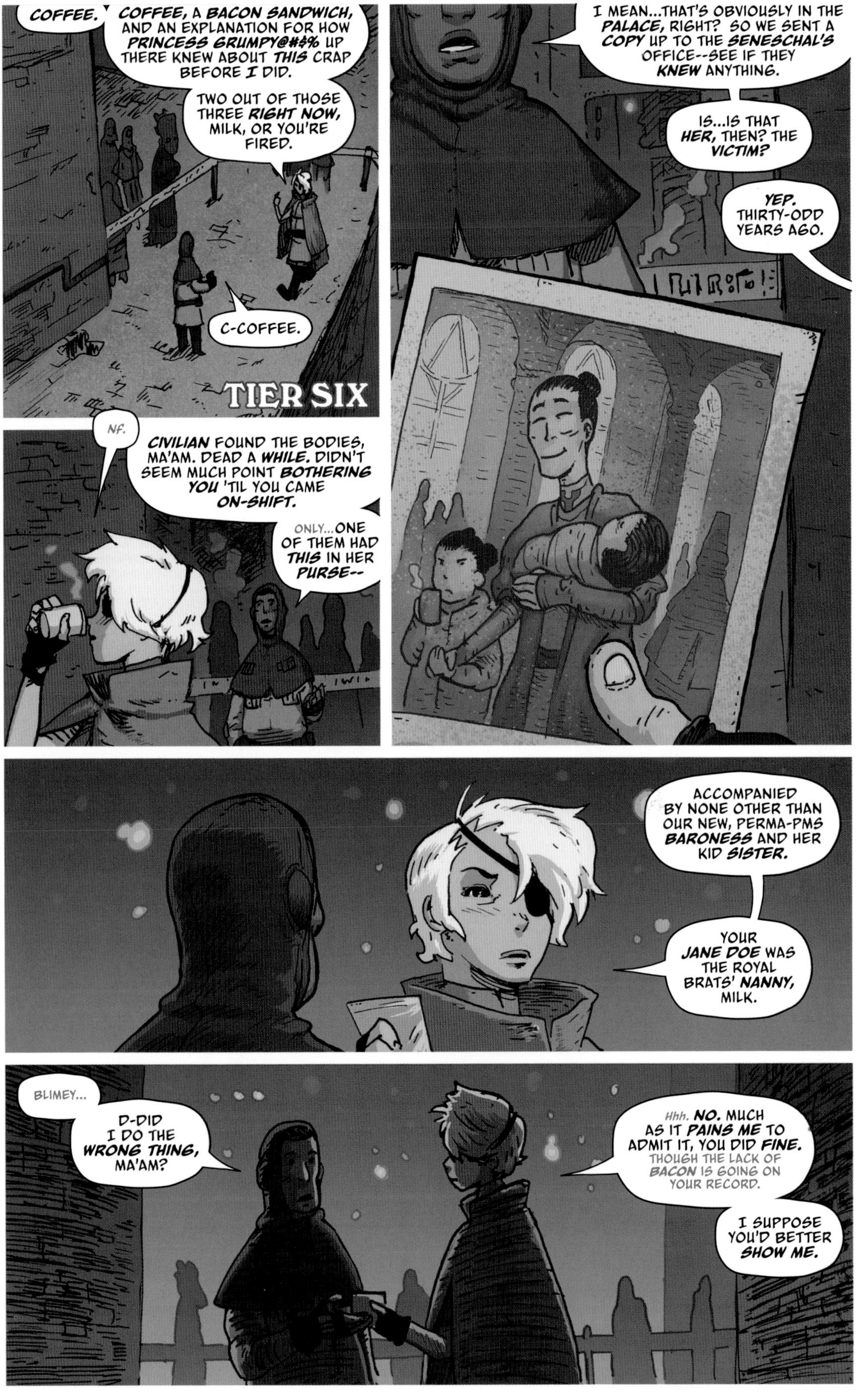
COFFEE.
COFFEE, A BACON SANDWICH, AND AN EXPLANATION FOR HOW PRINCESS GRUMPY@#$% UP THERE KNEW ABOUT THIS CRAP BEFORE I DID.
TWO OUT OF THOSE THREE RIGHT NOW, MILK, OR YOU'RE FIRED.
C-COFFEE.
TIER SIX
NF.
CIVILIAN FOUND THE BODIES, MA'AM. DEAD A WHILE. DIDN'T SEEM MUCH POINT BOTHERING YOU 'TIL YOU CAME ON-SHIFT.
ONLY...ONE OF THEM HAD THIS IN HER PURSE--
I MEAN...THAT'S OBVIOUSLY IN THE PALACE, RIGHT? SO WE SENT A COPY UP TO THE SENESCHAL'S OFFICE--SEE IF THEY KNEW ANYTHING.
IS...IS THAT HER, THEN? THE VICTIM?
YEP. THIRTY-ODD YEARS AGO.
ACCOMPANIED BY NONE OTHER THAN OUR NEW, PERMA-PMS BARONESS AND HER KID SISTER.
YOUR JANE DOE WAS THE ROYAL BRATS' NANNY, MILK.
BLIMEY...
D-DID I DO THE WRONG THING, MA'AM?
Hhh. NO. MUCH AS IT PAINS ME TO ADMIT IT, YOU DID FINE. THOUGH THE LACK OF BACON IS GOING ON YOUR RECORD.
I SUPPOSE YOU'D BETTER SHOW ME.

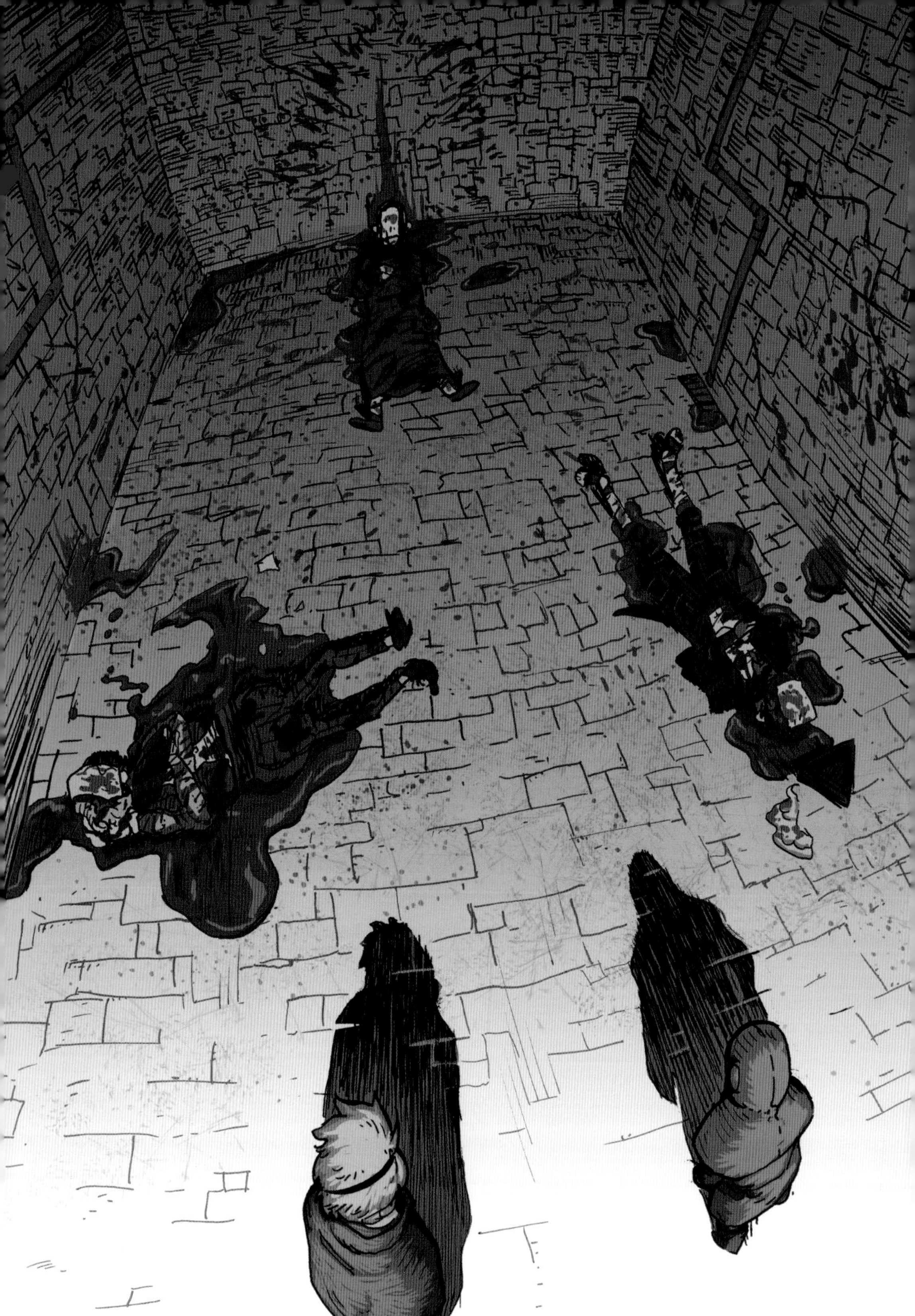

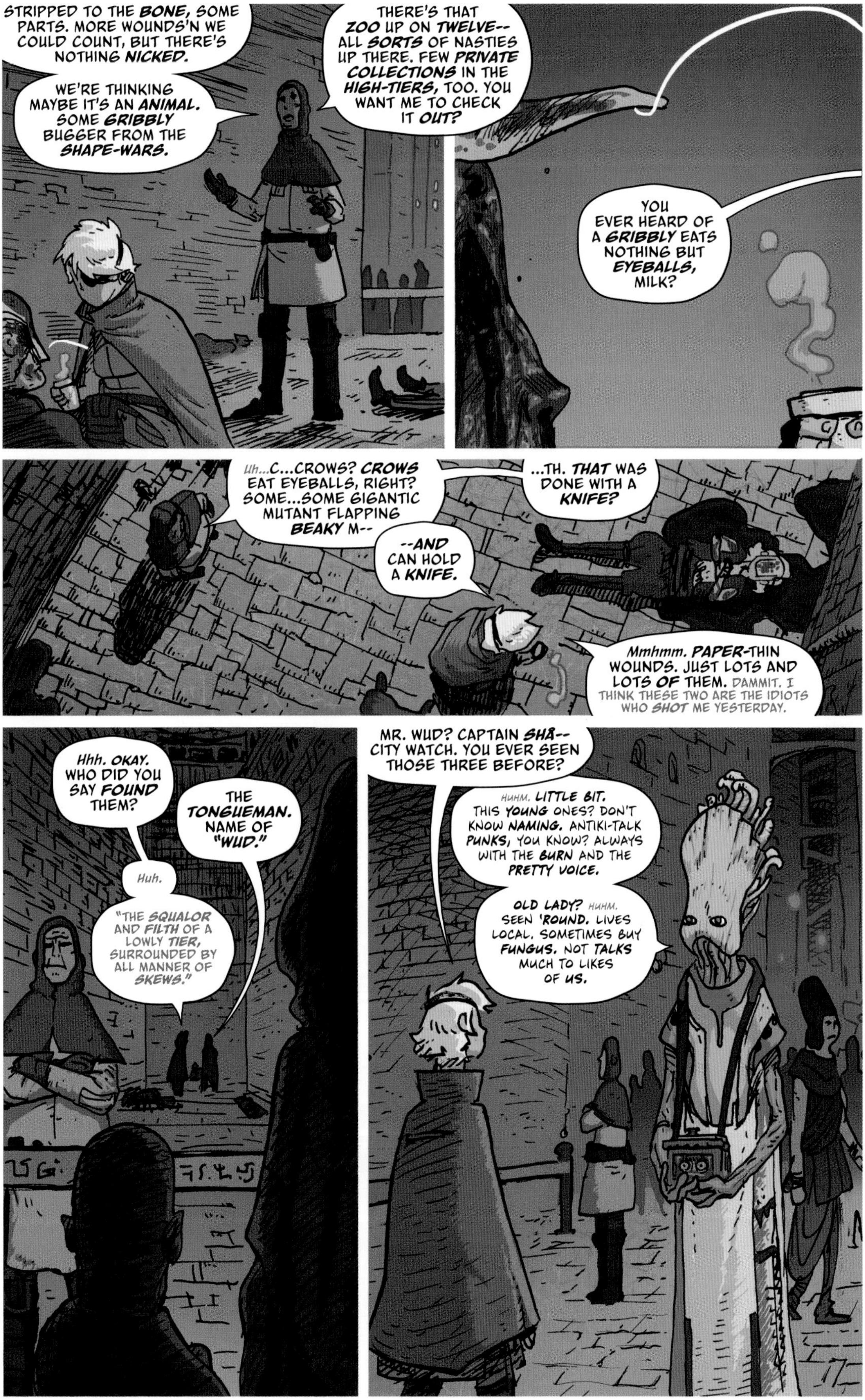
STRIPPED TO THE BONE, SOME PARTS. MORE WOUNDS'N WE COULD COUNT, BUT THERE'S NOTHING NICKED.
WE'RE THINKING MAYBE IT'S AN ANIMAL. SOME GRIBBLY BUGGER FROM THE SHAPE-WARS.
THERE'S THAT ZOO UP ON TWELVE-- ALL SORTS OF NASTIES UP THERE. FEW PRIVATE COLLECTIONS IN THE HIGH-TIERS, TOO. YOU WANT ME TO CHECK IT OUT?
YOU EVER HEARD OF A GRIBBLY EATS NOTHING BUT EYEBALLS, MILK?
Uh...C...CROWS? CROWS EAT EYEBALLS, RIGHT? SOME...SOME GIGANTIC MUTANT FLAPPING BEAKY M--
--AND CAN HOLD A KNIFE.
...TH. THAT WAS DONE WITH A KNIFE?
Mmhmm. PAPER-THIN WOUNDS. JUST LOTS AND LOTS OF THEM. DAMMIT. I THINK THESE TWO ARE THE IDIOTS WHO SHOT ME YESTERDAY.
Hhh. OKAY. WHO DID YOU SAY FOUND THEM?
THE TONGUEMAN. NAME OF "WUD."
Huh.
"THE SQUALOR AND FILTH OF A LOWLY TIER, SURROUNDED BY ALL MANNER OF SKEWS."
MR. WUD? CAPTAIN SHĀ-- CITY WATCH. YOU EVER SEEN THOSE THREE BEFORE?
HUHM. LITTLE BIT. THIS YOUNG ONES? DON'T KNOW NAMING. ANTIKI-TALK PUNKS, YOU KNOW? ALWAYS WITH THE BURN AND THE PRETTY VOICE.
OLD LADY? HUHM. SEEN 'ROUND. LIVES LOCAL. SOMETIMES BUY FUNGUS. NOT TALKS MUCH TO LIKES OF US.

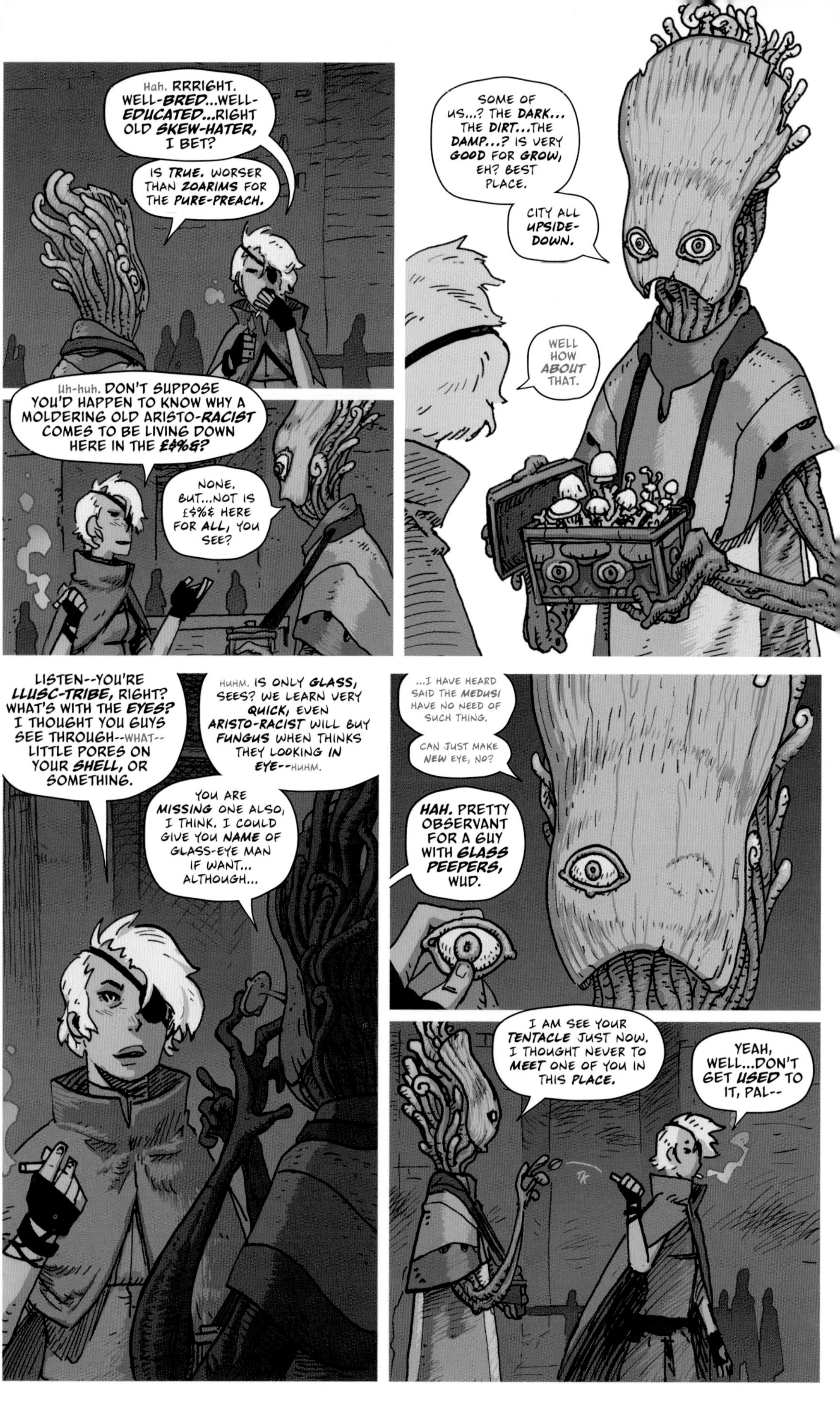

Hah. RRRIGHT. WELL-BRED...WELL-EDUCATED...RIGHT OLD SKEW-HATER, I BET?
IS TRUE. WORSER THAN ZOARIMS FOR THE PURE-PREACH.
Uh-huh. DON'T SUPPOSE YOU'D HAPPEN TO KNOW WHY A MOLDERING OLD ARISTO-RACIST COMES TO BE LIVING DOWN HERE IN THE £$%G?
NONE. BUT...NOT IS £$%& HERE FOR ALL, YOU SEE?
SOME OF US...? THE DARK... THE DIRT...THE DAMP...? IS VERY GOOD FOR GROW, EH? BEST PLACE.
CITY ALL UPSIDE-DOWN.
WELL HOW ABOUT THAT.
LISTEN--YOU'RE LLUSC-TRIBE, RIGHT? WHAT'S WITH THE EYES? I THOUGHT YOU GUYS SEE THROUGH--WHAT--LITTLE PORES ON YOUR SHELL, OR SOMETHING.
HUHM. IS ONLY GLASS, SEES? WE LEARN VERY QUICK, EVEN ARISTO-RACIST WILL BUY FUNGUS WHEN THINKS THEY LOOKING IN EYE--HUHM.
YOU ARE MISSING ONE ALSO, I THINK. I COULD GIVE YOU NAME OF GLASS-EYE MAN IF WANT... ALTHOUGH...
...I HAVE HEARD SAID THE MEDUSI HAVE NO NEED OF SUCH THING.
CAN JUST MAKE NEW EYE, NO?
HAH. PRETTY OBSERVANT FOR A GUY WITH GLASS PEEPERS, WUD.
I AM SEE YOUR TENTACLE JUST NOW. I THOUGHT NEVER TO MEET ONE OF YOU IN THIS PLACE.
YEAH, WELL...DON'T GET USED TO IT, PAL--

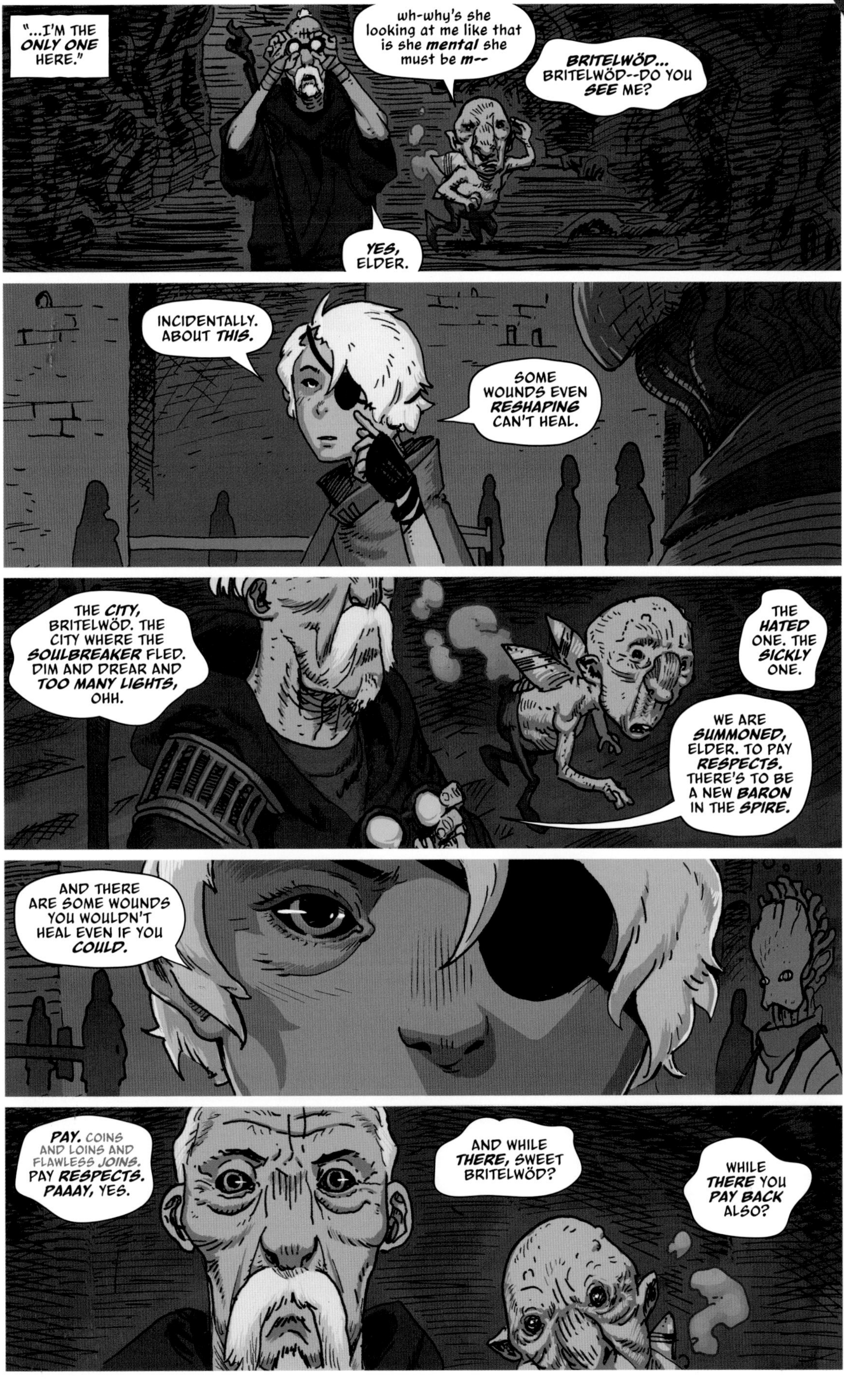
"...I'M THE ONLY ONE HERE."
wh-why's she looking at me like that is she mental she must be m--
BRITELWÖD... BRITELWÖD--DO YOU SEE ME?
YES, ELDER.
INCIDENTALLY. ABOUT THIS.
SOME WOUNDS EVEN RESHAPING CAN'T HEAL.
THE CITY, BRITELWÖD. THE CITY WHERE THE SOULBREAKER FLED. DIM AND DREAR AND TOO MANY LIGHTS, OHH.
THE HATED ONE. THE SICKLY ONE.
WE ARE SUMMONED, ELDER. TO PAY RESPECTS. THERE'S TO BE A NEW BARON IN THE SPIRE.
AND THERE ARE SOME WOUNDS YOU WOULDN'T HEAL EVEN IF YOU COULD.
PAY. COINS AND LOINS AND FLAWLESS JOINS. PAY RESPECTS. PAAAY, YES.
AND WHILE THERE, SWEET BRITELWÖD?
WHILE THERE YOU PAY BACK ALSO?

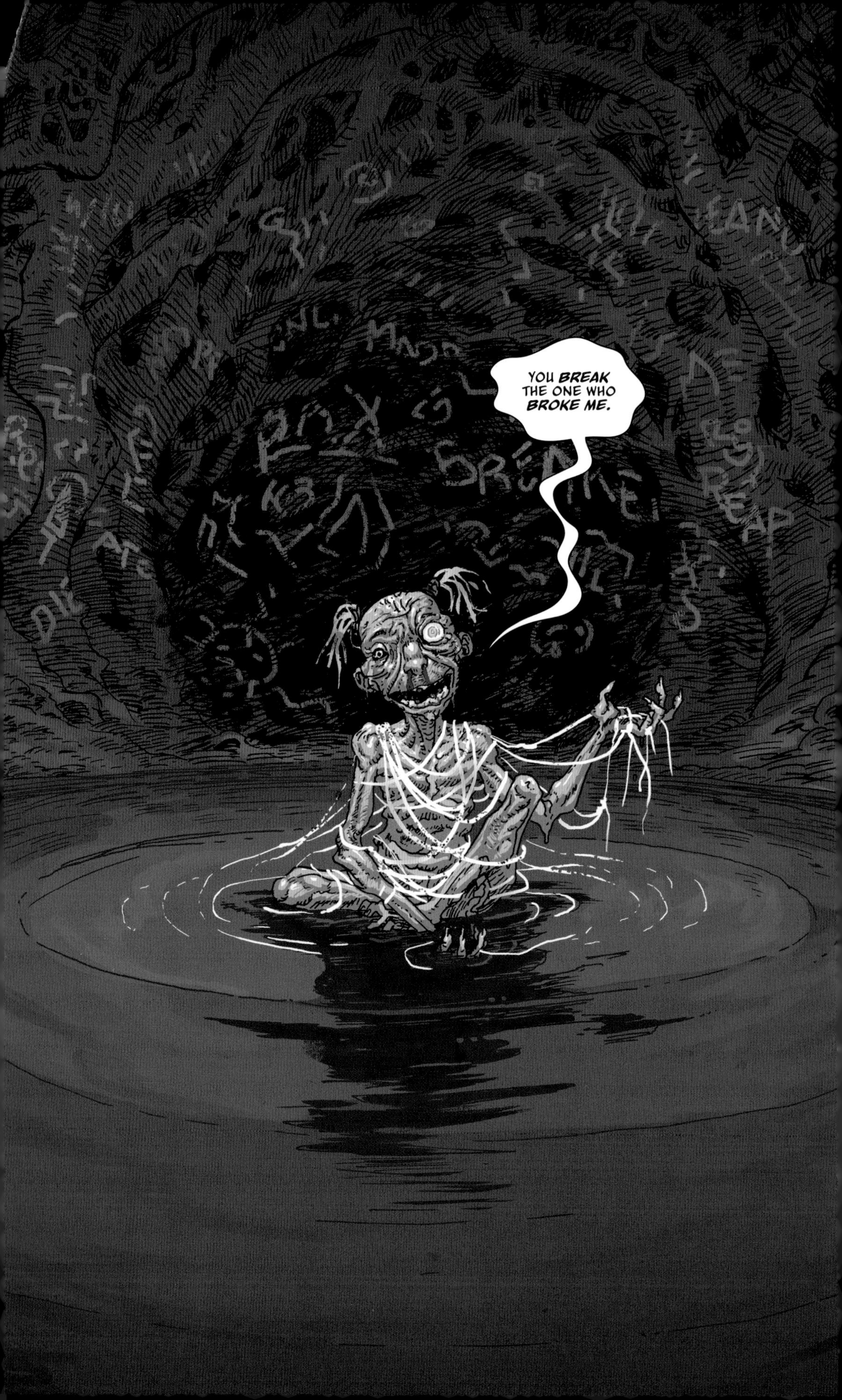
YOU *BREAK* THE ONE WHO *BROKE ME.*

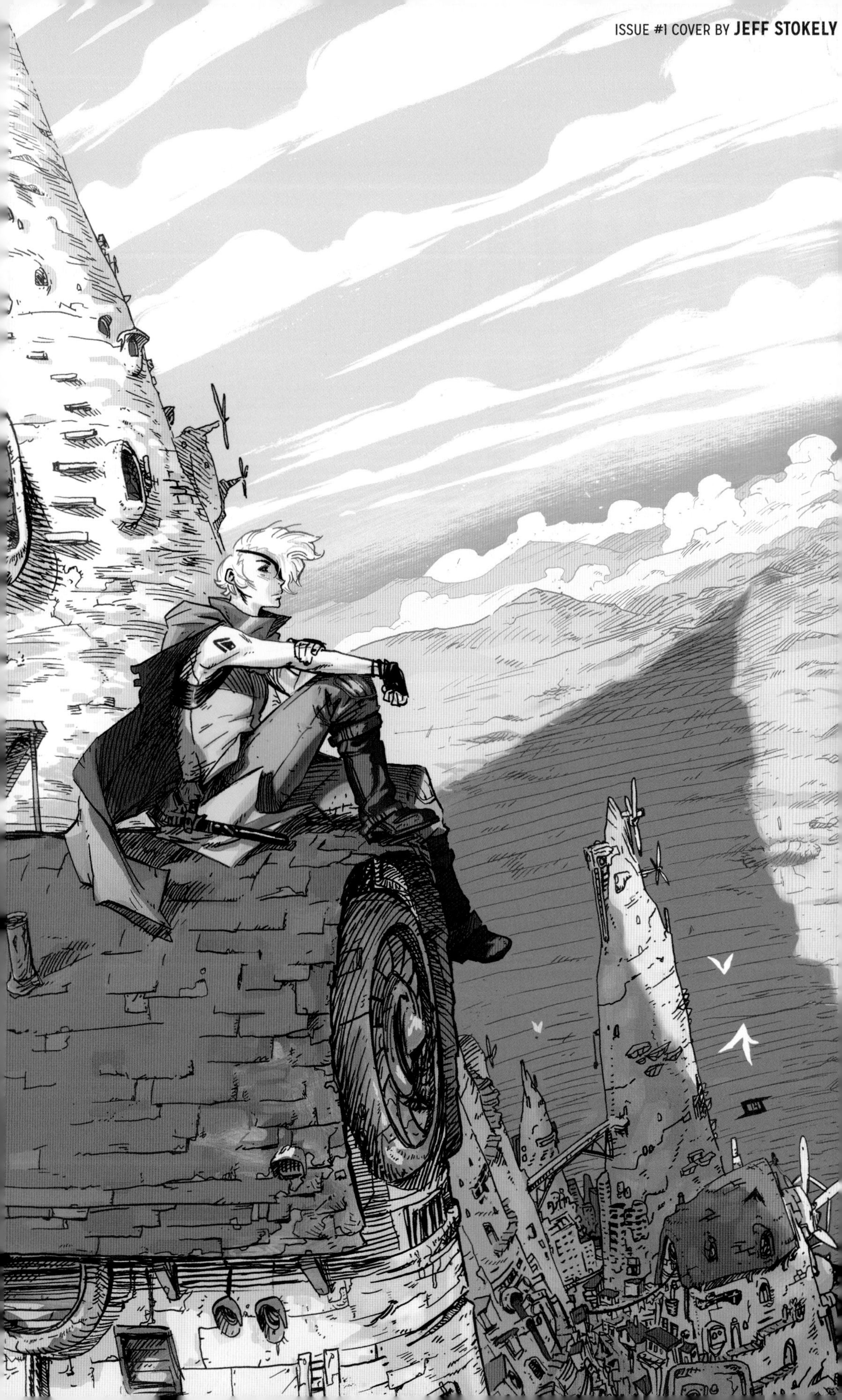

ISSUE #1 COVER BY **JEFF STOKELY**

CHAPTER TWO

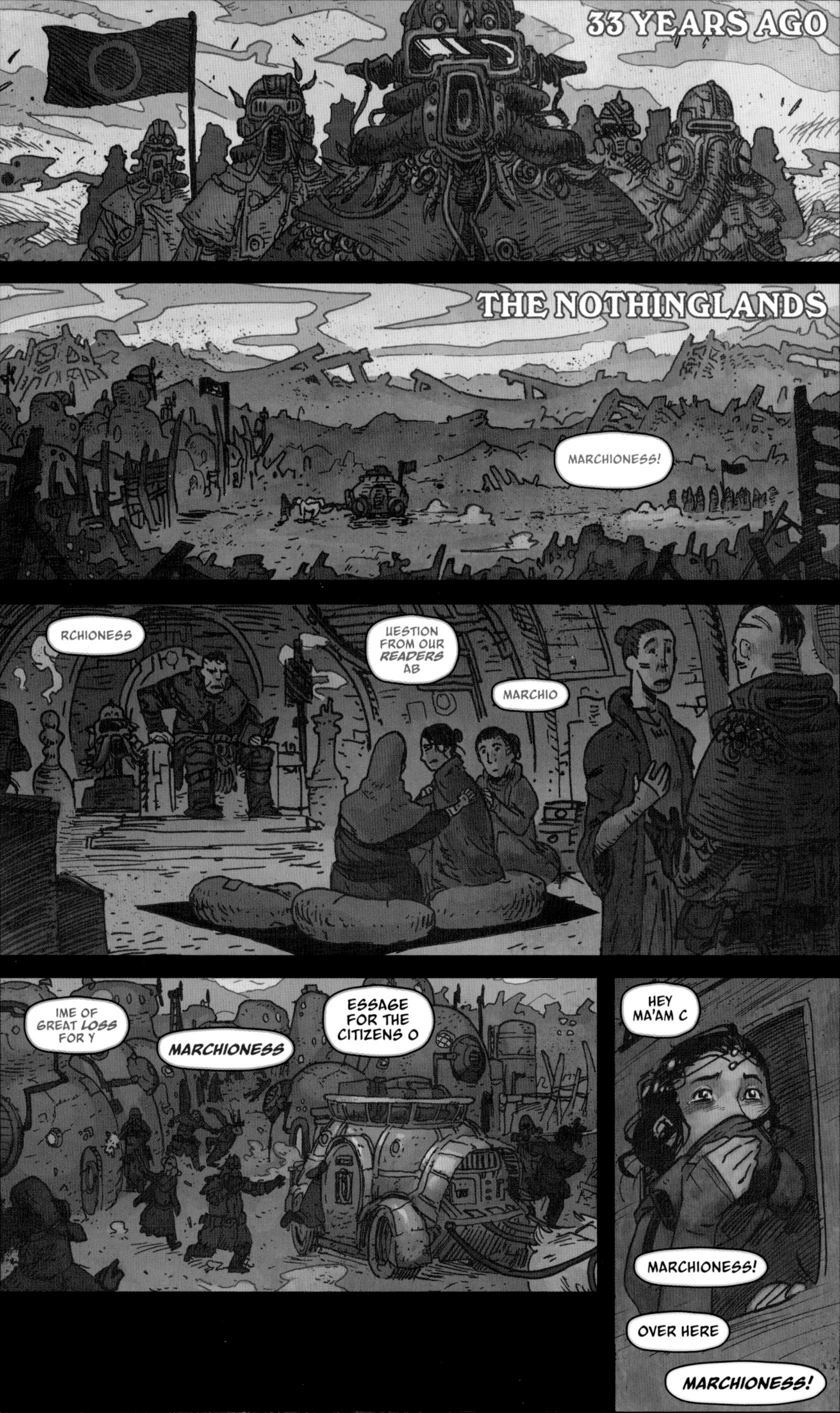
33 YEARS AGO
THE NOTHINGLANDS
MARCHIONESS!
RCHIONESS
UESTION FROM OUR READERS AB
MARCHIO
IME OF GREAT LOSS FOR Y
MARCHIONESS
ESSAGE FOR THE CITIZENS O
HEY MA'AM C
MARCHIONESS!
OVER HERE
MARCHIONESS!

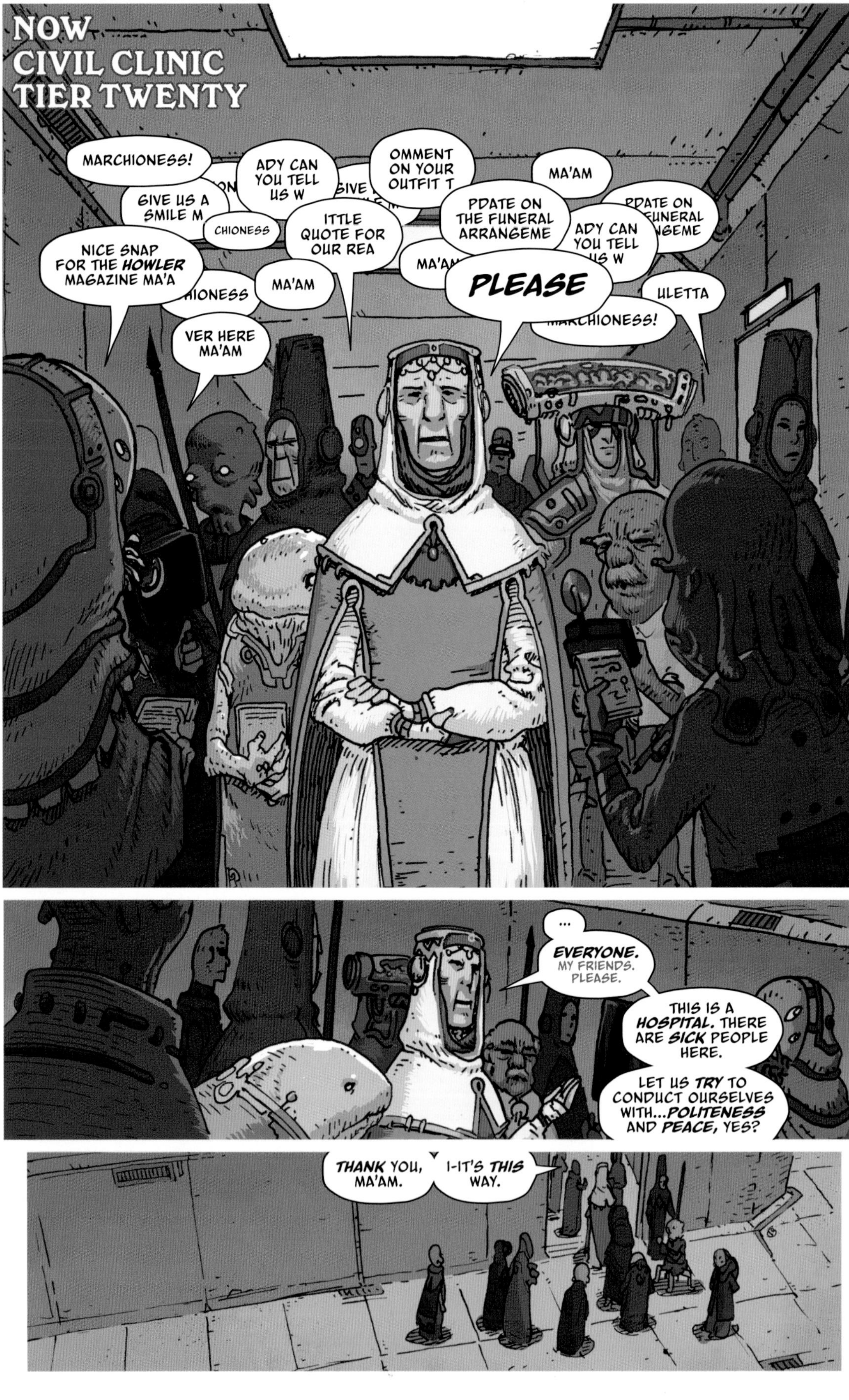
NOW
CIVIL CLINIC
TIER TWENTY
MARCHIONESS!
GIVE US A SMILE M
ADY CAN YOU TELL US W
CHIONESS
OMMENT ON YOUR OUTFIT T
ITTLE QUOTE FOR OUR REA
MA'AM
PDATE ON THE FUNERAL ARRANGEME
PDATE ON FUNERAL NGEME
ADY CAN YOU TELL US W
NICE SNAP FOR THE HOWLER MAGAZINE MA'A
HIONESS
MA'AM
MA'AM
PLEASE
ULETTA
MARCHIONESS!
VER HERE MA'AM
...
EVERYONE. MY FRIENDS. PLEASE.
THIS IS A HOSPITAL. THERE ARE SICK PEOPLE HERE.
LET US TRY TO CONDUCT OURSELVES WITH...POLITENESS AND PEACE, YES?
THANK YOU, MA'AM.
I-IT'S THIS WAY.

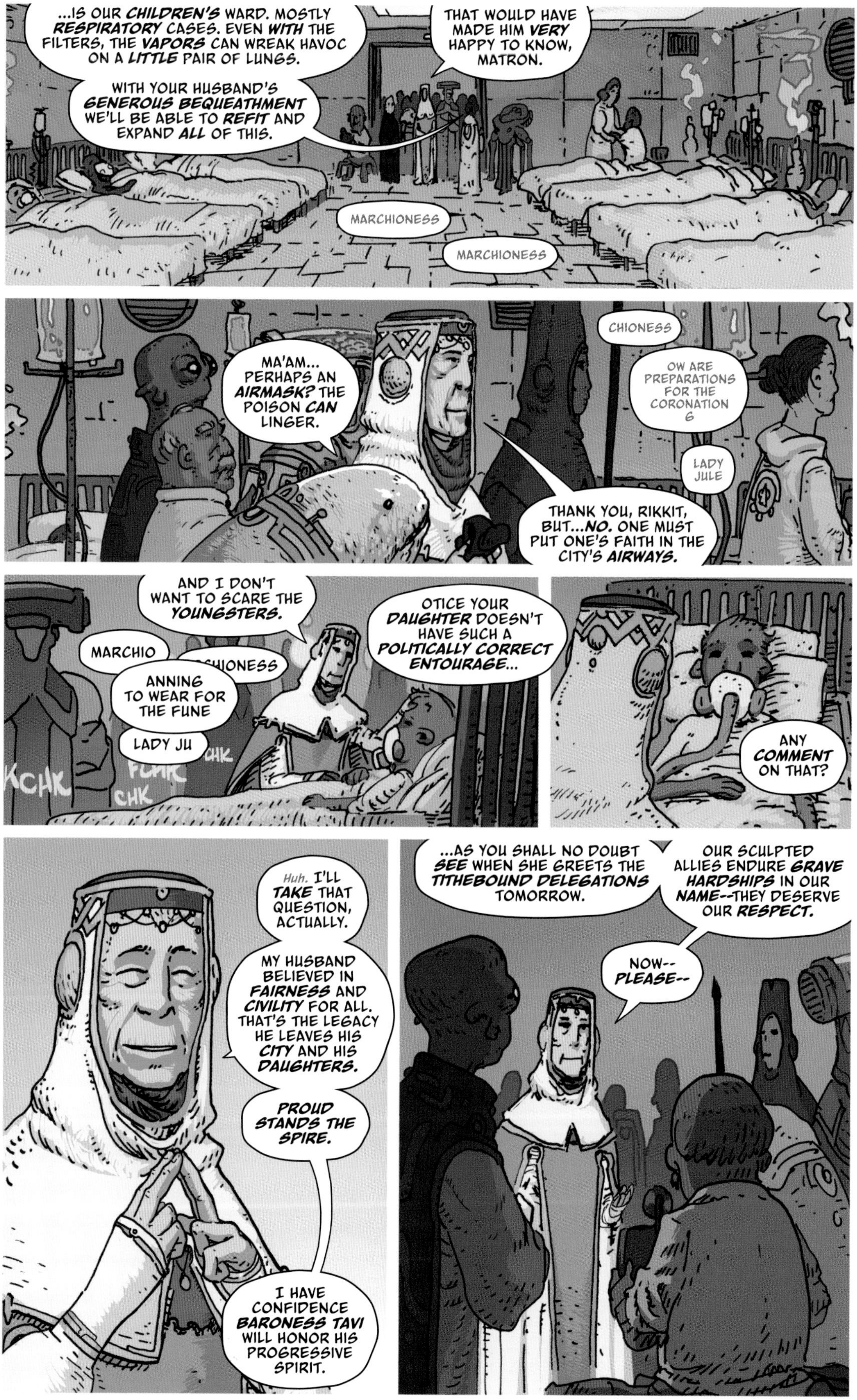

...IS OUR CHILDREN'S WARD. MOSTLY RESPIRATORY CASES. EVEN WITH THE FILTERS, THE VAPORS CAN WREAK HAVOC ON A LITTLE PAIR OF LUNGS.
WITH YOUR HUSBAND'S GENEROUS BEQUEATHMENT WE'LL BE ABLE TO REFIT AND EXPAND ALL OF THIS.
THAT WOULD HAVE MADE HIM VERY HAPPY TO KNOW, MATRON.
MARCHIONESS
MARCHIONESS
MA'AM... PERHAPS AN AIRMASK? THE POISON CAN LINGER.
CHIONESS
OW ARE PREPARATIONS FOR THE CORONATION
LADY JULE
THANK YOU, RIKKIT, BUT...NO. ONE MUST PUT ONE'S FAITH IN THE CITY'S AIRWAYS.
AND I DON'T WANT TO SCARE THE YOUNGSTERS.
MARCHIO
CHIONESS
ANNING TO WEAR FOR THE FUNE
LADY JU
KCHK
FCHK
CHK
CHK
OTICE YOUR DAUGHTER DOESN'T HAVE SUCH A POLITICALLY CORRECT ENTOURAGE...
ANY COMMENT ON THAT?
Huh. I'LL TAKE THAT QUESTION, ACTUALLY.
MY HUSBAND BELIEVED IN FAIRNESS AND CIVILITY FOR ALL. THAT'S THE LEGACY HE LEAVES HIS CITY AND HIS DAUGHTERS.
PROUD STANDS THE SPIRE.
I HAVE CONFIDENCE BARONESS TAVI WILL HONOR HIS PROGRESSIVE SPIRIT.
...AS YOU SHALL NO DOUBT SEE WHEN SHE GREETS THE TITHEBOUND DELEGATIONS TOMORROW.
OUR SCULPTED ALLIES ENDURE GRAVE HARDSHIPS IN OUR NAME--THEY DESERVE OUR RESPECT.
NOW-- PLEASE--

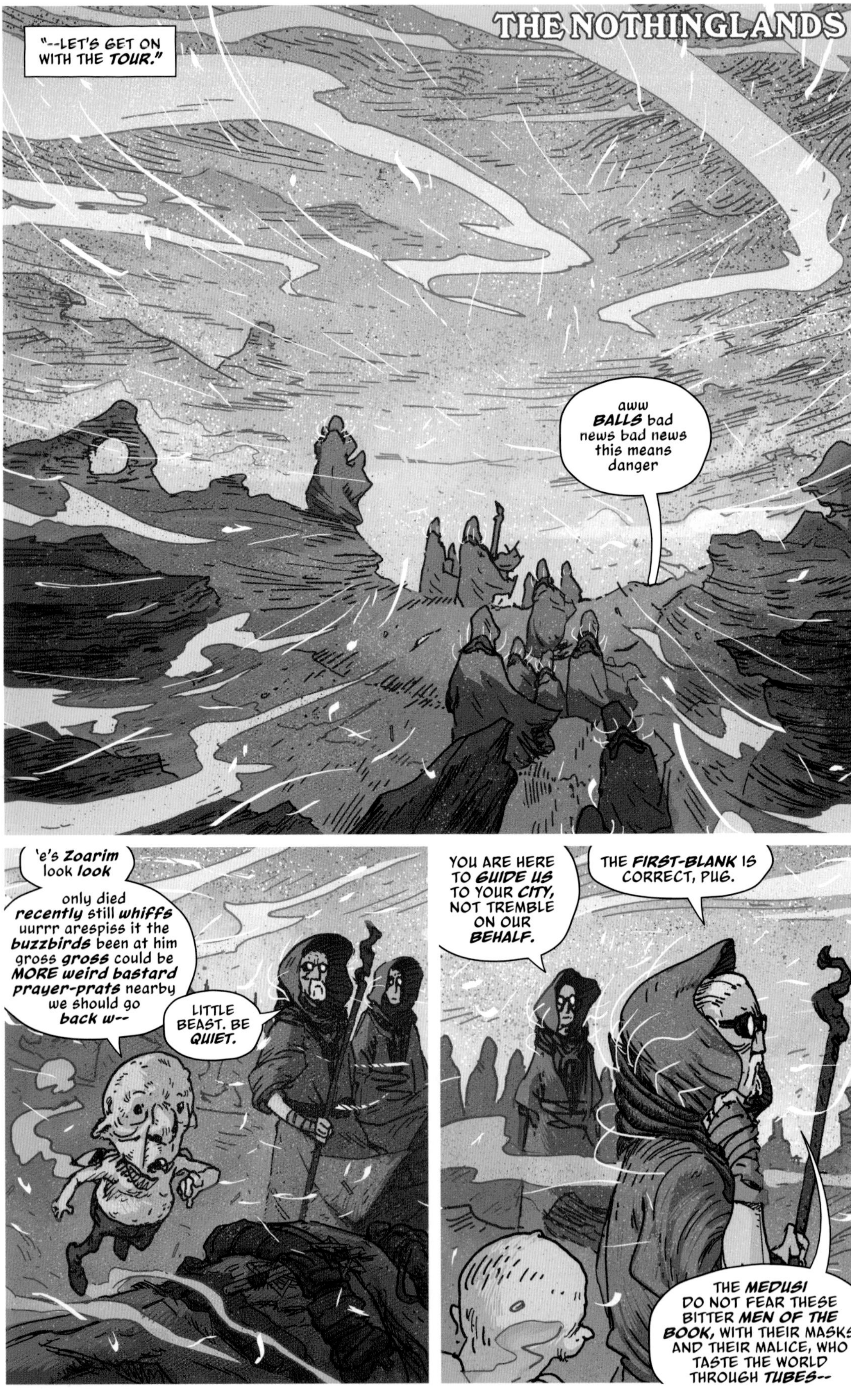
THE NOTHINGLANDS
"--LET'S GET ON WITH THE TOUR."
aww BALLS bad news bad news this means danger
'e's Zoarim look look
only died recently still whiffs uurrr arespiss it the buzzbirds been at him gross gross could be MORE weird bastard prayer-prats nearby we should go back w--
LITTLE BEAST. BE QUIET.
YOU ARE HERE TO GUIDE US TO YOUR CITY, NOT TREMBLE ON OUR BEHALF.
THE FIRST-BLANK IS CORRECT, PUG.
THE MEDUSI DO NOT FEAR THESE BITTER MEN OF THE BOOK, WITH THEIR MASKS AND THEIR MALICE, WHO TASTE THE WORLD THROUGH TUBES--

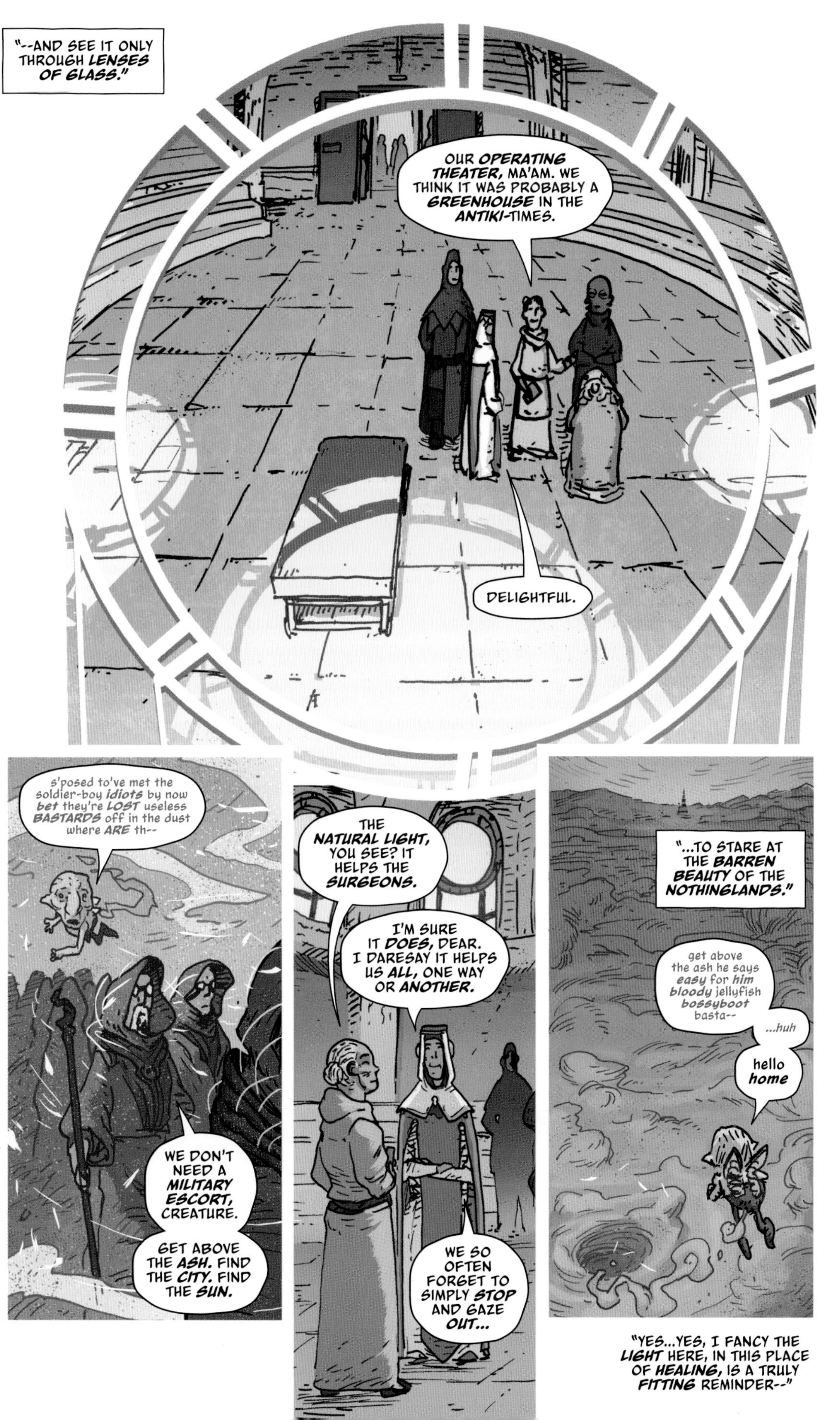
"--AND SEE IT ONLY THROUGH LENSES OF GLASS."
OUR OPERATING THEATER, MA'AM. WE THINK IT WAS PROBABLY A GREENHOUSE IN THE ANTIKI-TIMES.
DELIGHTFUL.
s'posed to've met the soldier-boy idiots by now bet they're LOST useless BASTARDS off in the dust where ARE th--
WE DON'T NEED A MILITARY ESCORT, CREATURE.
GET ABOVE THE ASH. FIND THE CITY. FIND THE SUN.
THE NATURAL LIGHT, YOU SEE? IT HELPS THE SURGEONS.
I'M SURE IT DOES, DEAR. I DARESAY IT HELPS US ALL, ONE WAY OR ANOTHER.
WE SO OFTEN FORGET TO SIMPLY STOP AND GAZE OUT...
"...TO STARE AT THE BARREN BEAUTY OF THE NOTHINGLANDS."
get above the ash he says easy for him bloody jellyfish bossyboot basta--
...huh
hello home
"YES...YES, I FANCY THE LIGHT HERE, IN THIS PLACE OF HEALING, IS A TRULY FITTING REMINDER--"

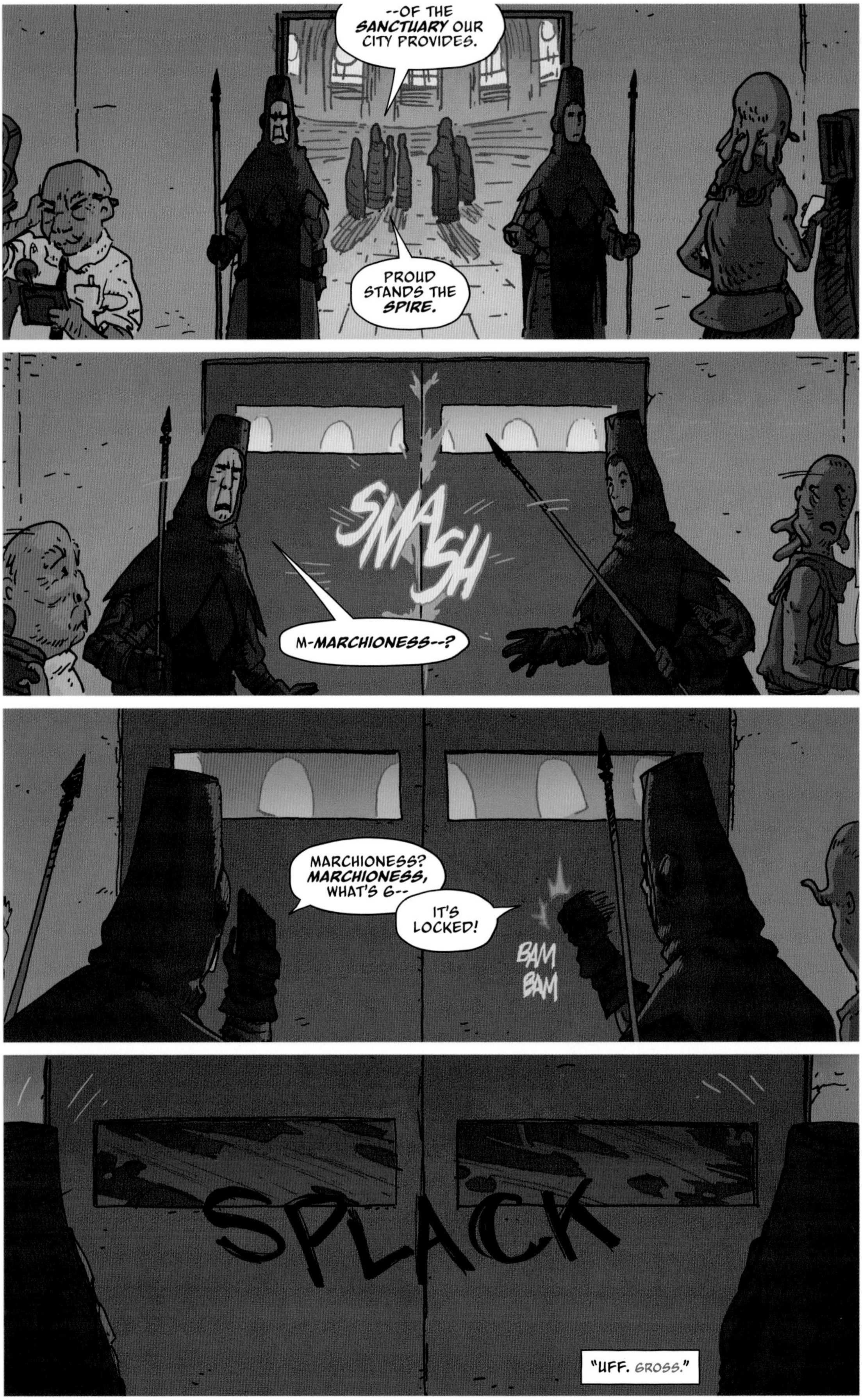
--OF THE SANCTUARY OUR CITY PROVIDES.
PROUD STANDS THE SPIRE.
SMASH
M-MARCHIONESS--?
MARCHIONESS? MARCHIONESS, WHAT'S G--
IT'S LOCKED!
BAM BAM
SPLACK
"UFF. GROSS."

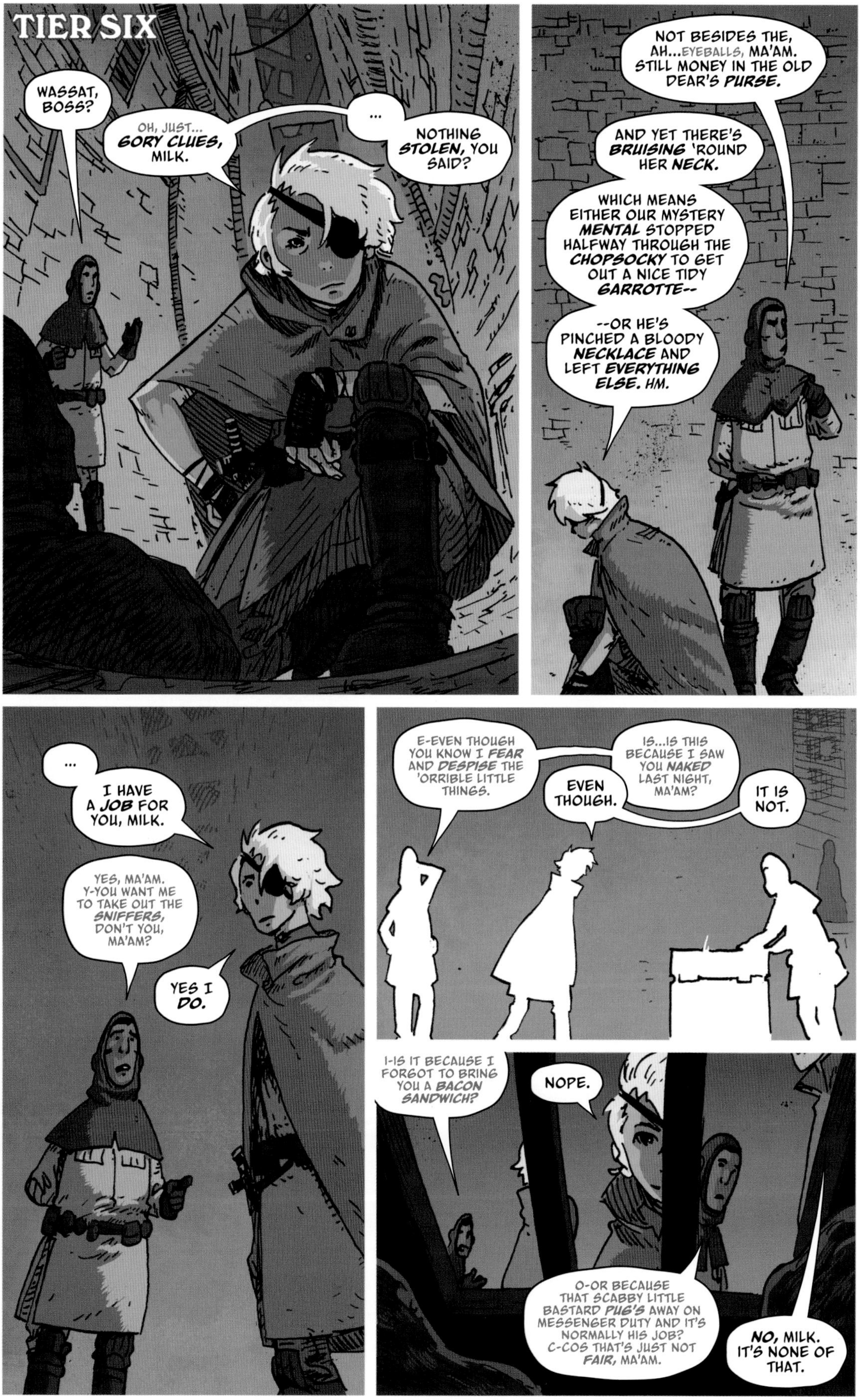
TIER SIX
WASSAT, BOSS?
OH, JUST... GORY CLUES, MILK.
...
NOTHING STOLEN, YOU SAID?
NOT BESIDES THE, AH...EYEBALLS, MA'AM. STILL MONEY IN THE OLD DEAR'S PURSE.
AND YET THERE'S BRUISING 'ROUND HER NECK.
WHICH MEANS EITHER OUR MYSTERY MENTAL STOPPED HALFWAY THROUGH THE CHOPSOCKY TO GET OUT A NICE TIDY GARROTTE--
--OR HE'S PINCHED A BLOODY NECKLACE AND LEFT EVERYTHING ELSE. HM.
...
I HAVE A JOB FOR YOU, MILK.
YES, MA'AM. Y-YOU WANT ME TO TAKE OUT THE SNIFFERS, DON'T YOU, MA'AM?
YES I DO.
E-EVEN THOUGH YOU KNOW I FEAR AND DESPISE THE 'ORRIBLE LITTLE THINGS.
EVEN THOUGH.
IS...IS THIS BECAUSE I SAW YOU NAKED LAST NIGHT, MA'AM?
IT IS NOT.
I-IS IT BECAUSE I FORGOT TO BRING YOU A BACON SANDWICH?
NOPE.
O-OR BECAUSE THAT SCABBY LITTLE BASTARD PUG'S AWAY ON MESSENGER DUTY AND IT'S NORMALLY HIS JOB? C-COS THAT'S JUST NOT FAIR, MA'AM.
NO, MILK. IT'S NONE OF THAT.

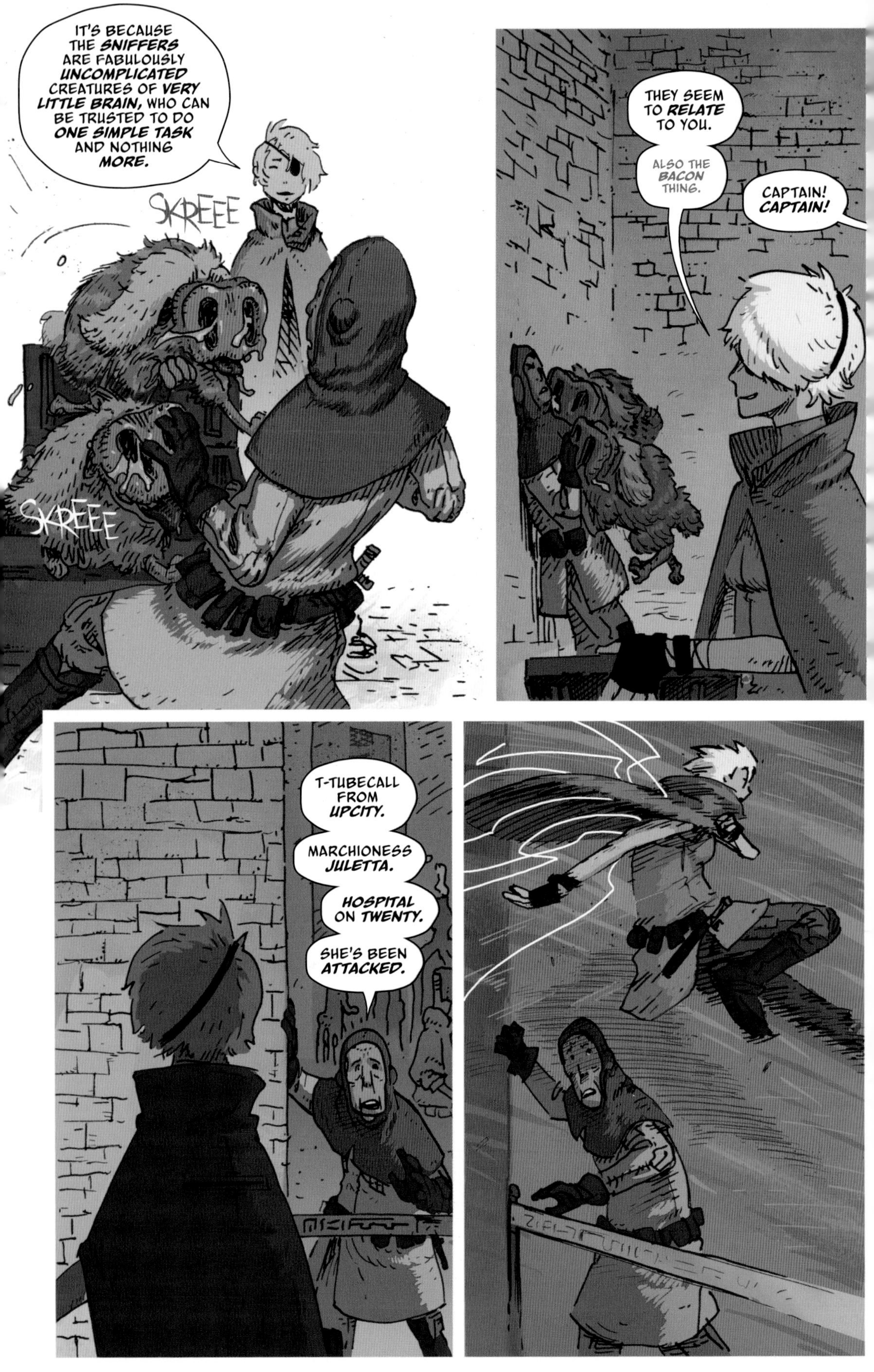
IT'S BECAUSE THE SNIFFERS ARE FABULOUSLY UNCOMPLICATED CREATURES OF VERY LITTLE BRAIN, WHO CAN BE TRUSTED TO DO ONE SIMPLE TASK AND NOTHING MORE.
SKREEE
SKREEE
THEY SEEM TO RELATE TO YOU.
ALSO THE BACON THING.
CAPTAIN! CAPTAIN!
T-TUBECALL FROM UPCITY.
MARCHIONESS JULETTA.
HOSPITAL ON TWENTY.
SHE'S BEEN ATTACKED.

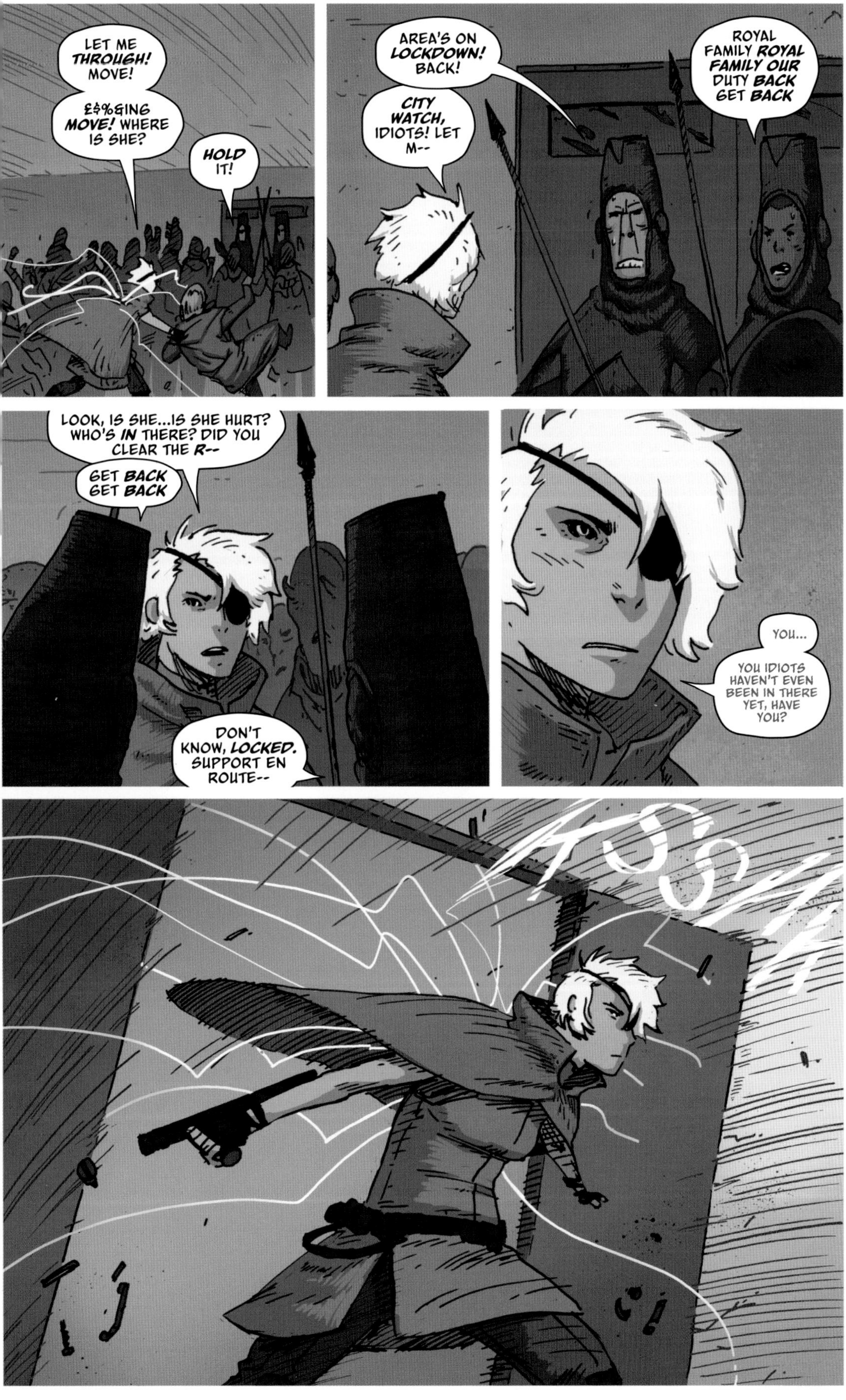
LET ME THROUGH! MOVE!
£$%&ING MOVE! WHERE IS SHE?
HOLD IT!
AREA'S ON LOCKDOWN! BACK!
CITY WATCH, IDIOTS! LET M--
ROYAL FAMILY ROYAL FAMILY OUR DUTY BACK GET BACK
LOOK, IS SHE...IS SHE HURT? WHO'S IN THERE? DID YOU CLEAR THE R--
GET BACK GET BACK
DON'T KNOW, LOCKED. SUPPORT EN ROUTE--
YOU...
YOU IDIOTS HAVEN'T EVEN BEEN IN THERE YET, HAVE YOU?
KSSHH

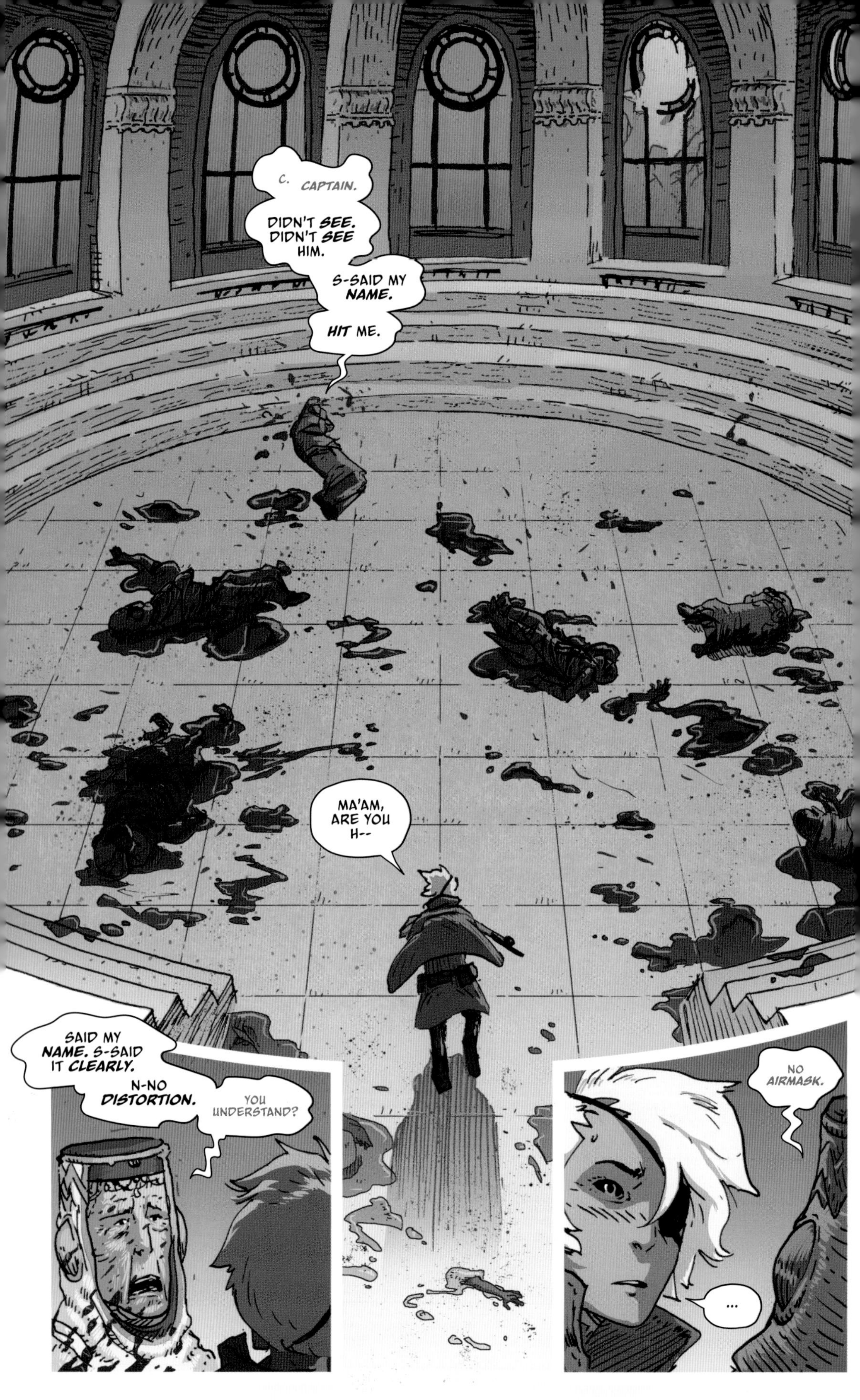
C. CAPTAIN.
DIDN'T SEE. DIDN'T SEE HIM.
S-SAID MY NAME.
HIT ME.
MA'AM, ARE YOU H--
SAID MY NAME. S-SAID IT CLEARLY.
N-NO DISTORTION.
YOU UNDERSTAND?
NO AIRMASK.
...

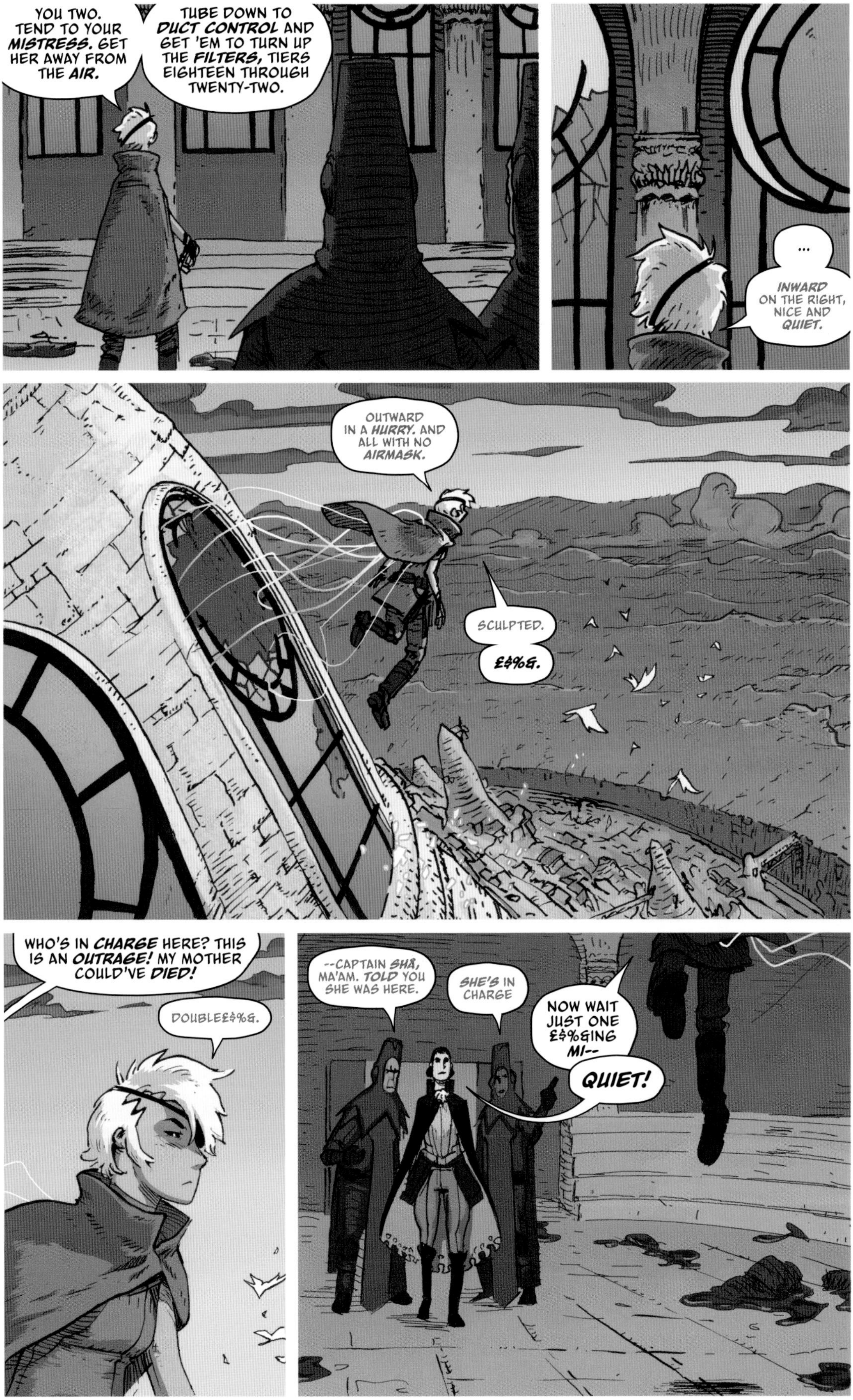
YOU TWO. TEND TO YOUR MISTRESS. GET HER AWAY FROM THE AIR.
TUBE DOWN TO DUCT CONTROL AND GET 'EM TO TURN UP THE FILTERS, TIERS EIGHTEEN THROUGH TWENTY-TWO.
...
INWARD ON THE RIGHT, NICE AND QUIET.
OUTWARD IN A HURRY. AND ALL WITH NO AIRMASK.
SCULPTED.
£$%&.
WHO'S IN CHARGE HERE? THIS IS AN OUTRAGE! MY MOTHER COULD'VE DIED!
DOUBLE£$%&.
--CAPTAIN SHĀ, MA'AM. TOLD YOU SHE WAS HERE.
SHE'S IN CHARGE
NOW WAIT JUST ONE £$%&ING MI--
QUIET!

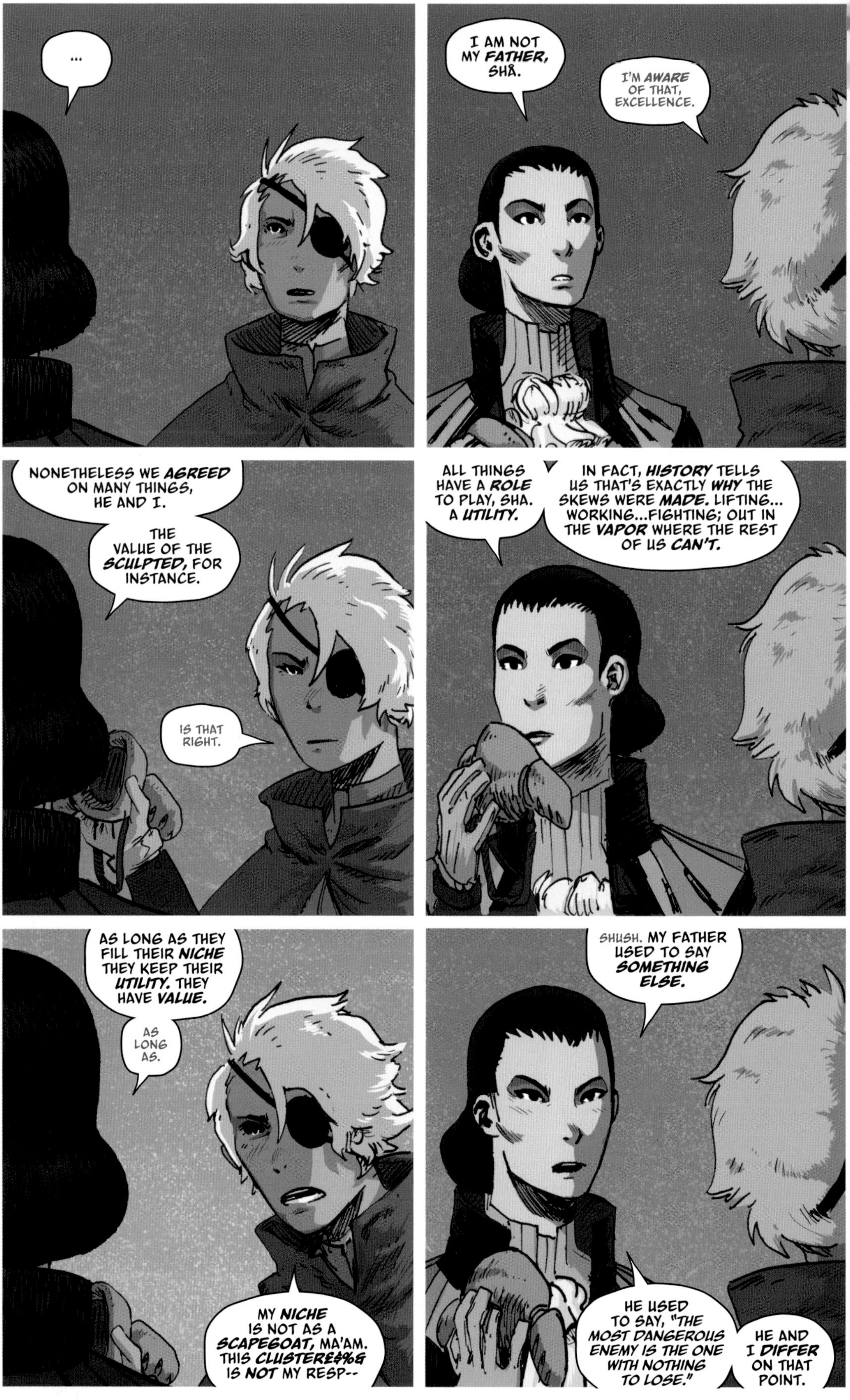
...
I AM NOT MY FATHER, SHĂ.
I'M AWARE OF THAT, EXCELLENCE.
NONETHELESS WE AGREED ON MANY THINGS, HE AND I.
THE VALUE OF THE SCULPTED, FOR INSTANCE.
IS THAT RIGHT.
ALL THINGS HAVE A ROLE TO PLAY, SHA. A UTILITY.
IN FACT, HISTORY TELLS US THAT'S EXACTLY WHY THE SKEWS WERE MADE. LIFTING... WORKING...FIGHTING; OUT IN THE VAPOR WHERE THE REST OF US CAN'T.
AS LONG AS THEY FILL THEIR NICHE THEY KEEP THEIR UTILITY. THEY HAVE VALUE.
AS LONG AS.
MY NICHE IS NOT AS A SCAPEGOAT, MA'AM. THIS CLUSTERE$%& IS NOT MY RESP--
SHUSH. MY FATHER USED TO SAY SOMETHING ELSE.
HE USED TO SAY, "THE MOST DANGEROUS ENEMY IS THE ONE WITH NOTHING TO LOSE."
HE AND I DIFFER ON THAT POINT.

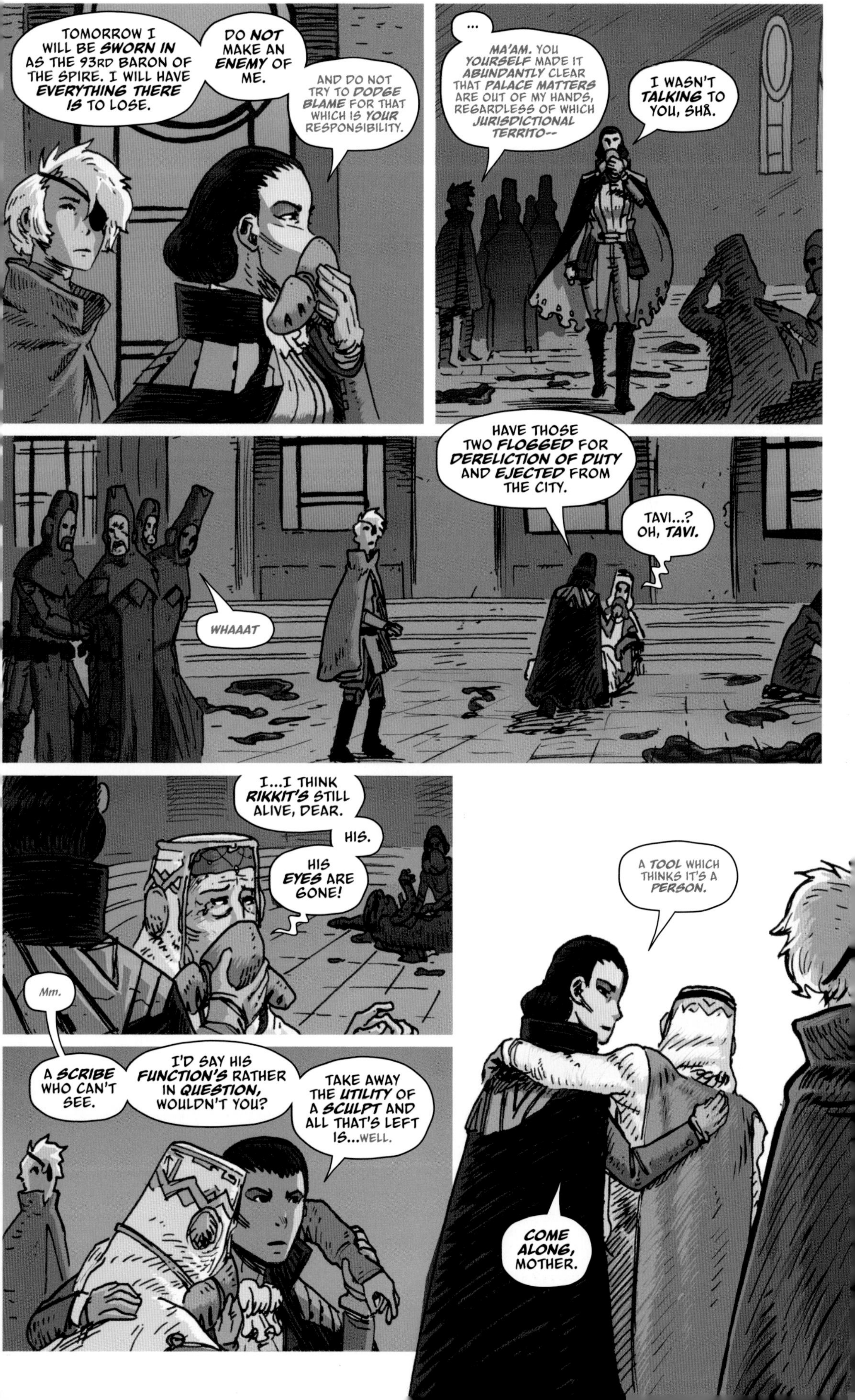
TOMORROW I WILL BE SWORN IN AS THE 93RD BARON OF THE SPIRE. I WILL HAVE EVERYTHING THERE IS TO LOSE.
DO NOT MAKE AN ENEMY OF ME.
AND DO NOT TRY TO DODGE BLAME FOR THAT WHICH IS YOUR RESPONSIBILITY.
...
MA'AM. YOU YOURSELF MADE IT ABUNDANTLY CLEAR THAT PALACE MATTERS ARE OUT OF MY HANDS, REGARDLESS OF WHICH JURISDICTIONAL TERRITO--
I WASN'T TALKING TO YOU, SHÅ.
HAVE THOSE TWO FLOGGED FOR DERELICTION OF DUTY AND EJECTED FROM THE CITY.
WHAAAT
TAVI...? OH, TAVI.
I...I THINK RIKKIT'S STILL ALIVE, DEAR.
HIS.
HIS EYES ARE GONE!
Mm.
A SCRIBE WHO CAN'T SEE.
I'D SAY HIS FUNCTION'S RATHER IN QUESTION, WOULDN'T YOU?
TAKE AWAY THE UTILITY OF A SCULPT AND ALL THAT'S LEFT IS...WELL.
A TOOL WHICH THINKS IT'S A PERSON.
COME ALONG, MOTHER.

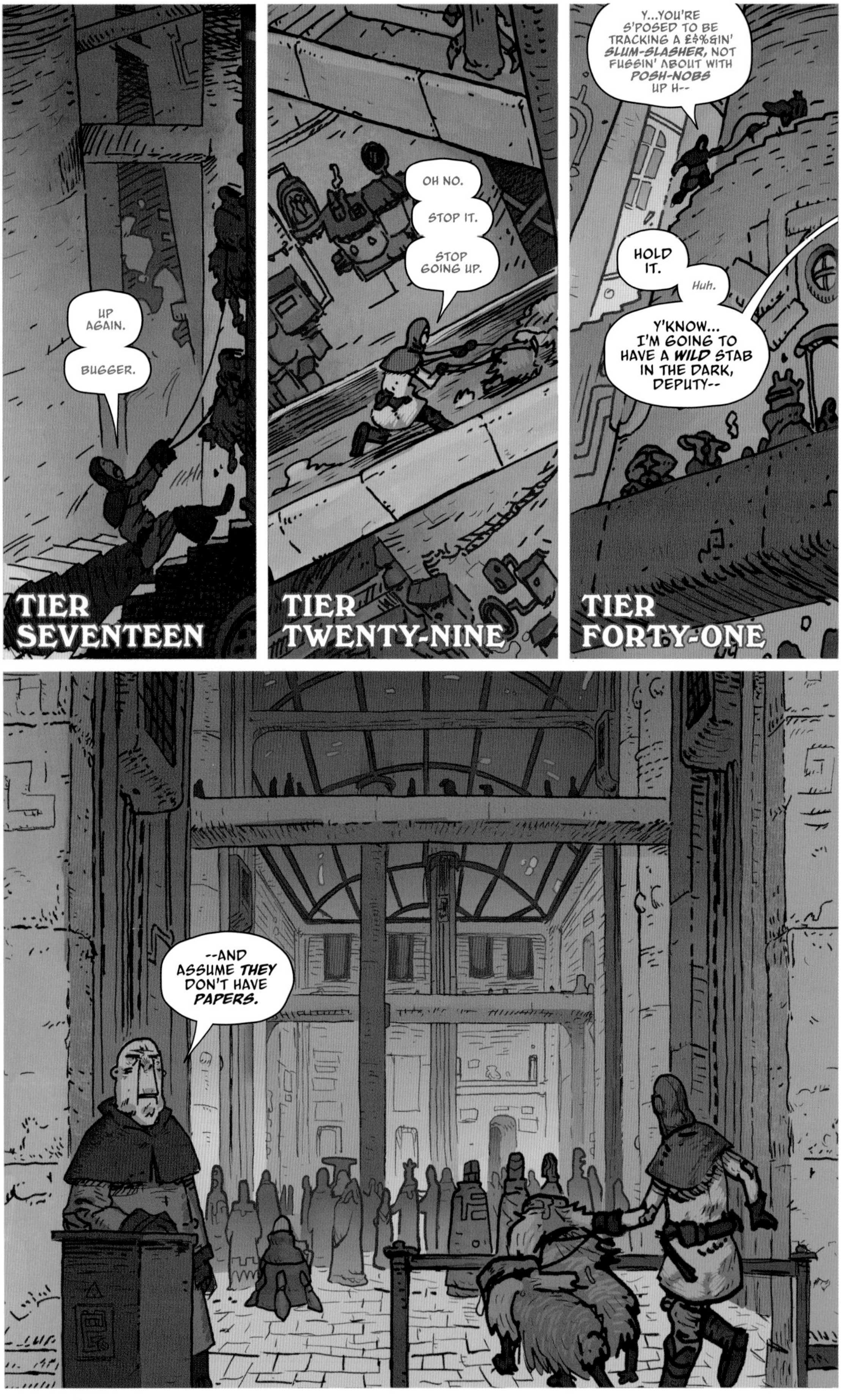
UP AGAIN.
BUGGER.
TIER SEVENTEEN
OH NO.
STOP IT.
STOP GOING UP.
TIER TWENTY-NINE
Y...YOU'RE S'POSED TO BE TRACKING A £$%&IN' SLUM-SLASHER, NOT FUSSIN' ABOUT WITH POSH-NOBS UP H--
HOLD IT.
Huh.
Y'KNOW... I'M GOING TO HAVE A WILD STAB IN THE DARK, DEPUTY--
TIER FORTY-ONE
--AND ASSUME THEY DON'T HAVE PAPERS.

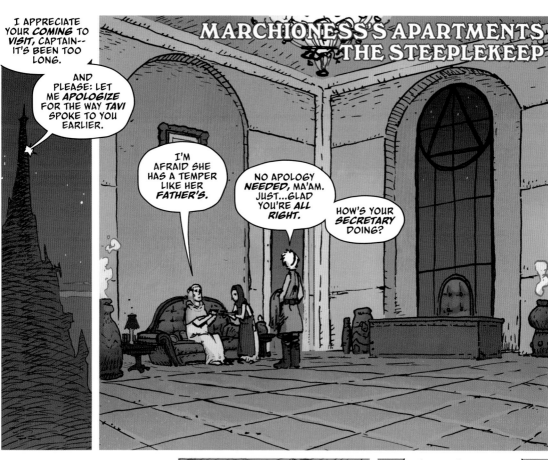

MARCHIONESS'S APARTMENTS THE STEEPLEKEEP
I APPRECIATE YOUR COMING TO VISIT, CAPTAIN-- IT'S BEEN TOO LONG.
AND PLEASE: LET ME APOLOGIZE FOR THE WAY TAVI SPOKE TO YOU EARLIER.
I'M AFRAID SHE HAS A TEMPER LIKE HER FATHER'S.
NO APOLOGY NEEDED, MA'AM. JUST...GLAD YOU'RE ALL RIGHT.
HOW'S YOUR SECRETARY DOING?
RIKKIT? OHHH, CONFUSED. FRIGHTENED. BUT WELL LOOKED AFTER, AT LEAST.
I WENT OVER TAVI'S HEAD AND HAD THE POOR FELLOW TAKEN TO THE ROYAL PHYSICIAN. IT'S THE LEAST WE COULD DO.
ALL THAT "UTILITY" NONSENSE-- REALLY.
ACTUALLY, I...I MIGHT LIKE TO SPEAK TO HIM, MA'AM. THE SCRIBE, I MEAN. HE MIGHT'VE SEEN SOMETHING.
NEVER AGAIN THOUGH, MM? POOR THING.
BUT...YES: OF COURSE. SPEAK TO WHOMEVER YOU WISH, DEAR. YOU HAVE MY FULL SANCTION IN INVESTIGATING ALL THIS. WHATEVER TAVI MAY SAY.
I'M, AH. I'M ACTUALLY SORT OF DOING THAT RIGHT NOW, MA'AM. SORRY.
IT WAS A... DIFFERENT MEMBER OF YOUR STAFF I CAME TO TALK ABOUT.
AH.
MADAM KEAN.

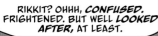

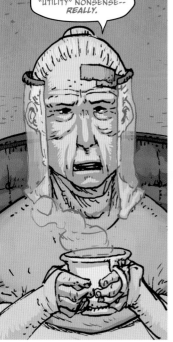

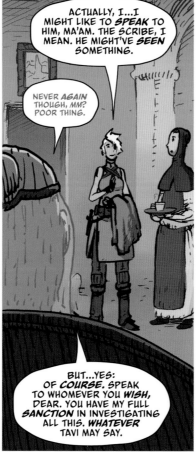

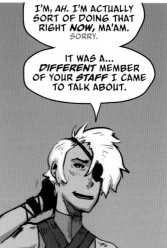

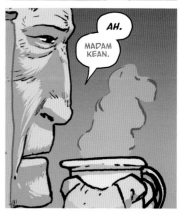

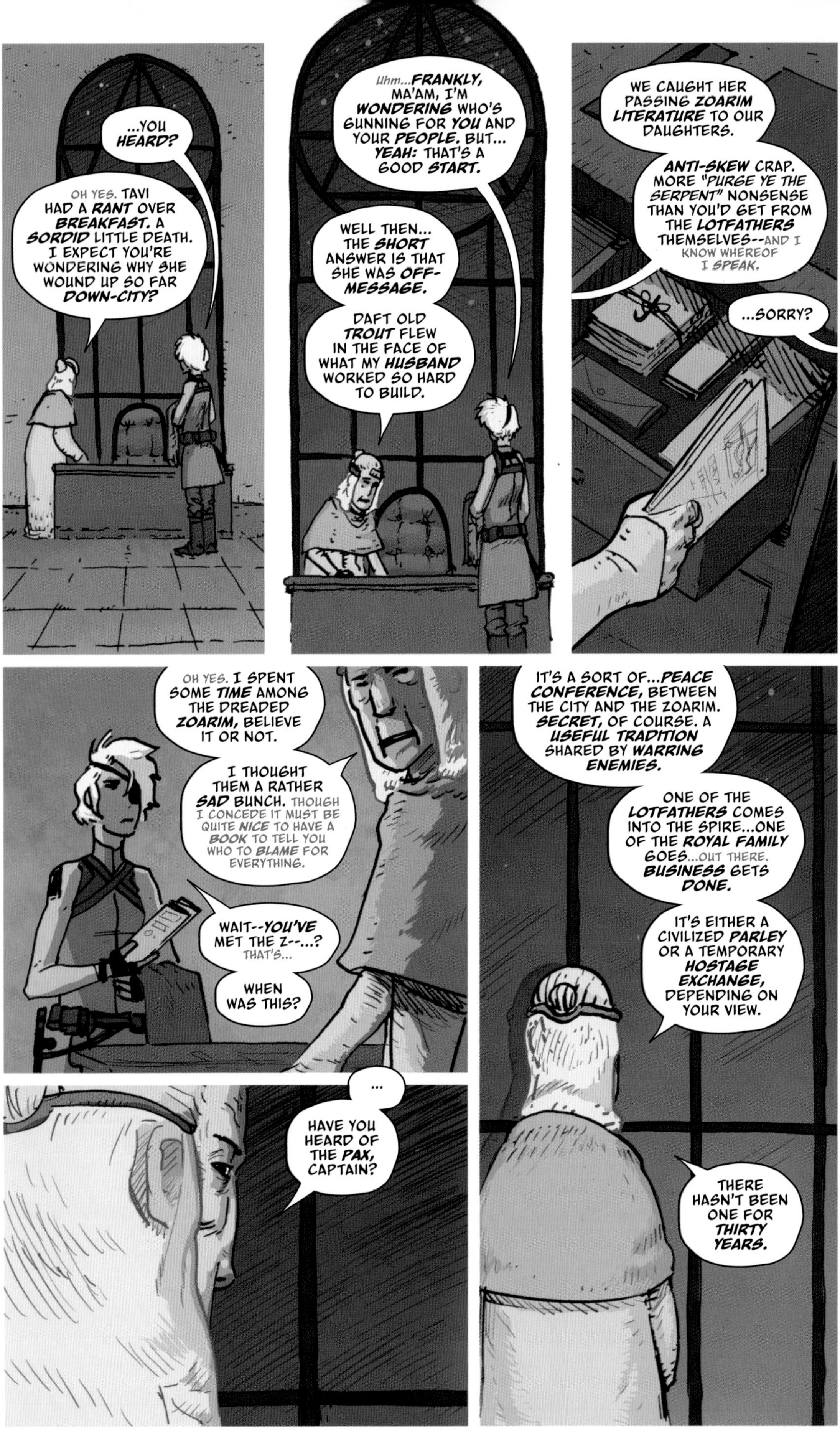
...YOU HEARD?
OH YES. TAVI HAD A RANT OVER BREAKFAST. A SORDID LITTLE DEATH. I EXPECT YOU'RE WONDERING WHY SHE WOUND UP SO FAR DOWN-CITY?
Uhm...FRANKLY, MA'AM, I'M WONDERING WHO'S GUNNING FOR YOU AND YOUR PEOPLE. BUT... YEAH: THAT'S A GOOD START.
WELL THEN... THE SHORT ANSWER IS THAT SHE WAS OFF-MESSAGE.
DAFT OLD TROUT FLEW IN THE FACE OF WHAT MY HUSBAND WORKED SO HARD TO BUILD.
WE CAUGHT HER PASSING ZOARIM LITERATURE TO OUR DAUGHTERS.
ANTI-SKEW CRAP. MORE "PURGE YE THE SERPENT" NONSENSE THAN YOU'D GET FROM THE LOTFATHERS THEMSELVES--AND I KNOW WHEREOF I SPEAK.
...SORRY?
OH YES. I SPENT SOME TIME AMONG THE DREADED ZOARIM, BELIEVE IT OR NOT.
I THOUGHT THEM A RATHER SAD BUNCH. THOUGH I CONCEDE IT MUST BE QUITE NICE TO HAVE A BOOK TO TELL YOU WHO TO BLAME FOR EVERYTHING.
WAIT--YOU'VE MET THE Z--...? THAT'S...
WHEN WAS THIS?
...
HAVE YOU HEARD OF THE PAX, CAPTAIN?
IT'S A SORT OF...PEACE CONFERENCE, BETWEEN THE CITY AND THE ZOARIM. SECRET, OF COURSE. A USEFUL TRADITION SHARED BY WARRING ENEMIES.
ONE OF THE LOTFATHERS COMES INTO THE SPIRE...ONE OF THE ROYAL FAMILY GOES...OUT THERE. BUSINESS GETS DONE.
IT'S EITHER A CIVILIZED PARLEY OR A TEMPORARY HOSTAGE EXCHANGE, DEPENDING ON YOUR VIEW.
THERE HASN'T BEEN ONE FOR THIRTY YEARS.

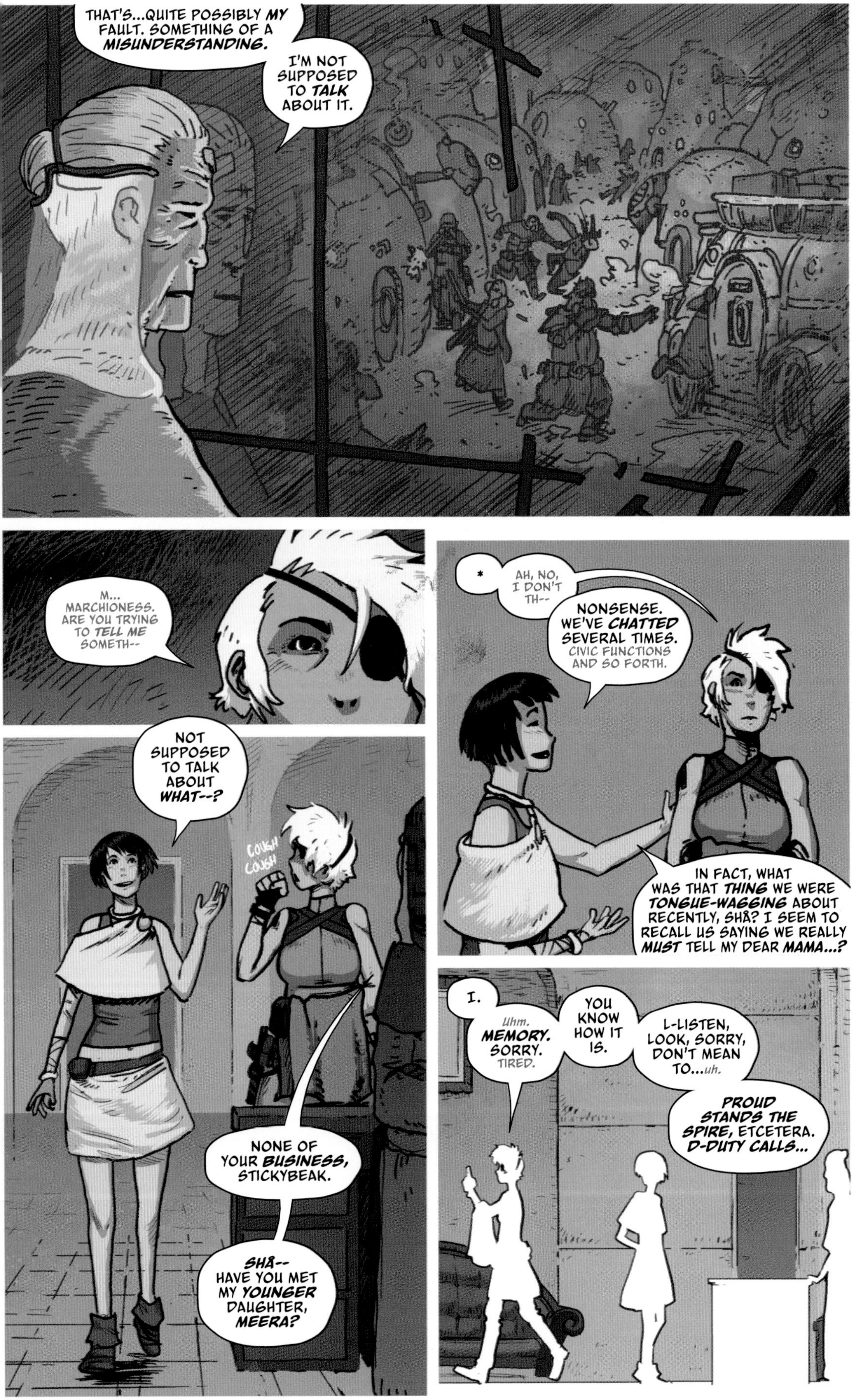
THAT'S...QUITE POSSIBLY MY FAULT. SOMETHING OF A MISUNDERSTANDING.
I'M NOT SUPPOSED TO TALK ABOUT IT.
M... MARCHIONESS. ARE YOU TRYING TO TELL ME SOMETH--
*
AH, NO, I DON'T TH--
NONSENSE. WE'VE CHATTED SEVERAL TIMES. CIVIC FUNCTIONS AND SO FORTH.
IN FACT, WHAT WAS THAT THING WE WERE TONGUE-WAGGING ABOUT RECENTLY, SHĀ? I SEEM TO RECALL US SAYING WE REALLY MUST TELL MY DEAR MAMA...?
NOT SUPPOSED TO TALK ABOUT WHAT--?
COUGH COUGH
NONE OF YOUR BUSINESS, STICKYBEAK.
SHĀ-- HAVE YOU MET MY YOUNGER DAUGHTER, MEERA?
I.
Uhm. MEMORY. SORRY. TIRED.
YOU KNOW HOW IT IS.
L-LISTEN, LOOK, SORRY, DON'T MEAN TO...uh.
PROUD STANDS THE SPIRE, ETCETERA. D-DUTY CALLS...

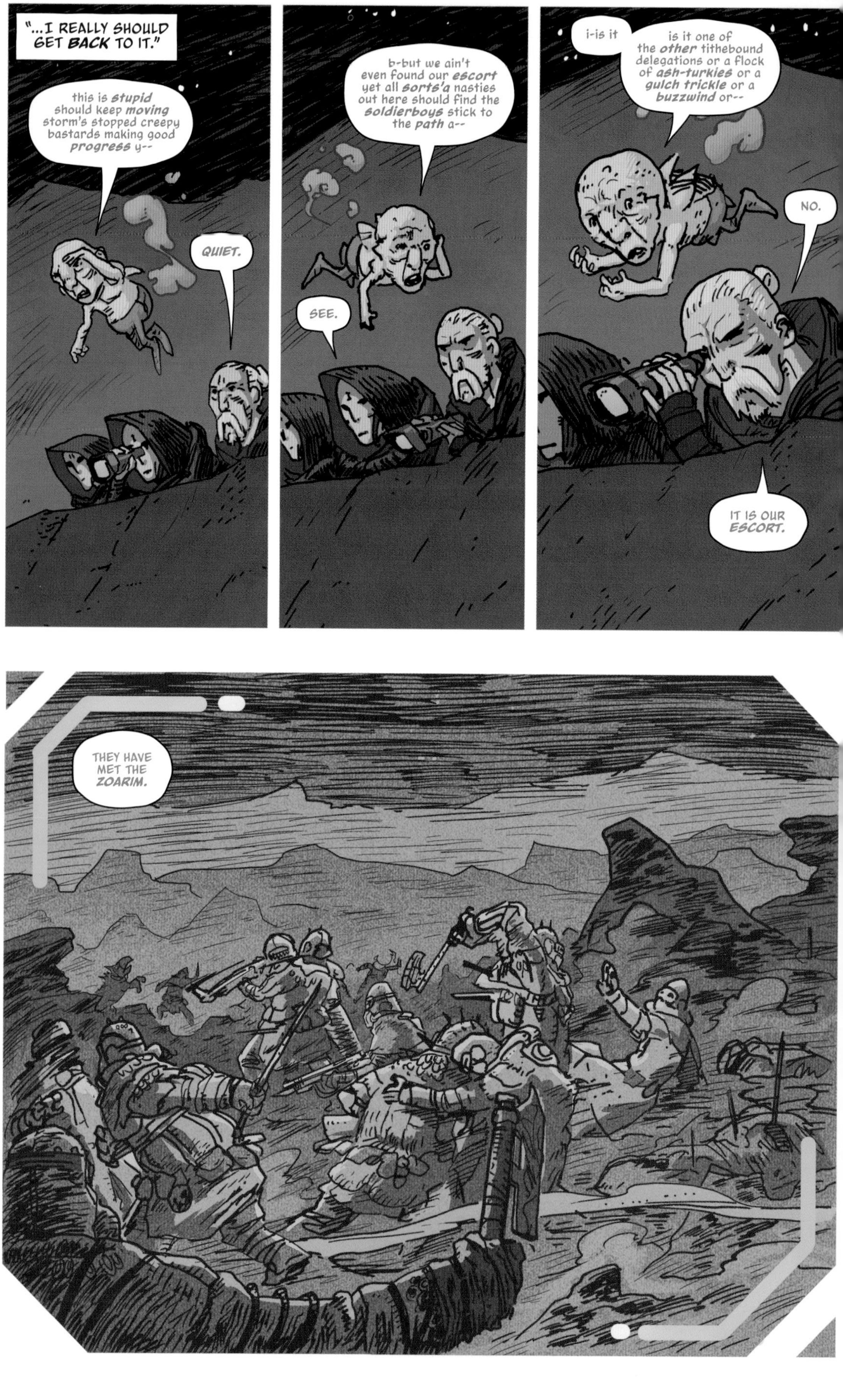
"...I REALLY SHOULD GET BACK TO IT."
this is stupid should keep moving storm's stopped creepy bastards making good progress y--
QUIET.
b-but we ain't even found our escort yet all sorts'a nasties out here should find the soldierboys stick to the path a--
SEE.
i-is it
is it one of the other tithebound delegations or a flock of ash-turkies or a gulch trickle or a buzzwind or--
NO.
IT IS OUR ESCORT.
THEY HAVE MET THE ZOARIM.

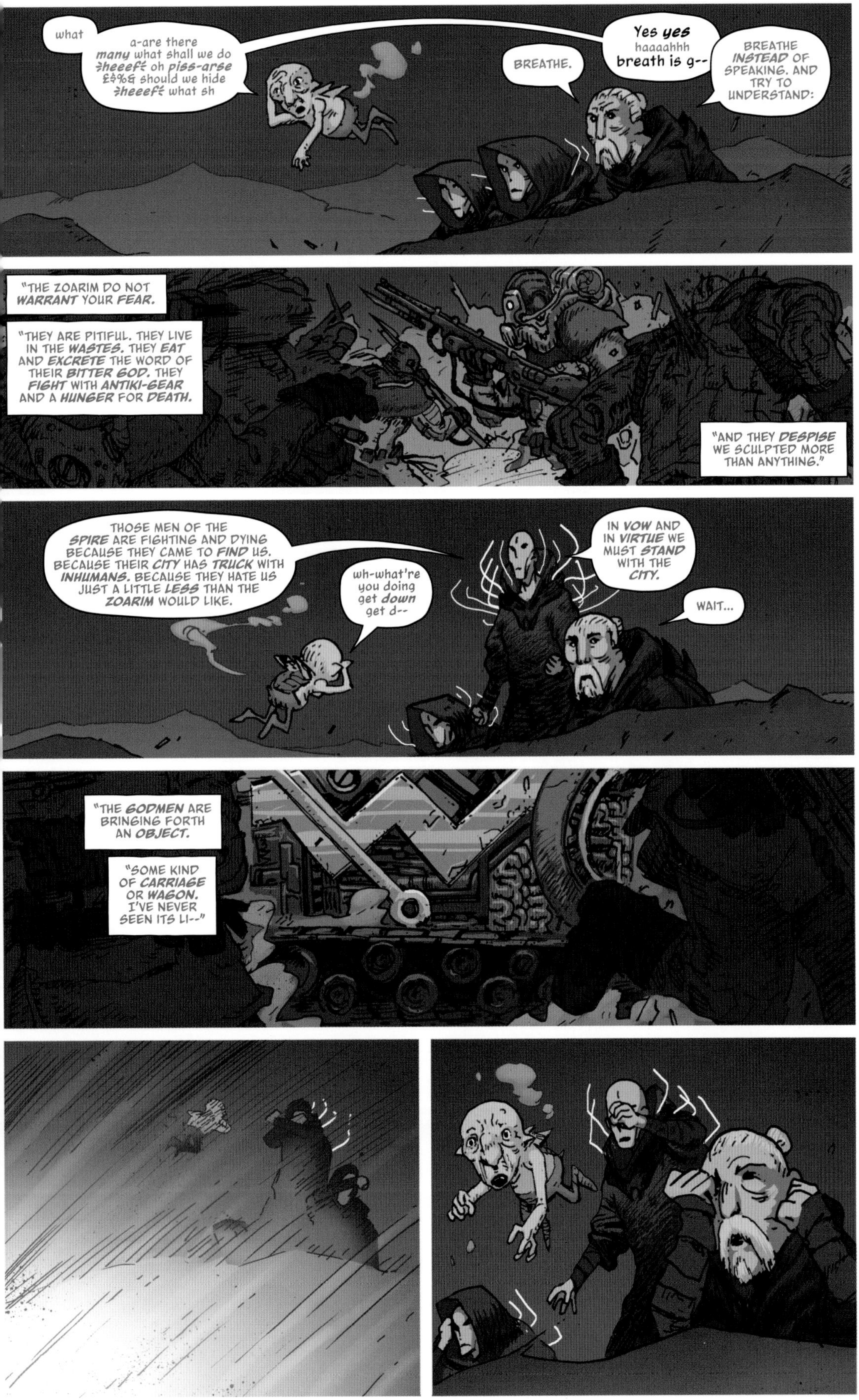
what
a-are there many what shall we do ≠heeef≠ oh piss-arse £$%& should we hide ≠heeef≠ what sh
Yes yes haaaahhh breath is g--
BREATHE.
BREATHE INSTEAD OF SPEAKING. AND TRY TO UNDERSTAND:
"THE ZOARIM DO NOT WARRANT YOUR FEAR.
"THEY ARE PITIFUL. THEY LIVE IN THE WASTES. THEY EAT AND EXCRETE THE WORD OF THEIR BITTER GOD. THEY FIGHT WITH ANTIKI-GEAR AND A HUNGER FOR DEATH.
"AND THEY DESPISE WE SCULPTED MORE THAN ANYTHING."
THOSE MEN OF THE SPIRE ARE FIGHTING AND DYING BECAUSE THEY CAME TO FIND US. BECAUSE THEIR CITY HAS TRUCK WITH INHUMANS. BECAUSE THEY HATE US JUST A LITTLE LESS THAN THE ZOARIM WOULD LIKE.
IN VOW AND IN VIRTUE WE MUST STAND WITH THE CITY.
wh-what're you doing get down get d--
WAIT...
"THE GODMEN ARE BRINGING FORTH AN OBJECT.
"SOME KIND OF CARRIAGE OR WAGON. I'VE NEVER SEEN ITS LI--"

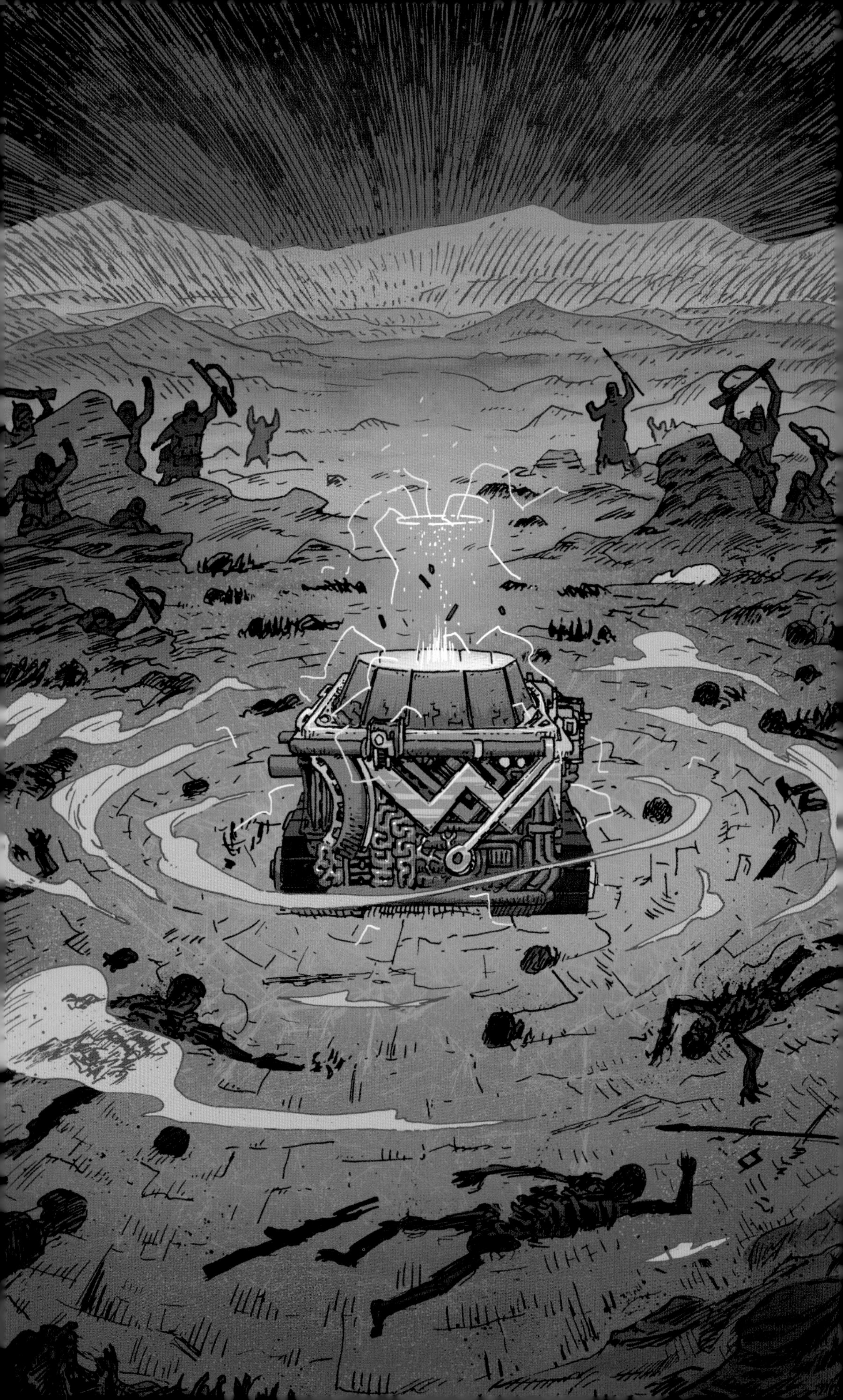

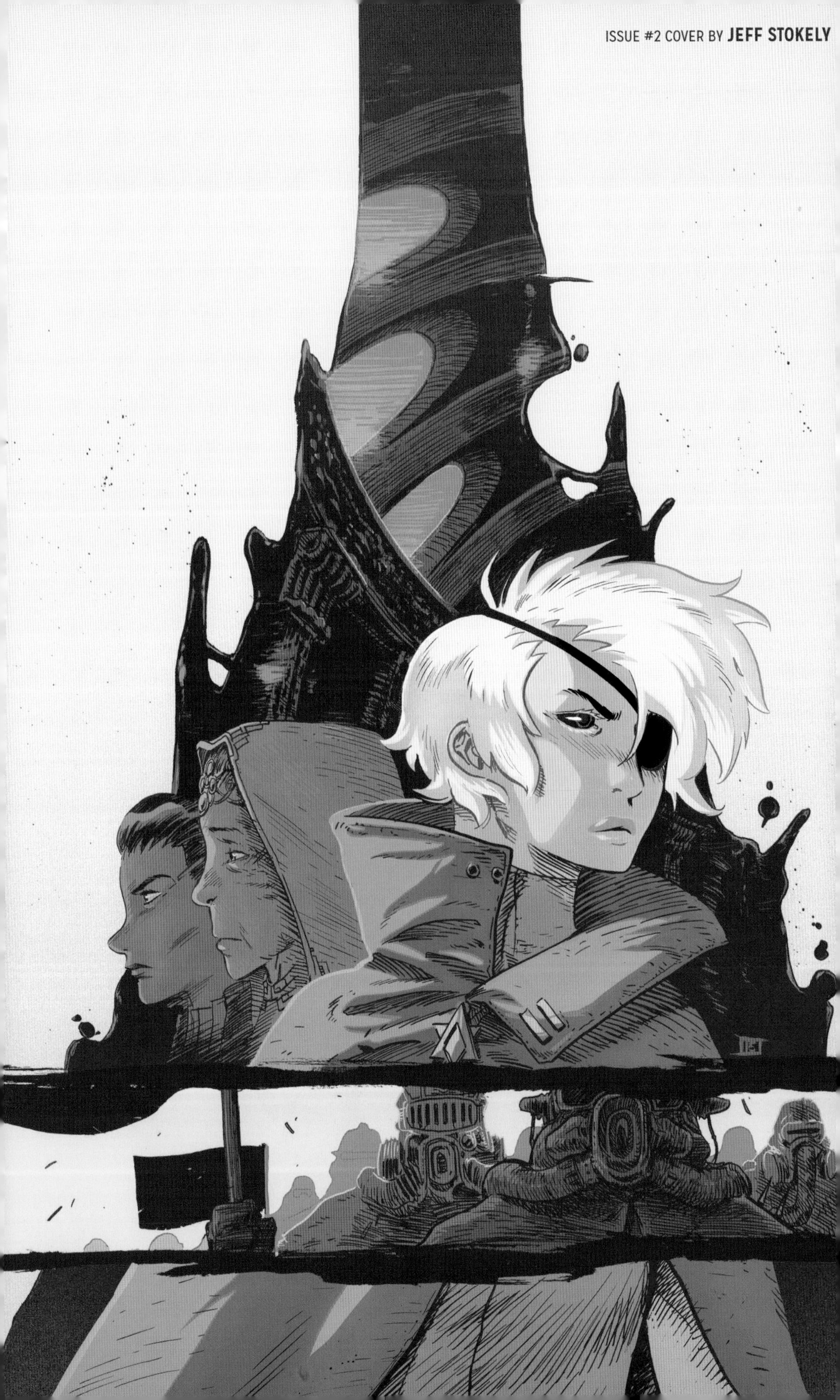

ISSUE #2 COVER BY **JEFF STOKELY**

CHAPTER THREE

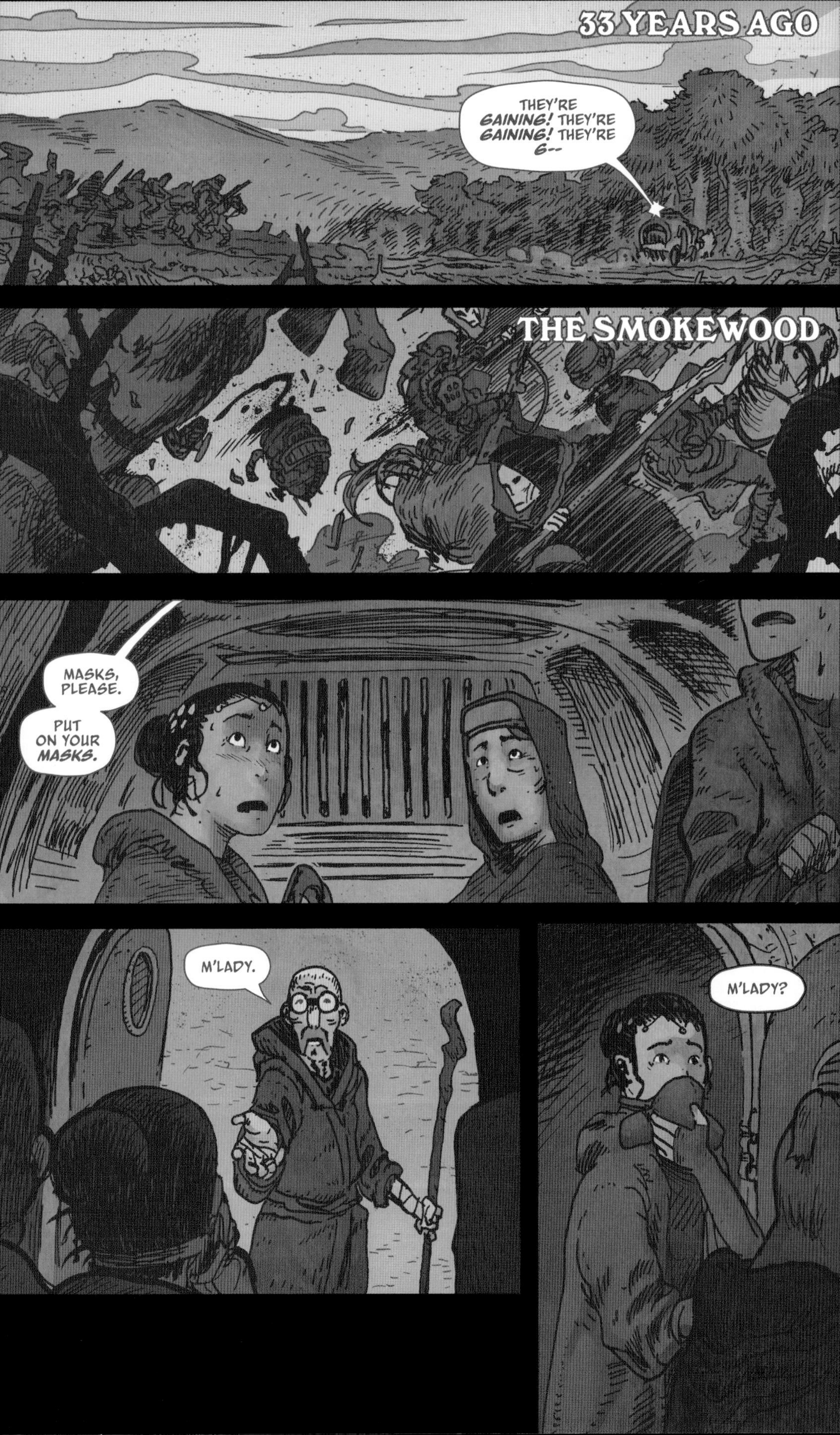
33 YEARS AGO
THEY'RE GAINING! THEY'RE GAINING! THEY'RE G--
THE SMOKEWOOD
MASKS, PLEASE.
PUT ON YOUR MASKS.
M'LADY.
M'LADY?

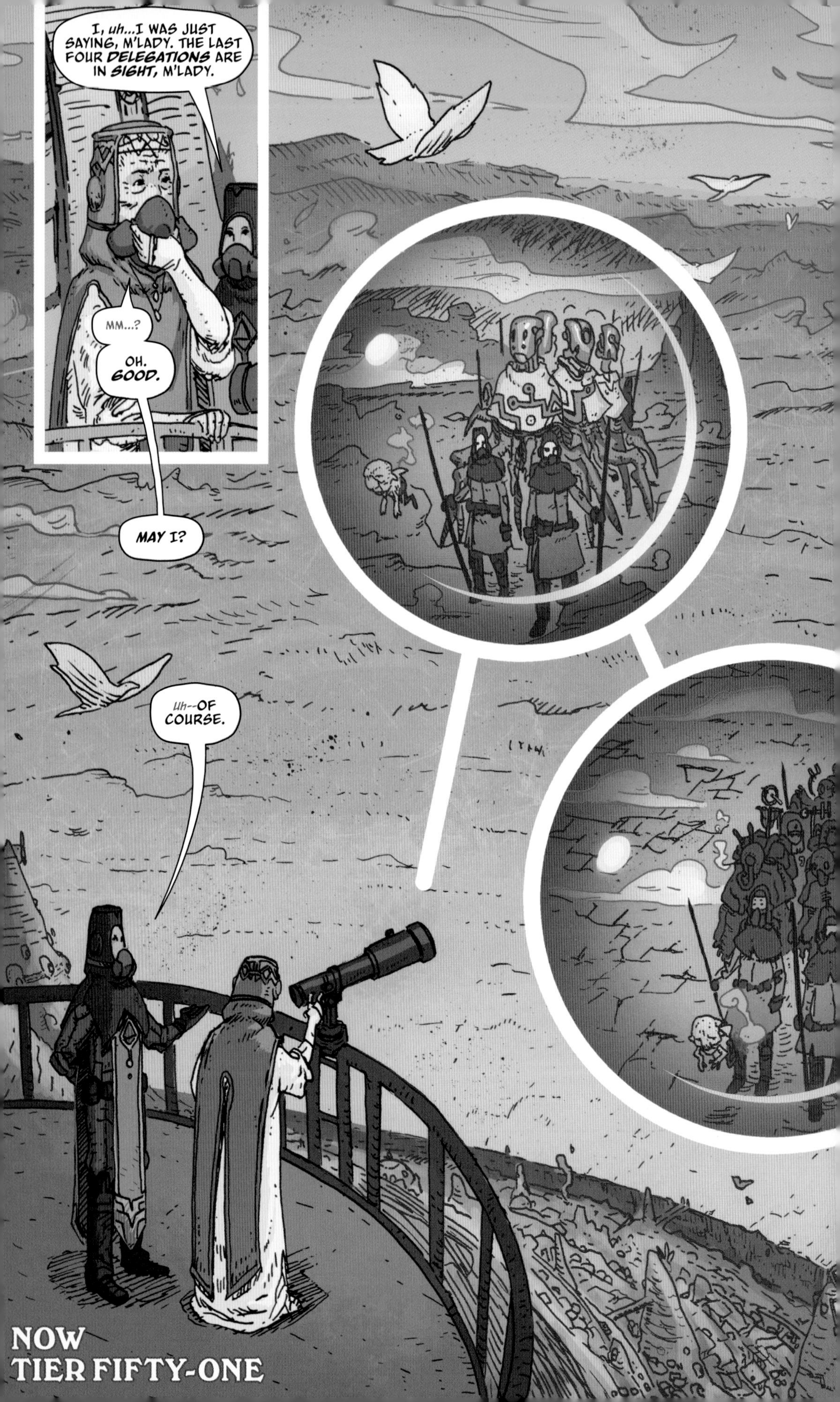
I, uh...I WAS JUST SAYING, M'LADY. THE LAST FOUR DELEGATIONS ARE IN SIGHT, M'LADY.
MM...?
OH. GOOD.
MAY I?
Uh--OF COURSE.
NOW
TIER FIFTY-ONE

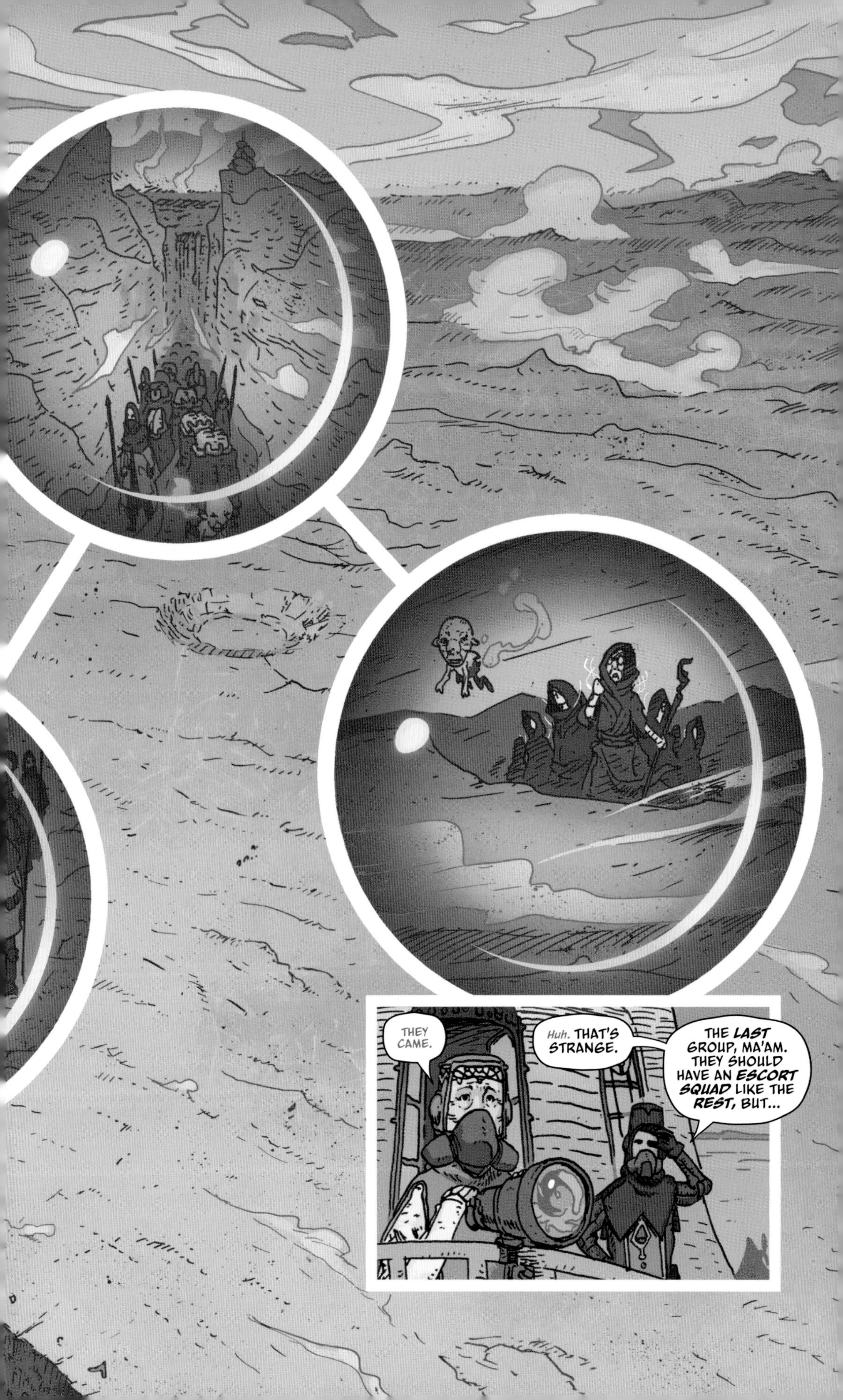
THEY CAME.
Huh. THAT'S STRANGE.
THE LAST GROUP, MA'AM. THEY SHOULD HAVE AN ESCORT SQUAD LIKE THE REST, BUT...

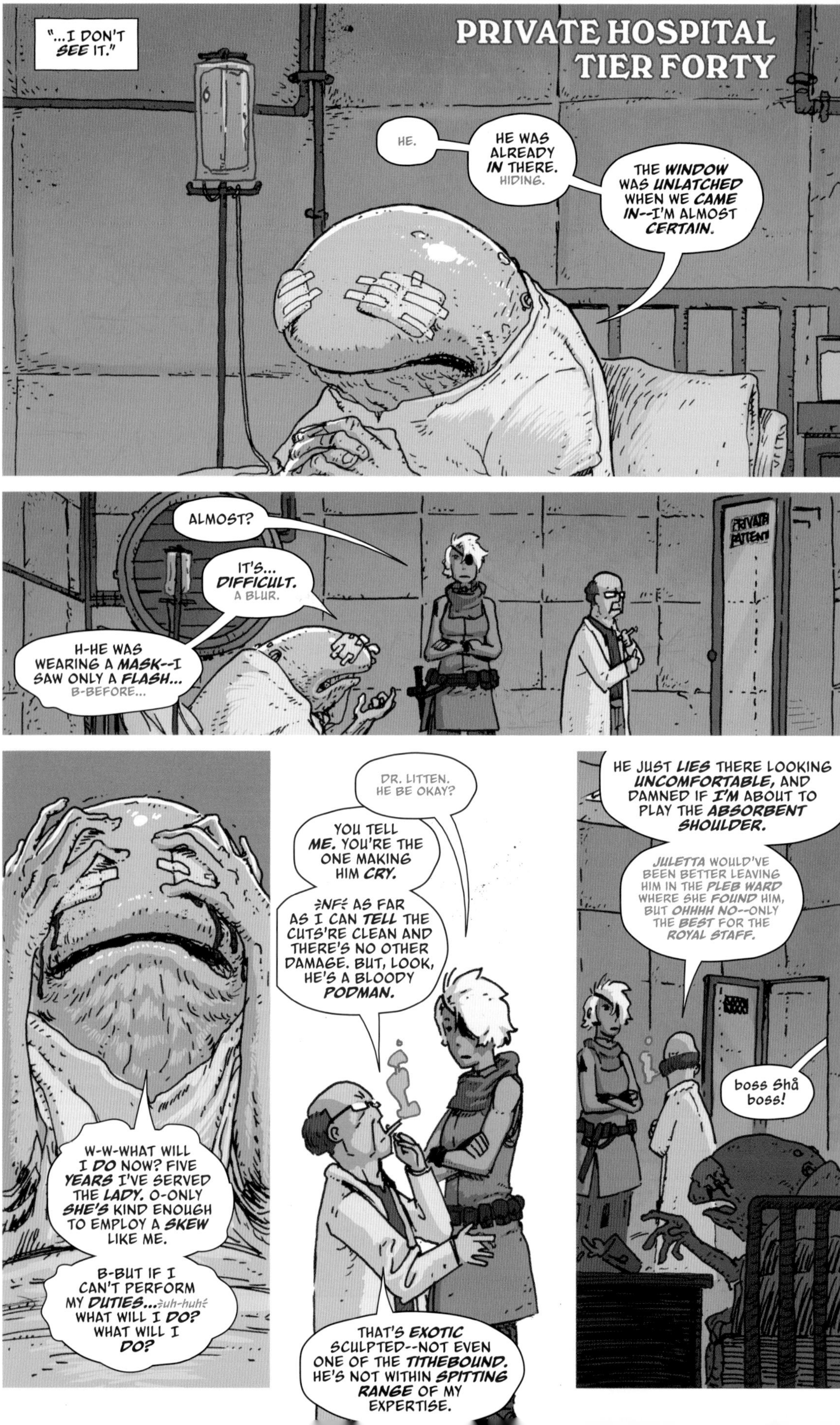
"...I DON'T SEE IT."
PRIVATE HOSPITAL TIER FORTY
HE.
HE WAS ALREADY IN THERE. HIDING.
THE WINDOW WAS UNLATCHED WHEN WE CAME IN--I'M ALMOST CERTAIN.
ALMOST?
IT'S... DIFFICULT. A BLUR.
H-HE WAS WEARING A MASK--I SAW ONLY A FLASH... B-BEFORE...
W-W-WHAT WILL I DO NOW? FIVE YEARS I'VE SERVED THE LADY. O-ONLY SHE'S KIND ENOUGH TO EMPLOY A SKEW LIKE ME.
B-BUT IF I CAN'T PERFORM MY DUTIES... ≑uh-huh≑ WHAT WILL I DO? WHAT WILL I DO?
DR. LITTEN. HE BE OKAY?
YOU TELL ME. YOU'RE THE ONE MAKING HIM CRY.
≑NF≑ AS FAR AS I CAN TELL THE CUTS'RE CLEAN AND THERE'S NO OTHER DAMAGE. BUT, LOOK, HE'S A BLOODY PODMAN.
THAT'S EXOTIC SCULPTED--NOT EVEN ONE OF THE TITHEBOUND. HE'S NOT WITHIN SPITTING RANGE OF MY EXPERTISE.
HE JUST LIES THERE LOOKING UNCOMFORTABLE, AND DAMNED IF I'M ABOUT TO PLAY THE ABSORBENT SHOULDER.
JULETTA WOULD'VE BEEN BETTER LEAVING HIM IN THE PLEB WARD WHERE SHE FOUND HIM, BUT OHHHH NO--ONLY THE BEST FOR THE ROYAL STAFF.
boss Shå boss!

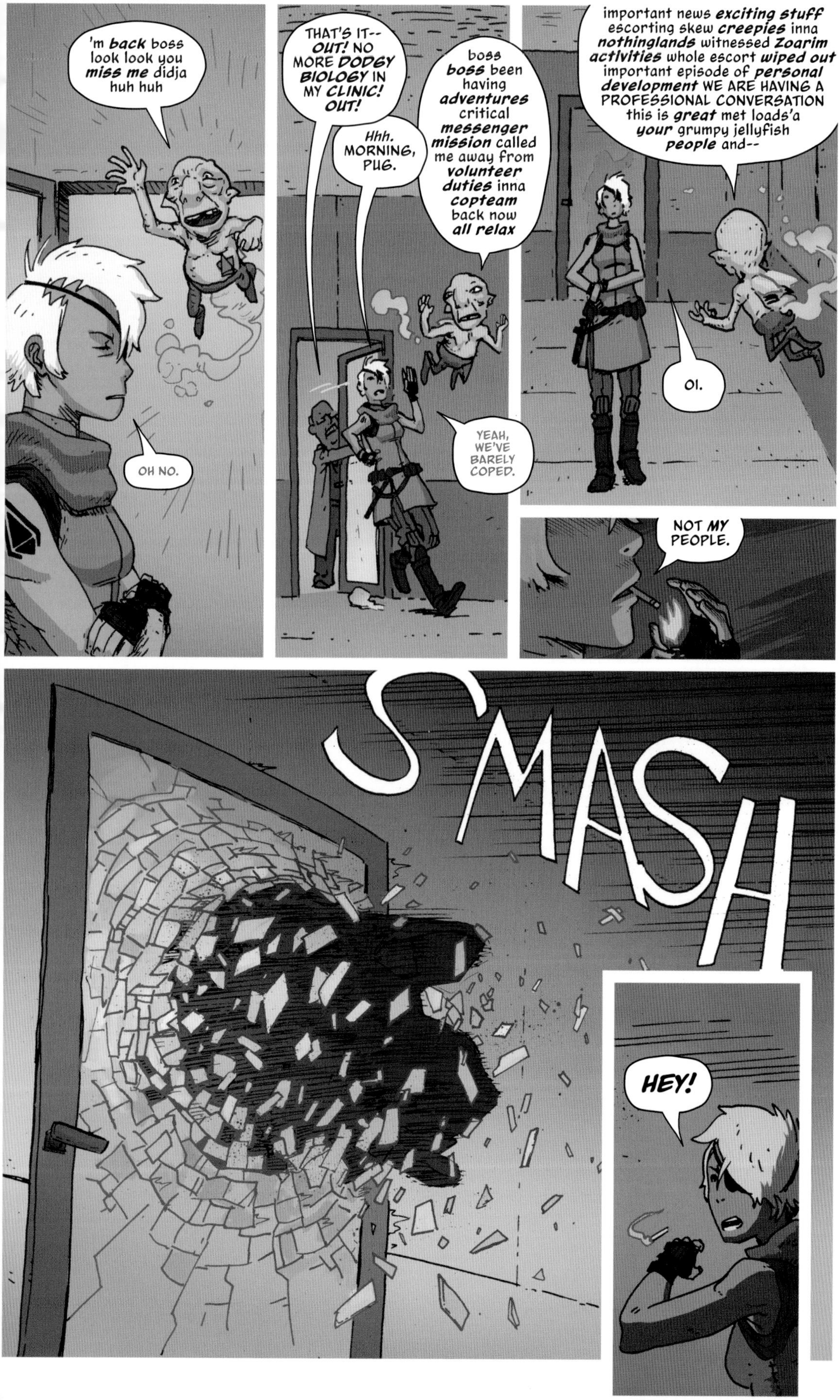

'm back boss look look you miss me didja huh huh
OH NO.
THAT'S IT-- OUT! NO MORE DODGY BIOLOGY IN MY CLINIC! OUT!
Hhh. MORNING, PUG.
boss boss been having adventures critical messenger mission called me away from volunteer duties inna copteam back now all relax
YEAH, WE'VE BARELY COPED.
important news exciting stuff escorting skew creepies inna nothinglands witnessed Zoarim activities whole escort wiped out important episode of personal development WE ARE HAVING A PROFESSIONAL CONVERSATION this is great met loads'a your grumpy jellyfish people and--
OI.
NOT MY PEOPLE.
SMASH
HEY!

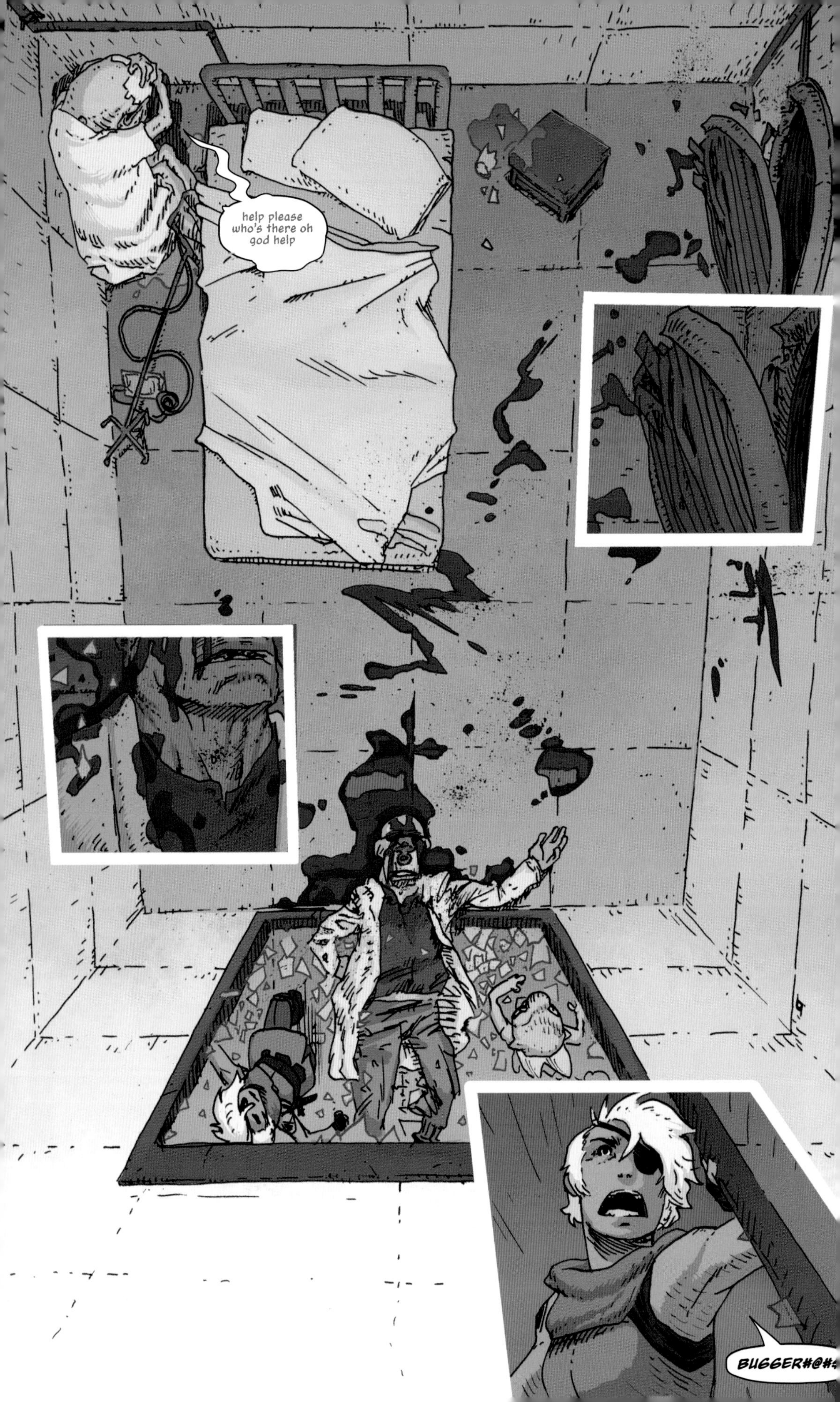
help please who's there oh god help
BUGGER#@#

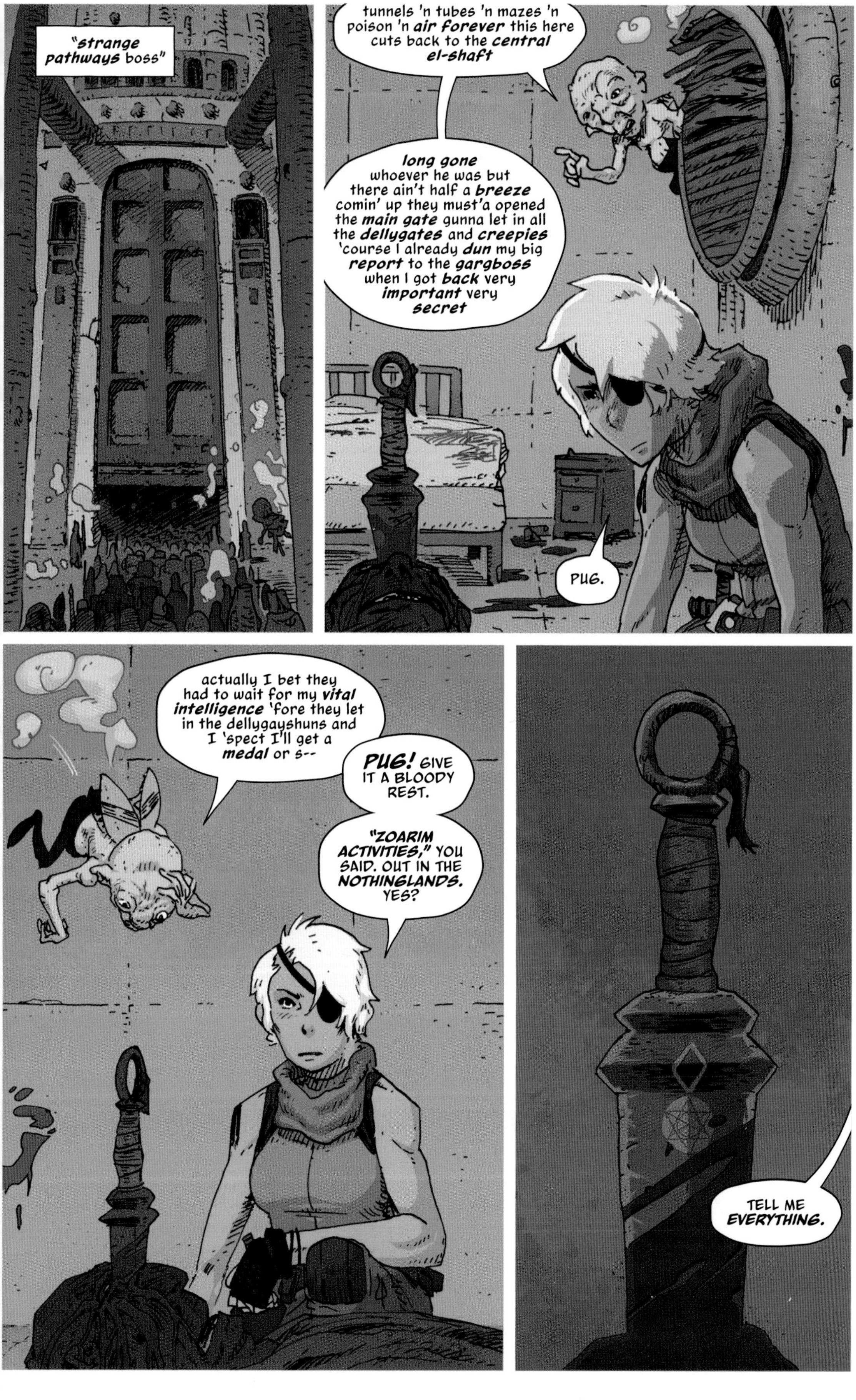
"strange pathways boss"
tunnels 'n tubes 'n mazes 'n poison 'n air forever this here cuts back to the central el-shaft
long gone whoever he was but there ain't half a breeze comin' up they must'a opened the main gate gunna let in all the dellygates and creepies 'course I already dun my big report to the gargboss when I got back very important very secret
PUG.
actually I bet they had to wait for my vital intelligence 'fore they let in the dellygayshuns and I 'spect I'll get a medal or s--
PUG! GIVE IT A BLOODY REST.
"ZOARIM ACTIVITIES," YOU SAID. OUT IN THE NOTHINGLANDS. YES?
TELL ME EVERYTHING.

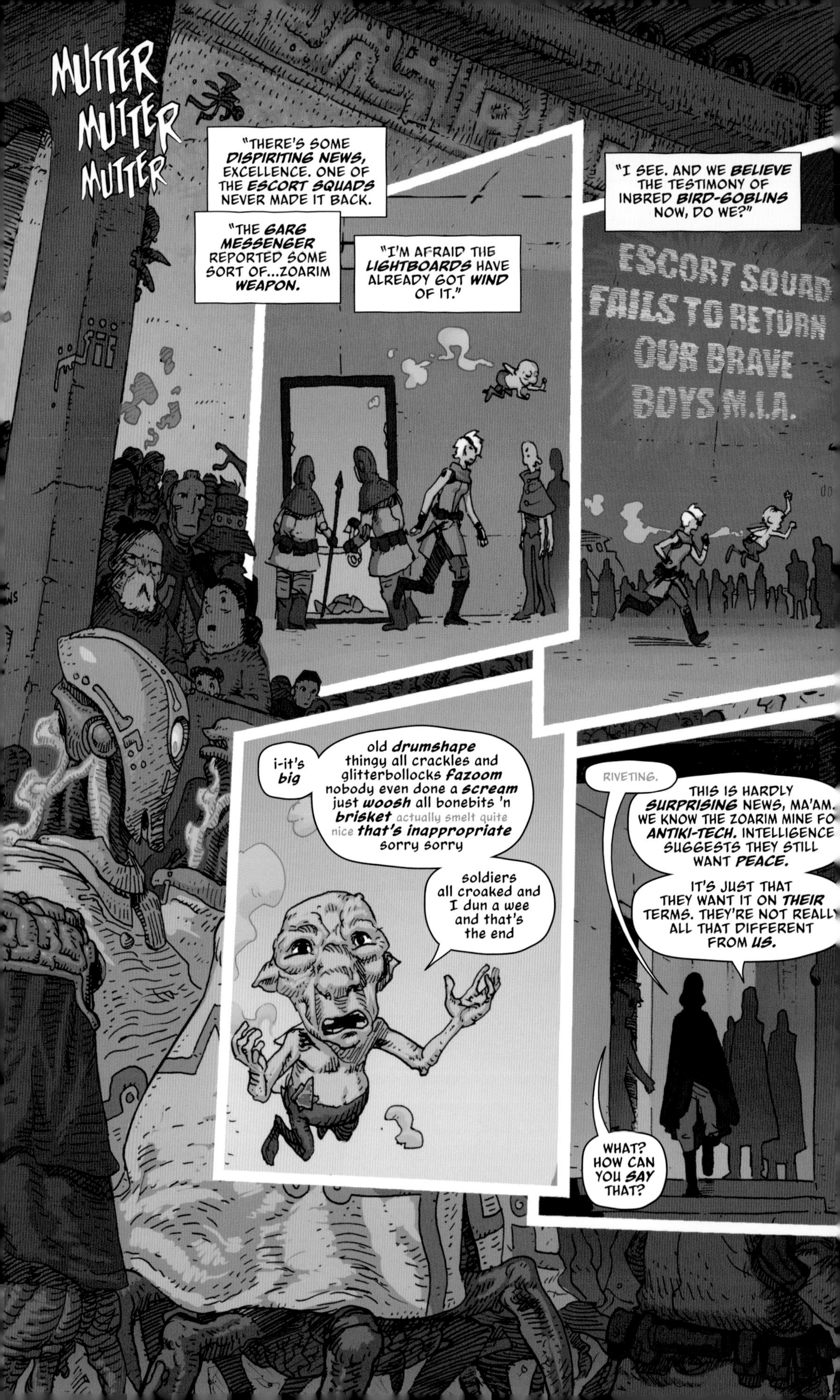

MUTTER MUTTER MUTTER
"THERE'S SOME DISPIRITING NEWS, EXCELLENCE. ONE OF THE ESCORT SQUADS NEVER MADE IT BACK.
"THE GARG MESSENGER REPORTED SOME SORT OF...ZOARIM WEAPON.
"I'M AFRAID THE LIGHTBOARDS HAVE ALREADY GOT WIND OF IT."
"I SEE. AND WE BELIEVE THE TESTIMONY OF INBRED BIRD-GOBLINS NOW, DO WE?"
ESCORT SQUAD FAILS TO RETURN OUR BRAVE BOYS M.I.A.
i-it's big
old drumshape thingy all crackles and glitterbollocks fazoom nobody even done a scream just woosh all bonebits 'n brisket actually smelt quite nice that's inappropriate sorry sorry
soldiers all croaked and I dun a wee and that's the end
RIVETING.
THIS IS HARDLY SURPRISING NEWS, MA'AM. WE KNOW THE ZOARIM MINE FO ANTIKI-TECH. INTELLIGENCE SUGGESTS THEY STILL WANT PEACE.
IT'S JUST THAT THEY WANT IT ON THEIR TERMS. THEY'RE NOT REALL ALL THAT DIFFERENT FROM US.
WHAT? HOW CAN YOU SAY THAT?

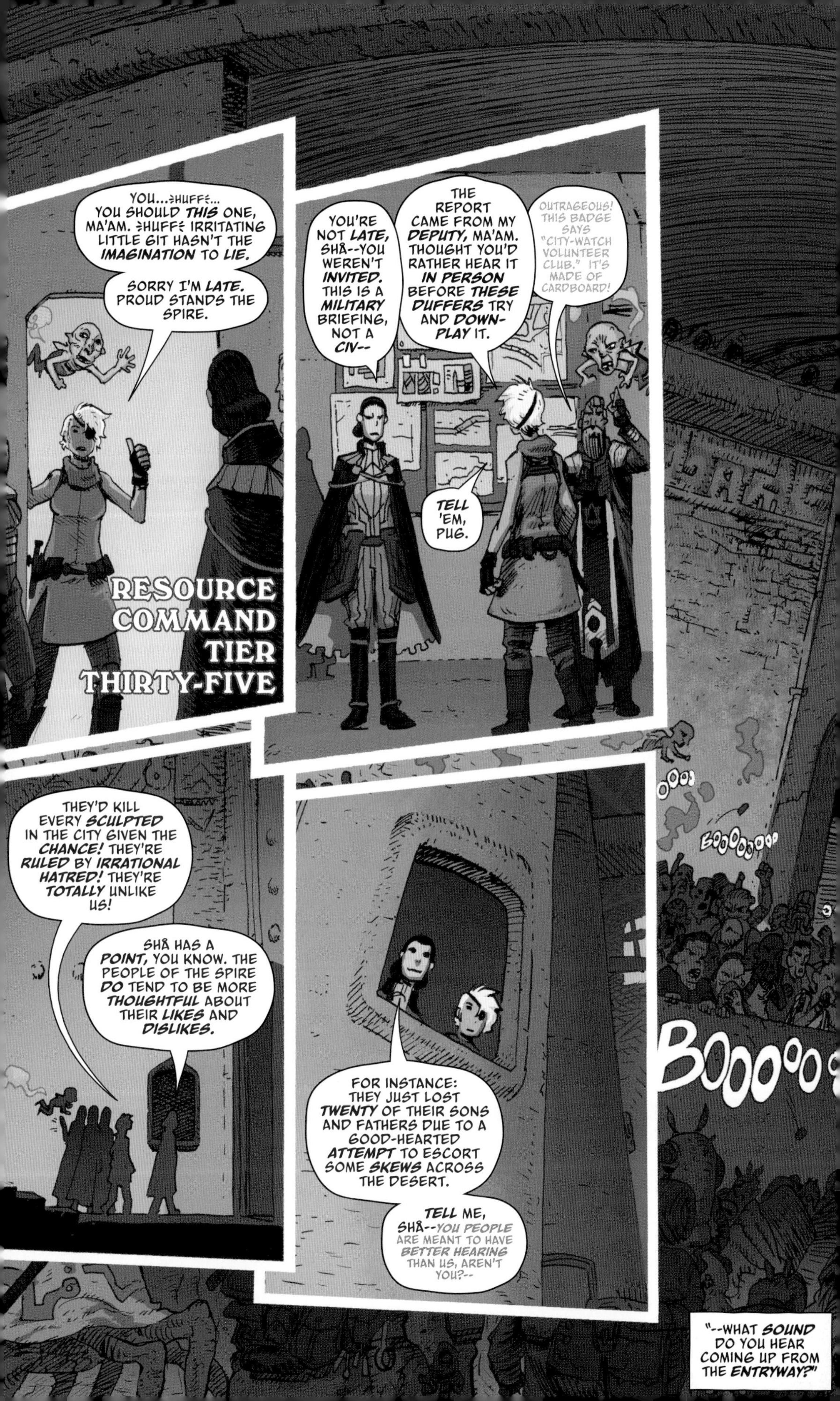

YOU...⋞HUFF⋟... YOU SHOULD THIS ONE, MA'AM. ⋞HUFF⋟ IRRITATING LITTLE GIT HASN'T THE IMAGINATION TO LIE.
SORRY I'M LATE. PROUD STANDS THE SPIRE.
RESOURCE COMMAND TIER THIRTY-FIVE
YOU'RE NOT LATE, SHÅ--YOU WEREN'T INVITED. THIS IS A MILITARY BRIEFING, NOT A CIV--
THE REPORT CAME FROM MY DEPUTY, MA'AM. THOUGHT YOU'D RATHER HEAR IT IN PERSON BEFORE THESE DUFFERS TRY AND DOWNPLAY IT.
OUTRAGEOUS! THIS BADGE SAYS "CITY-WATCH VOLUNTEER CLUB." IT'S MADE OF CARDBOARD!
TELL 'EM, PUG.
THEY'D KILL EVERY SCULPTED IN THE CITY GIVEN THE CHANCE! THEY'RE RULED BY IRRATIONAL HATRED! THEY'RE TOTALLY UNLIKE US!
SHÅ HAS A POINT, YOU KNOW. THE PEOPLE OF THE SPIRE DO TEND TO BE MORE THOUGHTFUL ABOUT THEIR LIKES AND DISLIKES.
FOR INSTANCE: THEY JUST LOST TWENTY OF THEIR SONS AND FATHERS DUE TO A GOOD-HEARTED ATTEMPT TO ESCORT SOME SKEWS ACROSS THE DESERT.
TELL ME, SHÅ--YOU PEOPLE ARE MEANT TO HAVE BETTER HEARING THAN US, AREN'T YOU?--
OOO
BOOOOOOOO
BOOOOO
"--WHAT SOUND DO YOU HEAR COMING UP FROM THE ENTRYWAY?"

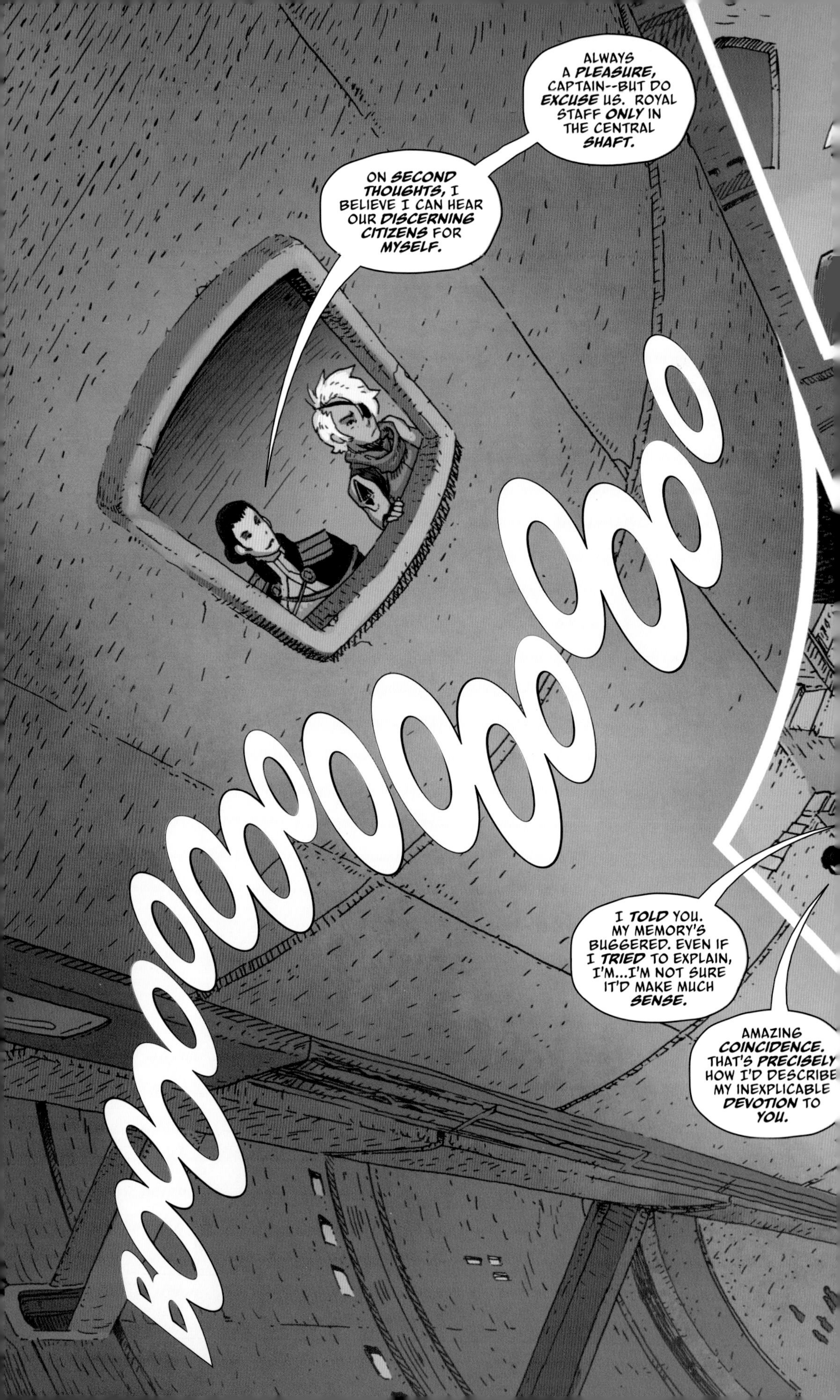
ALWAYS A PLEASURE, CAPTAIN--BUT DO EXCUSE US. ROYAL STAFF ONLY IN THE CENTRAL SHAFT.
ON SECOND THOUGHTS, I BELIEVE I CAN HEAR OUR DISCERNING CITIZENS FOR MYSELF.
BOOOOOOOOOOOOOOOO
I TOLD YOU. MY MEMORY'S BUGGERED. EVEN IF I TRIED TO EXPLAIN, I'M...I'M NOT SURE IT'D MAKE MUCH SENSE.
AMAZING COINCIDENCE. THAT'S PRECISELY HOW I'D DESCRIBE MY INEXPLICABLE DEVOTION TO YOU.

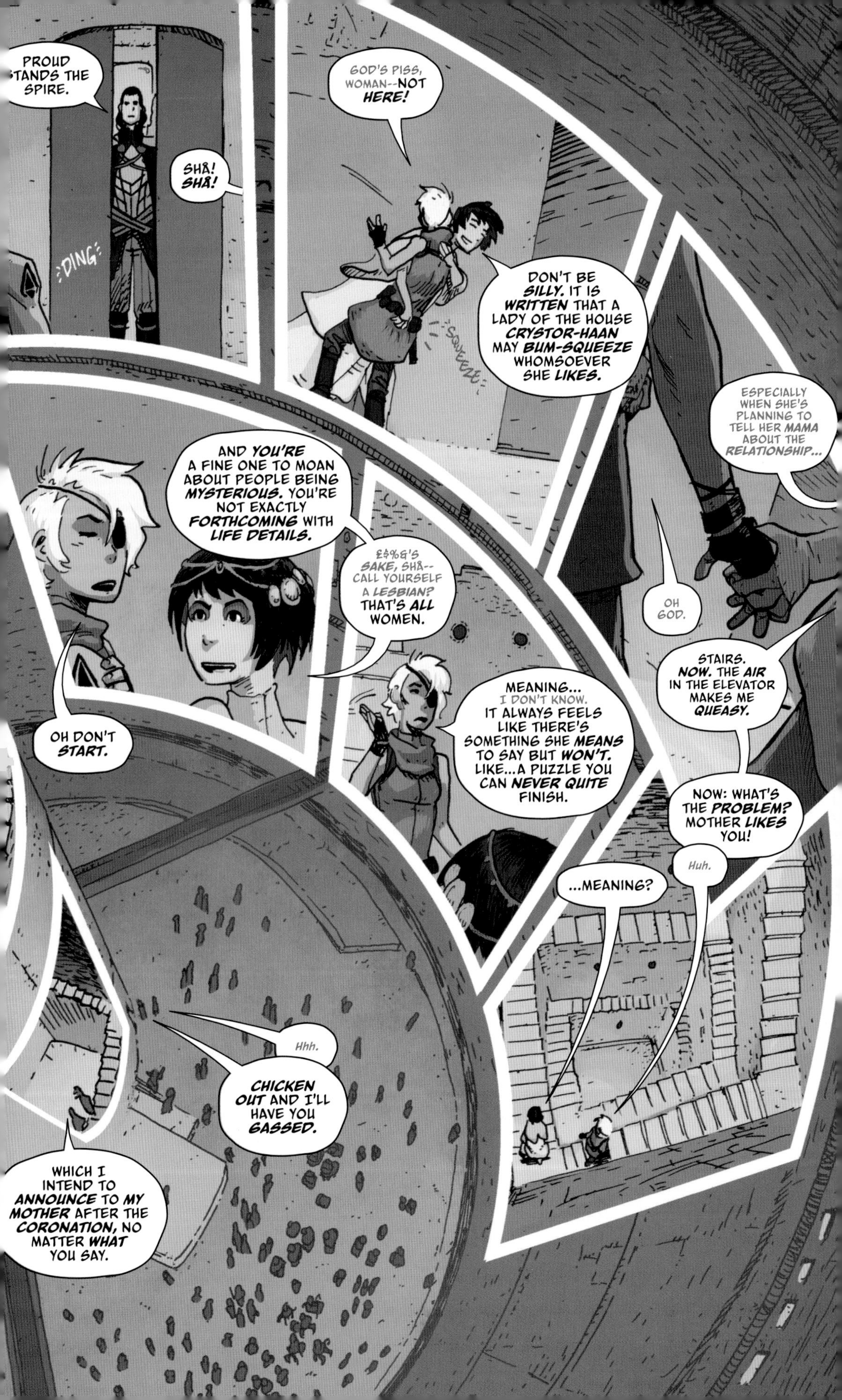
PROUD STANDS THE SPIRE.
SHÅ! SHÅ!
DING
GOD'S PISS, WOMAN--NOT HERE!
DON'T BE SILLY. IT IS WRITTEN THAT A LADY OF THE HOUSE CRYSTOR-HAAN MAY BUM-SQUEEZE WHOMSOEVER SHE LIKES.
SQUEEZE
SQUEEZE
ESPECIALLY WHEN SHE'S PLANNING TO TELL HER MAMA ABOUT THE RELATIONSHIP...
WHICH I INTEND TO ANNOUNCE TO MY MOTHER AFTER THE CORONATION, NO MATTER WHAT YOU SAY.
CHICKEN OUT AND I'LL HAVE YOU GASSED.
Hhh.
OH GOD.
STAIRS. NOW. THE AIR IN THE ELEVATOR MAKES ME QUEASY.
NOW: WHAT'S THE PROBLEM? MOTHER LIKES YOU!
Huh.
...MEANING?
MEANING... I DON'T KNOW. IT ALWAYS FEELS LIKE THERE'S SOMETHING SHE MEANS TO SAY BUT WON'T. LIKE...A PUZZLE YOU CAN NEVER QUITE FINISH.
AND YOU'RE A FINE ONE TO MOAN ABOUT PEOPLE BEING MYSTERIOUS. YOU'RE NOT EXACTLY FORTHCOMING WITH LIFE DETAILS.
OH DON'T START.
£$%&'S SAKE, SHÅ-- CALL YOURSELF A LESBIAN? THAT'S ALL WOMEN.

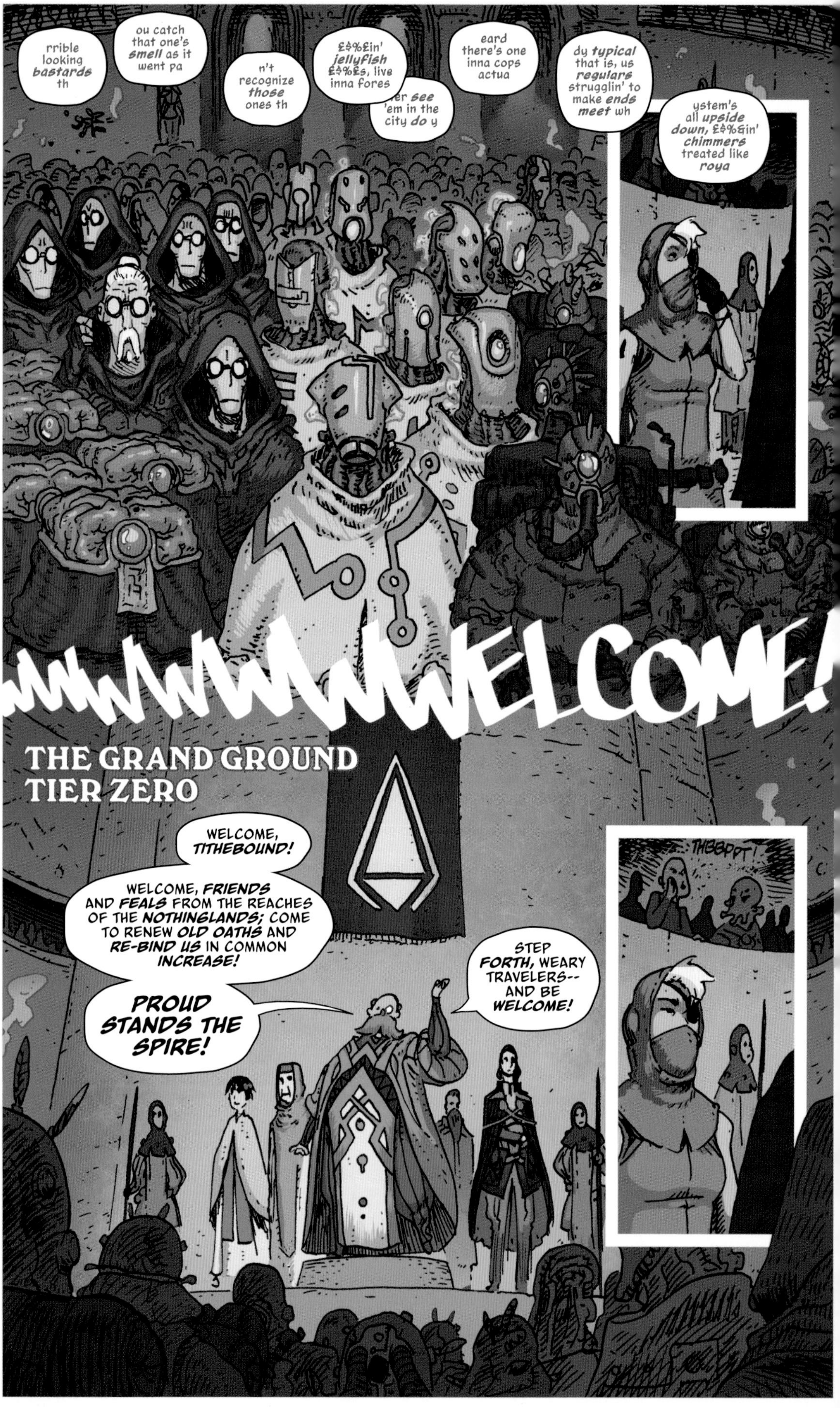

rrible looking bastards th
ou catch that one's smell as it went pa
n't recognize those ones th
£$%£in' jellyfish £$%£s, live inna fores
er see 'em in the city do y
eard there's one inna cops actua
dy typical that is, us regulars strugglin' to make ends meet wh
ystem's all upside down, £$%£in' chimmers treated like roya
WWWWWWWWELCOME!
THE GRAND GROUND TIER ZERO
WELCOME, TITHEBOUND!
WELCOME, FRIENDS AND FEALS FROM THE REACHES OF THE NOTHINGLANDS; COME TO RENEW OLD OATHS AND RE-BIND US IN COMMON INCREASE!
PROUD STANDS THE SPIRE!
STEP FORTH, WEARY TRAVELERS-- AND BE WELCOME!
THBBPPT!

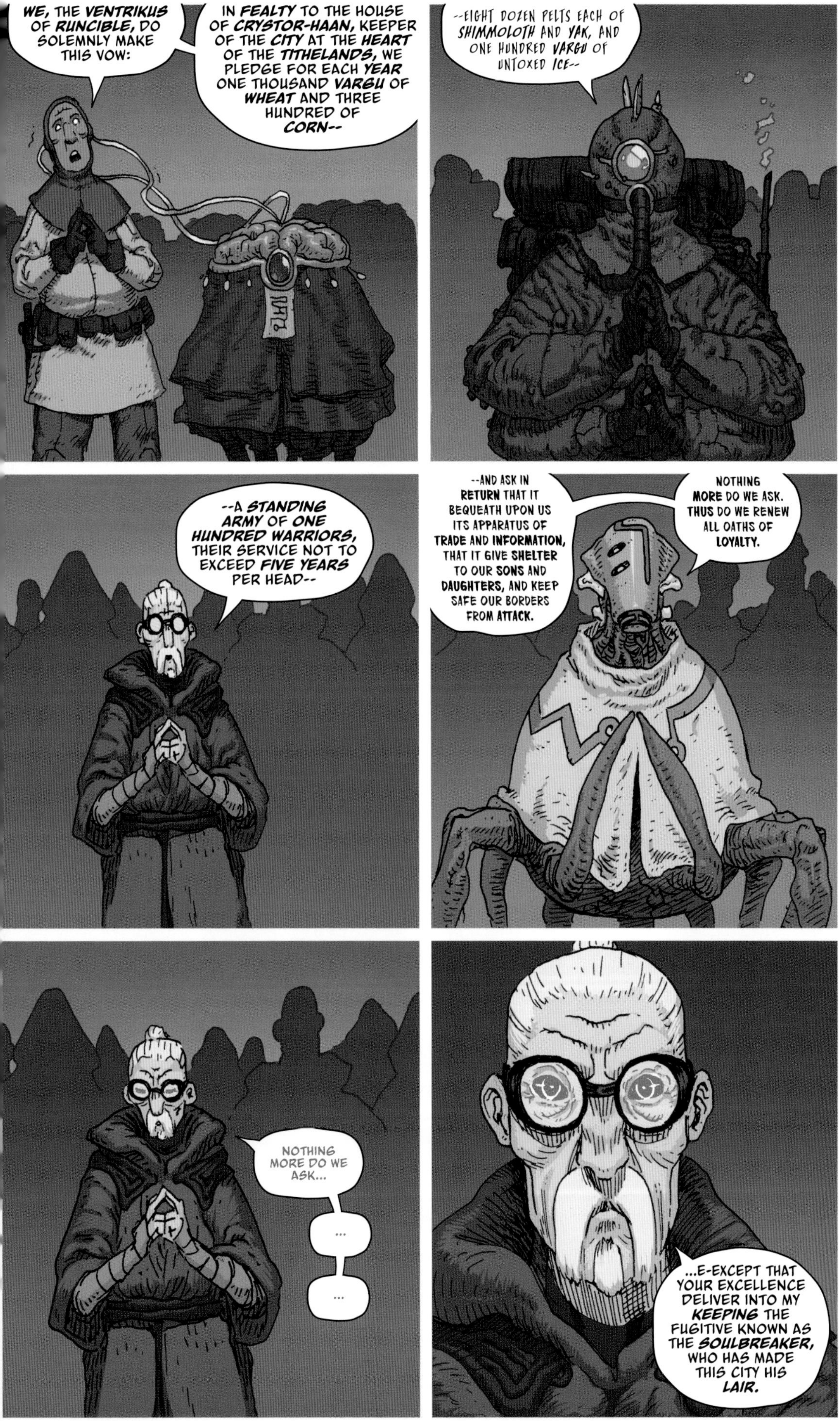
WE, THE VENTRIKUS OF RUNCIBLE, DO SOLEMNLY MAKE THIS VOW:
IN FEALTY TO THE HOUSE OF CRYSTOR-HAAN, KEEPER OF THE CITY AT THE HEART OF THE TITHELANDS, WE PLEDGE FOR EACH YEAR ONE THOUSAND VARGU OF WHEAT AND THREE HUNDRED OF CORN--
--EIGHT DOZEN PELTS EACH OF SHIMMOLOTH AND YAK, AND ONE HUNDRED VARGU OF UNTOXED ICE--
--A STANDING ARMY OF ONE HUNDRED WARRIORS, THEIR SERVICE NOT TO EXCEED FIVE YEARS PER HEAD--
--AND ASK IN RETURN THAT IT BEQUEATH UPON US ITS APPARATUS OF TRADE AND INFORMATION, THAT IT GIVE SHELTER TO OUR SONS AND DAUGHTERS, AND KEEP SAFE OUR BORDERS FROM ATTACK.
NOTHING MORE DO WE ASK. THUS DO WE RENEW ALL OATHS OF LOYALTY.
NOTHING MORE DO WE ASK...
...
...
...E-EXCEPT THAT YOUR EXCELLENCE DELIVER INTO MY KEEPING THE FUGITIVE KNOWN AS THE SOULBREAKER, WHO HAS MADE THIS CITY HIS LAIR.

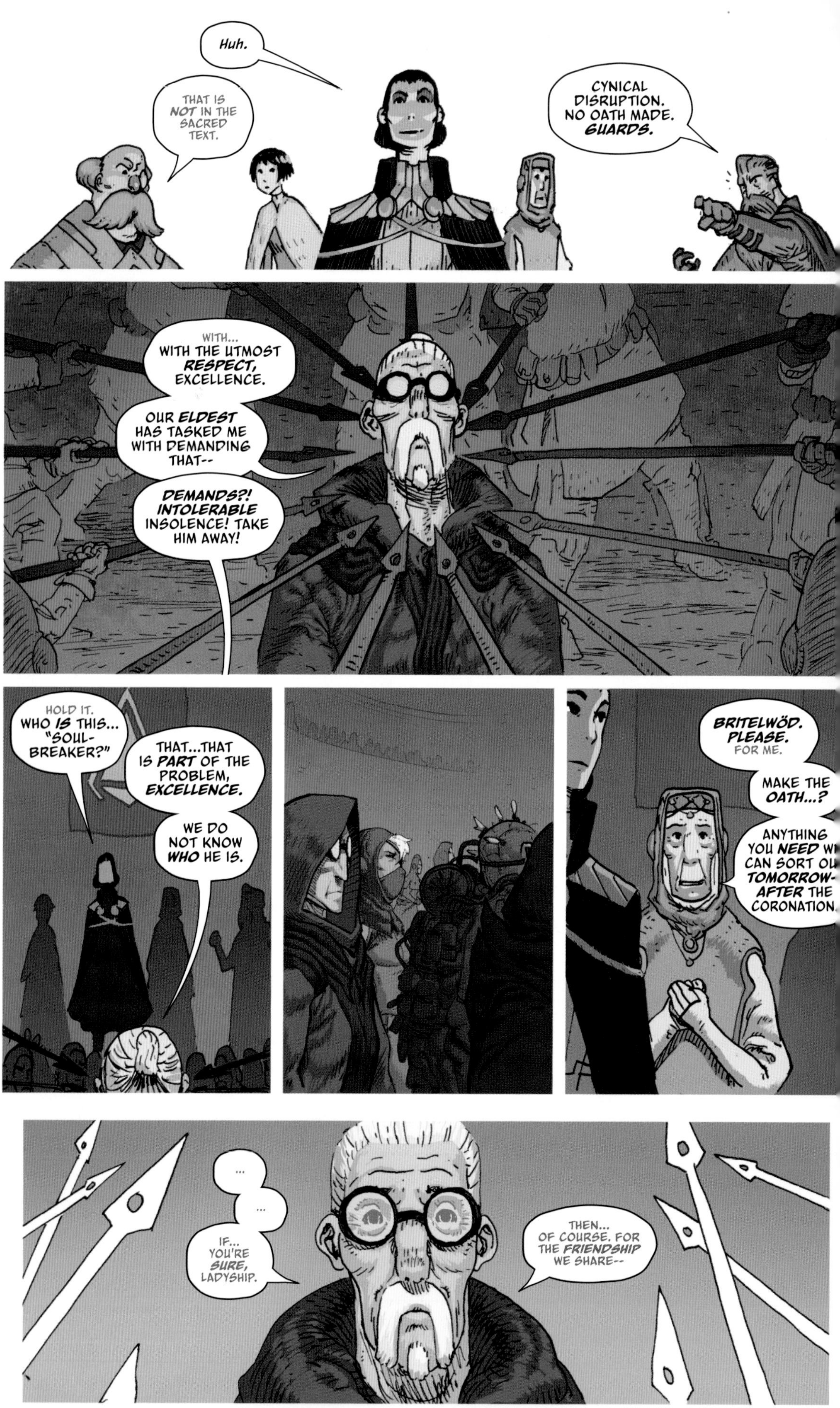
Huh.
THAT IS NOT IN THE SACRED TEXT.
CYNICAL DISRUPTION. NO OATH MADE. GUARDS.
WITH... WITH THE UTMOST RESPECT, EXCELLENCE.
OUR ELDEST HAS TASKED ME WITH DEMANDING THAT--
DEMANDS?! INTOLERABLE INSOLENCE! TAKE HIM AWAY!
HOLD IT. WHO IS THIS... "SOUL-BREAKER?"
THAT...THAT IS PART OF THE PROBLEM, EXCELLENCE.
WE DO NOT KNOW WHO HE IS.
BRITELWÖD. PLEASE. FOR ME.
MAKE THE OATH...?
...
...
IF... YOU'RE SURE, LADYSHIP.
THEN... OF COURSE. FOR THE FRIENDSHIP WE SHARE--

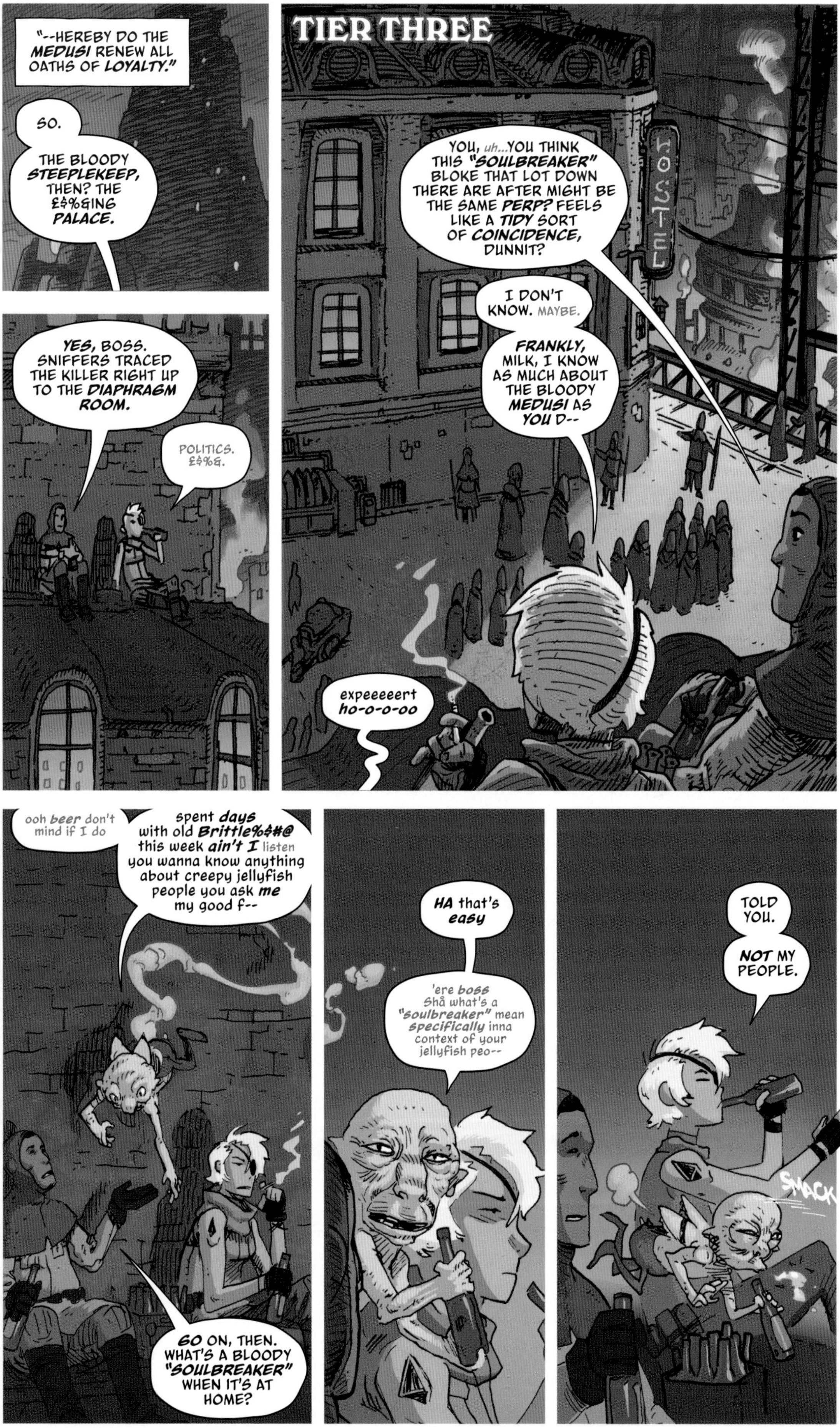
"--HEREBY DO THE *MEDUSI* RENEW ALL OATHS OF *LOYALTY.*"
SO.
THE BLOODY *STEEPLEKEEP,* THEN? THE £$%&ING *PALACE.*
YES, BOSS. SNIFFERS TRACED THE KILLER RIGHT UP TO THE *DIAPHRAGM ROOM.*
POLITICS. £$%&.
TIER THREE
HOSTEL
YOU, *uh*...YOU THINK THIS *"SOULBREAKER"* BLOKE THAT LOT DOWN THERE ARE AFTER MIGHT BE THE SAME *PERP?* FEELS LIKE A *TIDY* SORT OF *COINCIDENCE,* DUNNIT?
I DON'T KNOW. MAYBE.
FRANKLY, MILK, I KNOW AS MUCH ABOUT THE BLOODY *MEDUSI* AS *YOU* D--
expeeeeert *ho-o-o-oo*
ooh *beer* don't mind if I do
spent *days* with old *Brittle%$#@* this week *ain't I* listen you wanna know anything about creepy jellyfish people you ask *me* my good f--
GO ON, THEN. WHAT'S A BLOODY *"SOULBREAKER"* WHEN IT'S AT HOME?
HA that's *easy*
'ere *boss* Shå what's a *"soulbreaker"* mean *specifically* inna context of your jellyfish peo--
TOLD YOU.
NOT MY PEOPLE.
SMACK

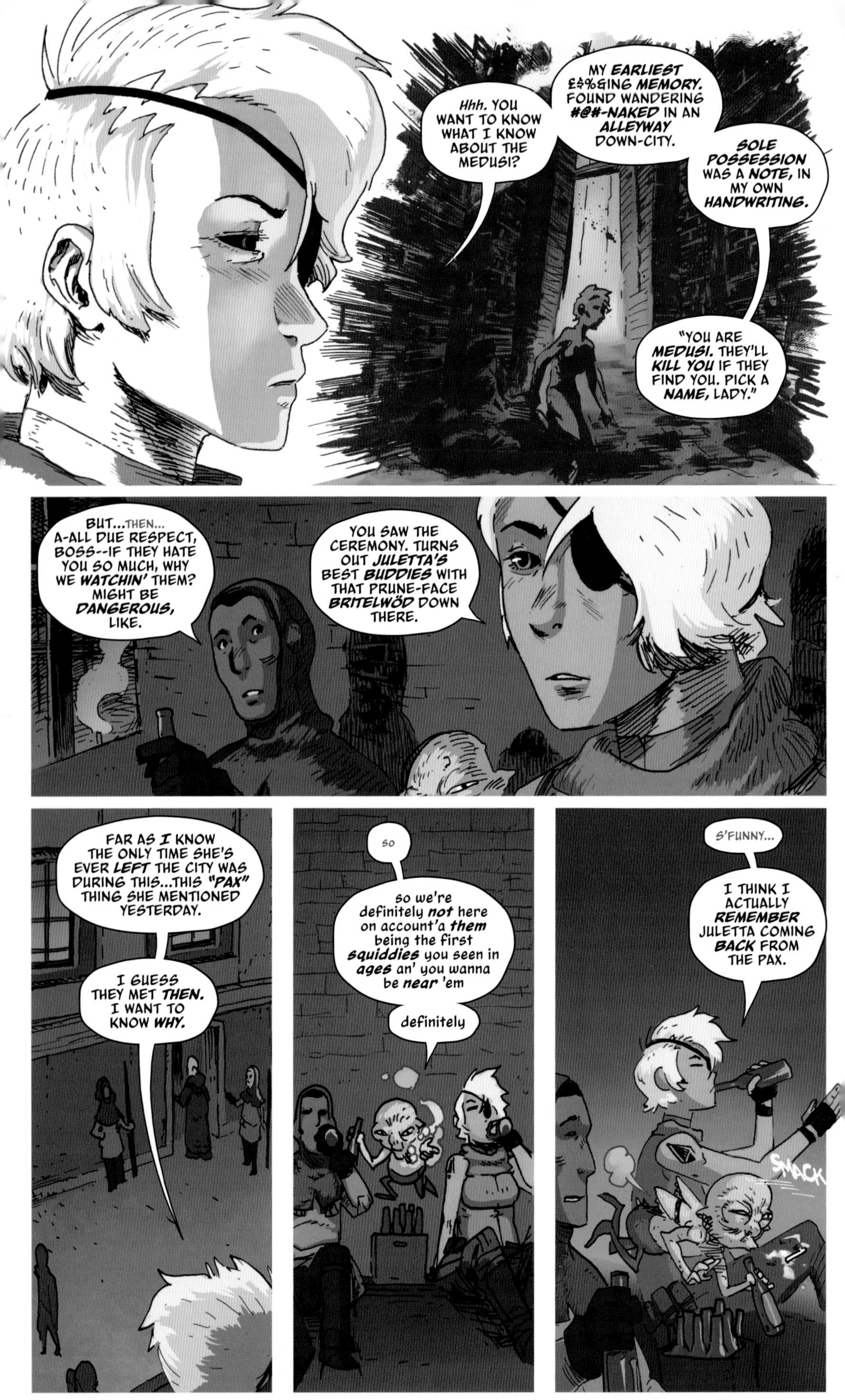
Hhh. YOU WANT TO KNOW WHAT I KNOW ABOUT THE MEDUSI?
MY EARLIEST £$%&ING MEMORY. FOUND WANDERING #@#-NAKED IN AN ALLEYWAY DOWN-CITY.
SOLE POSSESSION WAS A NOTE, IN MY OWN HANDWRITING.
"YOU ARE MEDUSI. THEY'LL KILL YOU IF THEY FIND YOU. PICK A NAME, LADY."
BUT...THEN... A-ALL DUE RESPECT, BOSS--IF THEY HATE YOU SO MUCH, WHY WE WATCHIN' THEM? MIGHT BE DANGEROUS, LIKE.
YOU SAW THE CEREMONY. TURNS OUT JULETTA'S BEST BUDDIES WITH THAT PRUNE-FACE BRITELWÖD DOWN THERE.
FAR AS I KNOW THE ONLY TIME SHE'S EVER LEFT THE CITY WAS DURING THIS...THIS "PAX" THING SHE MENTIONED YESTERDAY.
I GUESS THEY MET THEN. I WANT TO KNOW WHY.
so
so we're definitely not here on account'a them being the first squiddies you seen in ages an' you wanna be near 'em
definitely
S'FUNNY...
I THINK I ACTUALLY REMEMBER JULETTA COMING BACK FROM THE PAX.
SMACK

"THIS WAS...*EARLY DAYS*. NOT A COP YET. PART OF A *SKEW CREW* CLEANING THE *SHELL*."

"THERE'D BEEN *RUMORS* OF A *FLARE-UP* WITH THE *ZOARIM*--YOU KNOW HOW IT IS, NOTHING'S EVER *PUBLIC*."

"...THEN ONE DAY ALONG COMES A PAIR OF *ROYAL COACHES*. NO FANFARE, NO *ESCORT*..."

"I SUPPOSE IT'S LIKE SHE SAID: SOMETHING WENT *WRONG* OUT THERE."

TELL YOU *THIS*, THOUGH: JULETTA DIDN'T DO ANY *PUBLIC APPEARANCES* FOR A COUPLE OF YEARS *AFTER*.

'COURSE, THE *DAUGHTERS* CAME ALONG PRETTY FAST-- SO *"PROTECTING THE PRIVACY OF THE ROYAL INFANTS"* WORKED FINE AS AN EXCUSE.

NOW I'M *WONDERING*.

GLUP

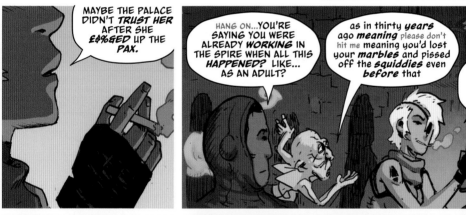

MAYBE THE PALACE DIDN'T *TRUST HER* AFTER SHE £$%&ED UP THE *PAX*.

HANG ON...YOU'RE SAYING YOU WERE ALREADY *WORKING* IN THE SPIRE WHEN ALL THIS *HAPPENED?* LIKE... AS AN ADULT?

as in thirty *years* ago *meaning* please don't hit me meaning you'd lost your *marbles* and pissed off the *squiddies* even *before* that

HA. I'LL MAKE DETECTIVES OF YOU *YET*, BOYS.

WE *MEDUSI* ARE *VERY* LONG-LI--

AAAAAH

AAA

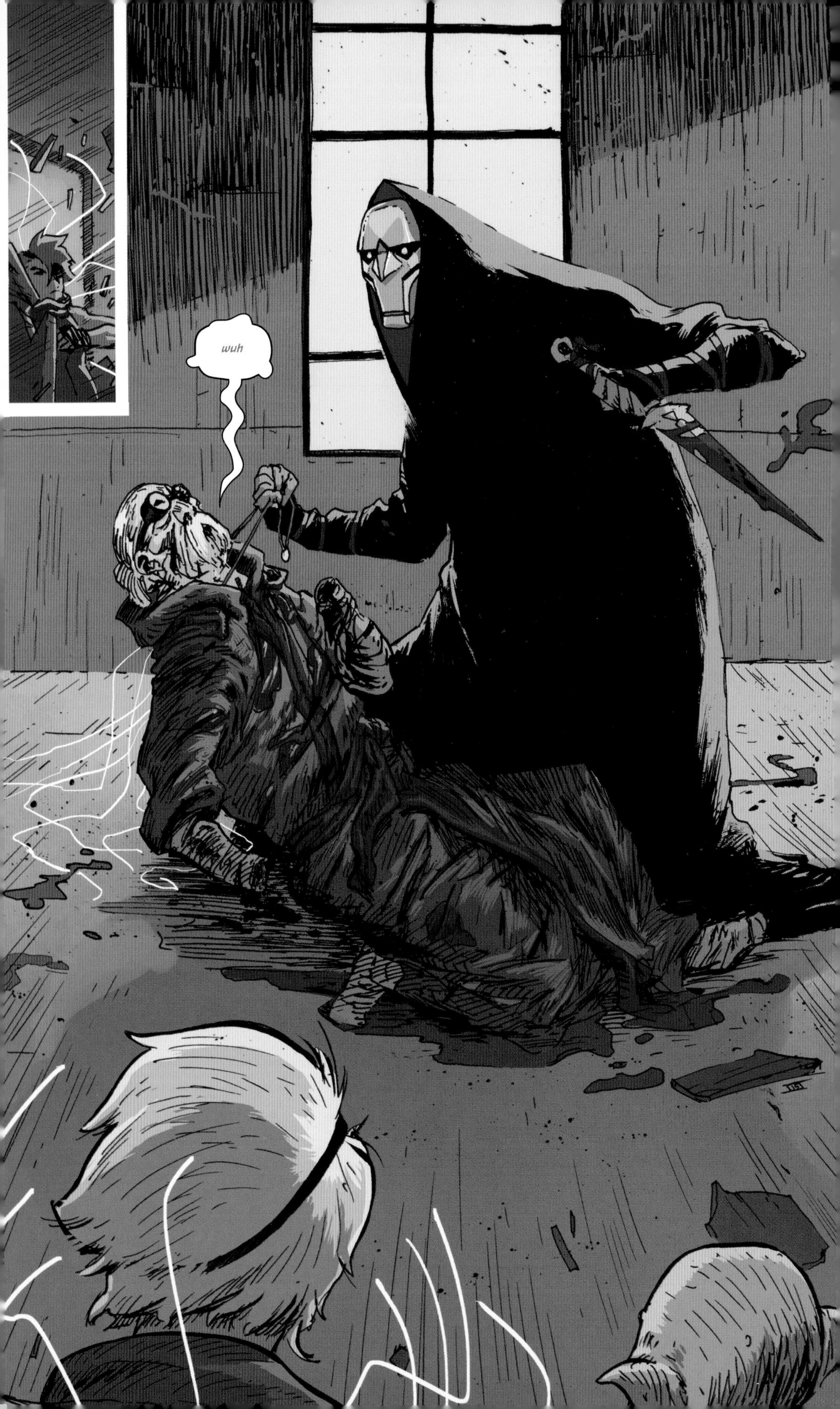
wuh

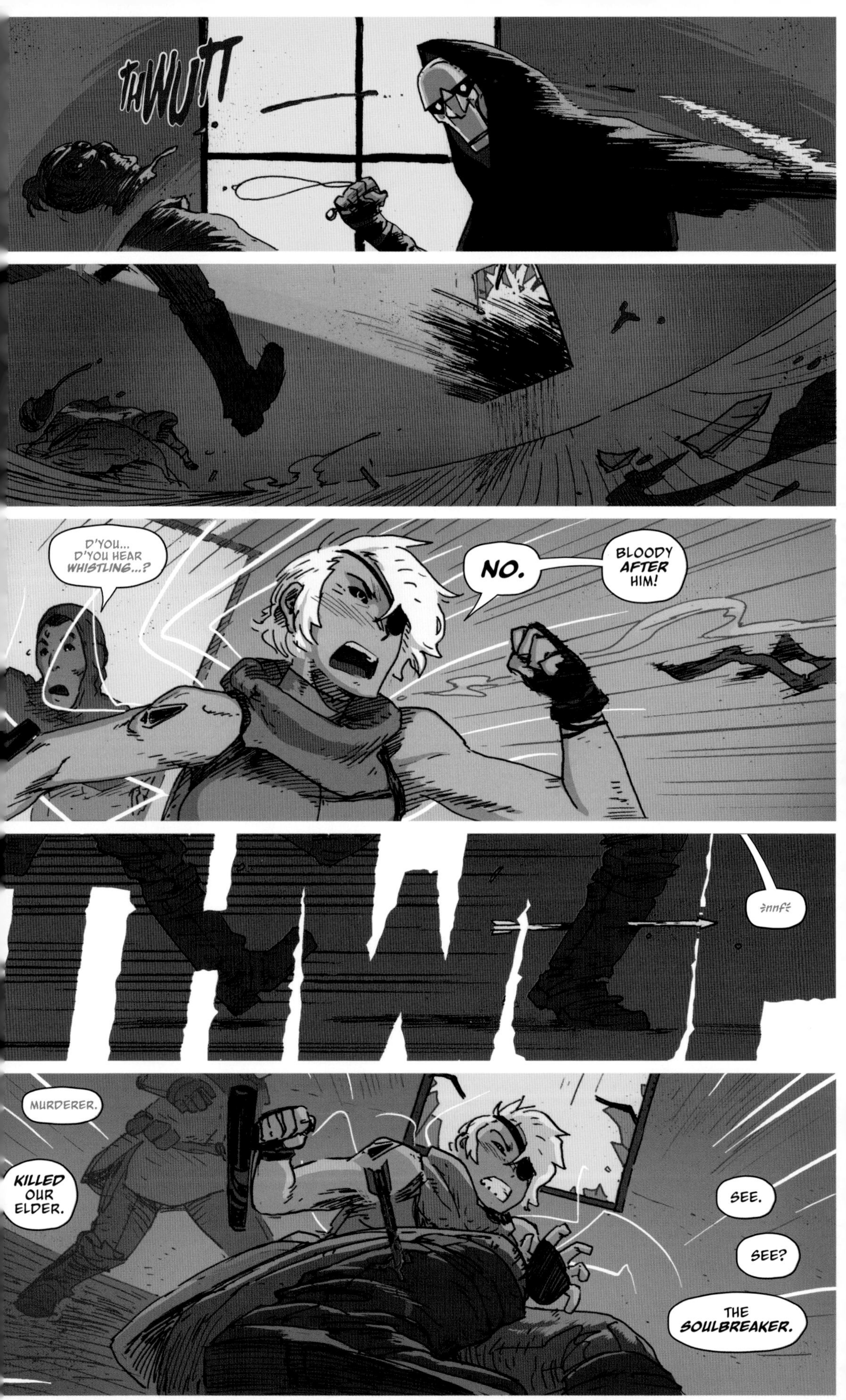
THWUT!
D'YOU... D'YOU HEAR WHISTLING...?
NO.
BLOODY AFTER HIM!
THWUP
nnf
MURDERER.
KILLED OUR ELDER.
SEE.
SEE?
THE SOULBREAKER.

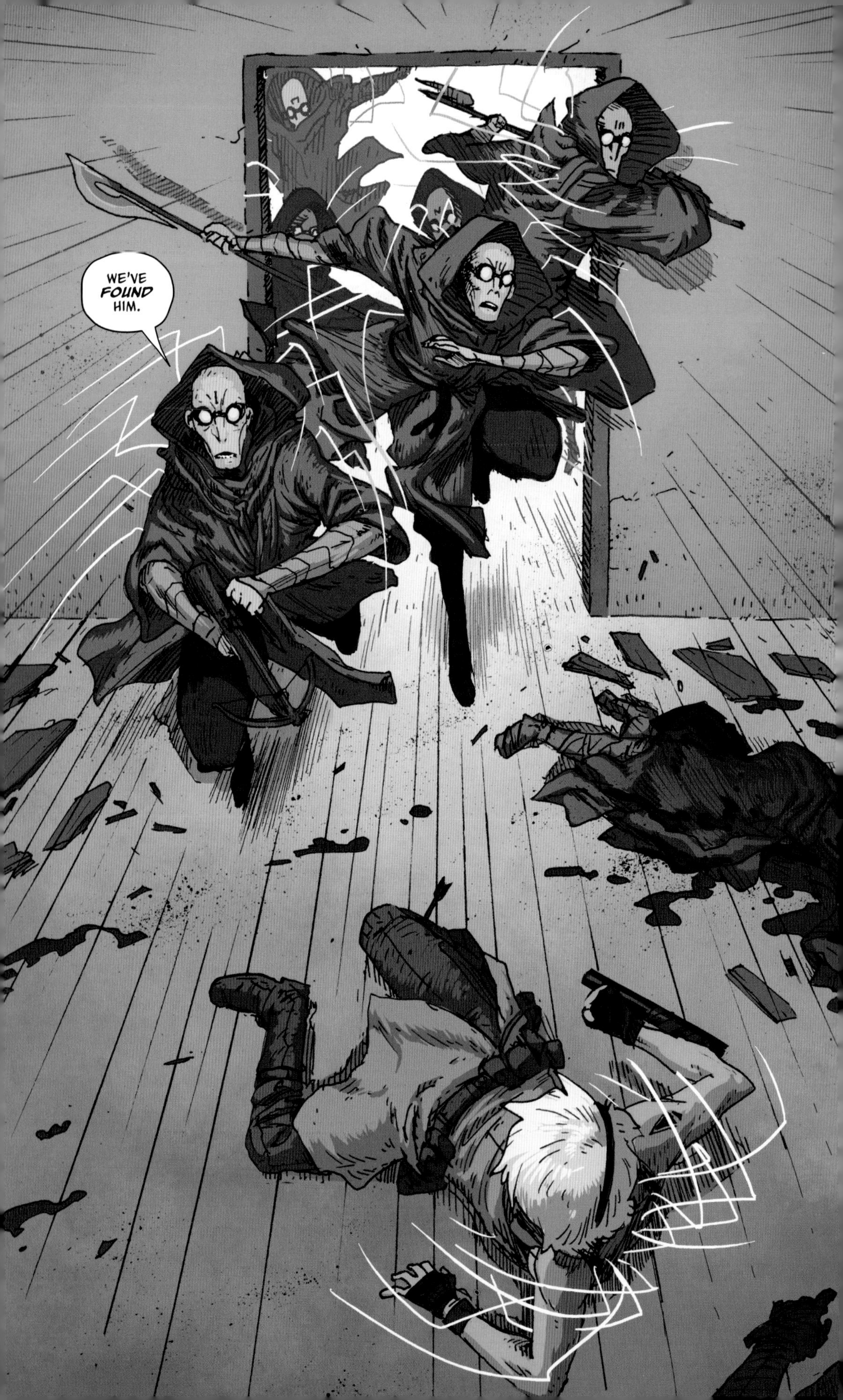
WE'VE *FOUND* HIM.

ISSUE #3 COVER BY **JEFF STOKELY**

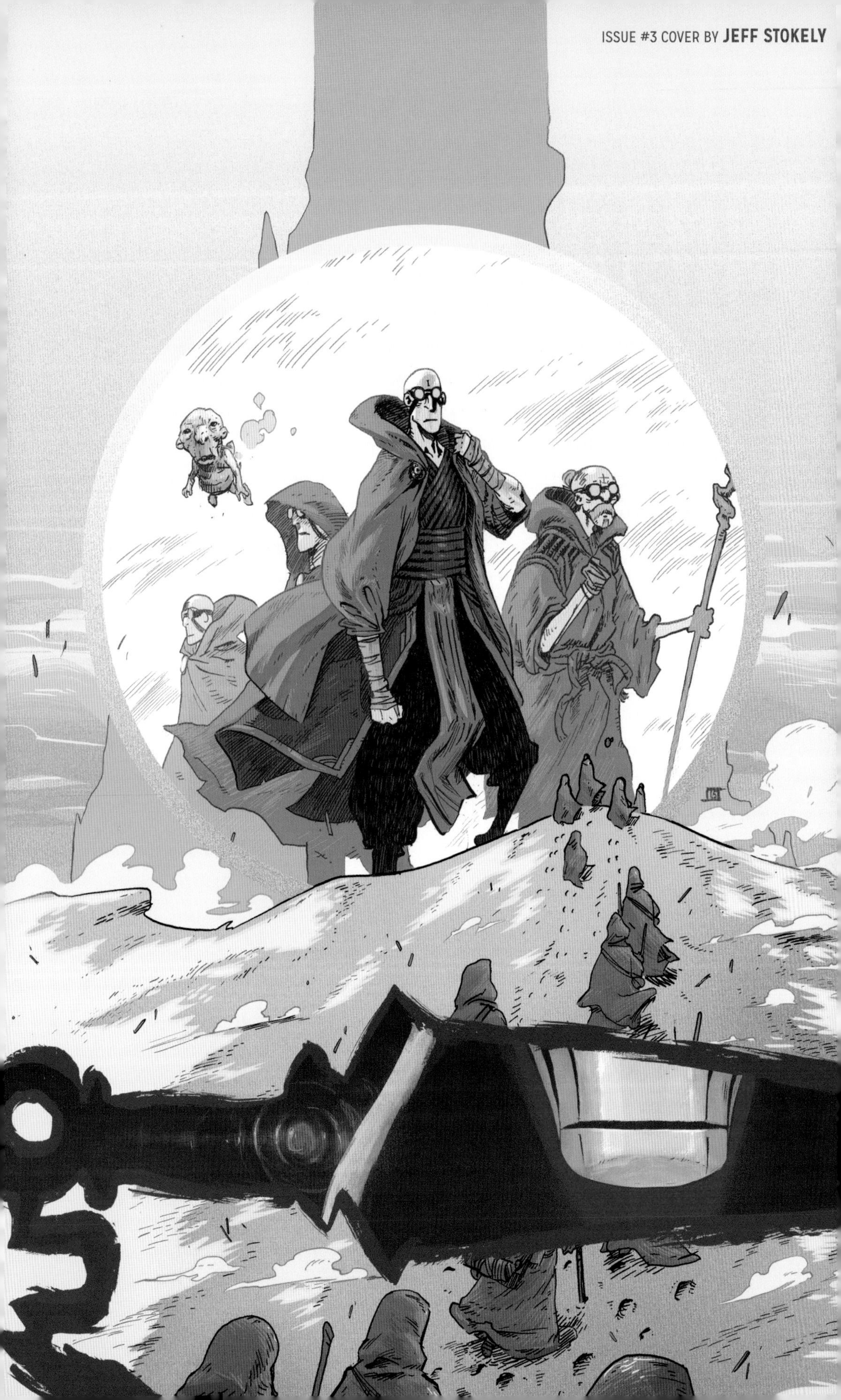

CHAPTER
FOUR

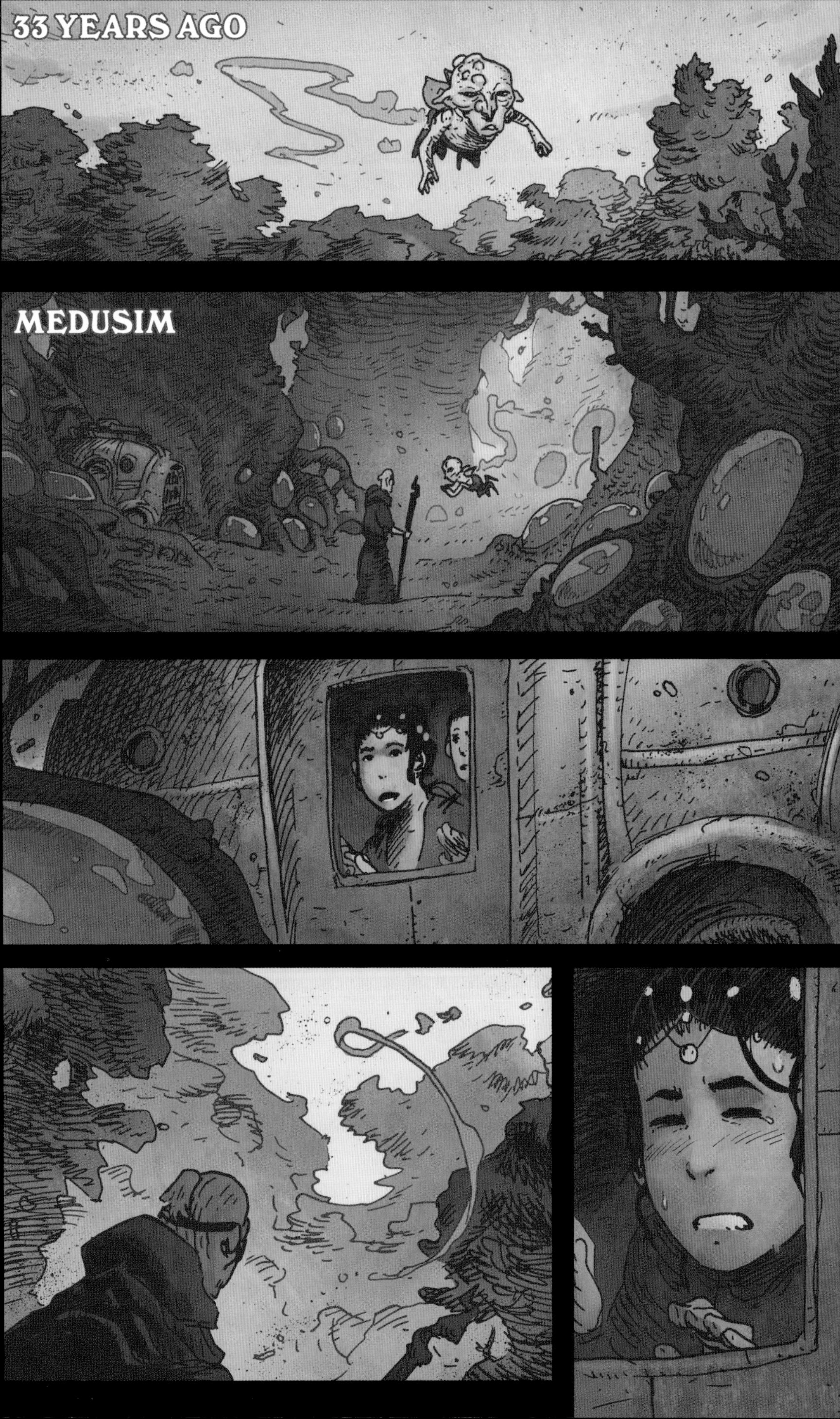
33 YEARS AGO
MEDUSIM

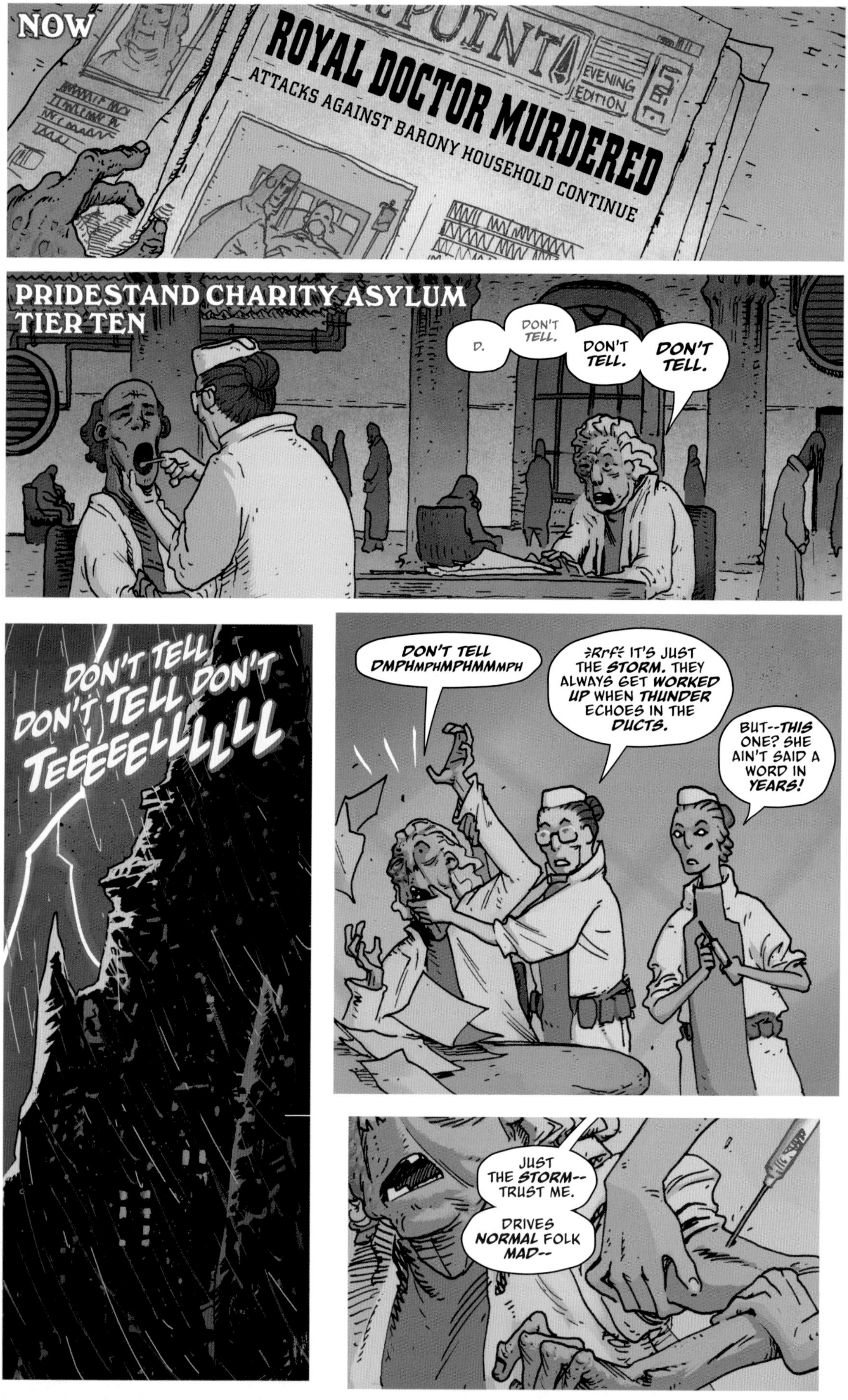
NOW
ROYAL DOCTOR MURDERED
ATTACKS AGAINST BARONY HOUSEHOLD CONTINUE
EVENING EDITION
PRIDESTAND CHARITY ASYLUM
TIER TEN
D.
DON'T TELL.
DON'T TELL.
DON'T TELL.
DON'T TELL DON'T TELL DON'T TELL DON'T TEEEEELLLLLL
DON'T TELL DMPHMPHMPHMMMPH
Rrf IT'S JUST THE STORM. THEY ALWAYS GET WORKED UP WHEN THUNDER ECHOES IN THE DUCTS.
BUT--THIS ONE? SHE AIN'T SAID A WORD IN YEARS!
JUST THE STORM--TRUST ME.
DRIVES NORMAL FOLK MAD--

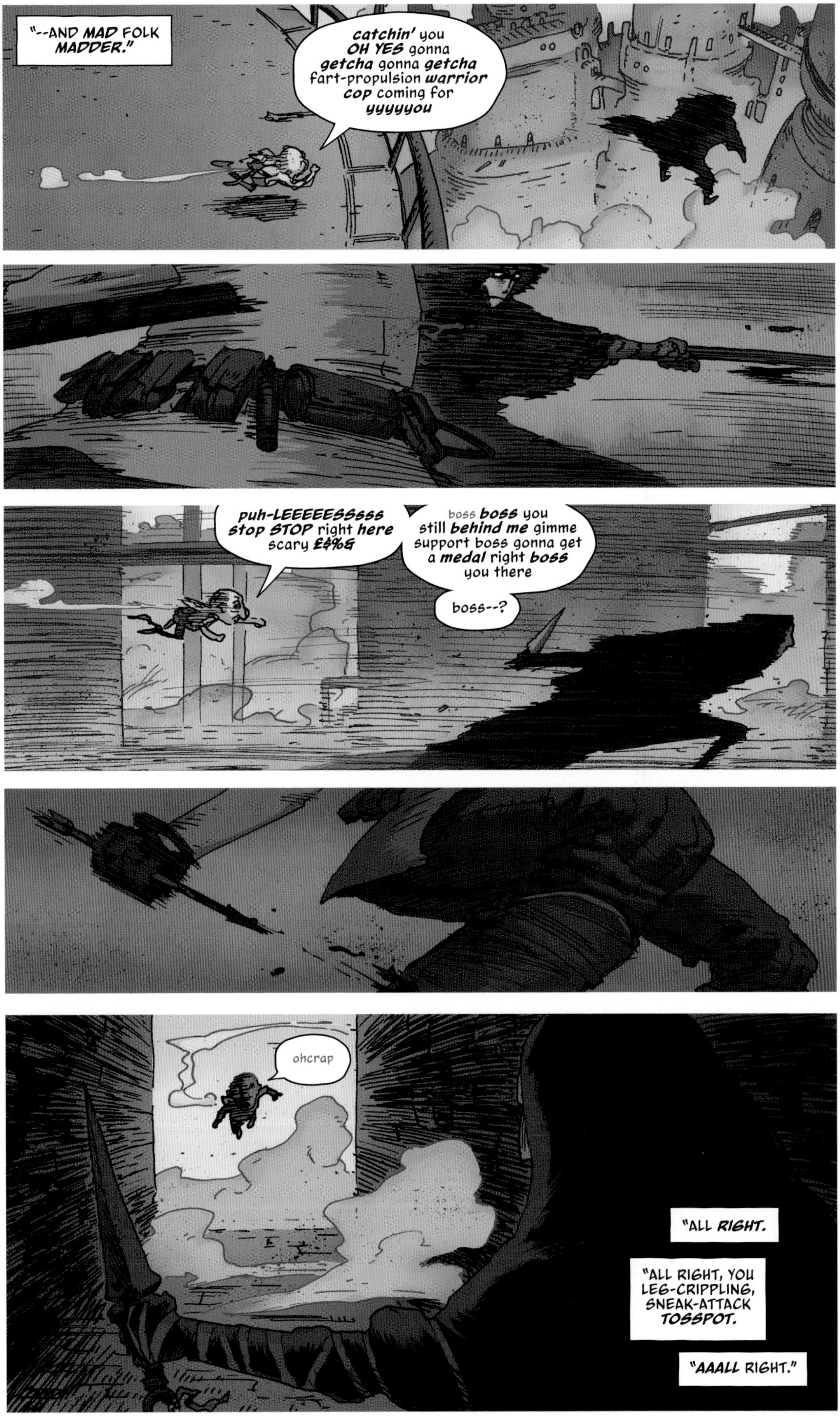
"--AND MAD FOLK MADDER."
catchin' you OH YES gonna getcha gonna getcha fart-propulsion warrior cop coming for yyyyyou
puh-LEEEEESSSSS stop STOP right here scary £$%G
boss boss you still behind me gimme support boss gonna get a medal right boss you there
boss--?
ohcrap
"ALL RIGHT.
"ALL RIGHT, YOU LEG-CRIPPLING, SNEAK-ATTACK TOSSPOT.
"AAALL RIGHT."

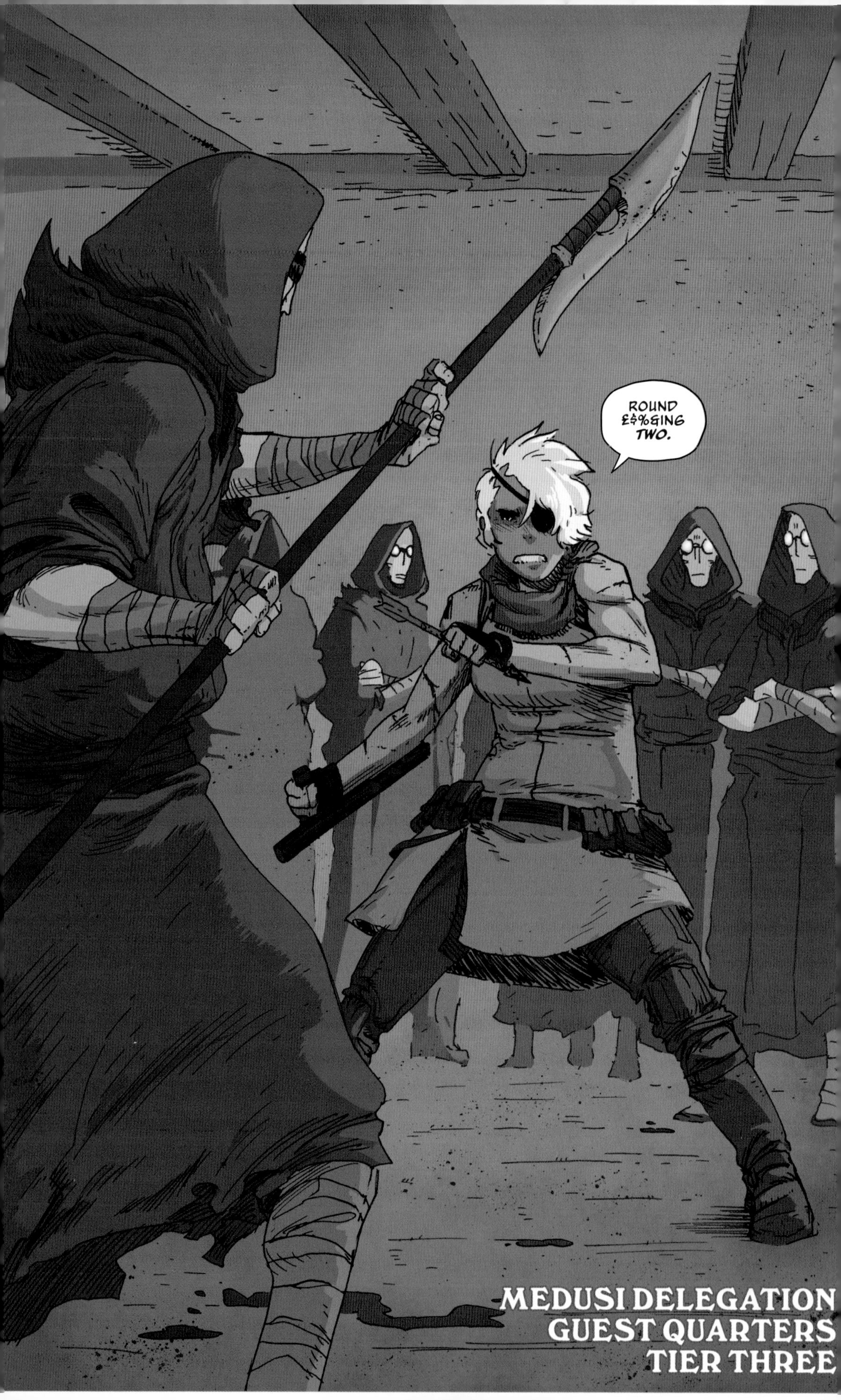
ROUND £$%&ING TWO.
MEDUSI DELEGATION GUEST QUARTERS TIER THREE

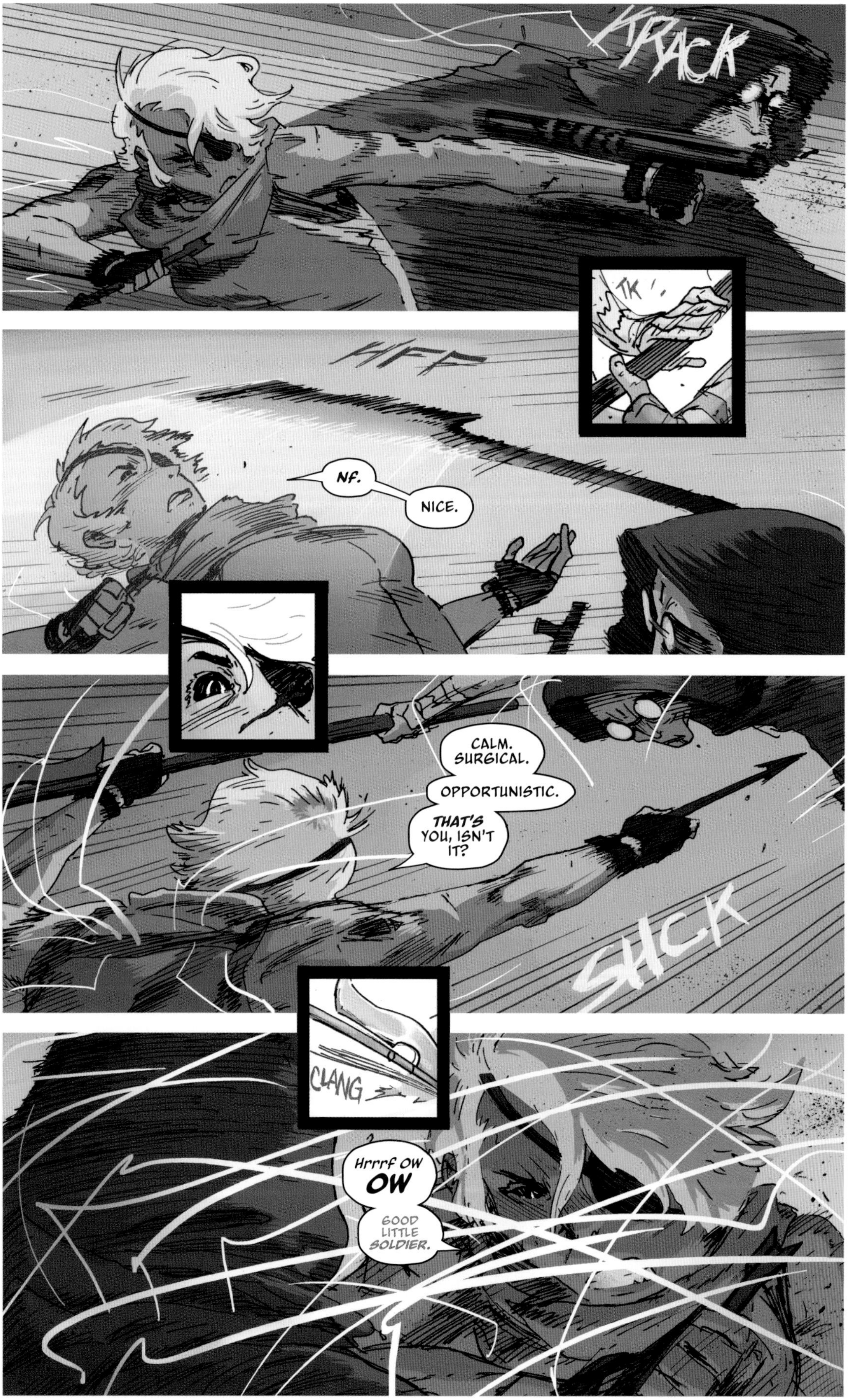
KRACK
TK
HFF
Nf.
NICE.
CALM. SURGICAL.
OPPORTUNISTIC.
THAT'S YOU, ISN'T IT?
SHCK
CLANG
Hrrrf OW OW
GOOD LITTLE SOLDIER.

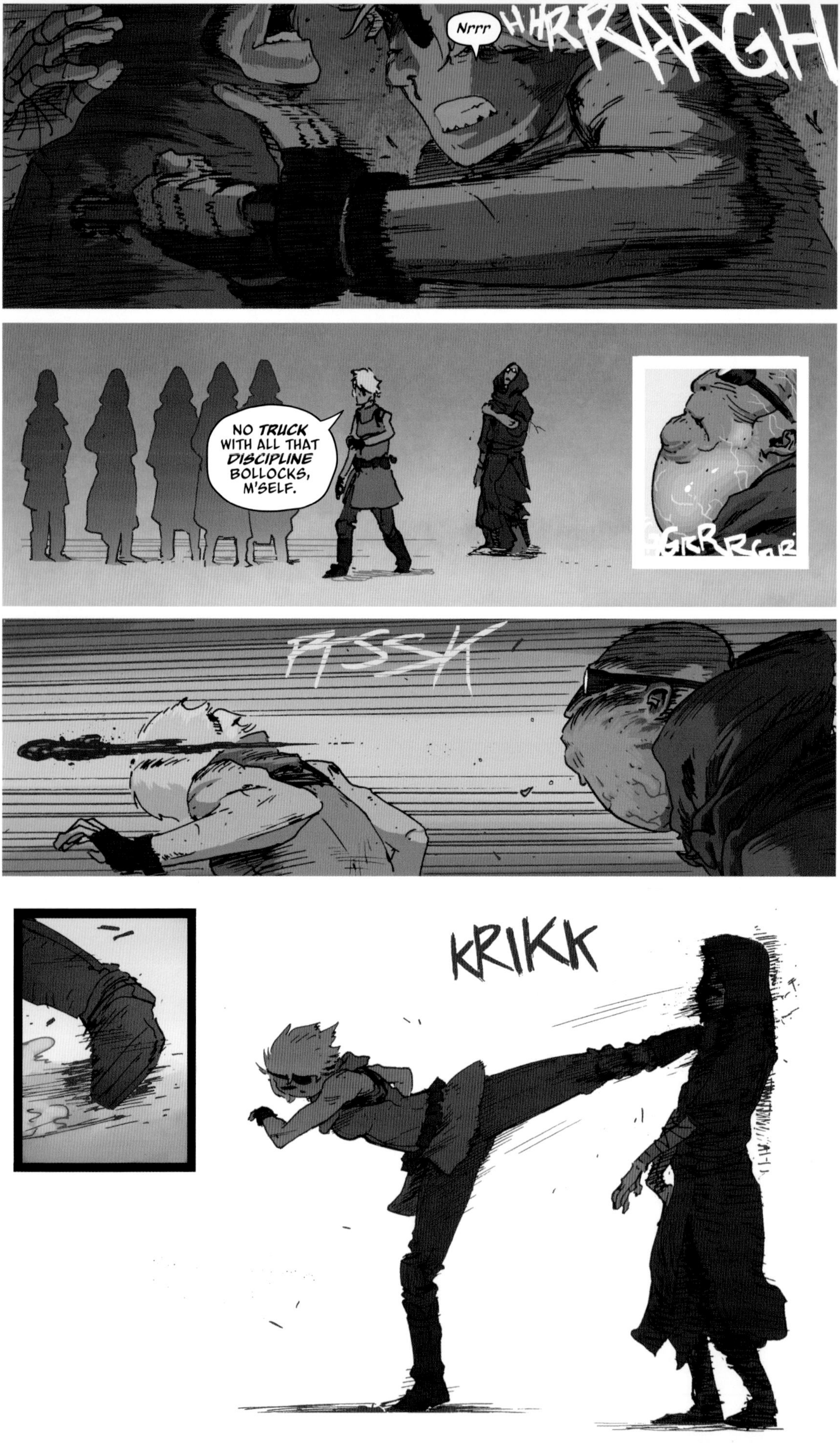
Nrrr
HHRRAAGH
NO TRUCK WITH ALL THAT DISCIPLINE BOLLOCKS, M'SELF.
GRRRGRR
KRIKK

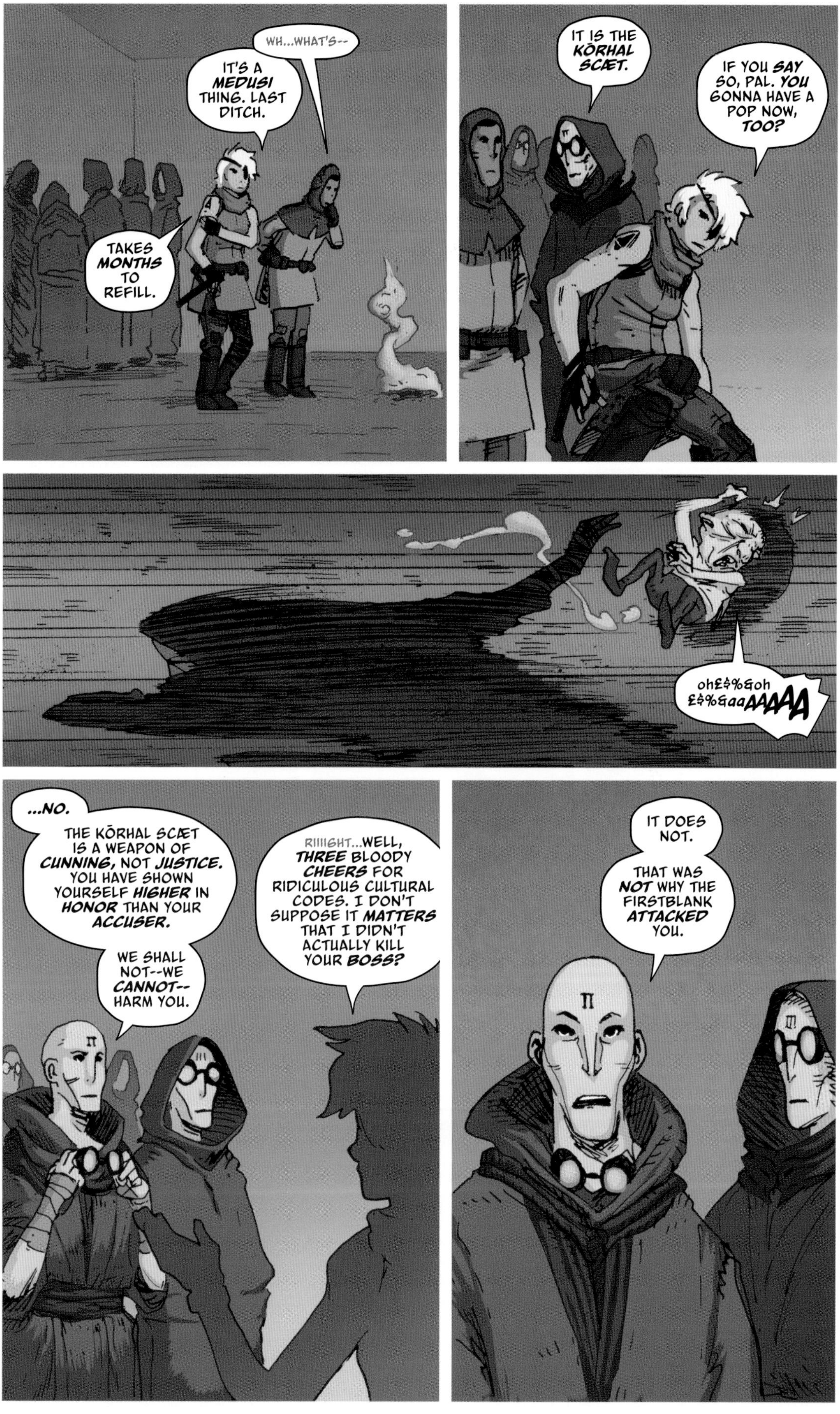
WH...WHAT'S--
IT'S A MEDUSI THING. LAST DITCH.
TAKES MONTHS TO REFILL.
IT IS THE KŌRHAL SCÆT.
IF YOU SAY SO, PAL. YOU GONNA HAVE A POP NOW, TOO?
oh£$%&oh £$%&aaAAAAA
...NO.
THE KŌRHAL SCÆT IS A WEAPON OF CUNNING, NOT JUSTICE. YOU HAVE SHOWN YOURSELF HIGHER IN HONOR THAN YOUR ACCUSER.
WE SHALL NOT--WE CANNOT--HARM YOU.
RIIIIGHT...WELL, THREE BLOODY CHEERS FOR RIDICULOUS CULTURAL CODES. I DON'T SUPPOSE IT MATTERS THAT I DIDN'T ACTUALLY KILL YOUR BOSS?
IT DOES NOT.
THAT WAS NOT WHY THE FIRSTBLANK ATTACKED YOU.

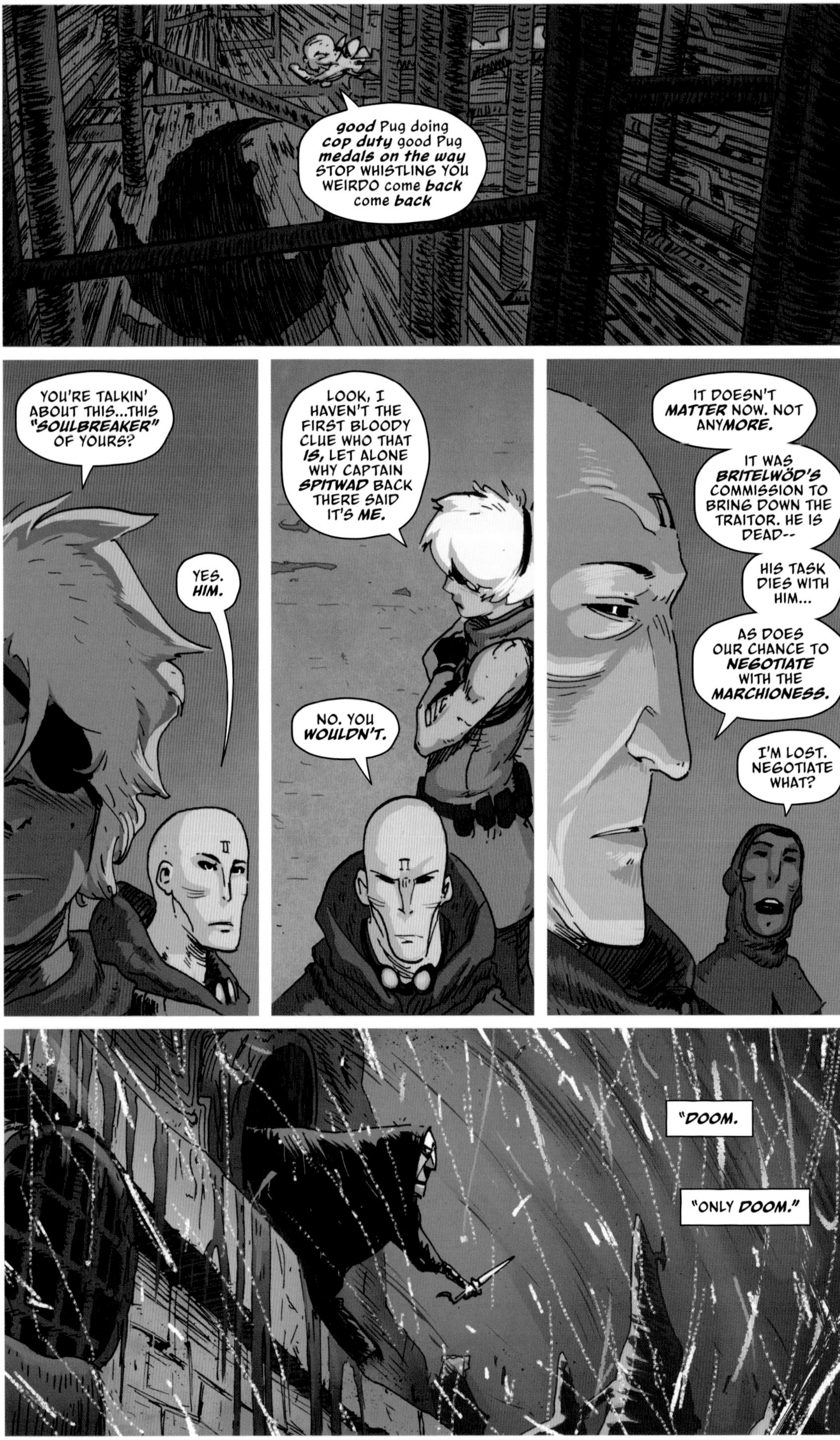
good Pug doing cop duty good Pug medals on the way STOP WHISTLING YOU WEIRDO come back come back
YOU'RE TALKIN' ABOUT THIS...THIS "SOULBREAKER" OF YOURS?
YES. HIM.
LOOK, I HAVEN'T THE FIRST BLOODY CLUE WHO THAT IS, LET ALONE WHY CAPTAIN SPITWAD BACK THERE SAID IT'S ME.
NO. YOU WOULDN'T.
IT DOESN'T MATTER NOW. NOT ANYMORE.
IT WAS BRITELWÖD'S COMMISSION TO BRING DOWN THE TRAITOR. HE IS DEAD--
HIS TASK DIES WITH HIM...
AS DOES OUR CHANCE TO NEGOTIATE WITH THE MARCHIONESS.
I'M LOST. NEGOTIATE WHAT?
"DOOM.
"ONLY DOOM."

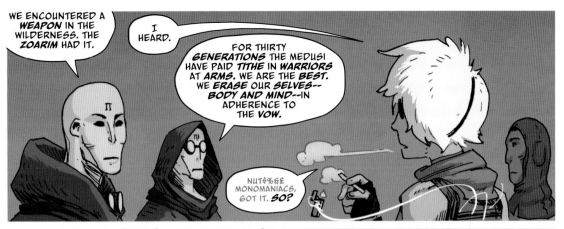

WE ENCOUNTERED A **WEAPON** IN THE WILDERNESS. THE **ZOARIM** HAD IT.

I HEARD.

FOR THIRTY **GENERATIONS** THE MEDUSI HAVE PAID **TITHE** IN **WARRIORS** AT **ARMS**. WE ARE THE **BEST**. WE **ERASE** OUR **SELVES**-- BODY AND MIND--IN ADHERENCE TO THE **VOW**.

NUT$%&£ MONOMANIACS, GOT IT. **SO?**

SHORTLY BEFORE Y-- ...SOMEONE...MURDERED OUR **LEADER**...

...THE **BARONESS** DECREED THAT THIRTY MEMBERS OF THIS DELEGATION BE **ARROGATED** INTO THE GARRISON.

IMMEDIATE DEPLOYMENT. A **SPECIAL** UNIT. **SCULPTED** TROOPS **ONLY**.

...

THE **WEAPON**. THAT SNEAKY **COW**.

"SHE'S SENDING OUT HER **DISPOSABLES** TO **DIE**."

WE WILL DO OUR **DUTY**. WE WILL **PERISH**, IF SO CALLED. THAT IS OUR **WAY**.

BUT...YOU ARE **OF** THIS CITY. YOU **KNOW** THESE...ROYALS. PERHAPS YOU CAN **SPEAK** TO THEM?

ARE YOU... ARE YOU **ACTUALLY** ASKING FOR MY **HELP?**

YOU ARE ONE OF **US**. WHATEVER **ELSE** YOU MAY BE.

DONN666

BOSS... BOSS, THAT'S THE B--

YEAH.

I...I HAVE TO **GO**...

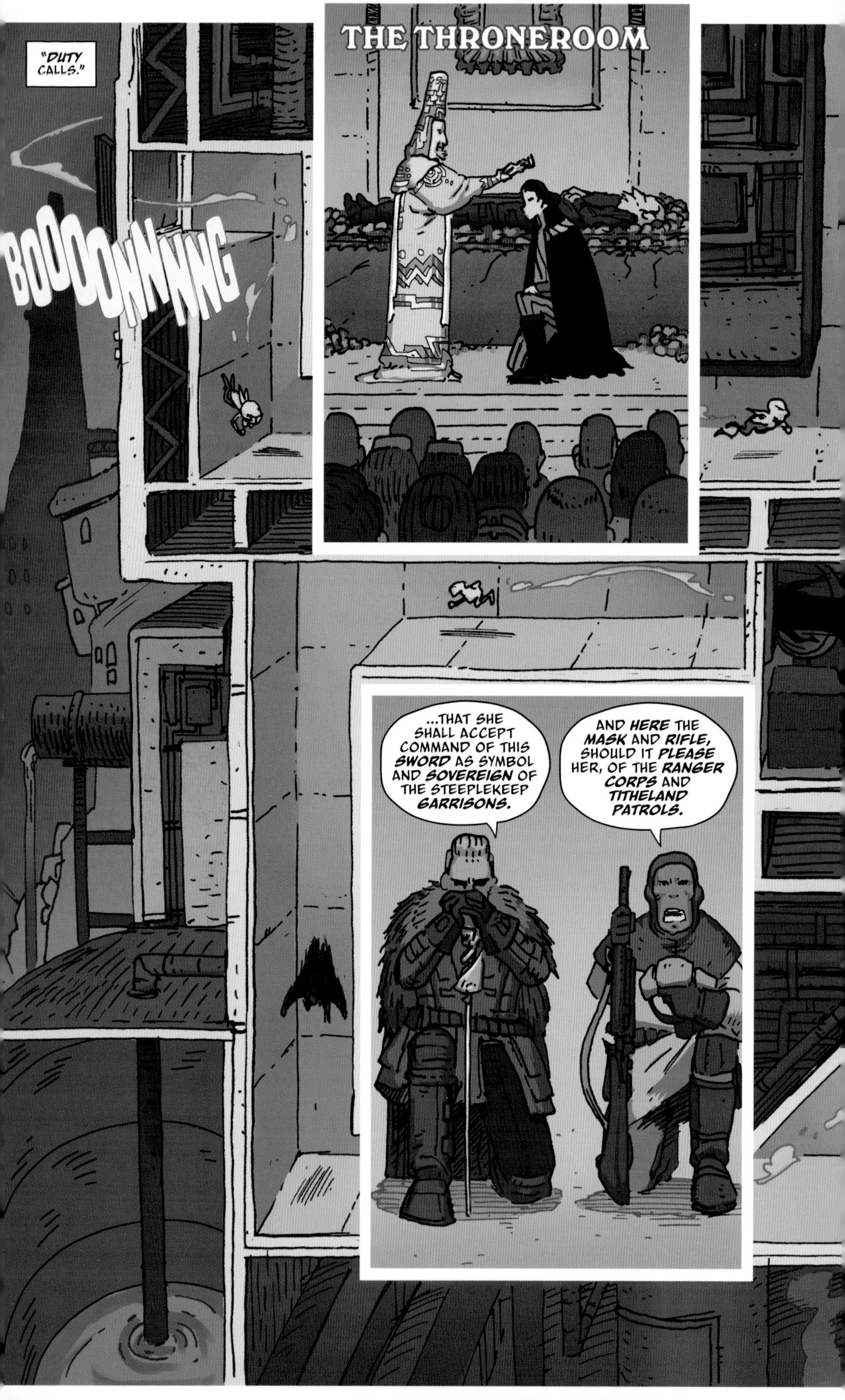
"DUTY CALLS."
BOOOONNNNG
THE THRONEROOM
...THAT SHE SHALL ACCEPT COMMAND OF THIS SWORD AS SYMBOL AND SOVEREIGN OF THE STEEPLEKEEP GARRISONS.
AND HERE THE MASK AND RIFLE, SHOULD IT PLEASE HER, OF THE RANGER CORPS AND TITHELAND PATROLS.

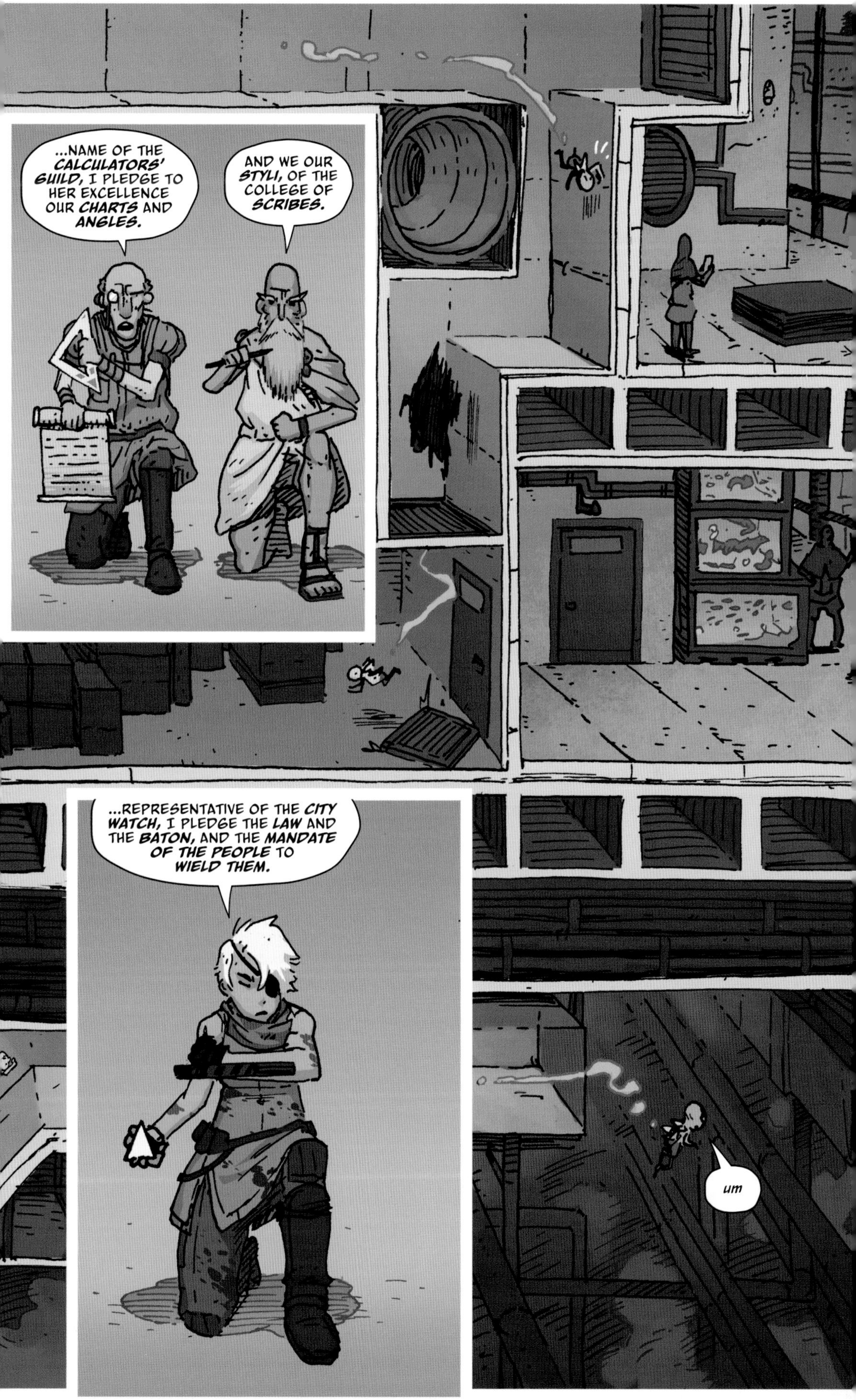
...NAME OF THE CALCULATORS' GUILD, I PLEDGE TO HER EXCELLENCE OUR CHARTS AND ANGLES.
AND WE OUR STYLI, OF THE COLLEGE OF SCRIBES.
...REPRESENTATIVE OF THE CITY WATCH, I PLEDGE THE LAW AND THE BATON, AND THE MANDATE OF THE PEOPLE TO WIELD THEM.
um

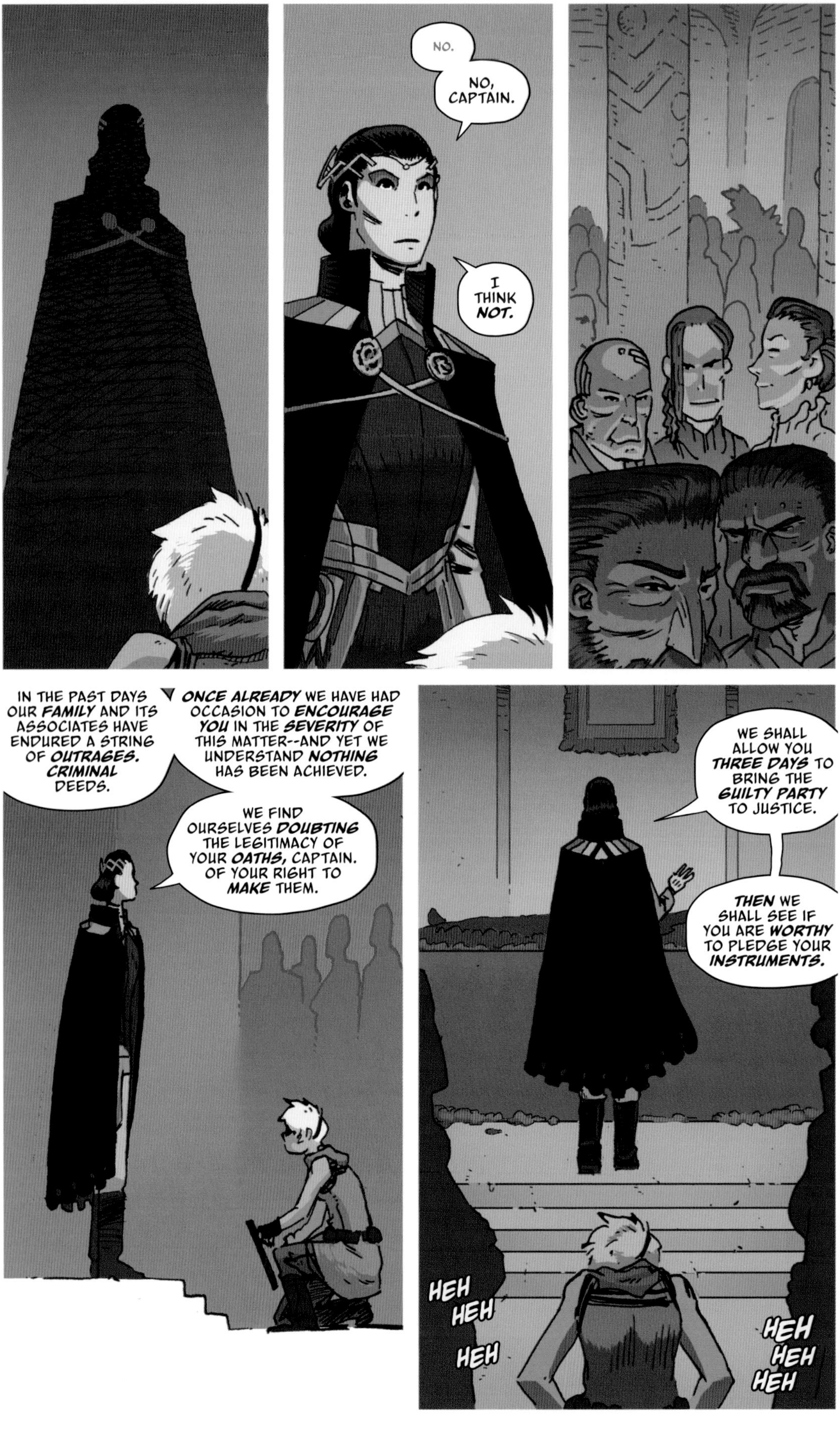
NO.
NO, CAPTAIN.
I THINK NOT.
IN THE PAST DAYS OUR FAMILY AND ITS ASSOCIATES HAVE ENDURED A STRING OF OUTRAGES. CRIMINAL DEEDS.
ONCE ALREADY WE HAVE HAD OCCASION TO ENCOURAGE YOU IN THE SEVERITY OF THIS MATTER--AND YET WE UNDERSTAND NOTHING HAS BEEN ACHIEVED.
WE FIND OURSELVES DOUBTING THE LEGITIMACY OF YOUR OATHS, CAPTAIN. OF YOUR RIGHT TO MAKE THEM.
WE SHALL ALLOW YOU THREE DAYS TO BRING THE GUILTY PARTY TO JUSTICE.
THEN WE SHALL SEE IF YOU ARE WORTHY TO PLEDGE YOUR INSTRUMENTS.
HEH HEH HEH
HEH HEH HEH

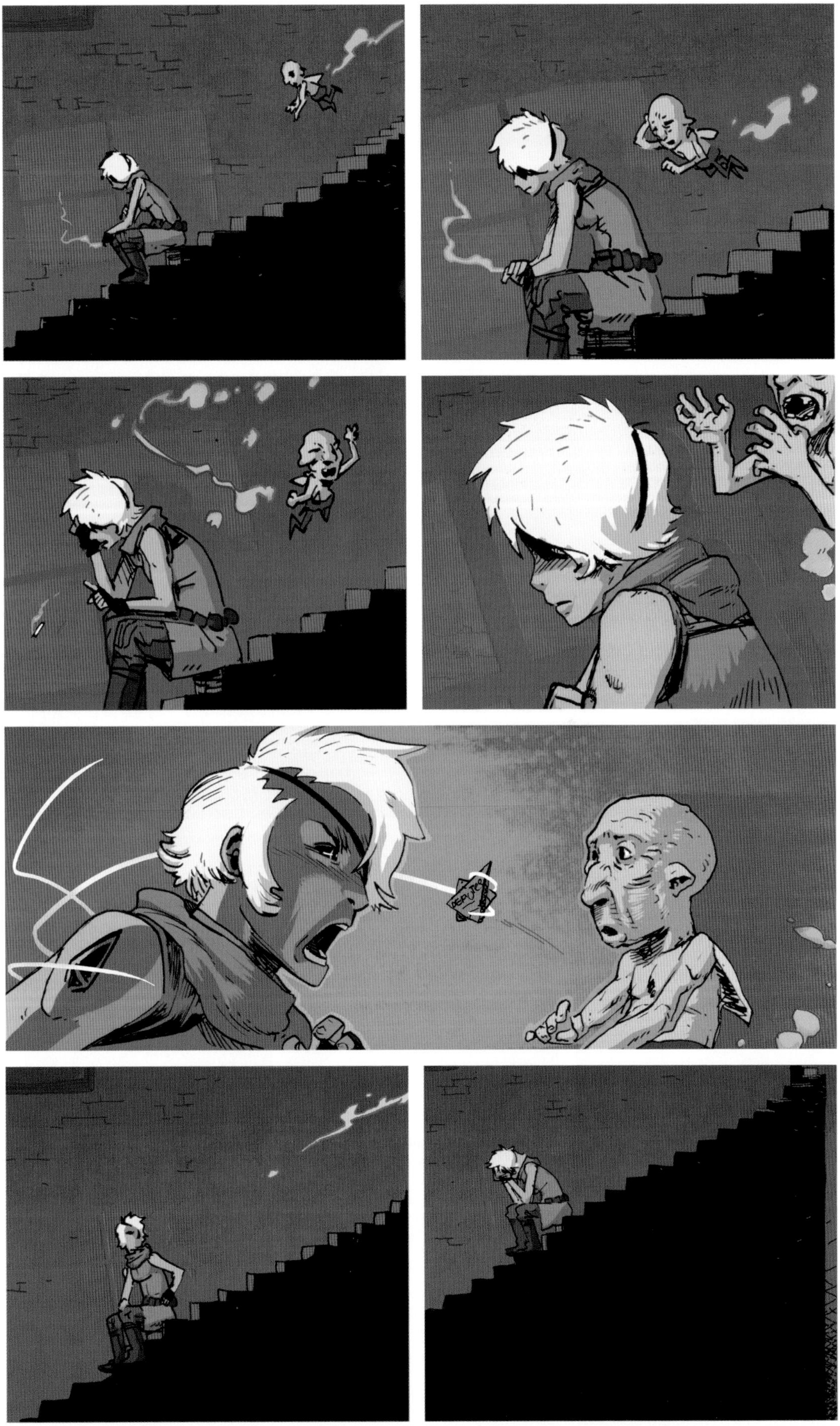

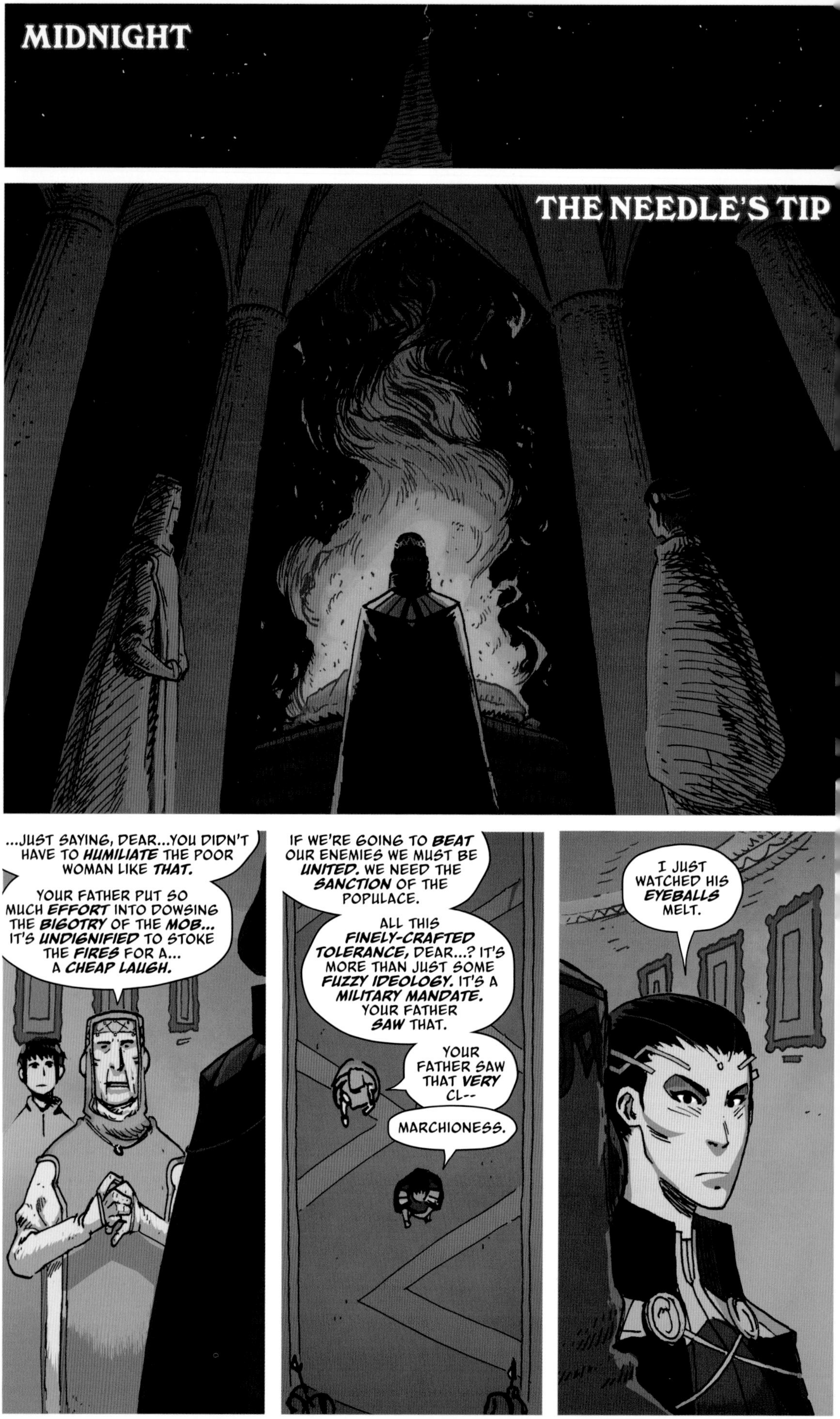
MIDNIGHT
THE NEEDLE'S TIP
...JUST SAYING, DEAR...YOU DIDN'T HAVE TO HUMILIATE THE POOR WOMAN LIKE THAT.
YOUR FATHER PUT SO MUCH EFFORT INTO DOWSING THE BIGOTRY OF THE MOB... IT'S UNDIGNIFIED TO STOKE THE FIRES FOR A... A CHEAP LAUGH.
IF WE'RE GOING TO BEAT OUR ENEMIES WE MUST BE UNITED. WE NEED THE SANCTION OF THE POPULACE.
ALL THIS FINELY-CRAFTED TOLERANCE, DEAR...? IT'S MORE THAN JUST SOME FUZZY IDEOLOGY. IT'S A MILITARY MANDATE. YOUR FATHER SAW THAT.
YOUR FATHER SAW THAT VERY CL--
MARCHIONESS.
I JUST WATCHED HIS EYEBALLS MELT.

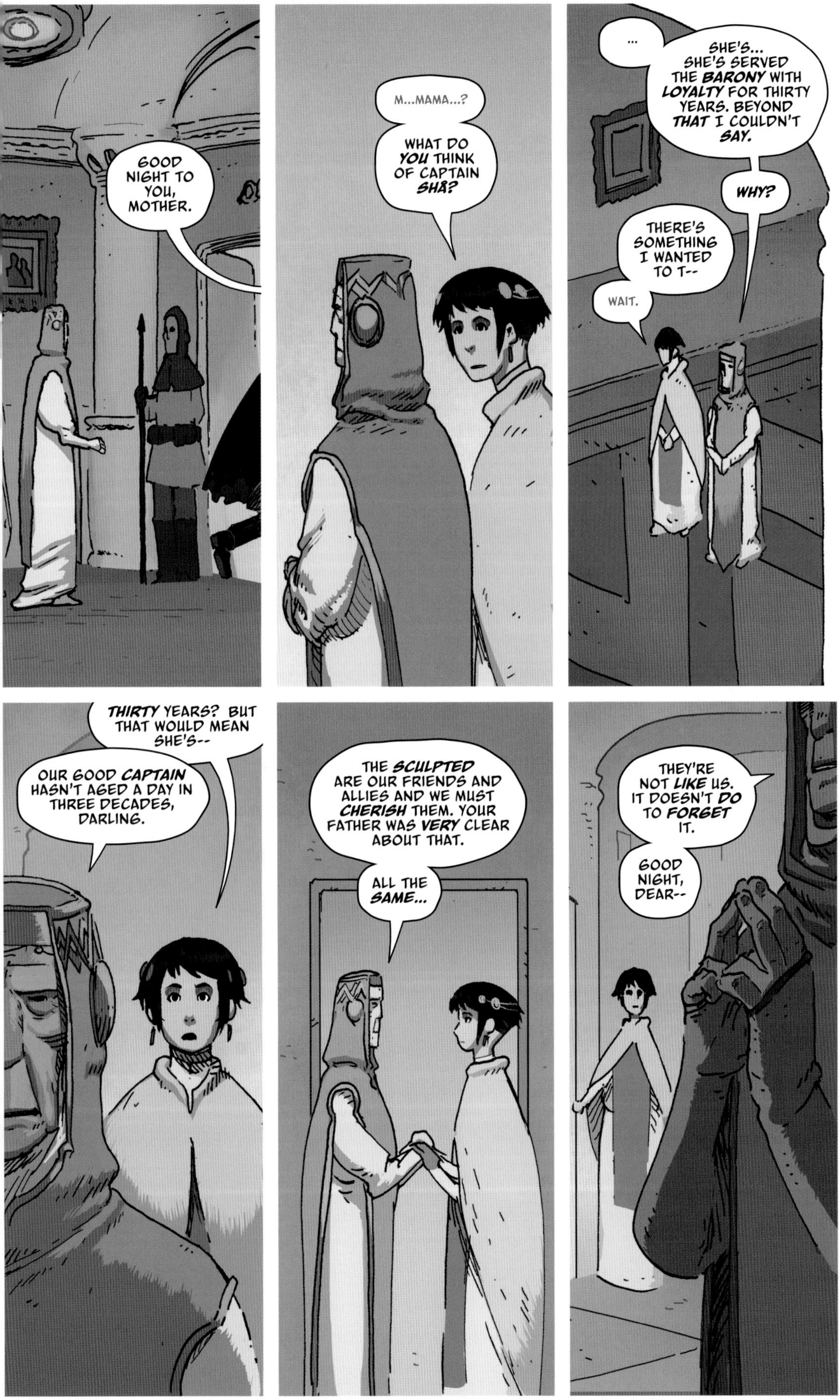
GOOD NIGHT TO YOU, MOTHER.
M...MAMA...?
WHAT DO YOU THINK OF CAPTAIN SHĀ?
...
SHE'S... SHE'S SERVED THE BARONY WITH LOYALTY FOR THIRTY YEARS. BEYOND THAT I COULDN'T SAY.
WHY?
THERE'S SOMETHING I WANTED TO T--
WAIT.
THIRTY YEARS? BUT THAT WOULD MEAN SHE'S--
OUR GOOD CAPTAIN HASN'T AGED A DAY IN THREE DECADES, DARLING.
THE SCULPTED ARE OUR FRIENDS AND ALLIES AND WE MUST CHERISH THEM. YOUR FATHER WAS VERY CLEAR ABOUT THAT.
ALL THE SAME...
THEY'RE NOT LIKE US. IT DOESN'T DO TO FORGET IT.
GOOD NIGHT, DEAR--

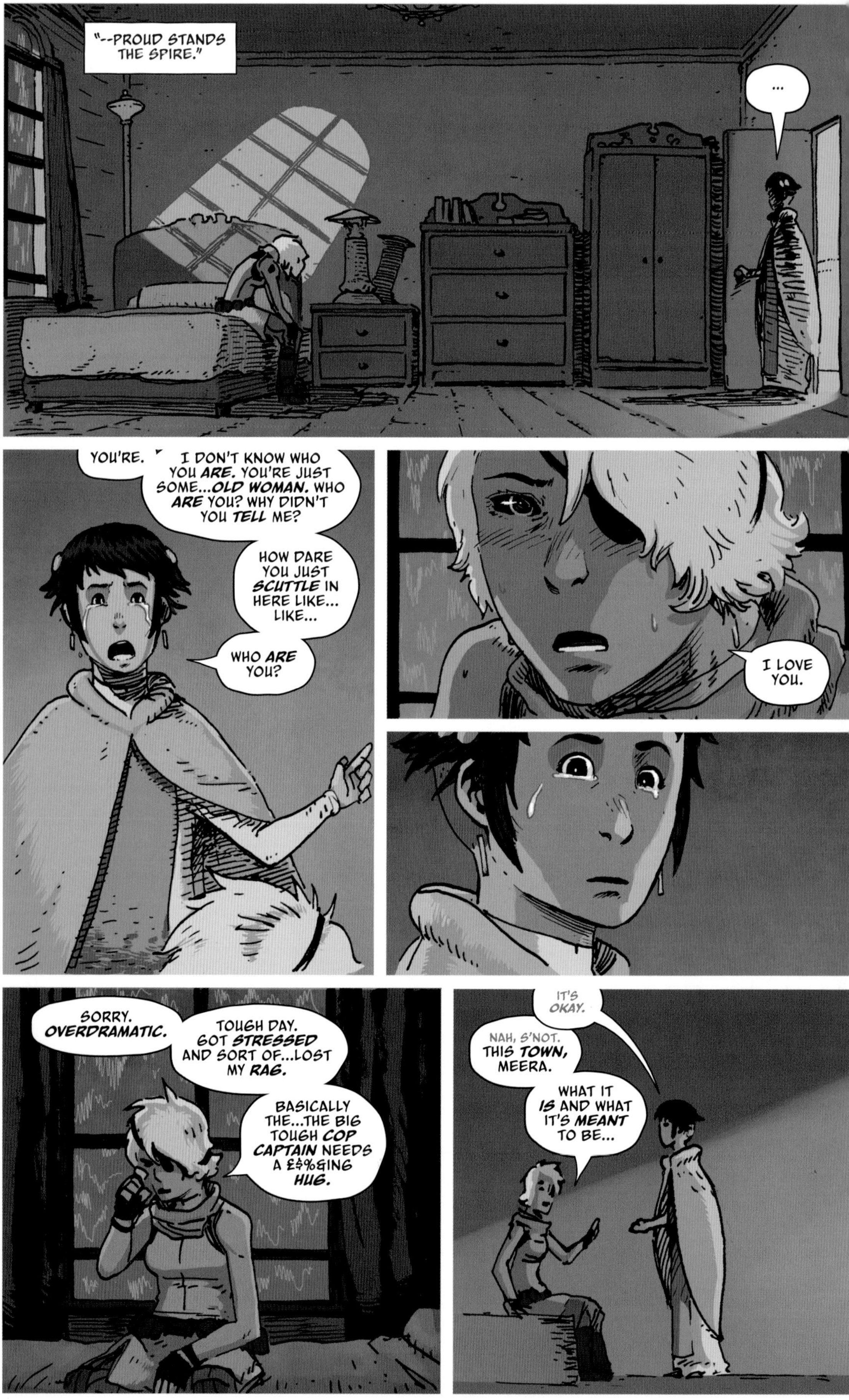
"--PROUD STANDS THE SPIRE."
...
YOU'RE.
I DON'T KNOW WHO YOU ARE. YOU'RE JUST SOME...OLD WOMAN. WHO ARE YOU? WHY DIDN'T YOU TELL ME?
HOW DARE YOU JUST SCUTTLE IN HERE LIKE... LIKE...
WHO ARE YOU?
I LOVE YOU.
SORRY. OVERDRAMATIC.
TOUGH DAY. GOT STRESSED AND SORT OF...LOST MY RAG.
BASICALLY THE...THE BIG TOUGH COP CAPTAIN NEEDS A £$%&ING HUG.
IT'S OKAY.
NAH, S'NOT. THIS TOWN, MEERA.
WHAT IT IS AND WHAT IT'S MEANT TO BE...

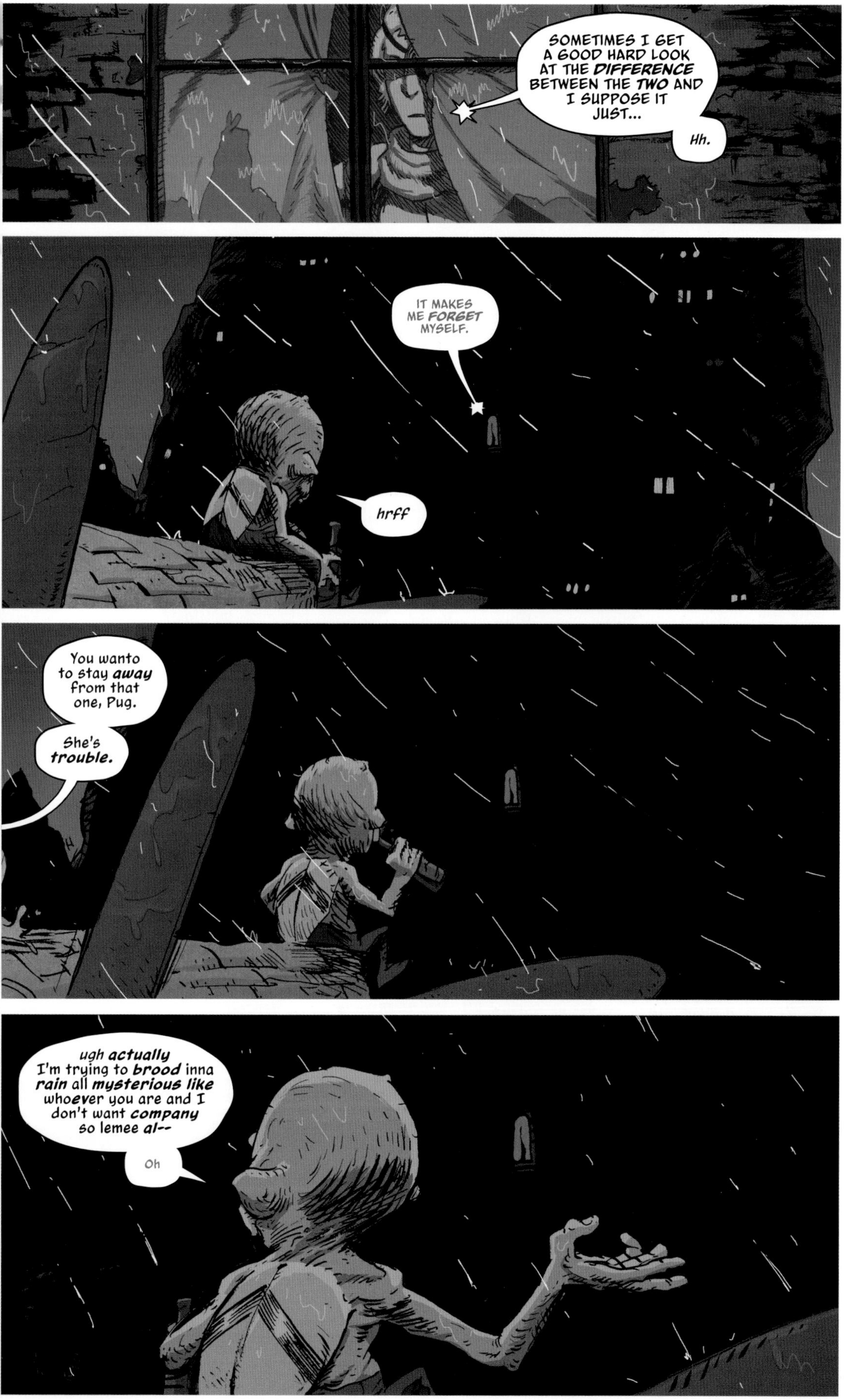
SOMETIMES I GET A GOOD HARD LOOK AT THE *DIFFERENCE* BETWEEN THE *TWO* AND I SUPPOSE IT JUST...
Hh.
IT MAKES ME *FORGET* MYSELF.
hrff
You wanto to stay *away* from that one, Pug.
She's *trouble.*
ugh *actually* I'm trying to *brood* inna *rain* all *mysterious like* who*ever* you are and I don't want *company* so lemee *al--*
Oh

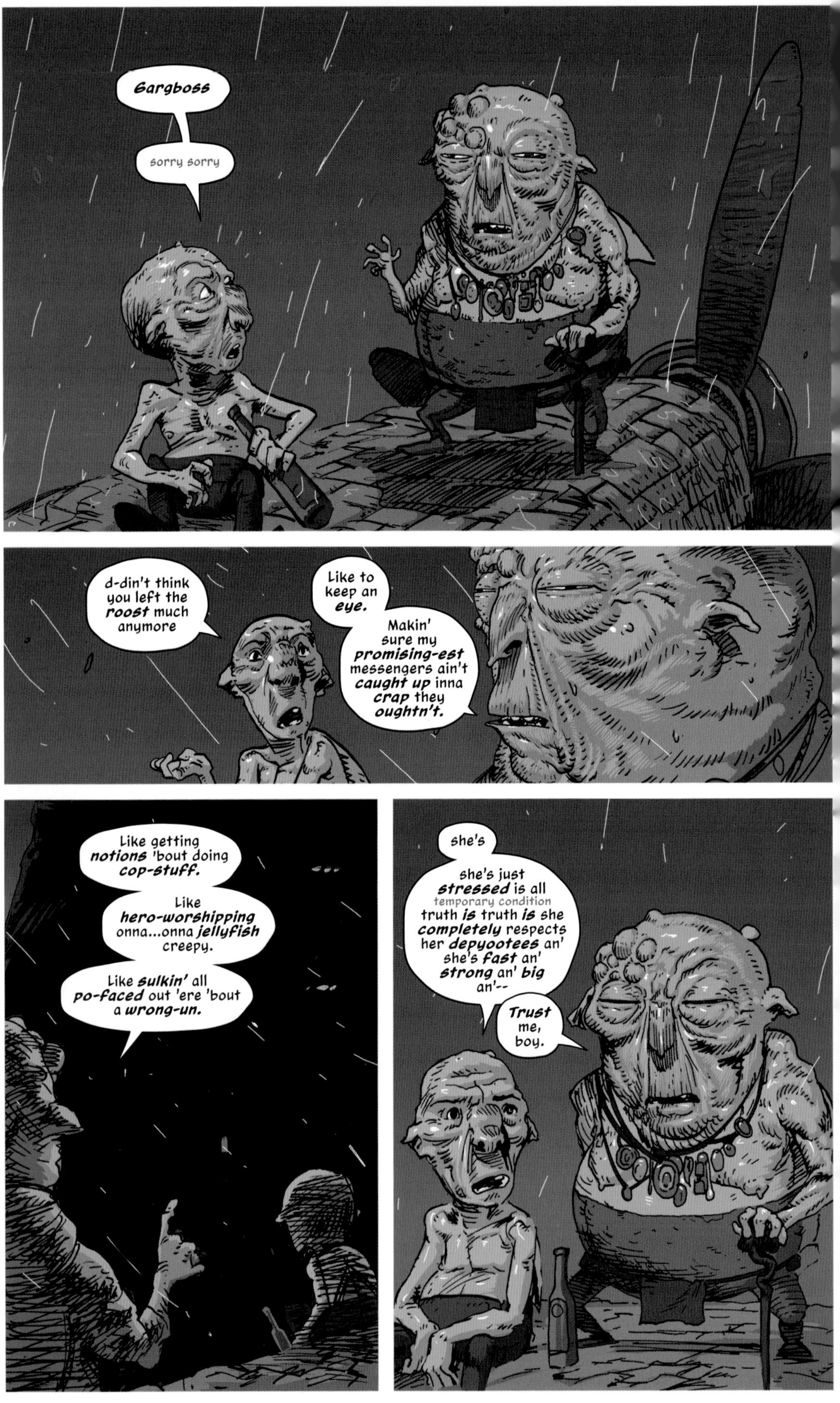

Gargboss
sorry sorry
d-din't think you left the roost much anymore
Like to keep an eye.
Makin' sure my promising-est messengers ain't caught up inna crap they oughtn't.
Like getting notions 'bout doing cop-stuff.
Like hero-worshipping onna...onna jellyfish creepy.
Like sulkin' all po-faced out 'ere 'bout a wrong-un.
she's
she's just stressed is all
temporary condition
truth is truth is she completely respects her depyootees an' she's fast an' strong an' big an'--
Trust me, boy.

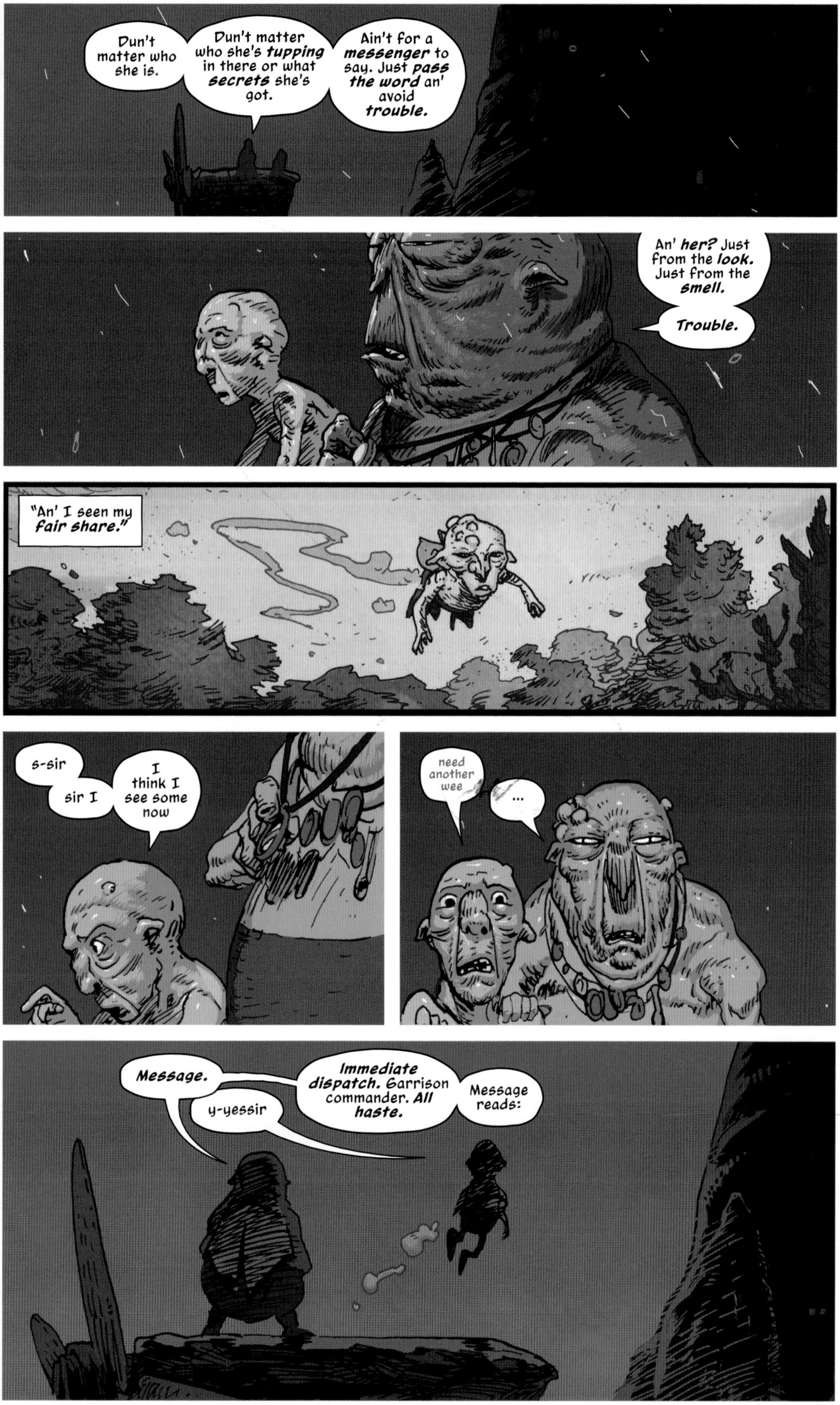

Dun't matter who she is.
Dun't matter who she's *tupping* in there or what *secrets* she's got.
Ain't for a *messenger* to say. Just *pass the word* an' avoid *trouble.*
An' *her?* Just from the *look.* Just from the *smell.*
Trouble.
"An' I seen my *fair share."*
s-sir
sir I
I think I see some now
need another wee
...
Message.
y-yessir
Immediate dispatch. Garrison commander. *All haste.*
Message reads:

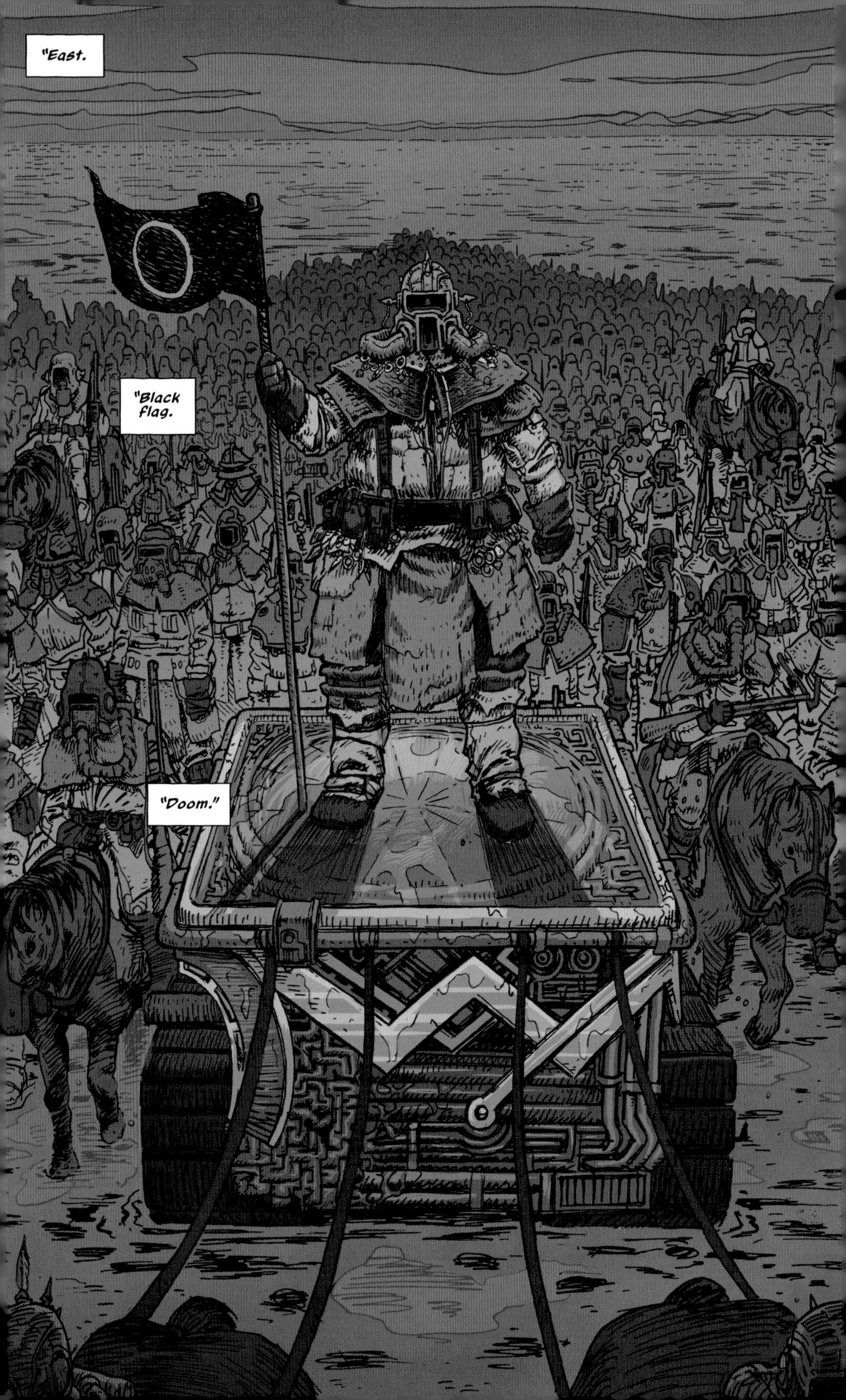
"East.
"Black flag.
"Doom."

ISSUE #4 COVER BY
JEFF STOKELY

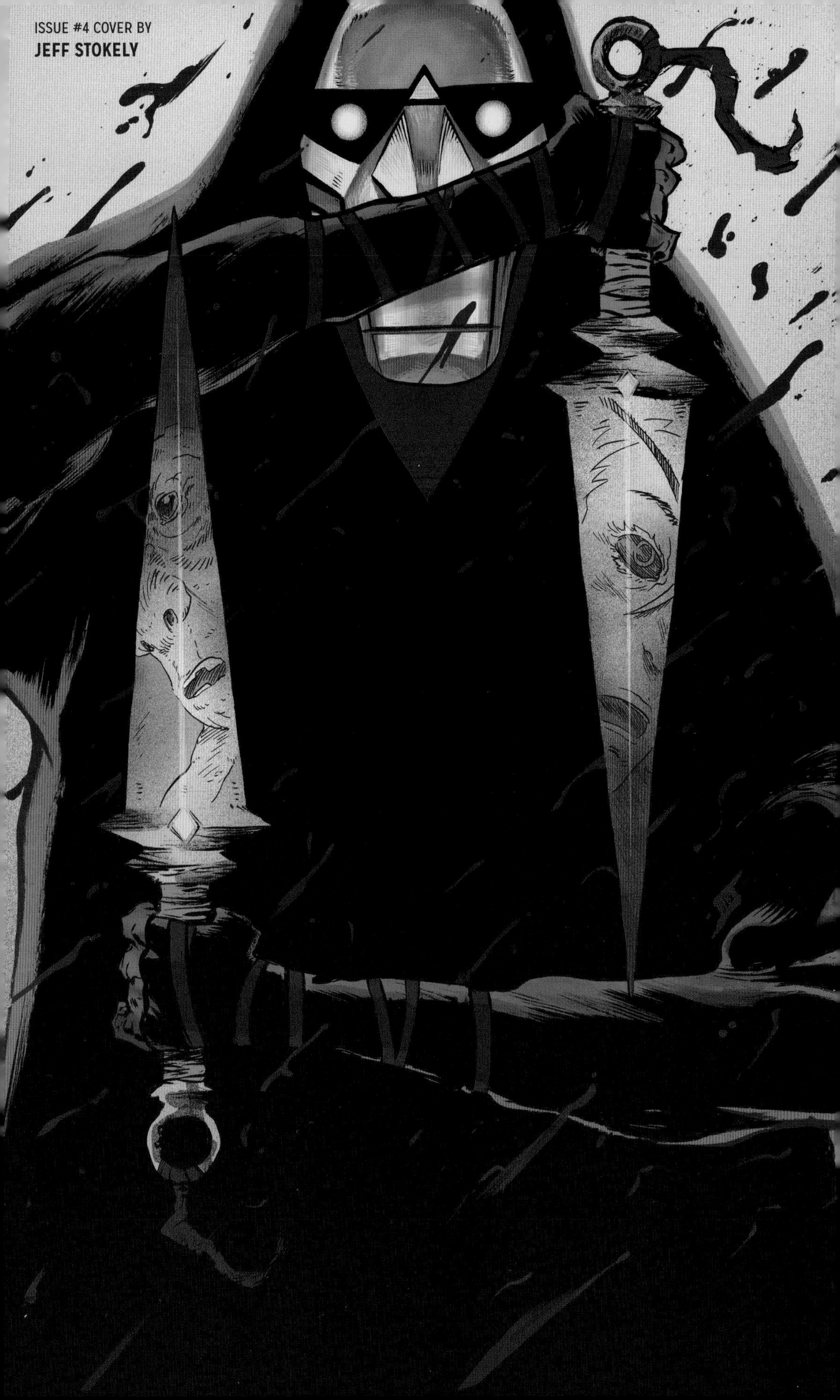

CHAPTER
FIVE

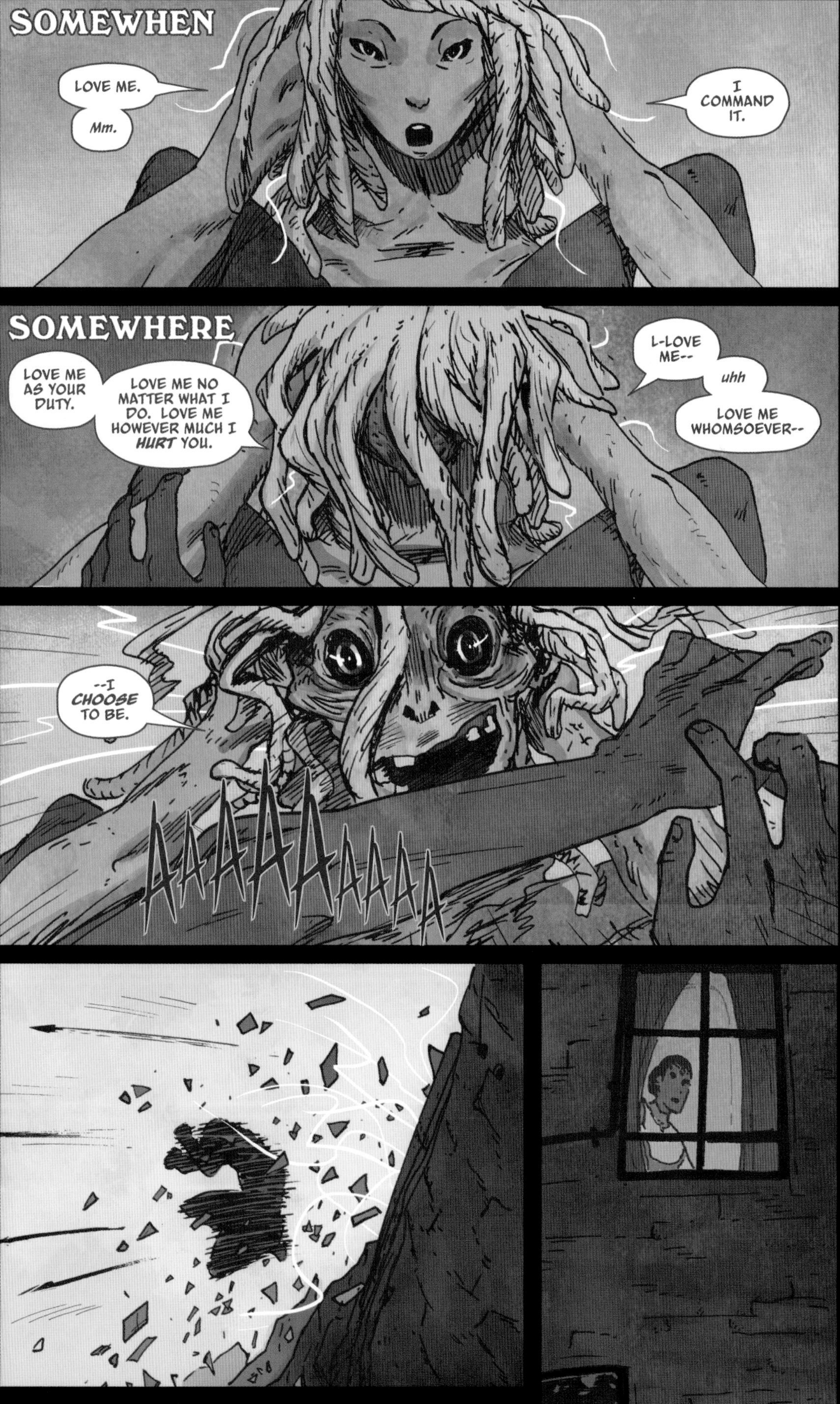
SOMEWHEN
LOVE ME.
Mm.
I COMMAND IT.
SOMEWHERE
LOVE ME AS YOUR DUTY.
LOVE ME NO MATTER WHAT I DO. LOVE ME HOWEVER MUCH I HURT YOU.
L-LOVE ME--
uhh
LOVE ME WHOMSOEVER--
--I CHOOSE TO BE.
AAAAAAAAAA

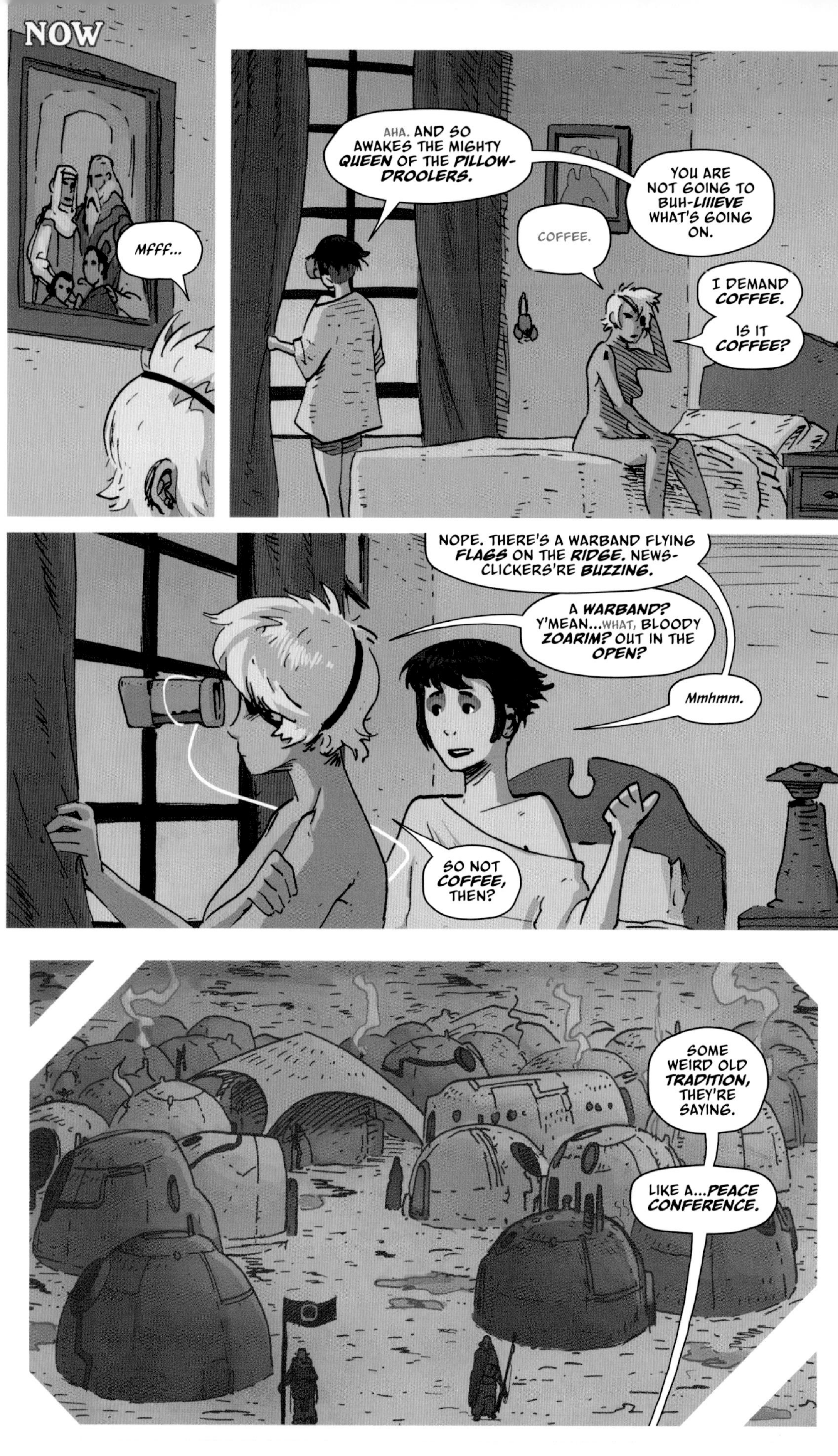
NOW
Mfff...
AHA. AND SO AWAKES THE MIGHTY QUEEN OF THE PILLOW-DROOLERS.
YOU ARE NOT GOING TO BUH-LIIIEVE WHAT'S GOING ON.
COFFEE.
I DEMAND COFFEE.
IS IT COFFEE?
NOPE. THERE'S A WARBAND FLYING FLAGS ON THE RIDGE. NEWS-CLICKERS'RE BUZZING.
A WARBAND? Y'MEAN...WHAT, BLOODY ZOARIM? OUT IN THE OPEN?
Mmhmm.
SO NOT COFFEE, THEN?
SOME WEIRD OLD TRADITION, THEY'RE SAYING.
LIKE A...PEACE CONFERENCE.

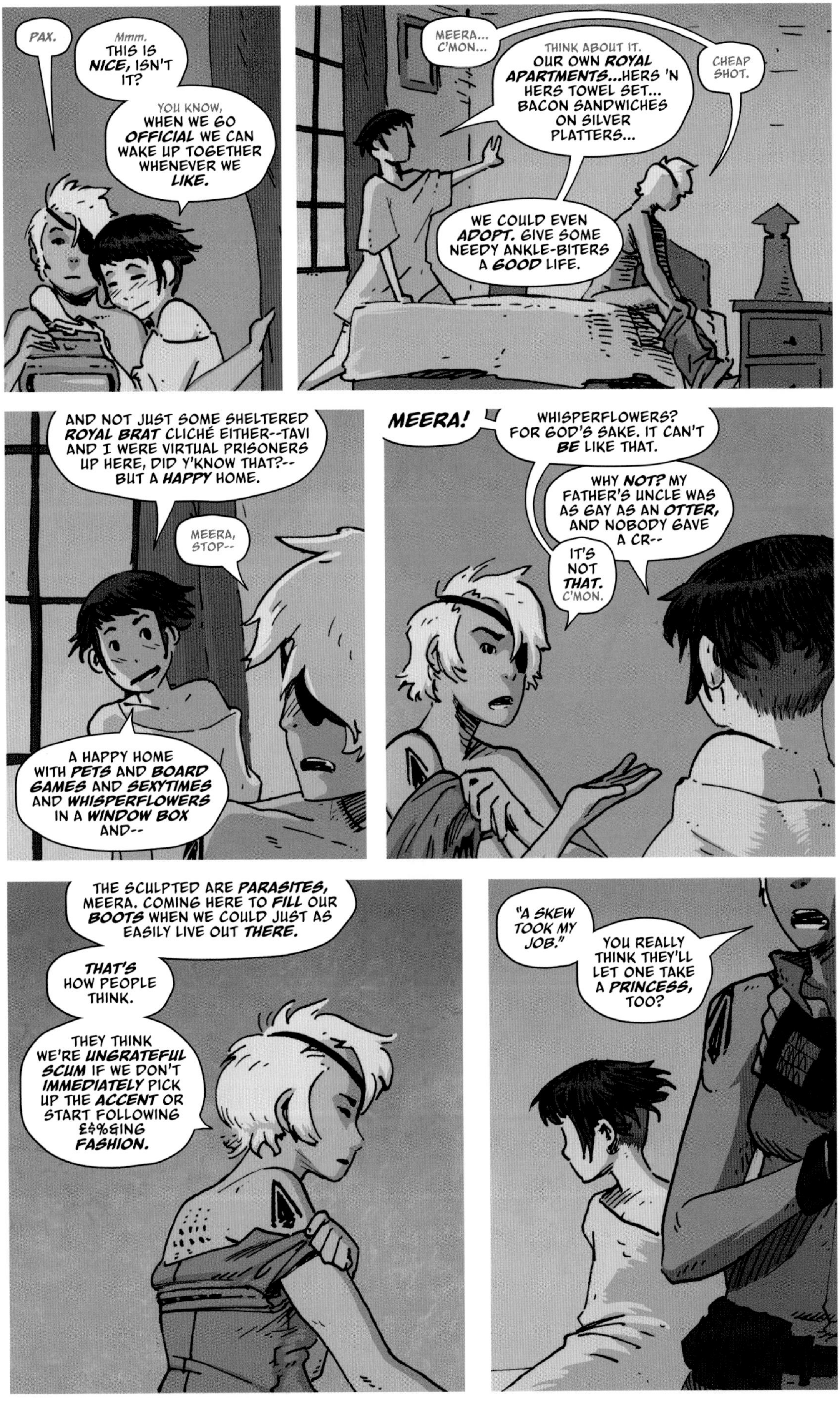
PAX.
Mmm. THIS IS NICE, ISN'T IT?
YOU KNOW, WHEN WE GO OFFICIAL WE CAN WAKE UP TOGETHER WHENEVER WE LIKE.
MEERA... C'MON...
THINK ABOUT IT. OUR OWN ROYAL APARTMENTS...HERS 'N HERS TOWEL SET... BACON SANDWICHES ON SILVER PLATTERS...
CHEAP SHOT.
WE COULD EVEN ADOPT. GIVE SOME NEEDY ANKLE-BITERS A GOOD LIFE.
AND NOT JUST SOME SHELTERED ROYAL BRAT CLICHÉ EITHER--TAVI AND I WERE VIRTUAL PRISONERS UP HERE, DID Y'KNOW THAT?--BUT A HAPPY HOME.
MEERA, STOP--
A HAPPY HOME WITH PETS AND BOARD GAMES AND SEXYTIMES AND WHISPERFLOWERS IN A WINDOW BOX AND--
MEERA!
WHISPERFLOWERS? FOR GOD'S SAKE. IT CAN'T BE LIKE THAT.
WHY NOT? MY FATHER'S UNCLE WAS AS GAY AS AN OTTER, AND NOBODY GAVE A CR--
IT'S NOT THAT. C'MON.
THE SCULPTED ARE PARASITES, MEERA. COMING HERE TO FILL OUR BOOTS WHEN WE COULD JUST AS EASILY LIVE OUT THERE.
THAT'S HOW PEOPLE THINK.
THEY THINK WE'RE UNGRATEFUL SCUM IF WE DON'T IMMEDIATELY PICK UP THE ACCENT OR START FOLLOWING £$%&ING FASHION.
"A SKEW TOOK MY JOB."
YOU REALLY THINK THEY'LL LET ONE TAKE A PRINCESS, TOO?

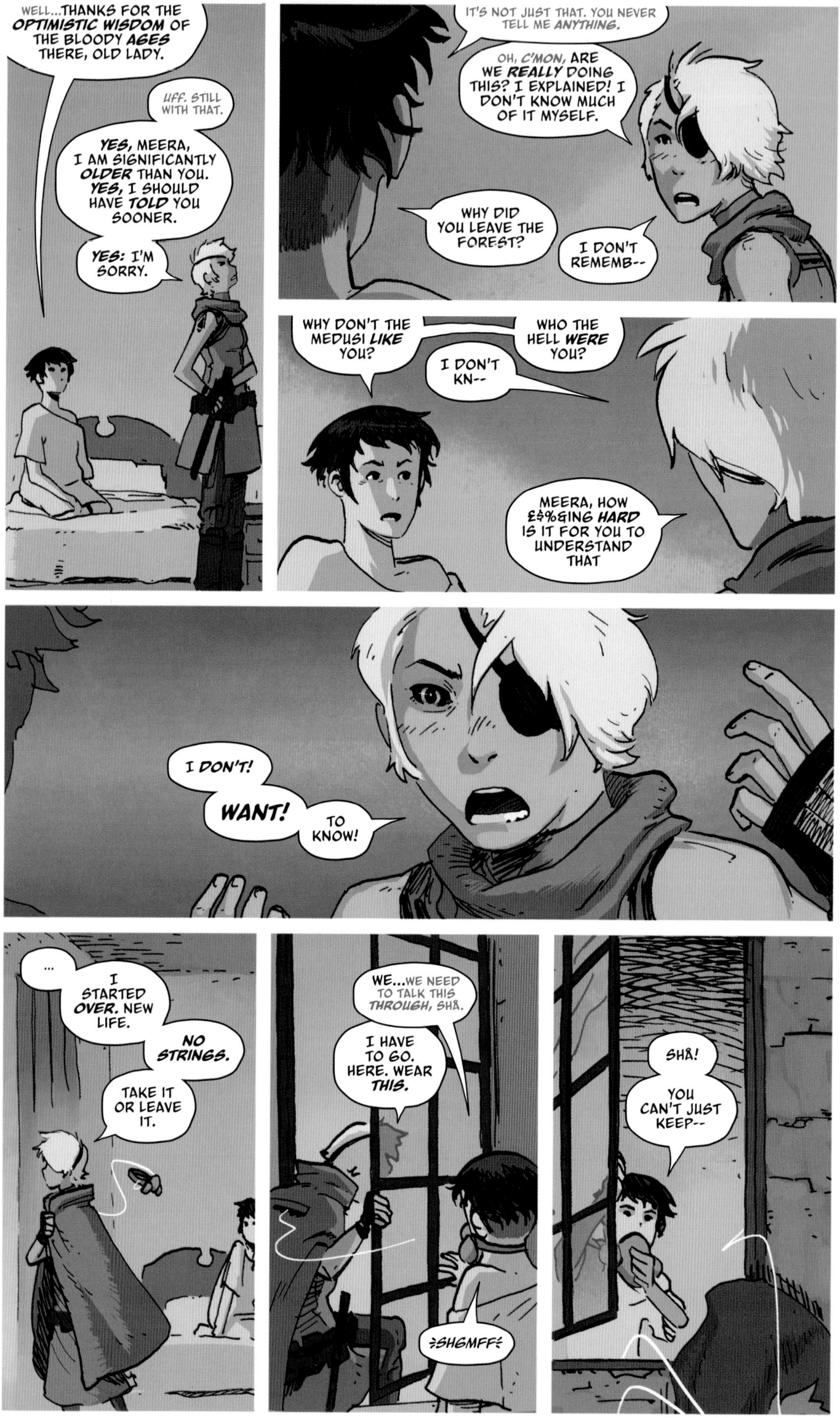
WELL...THANKS FOR THE OPTIMISTIC WISDOM OF THE BLOODY AGES THERE, OLD LADY.
UFF. STILL WITH THAT.
YES, MEERA, I AM SIGNIFICANTLY OLDER THAN YOU. YES, I SHOULD HAVE TOLD YOU SOONER.
YES: I'M SORRY.
IT'S NOT JUST THAT. YOU NEVER TELL ME ANYTHING.
OH, C'MON, ARE WE REALLY DOING THIS? I EXPLAINED! I DON'T KNOW MUCH OF IT MYSELF.
WHY DID YOU LEAVE THE FOREST?
I DON'T REMEMB--
WHY DON'T THE MEDUSI LIKE YOU?
I DON'T KN--
WHO THE HELL WERE YOU?
MEERA, HOW £$%&ING HARD IS IT FOR YOU TO UNDERSTAND THAT
I DON'T!
WANT!
TO KNOW!
...
I STARTED OVER. NEW LIFE.
NO STRINGS.
TAKE IT OR LEAVE IT.
WE...WE NEED TO TALK THIS THROUGH, SHÅ.
I HAVE TO GO. HERE. WEAR THIS.
SHGMFF
SHÅ!
YOU CAN'T JUST KEEP--

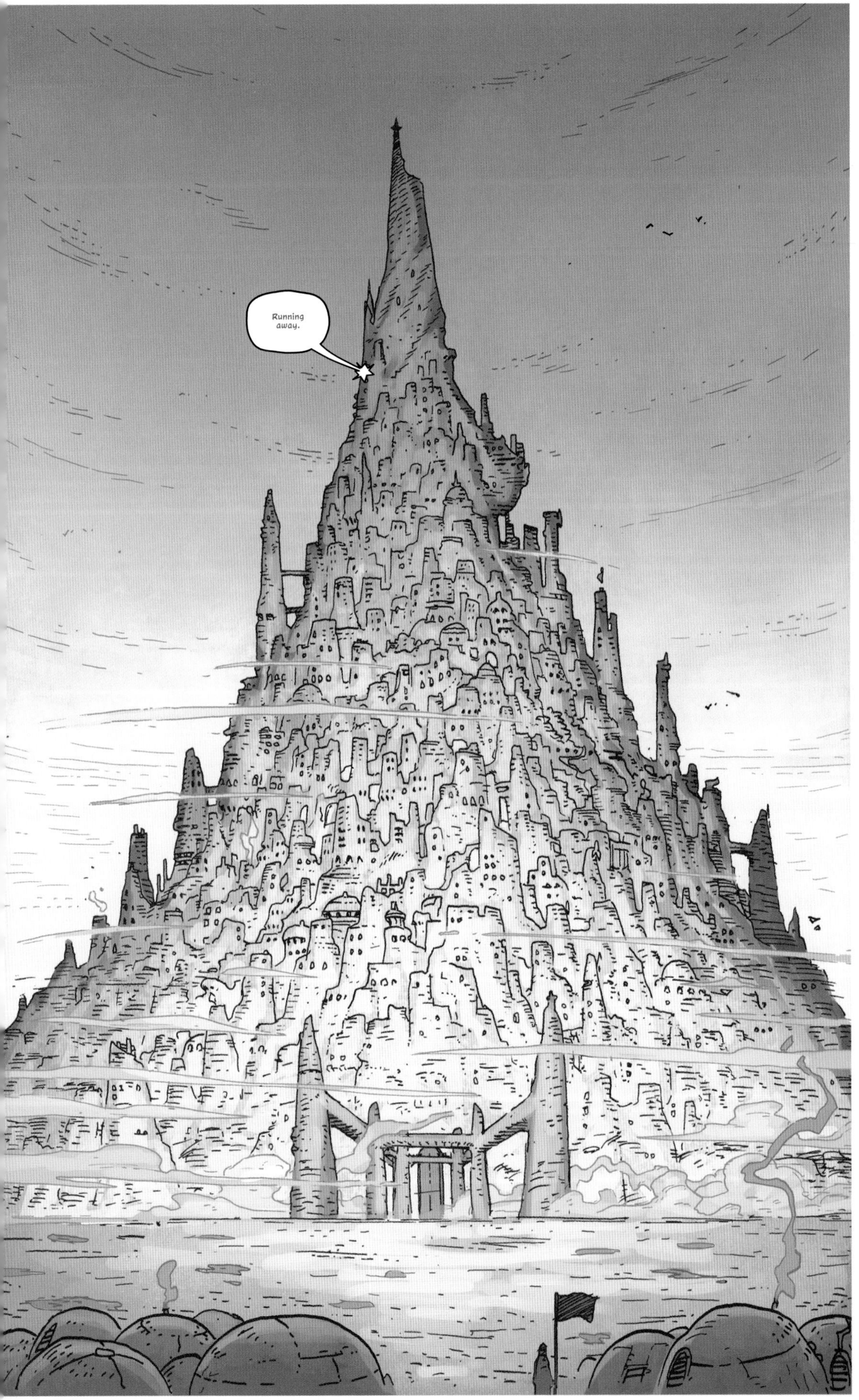
Running away.

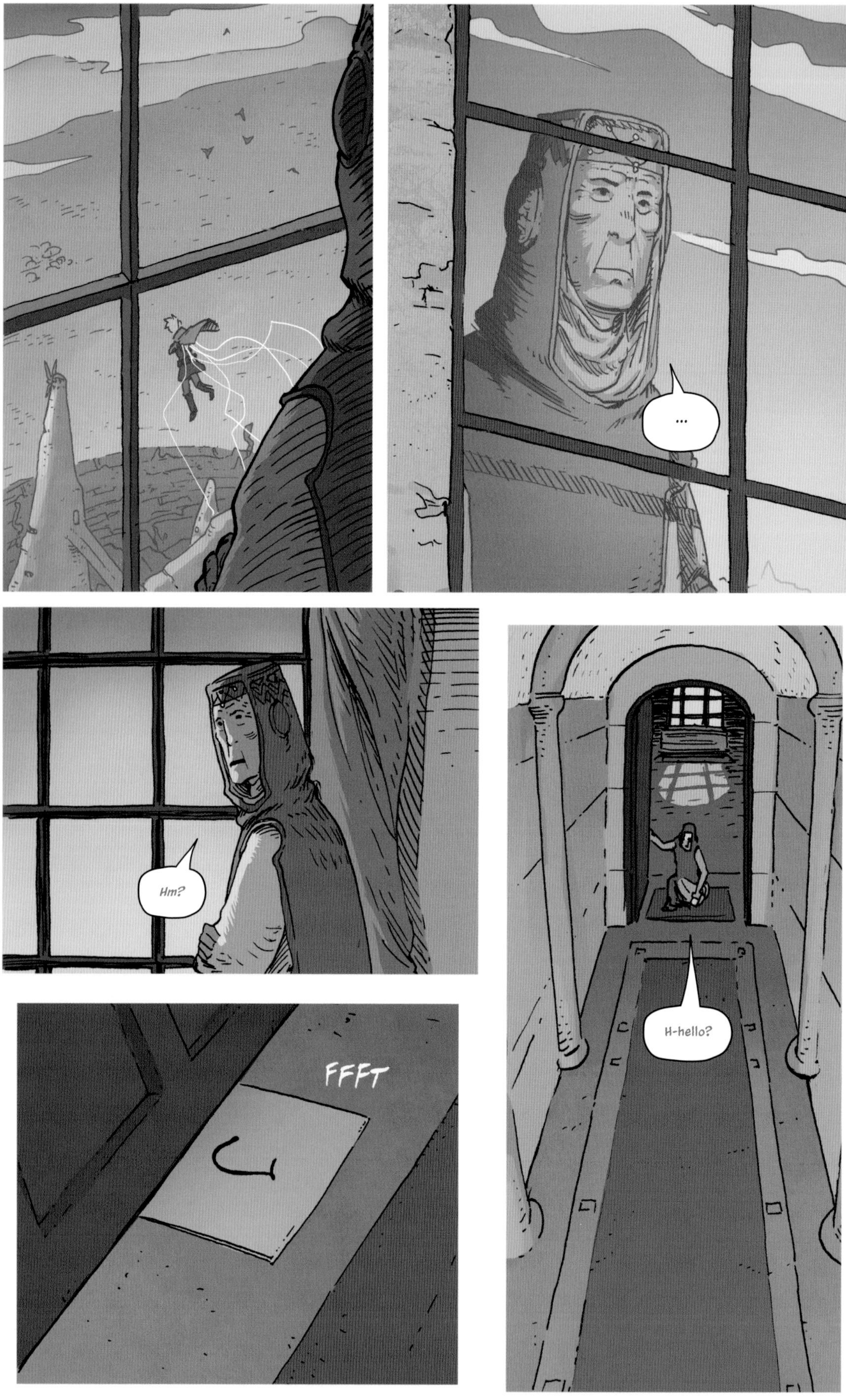
...
Hm?
FFFT
H-hello?

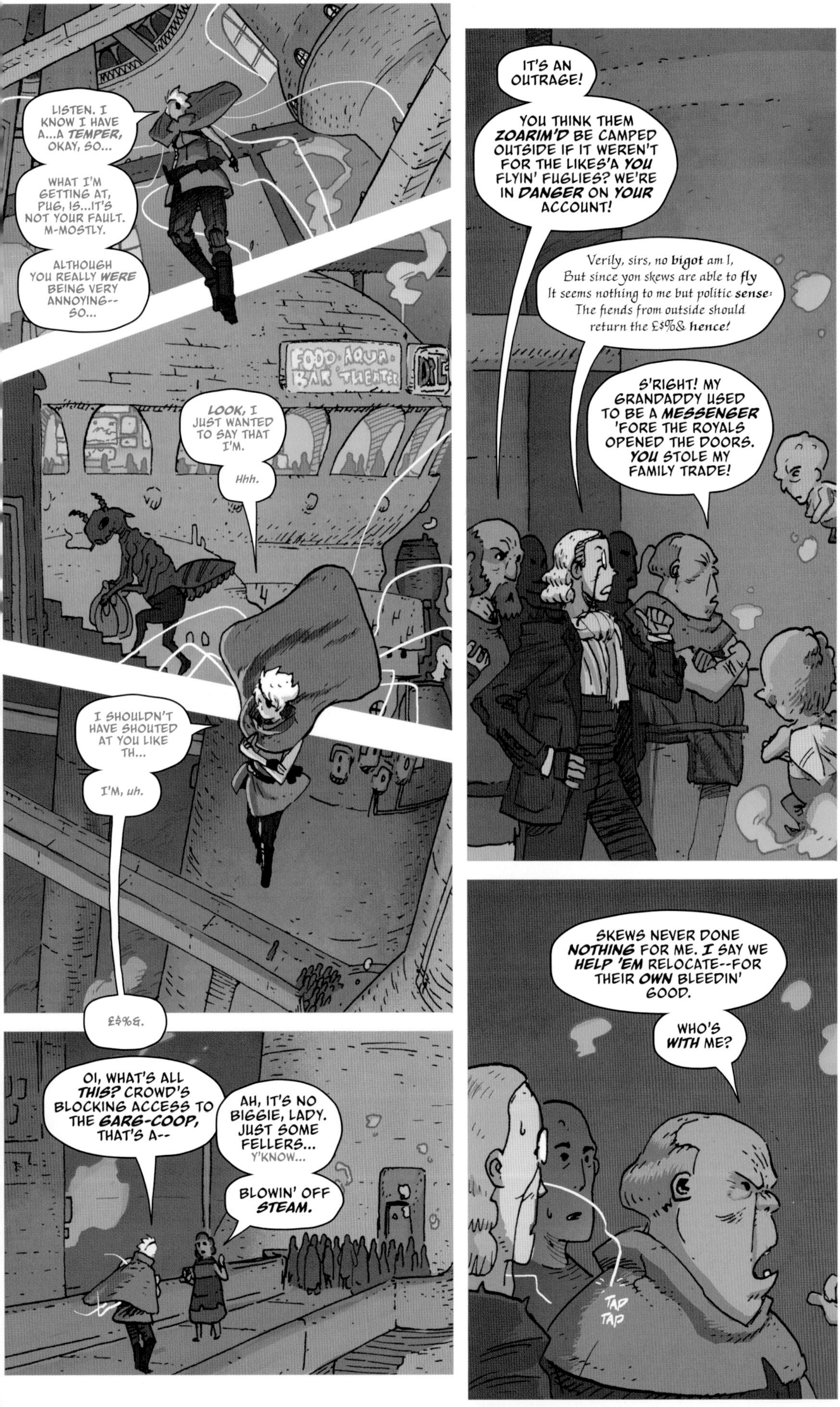
LISTEN. I KNOW I HAVE A...A TEMPER, OKAY, SO...
WHAT I'M GETTING AT, PUG, IS...IT'S NOT YOUR FAULT. M-MOSTLY.
ALTHOUGH YOU REALLY WERE BEING VERY ANNOYING-- SO...
FOOD · AQUA · BAR · THEATER
LOOK, I JUST WANTED TO SAY THAT I'M.
Hhh.
I SHOULDN'T HAVE SHOUTED AT YOU LIKE TH...
I'M, uh.
£$%&.
OI, WHAT'S ALL THIS? CROWD'S BLOCKING ACCESS TO THE GARG-COOP, THAT'S A--
AH, IT'S NO BIGGIE, LADY. JUST SOME FELLERS... Y'KNOW...
BLOWIN' OFF STEAM.
IT'S AN OUTRAGE!
YOU THINK THEM ZOARIM'D BE CAMPED OUTSIDE IF IT WEREN'T FOR THE LIKES'A YOU FLYIN' FUGLIES? WE'RE IN DANGER ON YOUR ACCOUNT!
Verily, sirs, no bigot am I, But since yon skews are able to fly It seems nothing to me but politic sense: The fiends from outside should return the £$%& hence!
S'RIGHT! MY GRANDADDY USED TO BE A MESSENGER 'FORE THE ROYALS OPENED THE DOORS. YOU STOLE MY FAMILY TRADE!
SKEWS NEVER DONE NOTHING FOR ME. I SAY WE HELP 'EM RELOCATE--FOR THEIR OWN BLEEDIN' GOOD.
WHO'S WITH ME?
TAP TAP

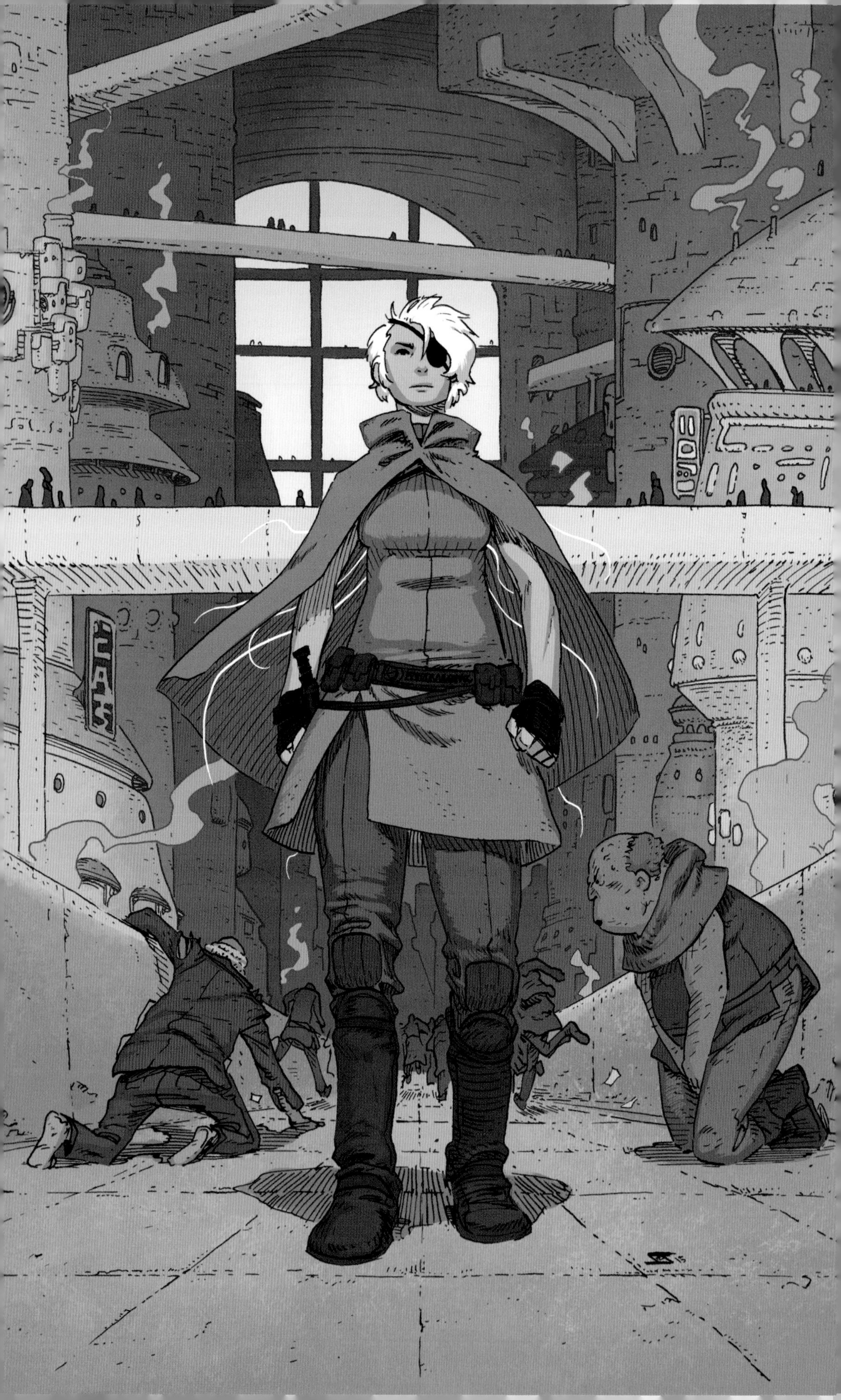

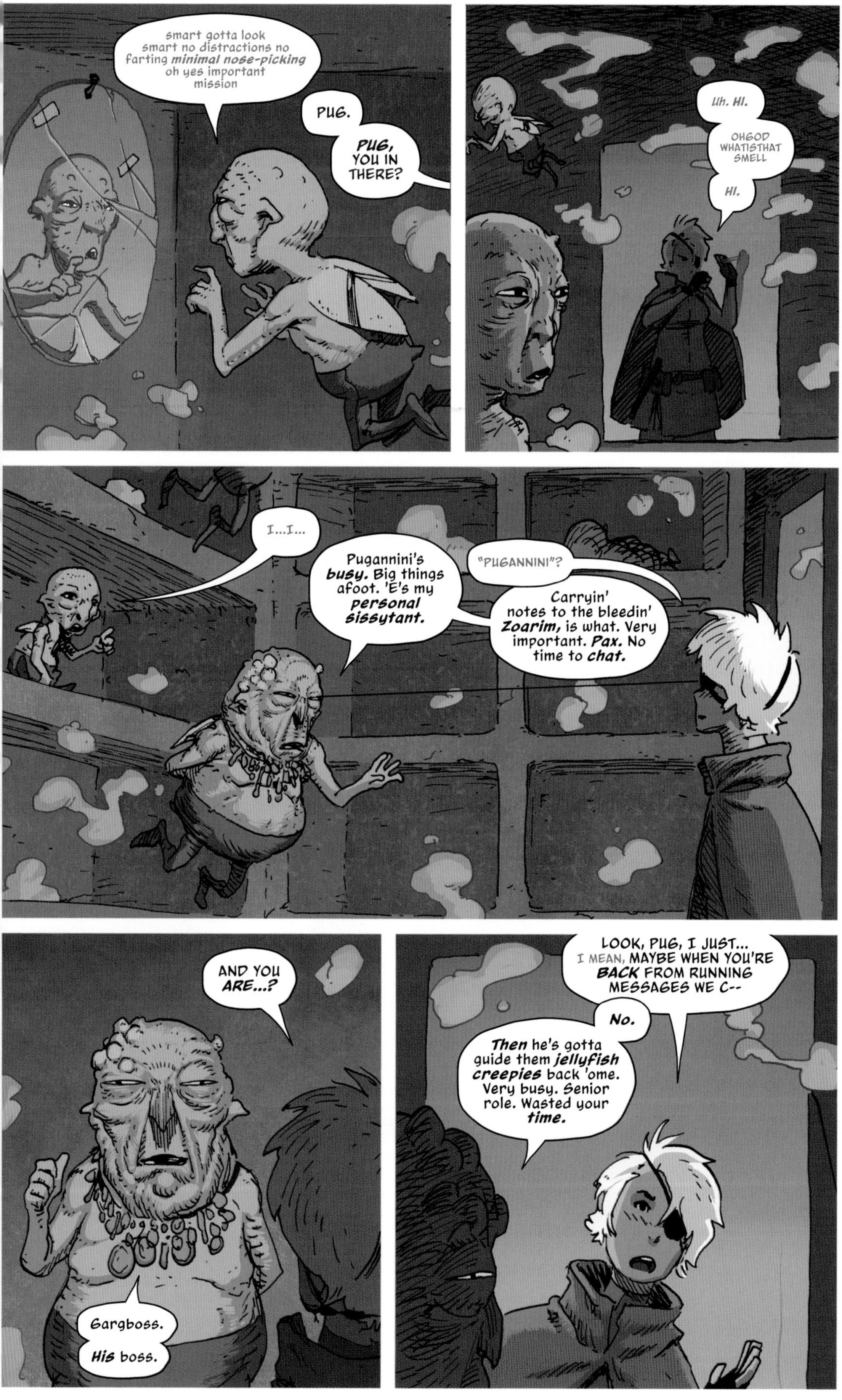
smart gotta look smart no distractions no farting *minimal nose-picking* oh yes important mission
PUG.
PUG, YOU IN THERE?
Uh. HI.
OHGOD WHATISTHAT SMELL
HI.
I...I...
Pugannini's *busy.* Big things afoot. 'E's my *personal sissytant.*
"PUGANNINI"?
Carryin' notes to the bleedin' *Zoarim,* is what. Very important. *Pax.* No time to *chat.*
AND YOU *ARE...?*
Gargboss.
His boss.
LOOK, PUG, I JUST... I MEAN, MAYBE WHEN YOU'RE *BACK* FROM RUNNING MESSAGES WE C--
No.
Then he's gotta guide them *jellyfish creepies* back 'ome. Very busy. Senior role. Wasted your *time.*

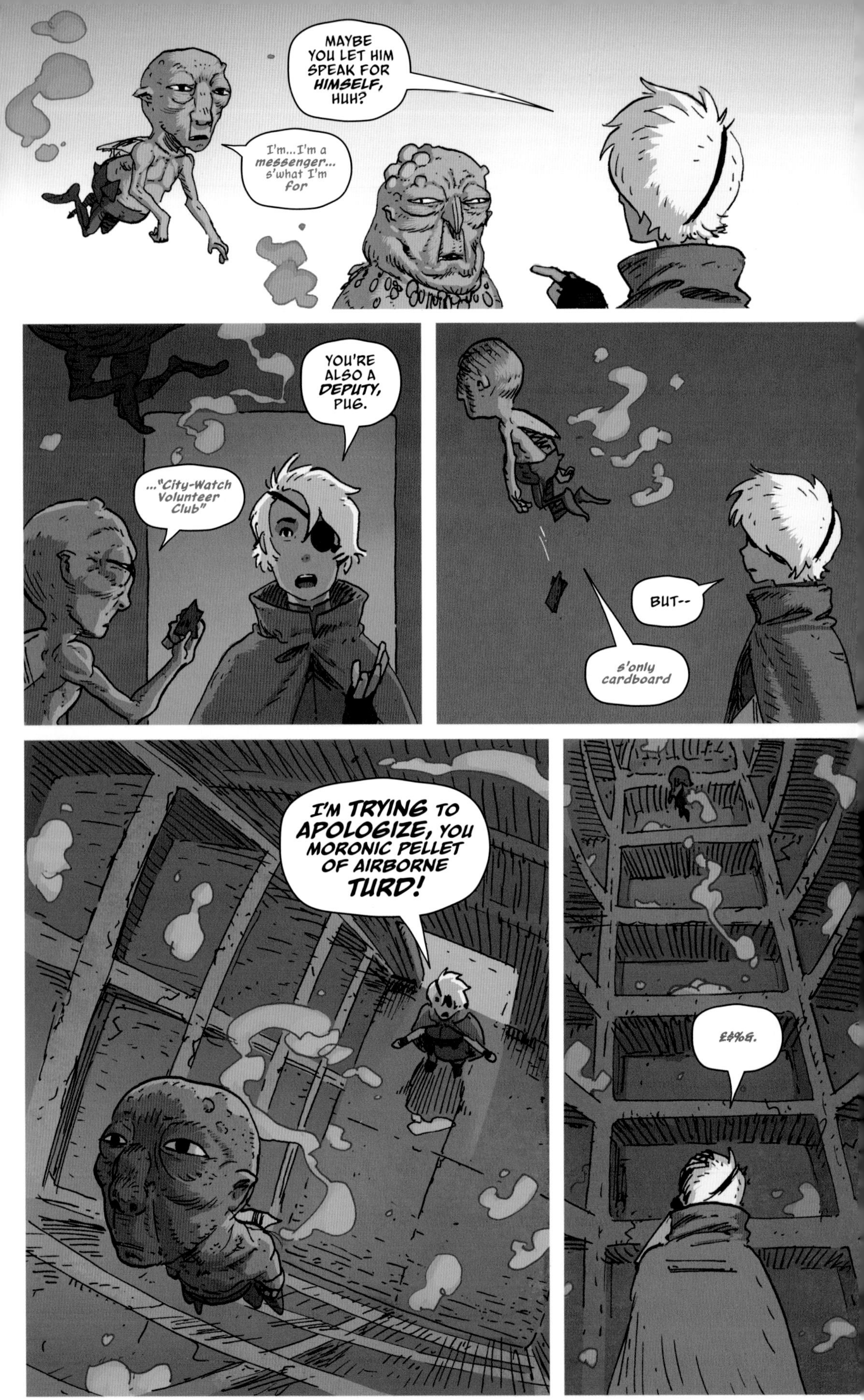

MAYBE YOU LET HIM SPEAK FOR HIMSELF, HUH?
I'm...I'm a messenger... s'what I'm for
YOU'RE ALSO A DEPUTY, PUG.
..."City-Watch Volunteer Club"
BUT--
s'only cardboard
I'M TRYING TO APOLOGIZE, YOU MORONIC PELLET OF AIRBORNE TURD!
£$%G.

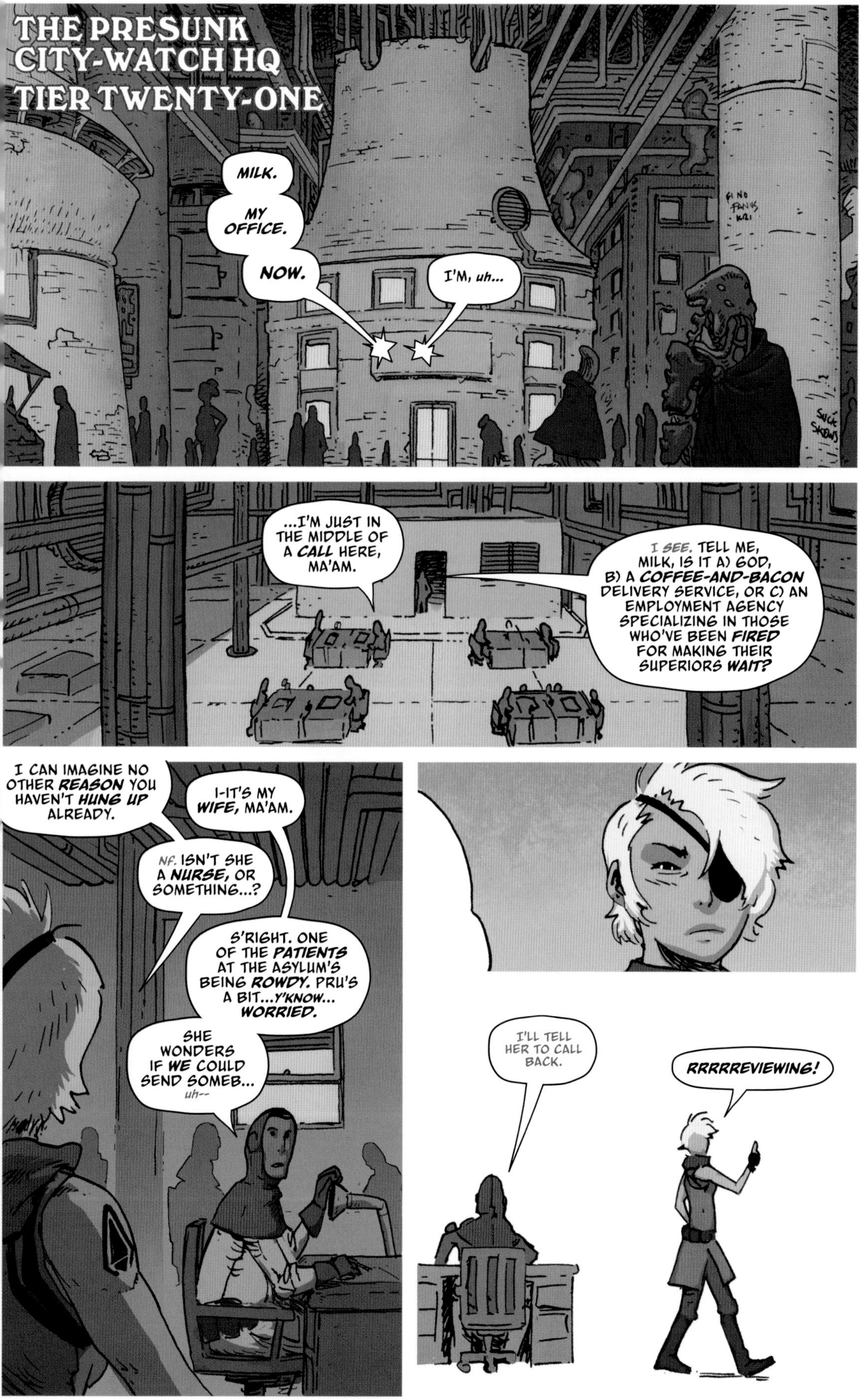
THE PRESUNK CITY-WATCH HQ TIER TWENTY-ONE
MILK.
MY OFFICE.
NOW.
I'M, uh...
...I'M JUST IN THE MIDDLE OF A CALL HERE, MA'AM.
I SEE. TELL ME, MILK, IS IT A) GOD, B) A COFFEE-AND-BACON DELIVERY SERVICE, OR C) AN EMPLOYMENT AGENCY SPECIALIZING IN THOSE WHO'VE BEEN FIRED FOR MAKING THEIR SUPERIORS WAIT?
I CAN IMAGINE NO OTHER REASON YOU HAVEN'T HUNG UP ALREADY.
I-IT'S MY WIFE, MA'AM.
NF. ISN'T SHE A NURSE, OR SOMETHING...?
S'RIGHT. ONE OF THE PATIENTS AT THE ASYLUM'S BEING ROWDY. PRU'S A BIT...Y'KNOW... WORRIED.
SHE WONDERS IF WE COULD SEND SOMEB... uh--
I'LL TELL HER TO CALL BACK.
RRRRREVIEWING!

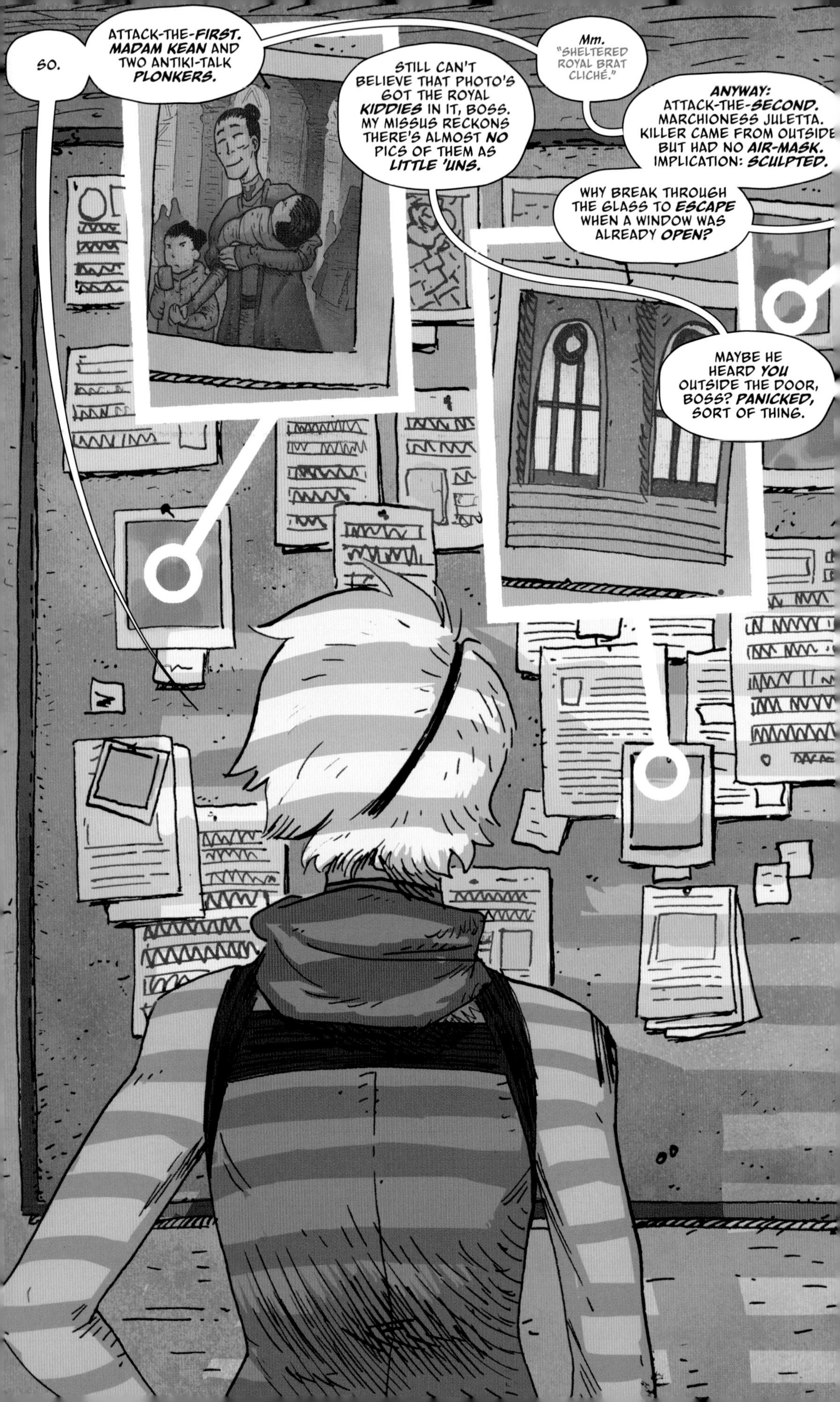
SO.
ATTACK-THE-FIRST. MADAM KEAN AND TWO ANTIKI-TALK PLONKERS.
STILL CAN'T BELIEVE THAT PHOTO'S GOT THE ROYAL KIDDIES IN IT, BOSS. MY MISSUS RECKONS THERE'S ALMOST NO PICS OF THEM AS LITTLE 'UNS.
Mm. "SHELTERED ROYAL BRAT CLICHÉ."
ANYWAY: ATTACK-THE-SECOND. MARCHIONESS JULETTA. KILLER CAME FROM OUTSIDE BUT HAD NO AIR-MASK. IMPLICATION: SCULPTED.
WHY BREAK THROUGH THE GLASS TO ESCAPE WHEN A WINDOW WAS ALREADY OPEN?
MAYBE HE HEARD YOU OUTSIDE THE DOOR, BOSS? PANICKED, SORT OF THING.

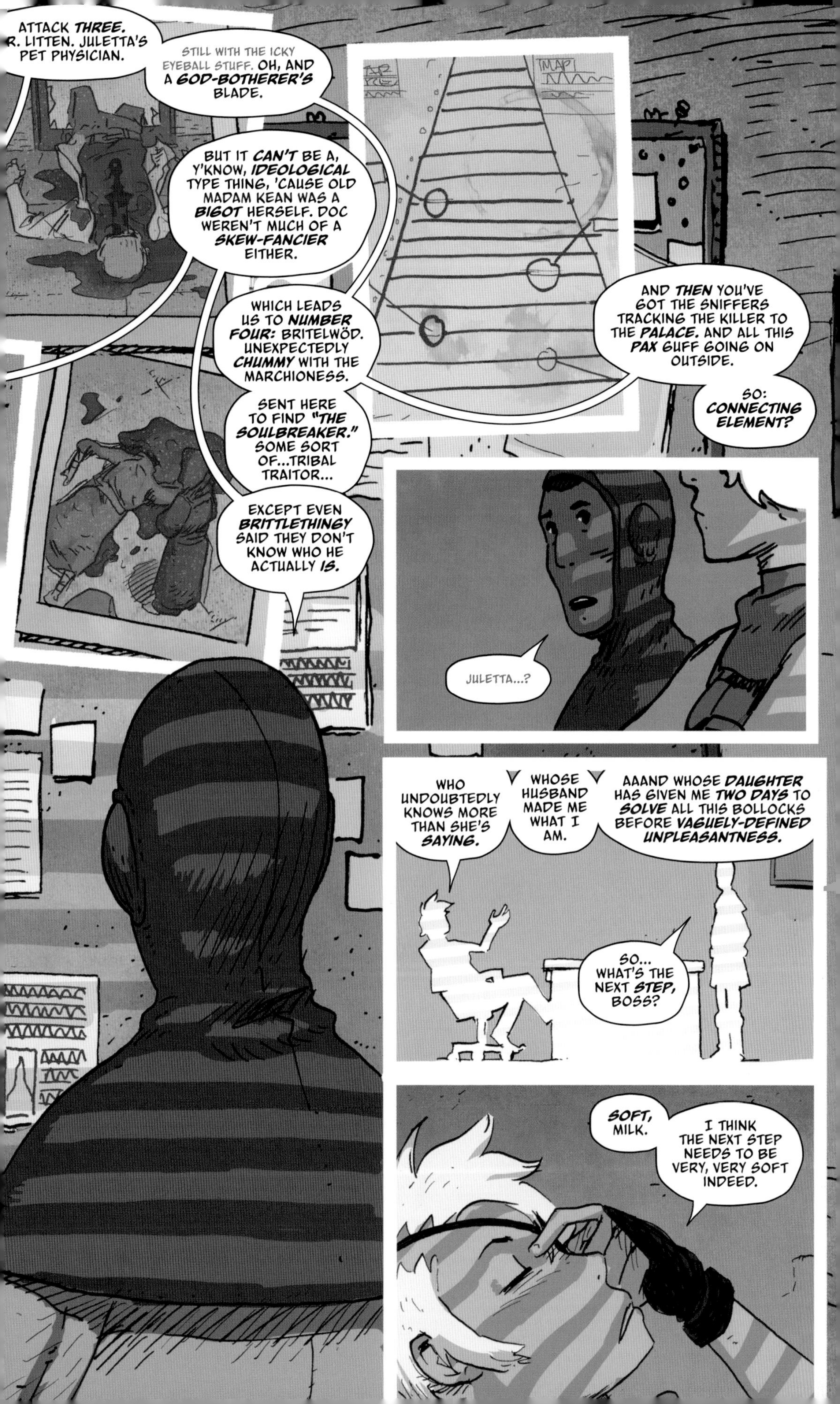

ATTACK THREE. R. LITTEN. JULETTA'S PET PHYSICIAN.
STILL WITH THE ICKY EYEBALL STUFF. OH, AND A GOD-BOTHERER'S BLADE.
BUT IT CAN'T BE A, Y'KNOW, IDEOLOGICAL TYPE THING, 'CAUSE OLD MADAM KEAN WAS A BIGOT HERSELF. DOC WEREN'T MUCH OF A SKEW-FANCIER EITHER.
WHICH LEADS US TO NUMBER FOUR: BRITELWÖD. UNEXPECTEDLY CHUMMY WITH THE MARCHIONESS.
SENT HERE TO FIND "THE SOULBREAKER." SOME SORT OF...TRIBAL TRAITOR...
EXCEPT EVEN BRITTLETHINGY SAID THEY DON'T KNOW WHO HE ACTUALLY IS.
AND THEN YOU'VE GOT THE SNIFFERS TRACKING THE KILLER TO THE PALACE. AND ALL THIS PAX GUFF GOING ON OUTSIDE.
SO: CONNECTING ELEMENT?
JULETTA...?
WHO UNDOUBTEDLY KNOWS MORE THAN SHE'S SAYING.
WHOSE HUSBAND MADE ME WHAT I AM.
AAAND WHOSE DAUGHTER HAS GIVEN ME TWO DAYS TO SOLVE ALL THIS BOLLOCKS BEFORE VAGUELY-DEFINED UNPLEASANTNESS.
SO... WHAT'S THE NEXT STEP, BOSS?
SOFT, MILK.
I THINK THE NEXT STEP NEEDS TO BE VERY, VERY SOFT INDEED.

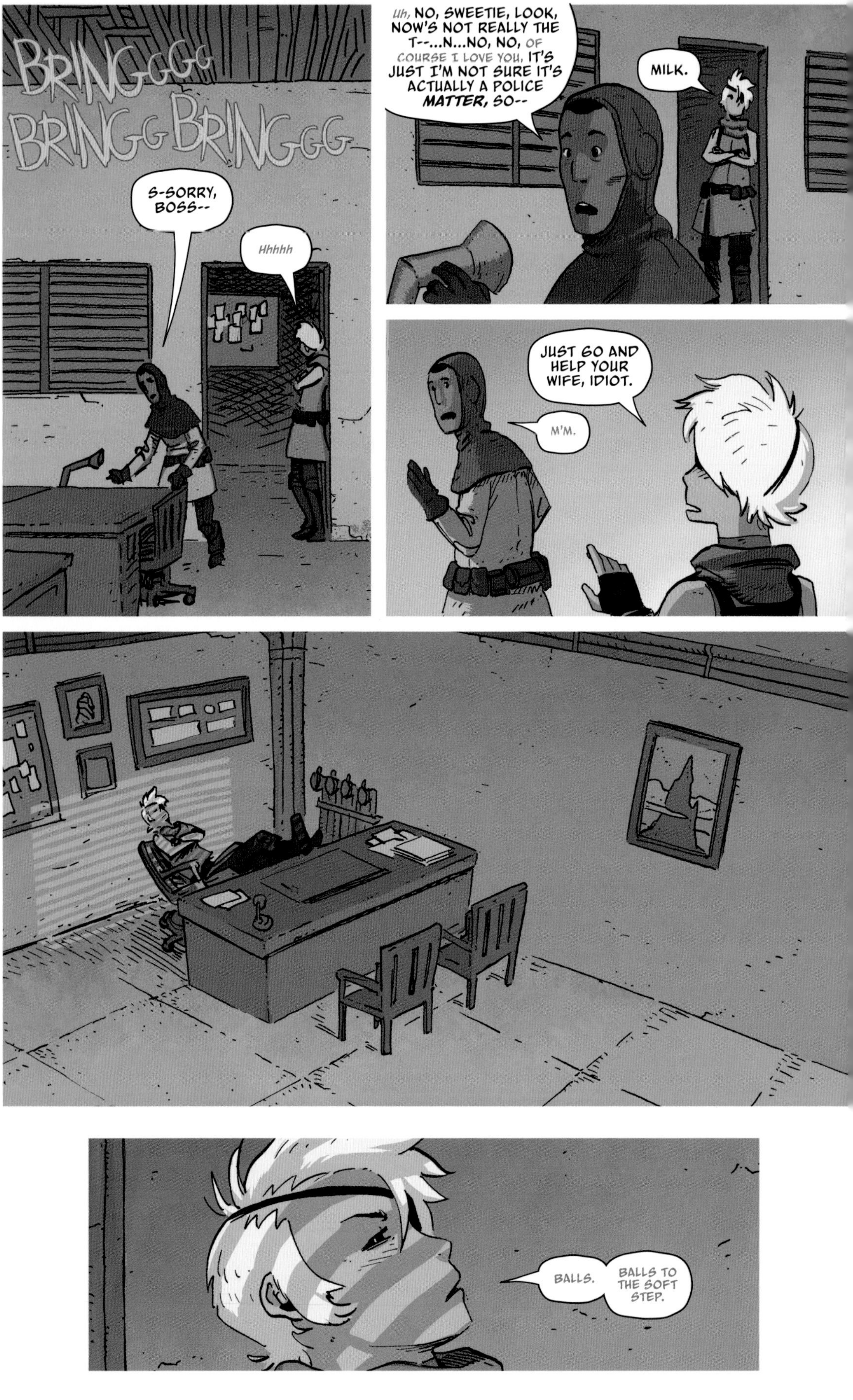

BRINGGGG BRINGG BRINGGG
S-SORRY, BOSS--
Hhhhh
Uh, NO, SWEETIE, LOOK, NOW'S NOT REALLY THE T--...N...NO, NO, OF COURSE I LOVE YOU, IT'S JUST I'M NOT SURE IT'S ACTUALLY A POLICE MATTER, SO--
MILK.
JUST GO AND HELP YOUR WIFE, IDIOT.
M'M.
BALLS.
BALLS TO THE SOFT STEP.

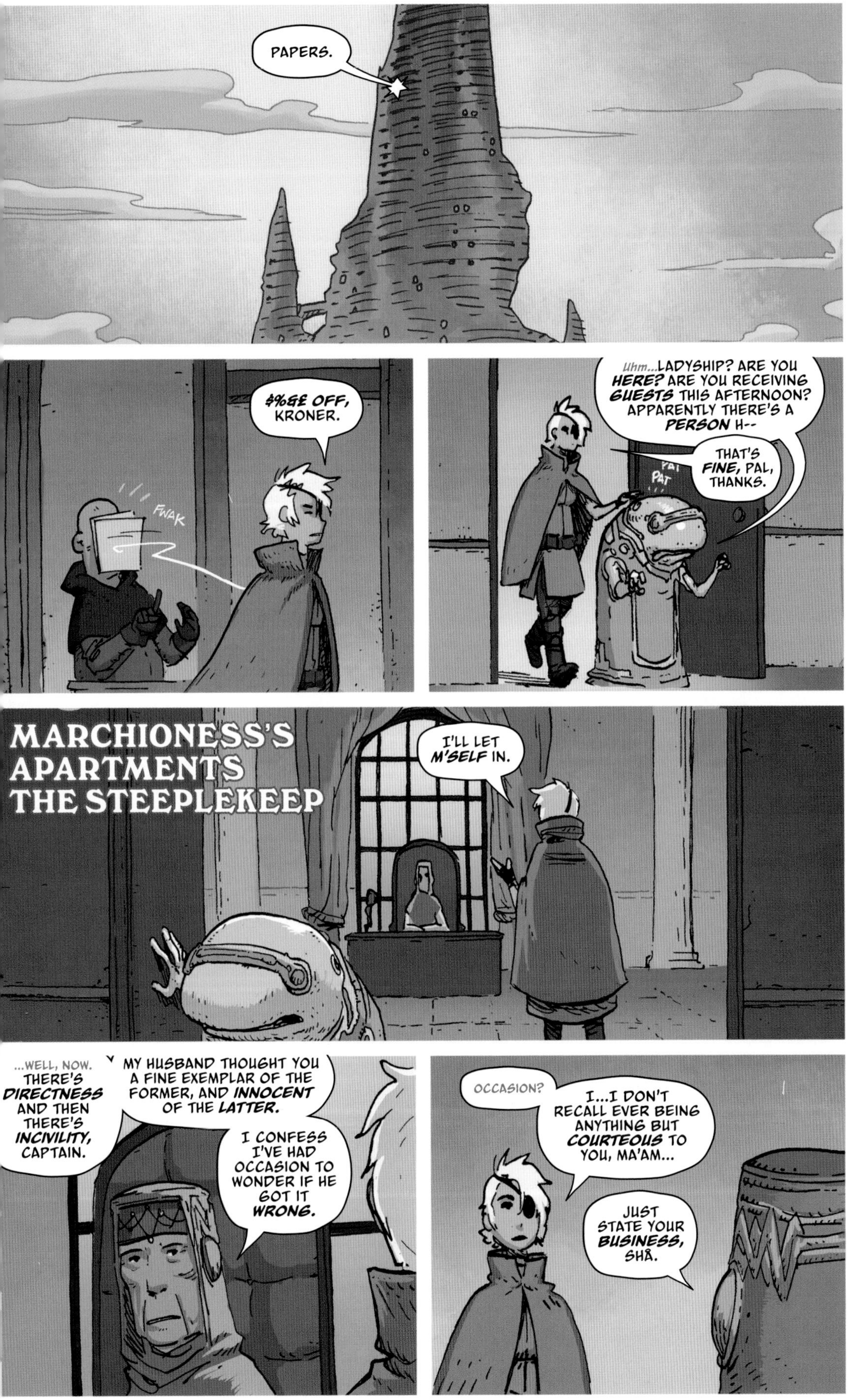

PAPERS.
$%&E OFF, KRONER.
FWAK
Uhm...LADYSHIP? ARE YOU HERE? ARE YOU RECEIVING GUESTS THIS AFTERNOON? APPARENTLY THERE'S A PERSON H--
PAT PAT
THAT'S FINE, PAL, THANKS.
MARCHIONESS'S APARTMENTS THE STEEPLEKEEP
I'LL LET M'SELF IN.
...WELL, NOW. THERE'S DIRECTNESS AND THEN THERE'S INCIVILITY, CAPTAIN.
MY HUSBAND THOUGHT YOU A FINE EXEMPLAR OF THE FORMER, AND INNOCENT OF THE LATTER.
I CONFESS I'VE HAD OCCASION TO WONDER IF HE GOT IT WRONG.
OCCASION?
I...I DON'T RECALL EVER BEING ANYTHING BUT COURTEOUS TO YOU, MA'AM...
JUST STATE YOUR BUSINESS, SHÅ.

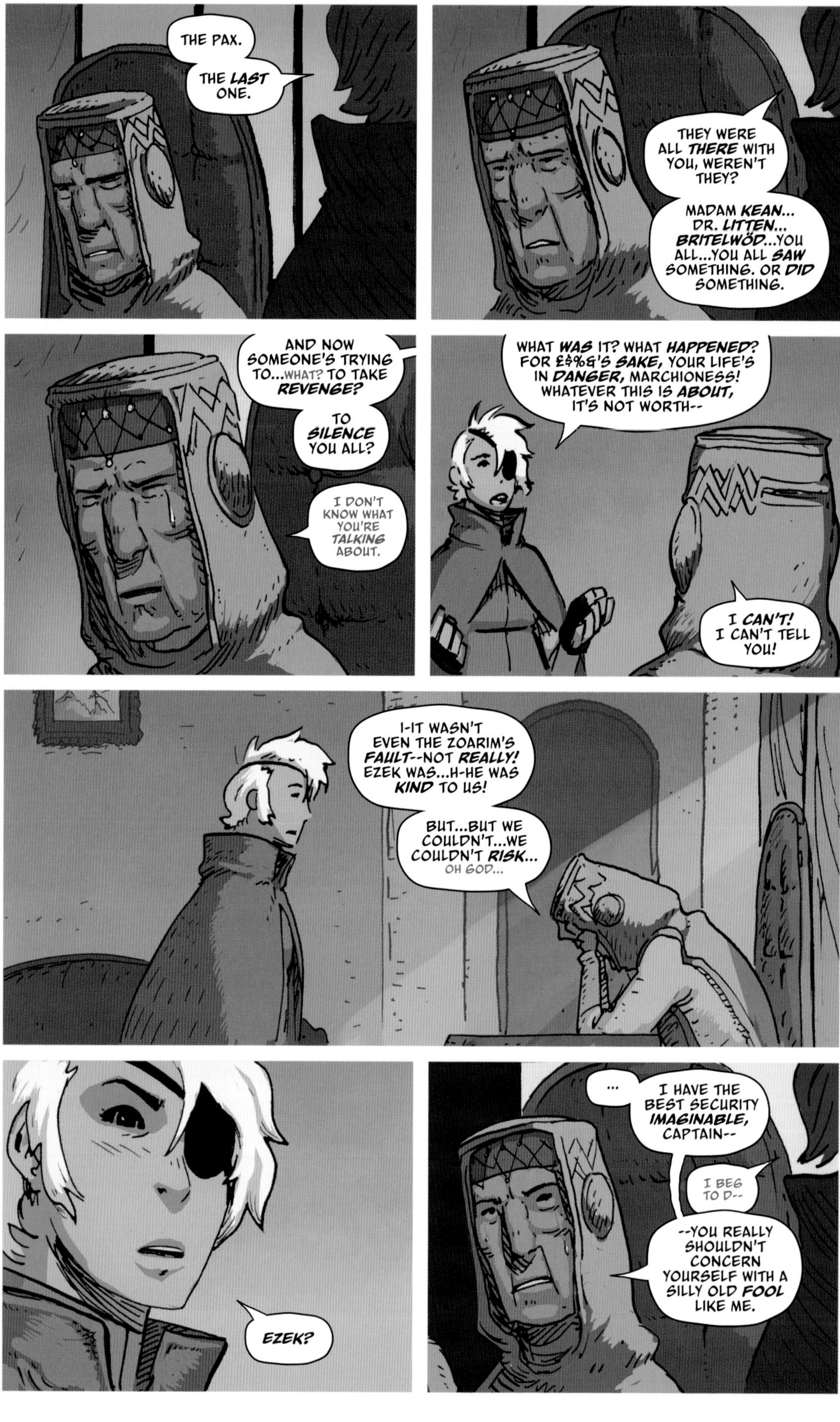

THE PAX.
THE LAST ONE.
THEY WERE ALL THERE WITH YOU, WEREN'T THEY?
MADAM KEAN... DR. LITTEN... BRITELWÖD...YOU ALL...YOU ALL SAW SOMETHING. OR DID SOMETHING.
AND NOW SOMEONE'S TRYING TO...WHAT? TO TAKE REVENGE?
TO SILENCE YOU ALL?
I DON'T KNOW WHAT YOU'RE TALKING ABOUT.
WHAT WAS IT? WHAT HAPPENED? FOR £$%&'S SAKE, YOUR LIFE'S IN DANGER, MARCHIONESS! WHATEVER THIS IS ABOUT, IT'S NOT WORTH--
I CAN'T! I CAN'T TELL YOU!
I-IT WASN'T EVEN THE ZOARIM'S FAULT--NOT REALLY! EZEK WAS...H-HE WAS KIND TO US!
BUT...BUT WE COULDN'T...WE COULDN'T RISK... OH GOD...
EZEK?
...
I HAVE THE BEST SECURITY IMAGINABLE, CAPTAIN--
I BEG TO D--
--YOU REALLY SHOULDN'T CONCERN YOURSELF WITH A SILLY OLD FOOL LIKE ME.

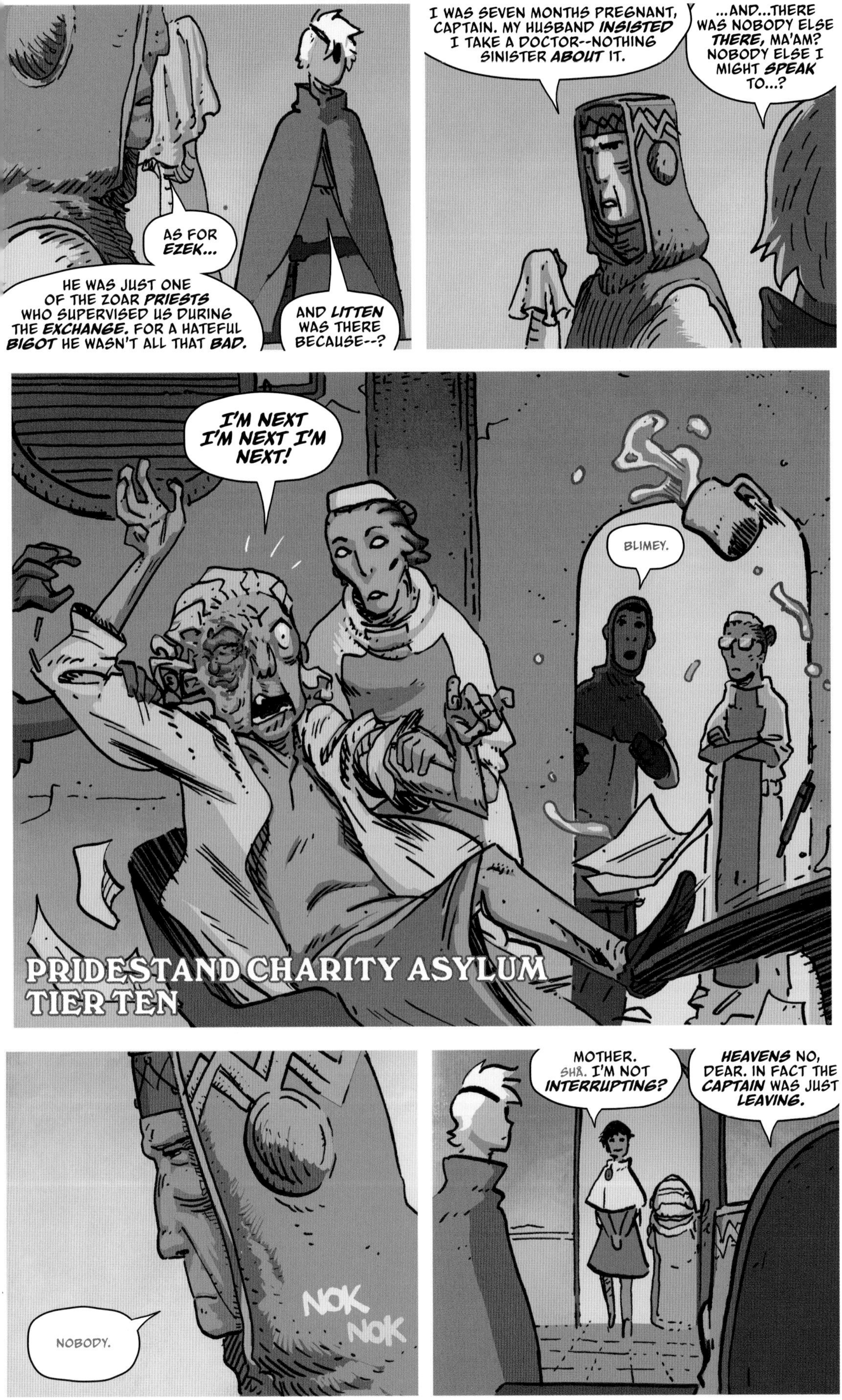
AS FOR EZEK...
HE WAS JUST ONE OF THE ZOAR PRIESTS WHO SUPERVISED US DURING THE EXCHANGE. FOR A HATEFUL BIGOT HE WASN'T ALL THAT BAD.
AND LITTEN WAS THERE BECAUSE--?
I WAS SEVEN MONTHS PREGNANT, CAPTAIN. MY HUSBAND INSISTED I TAKE A DOCTOR--NOTHING SINISTER ABOUT IT.
...AND...THERE WAS NOBODY ELSE THERE, MA'AM? NOBODY ELSE I MIGHT SPEAK TO...?
I'M NEXT I'M NEXT I'M NEXT!
BLIMEY.
PRIDESTAND CHARITY ASYLUM
TIER TEN
NOK
NOK
NOBODY.
MOTHER. SHÅ. I'M NOT INTERRUPTING?
HEAVENS NO, DEAR. IN FACT THE CAPTAIN WAS JUST LEAVING.

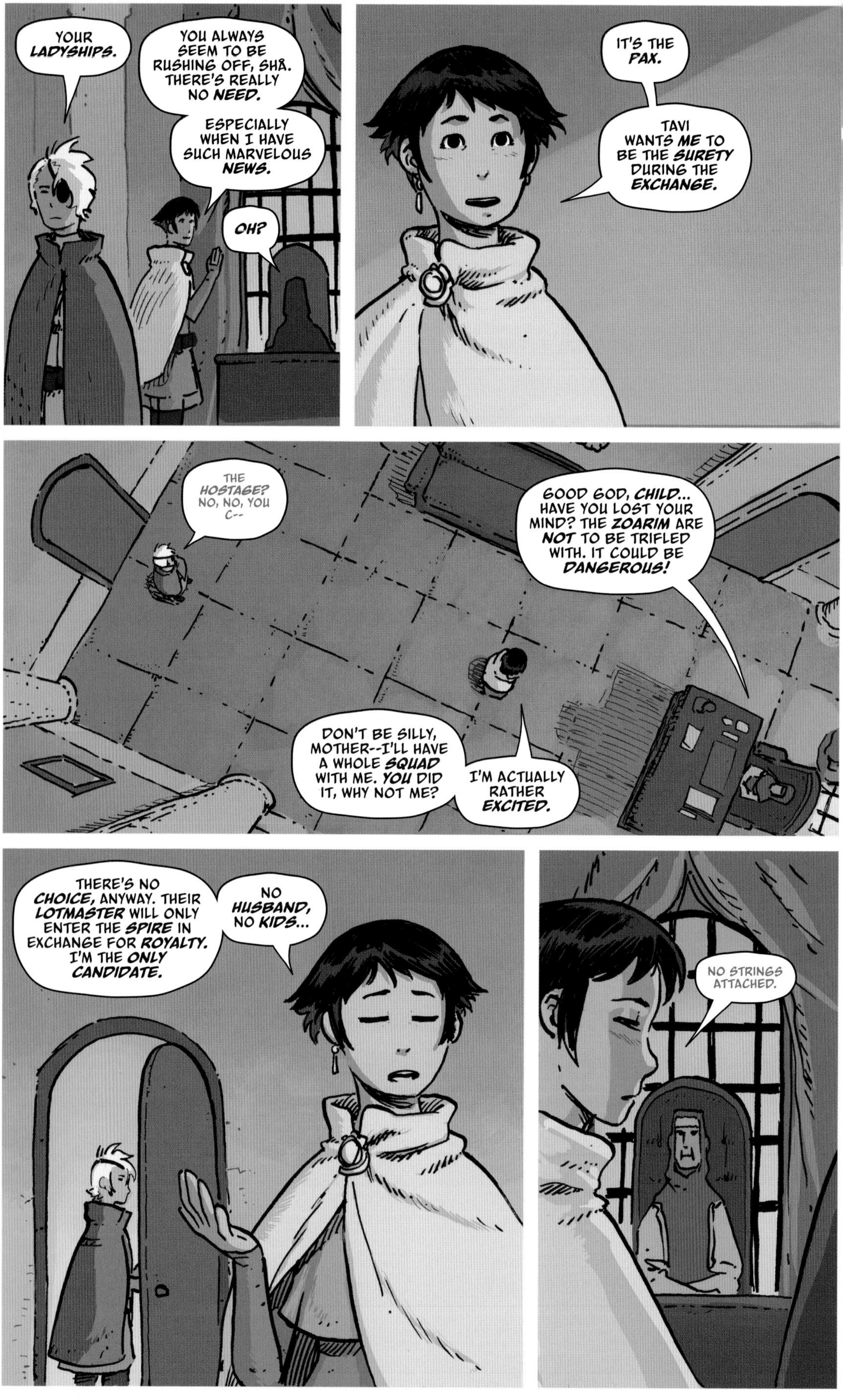
YOUR LADYSHIPS.
YOU ALWAYS SEEM TO BE RUSHING OFF, SHĂ. THERE'S REALLY NO NEED.
ESPECIALLY WHEN I HAVE SUCH MARVELOUS NEWS.
OH?
IT'S THE PAX.
TAVI WANTS ME TO BE THE SURETY DURING THE EXCHANGE.
THE HOSTAGE? NO, NO, YOU C--
GOOD GOD, CHILD... HAVE YOU LOST YOUR MIND? THE ZOARIM ARE NOT TO BE TRIFLED WITH. IT COULD BE DANGEROUS!
DON'T BE SILLY, MOTHER--I'LL HAVE A WHOLE SQUAD WITH ME. YOU DID IT, WHY NOT ME?
I'M ACTUALLY RATHER EXCITED.
THERE'S NO CHOICE, ANYWAY. THEIR LOTMASTER WILL ONLY ENTER THE SPIRE IN EXCHANGE FOR ROYALTY. I'M THE ONLY CANDIDATE.
NO HUSBAND, NO KIDS...
NO STRINGS ATTACHED.

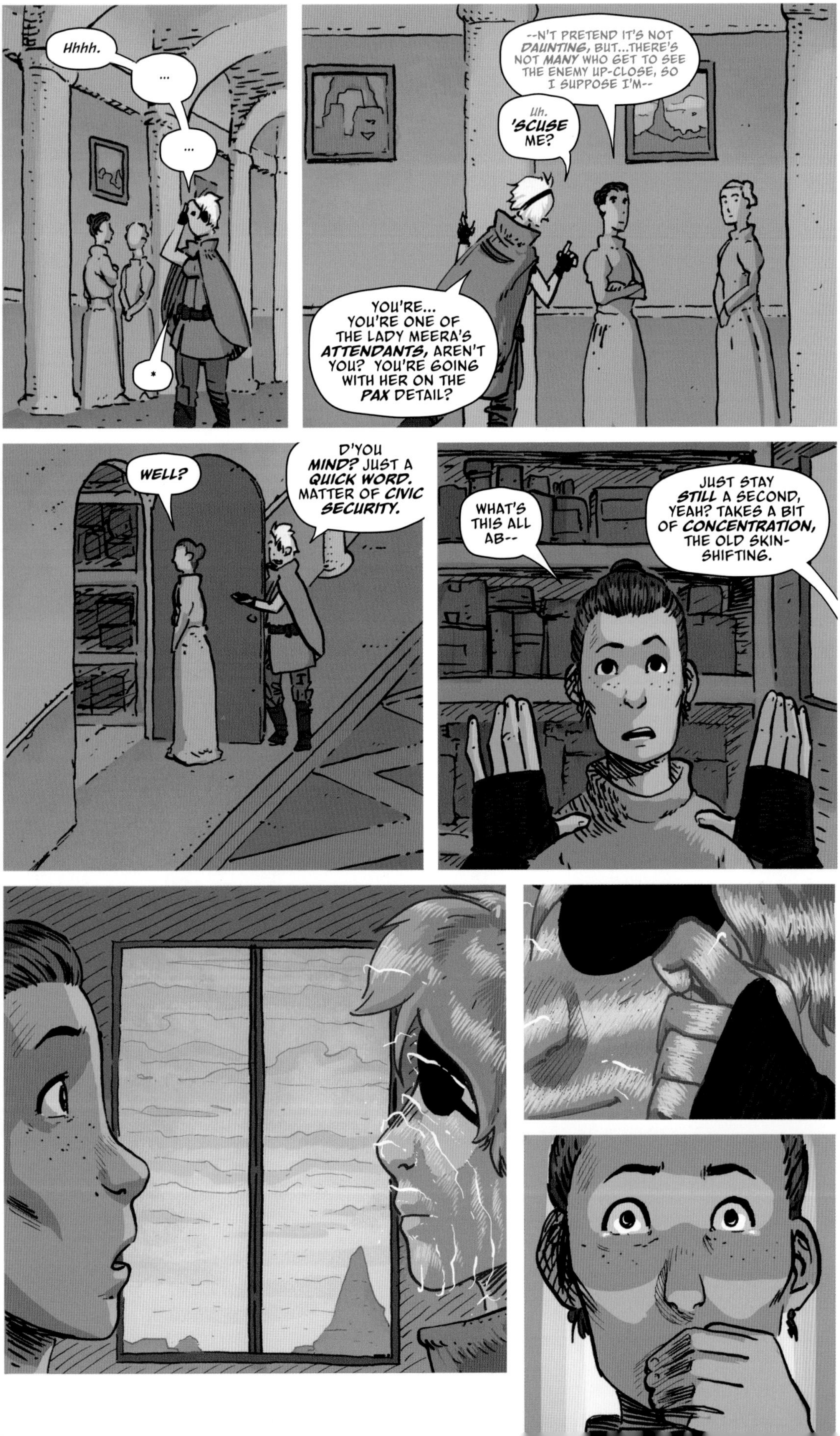

Hhhh.
...
...
*
--N'T PRETEND IT'S NOT DAUNTING, BUT...THERE'S NOT MANY WHO GET TO SEE THE ENEMY UP-CLOSE, SO I SUPPOSE I'M--
Uh. 'SCUSE ME?
YOU'RE... YOU'RE ONE OF THE LADY MEERA'S ATTENDANTS, AREN'T YOU? YOU'RE GOING WITH HER ON THE PAX DETAIL?
WELL?
D'YOU MIND? JUST A QUICK WORD. MATTER OF CIVIC SECURITY.
WHAT'S THIS ALL AB--
JUST STAY STILL A SECOND, YEAH? TAKES A BIT OF CONCENTRATION, THE OLD SKIN-SHIFTING.

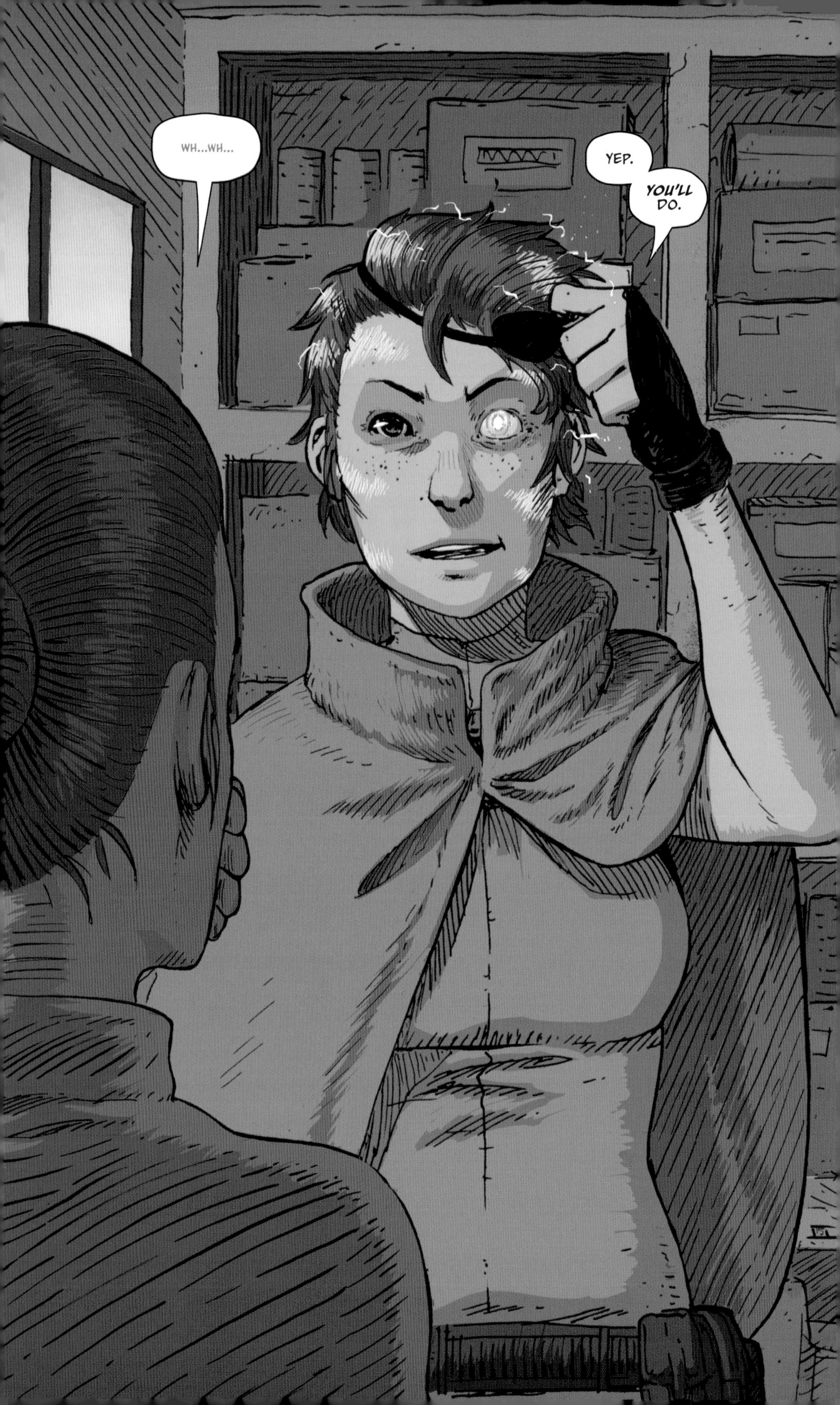
WH...WH...
YEP.
YOU'LL DO.

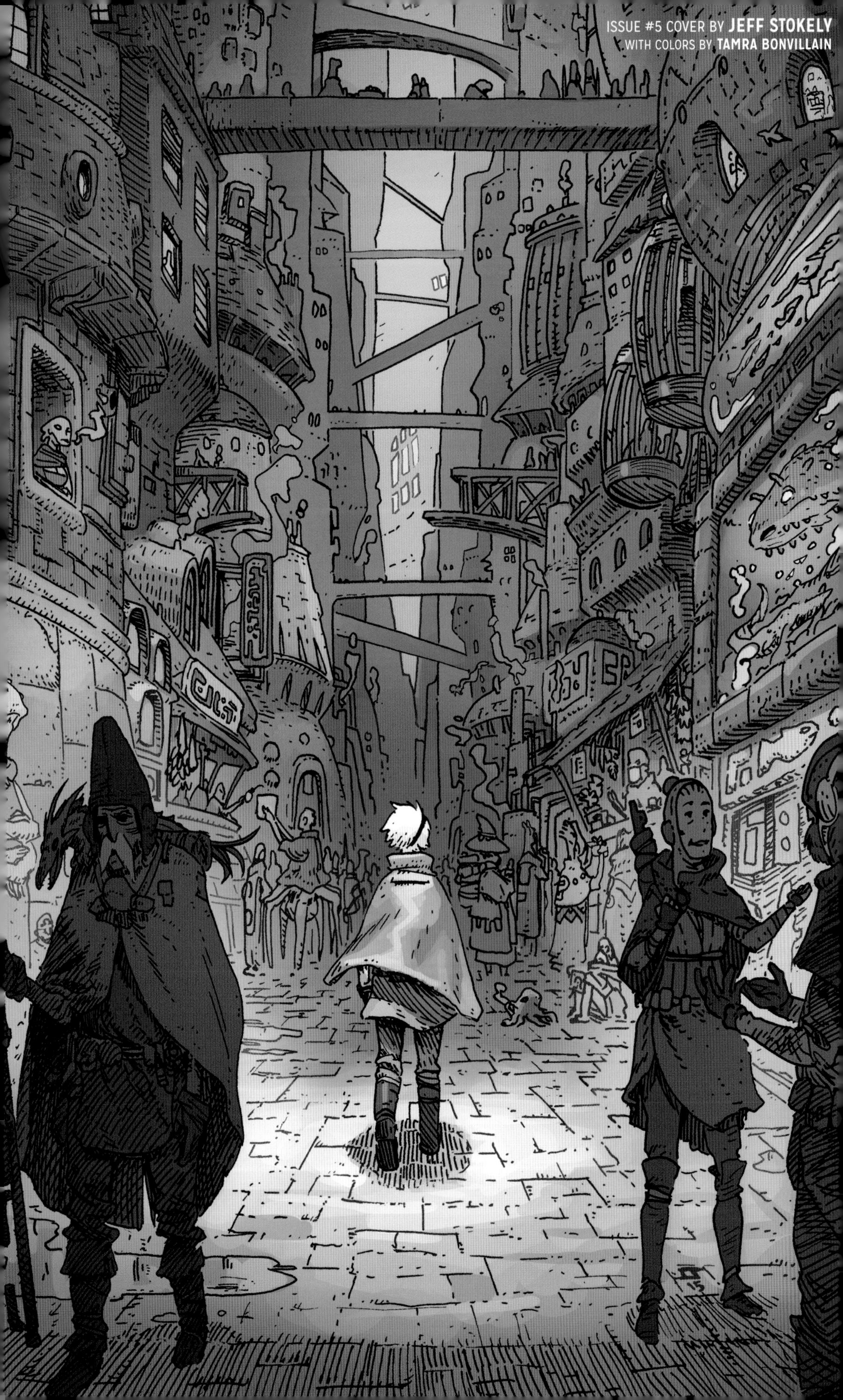

ISSUE #5 COVER BY **JEFF STOKELY**
WITH COLORS BY **TAMRA BONVILLAIN**

CHAPTER SIX

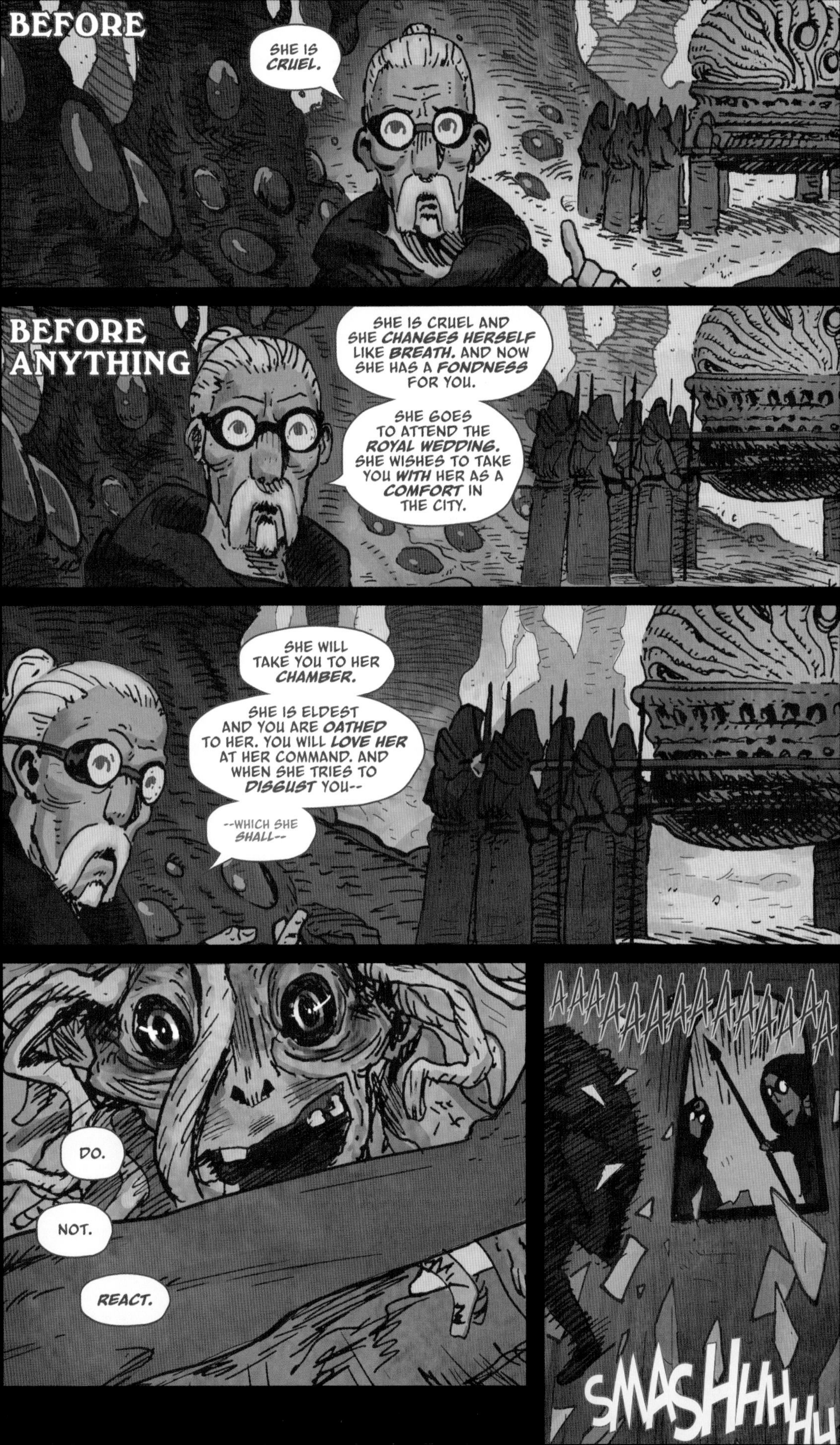
BEFORE
SHE IS CRUEL.
BEFORE ANYTHING
SHE IS CRUEL AND SHE CHANGES HERSELF LIKE BREATH. AND NOW SHE HAS A FONDNESS FOR YOU.
SHE GOES TO ATTEND THE ROYAL WEDDING. SHE WISHES TO TAKE YOU WITH HER AS A COMFORT IN THE CITY.
SHE WILL TAKE YOU TO HER CHAMBER.
SHE IS ELDEST AND YOU ARE OATHED TO HER. YOU WILL LOVE HER AT HER COMMAND. AND WHEN SHE TRIES TO DISGUST YOU--
--WHICH SHE SHALL--
DO.
NOT.
REACT.
AAAAAAAAAAAAAAA
SMASHHHHHH

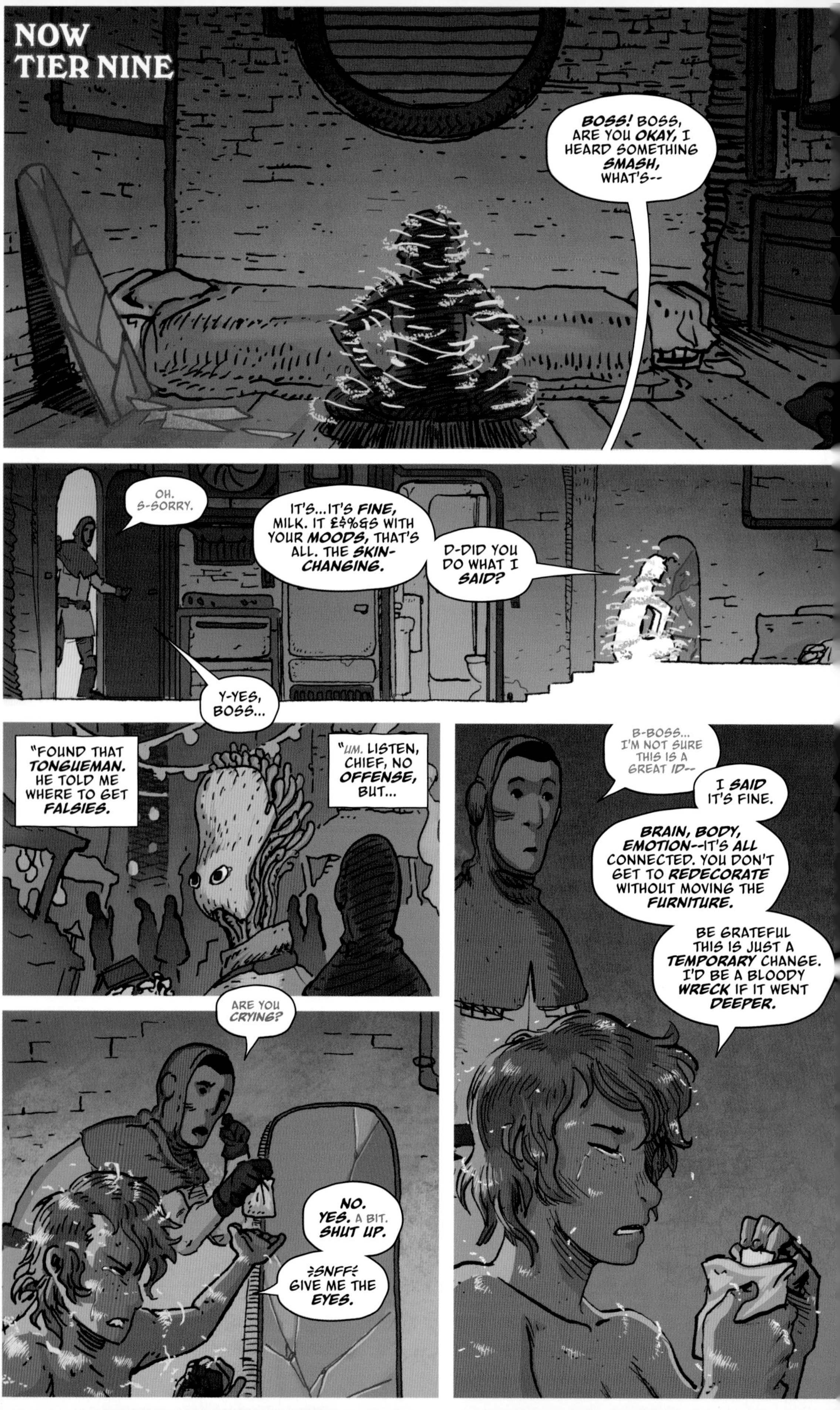
NOW
TIER NINE
BOSS! BOSS, ARE YOU OKAY, I HEARD SOMETHING SMASH, WHAT'S--
OH. S-SORRY.
IT'S...IT'S FINE, MILK. IT £$%&$ WITH YOUR MOODS, THAT'S ALL. THE SKIN-CHANGING.
D-DID YOU DO WHAT I SAID?
Y-YES, BOSS...
"FOUND THAT TONGUEMAN. HE TOLD ME WHERE TO GET FALSIES.
"UM. LISTEN, CHIEF, NO OFFENSE, BUT...
ARE YOU CRYING?
NO. YES. A BIT. SHUT UP.
SNFF GIVE ME THE EYES.
B-BOSS... I'M NOT SURE THIS IS A GREAT ID--
I SAID IT'S FINE.
BRAIN, BODY, EMOTION--IT'S ALL CONNECTED. YOU DON'T GET TO REDECORATE WITHOUT MOVING THE FURNITURE.
BE GRATEFUL THIS IS JUST A TEMPORARY CHANGE. I'D BE A BLOODY WRECK IF IT WENT DEEPER.

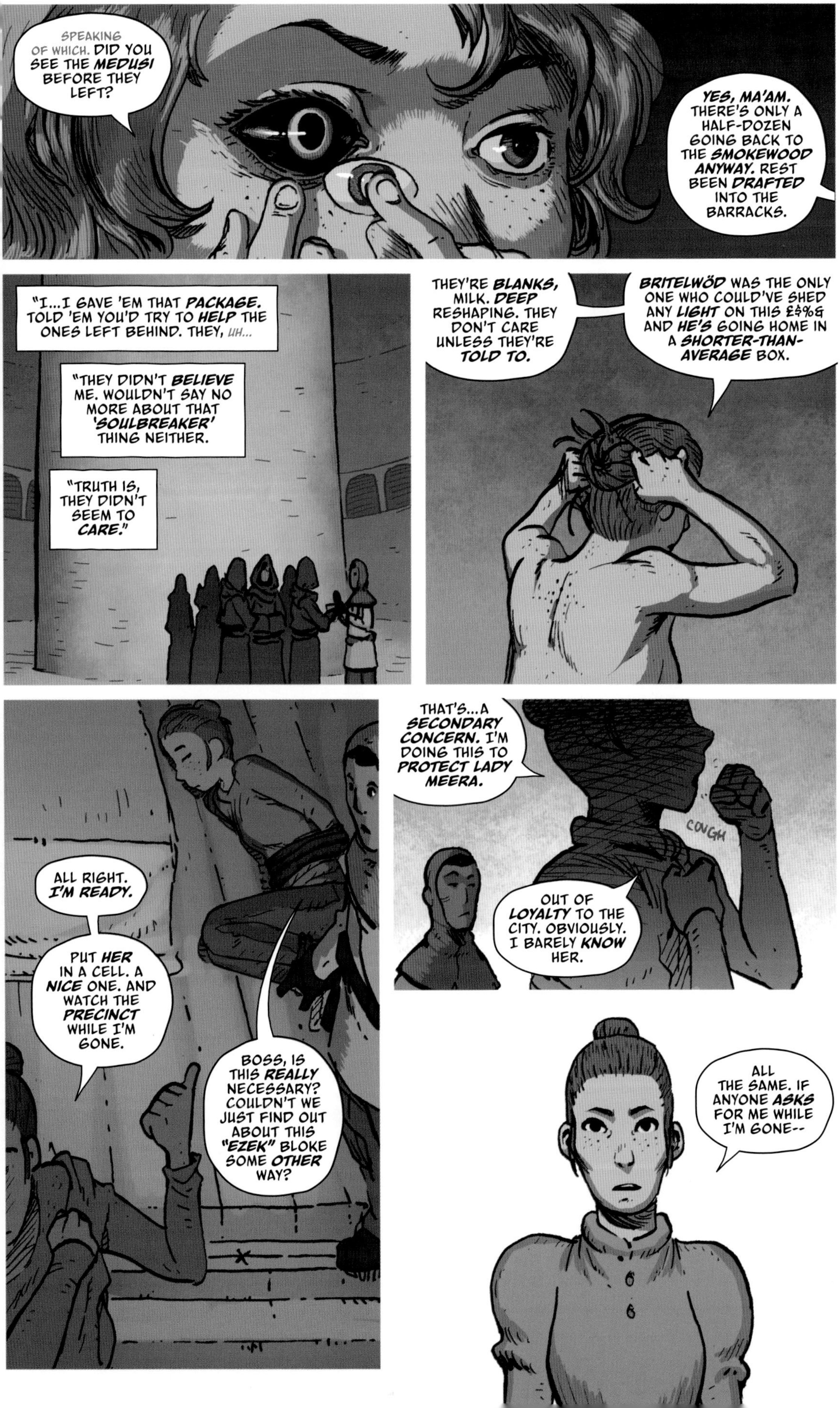
SPEAKING OF WHICH. DID YOU SEE THE *MEDUSI* BEFORE THEY LEFT?
YES, MA'AM. THERE'S ONLY A HALF-DOZEN GOING BACK TO THE *SMOKEWOOD ANYWAY.* REST BEEN *DRAFTED* INTO THE BARRACKS.
"I...I GAVE 'EM THAT *PACKAGE.* TOLD 'EM YOU'D TRY TO *HELP* THE ONES LEFT BEHIND. THEY, UH...
"THEY DIDN'T *BELIEVE* ME. WOULDN'T SAY NO MORE ABOUT THAT *'SOULBREAKER'* THING NEITHER.
"TRUTH IS, THEY DIDN'T SEEM TO *CARE.*"
THEY'RE *BLANKS,* MILK. *DEEP* RESHAPING. THEY DON'T CARE UNLESS THEY'RE *TOLD TO.*
BRITELWÖD WAS THE ONLY ONE WHO COULD'VE SHED ANY *LIGHT* ON THIS £$%& AND *HE'S* GOING HOME IN A *SHORTER-THAN-AVERAGE* BOX.
ALL RIGHT. *I'M READY.*
PUT *HER* IN A CELL. A *NICE* ONE. AND WATCH THE *PRECINCT* WHILE I'M GONE.
BOSS, IS THIS *REALLY* NECESSARY? COULDN'T WE JUST FIND OUT ABOUT THIS *"EZEK"* BLOKE SOME *OTHER* WAY?
THAT'S...A *SECONDARY CONCERN.* I'M DOING THIS TO *PROTECT LADY MEERA.*
COUGH
OUT OF *LOYALTY* TO THE CITY. OBVIOUSLY. I BARELY *KNOW* HER.
ALL THE SAME. IF ANYONE *ASKS* FOR ME WHILE I'M GONE--

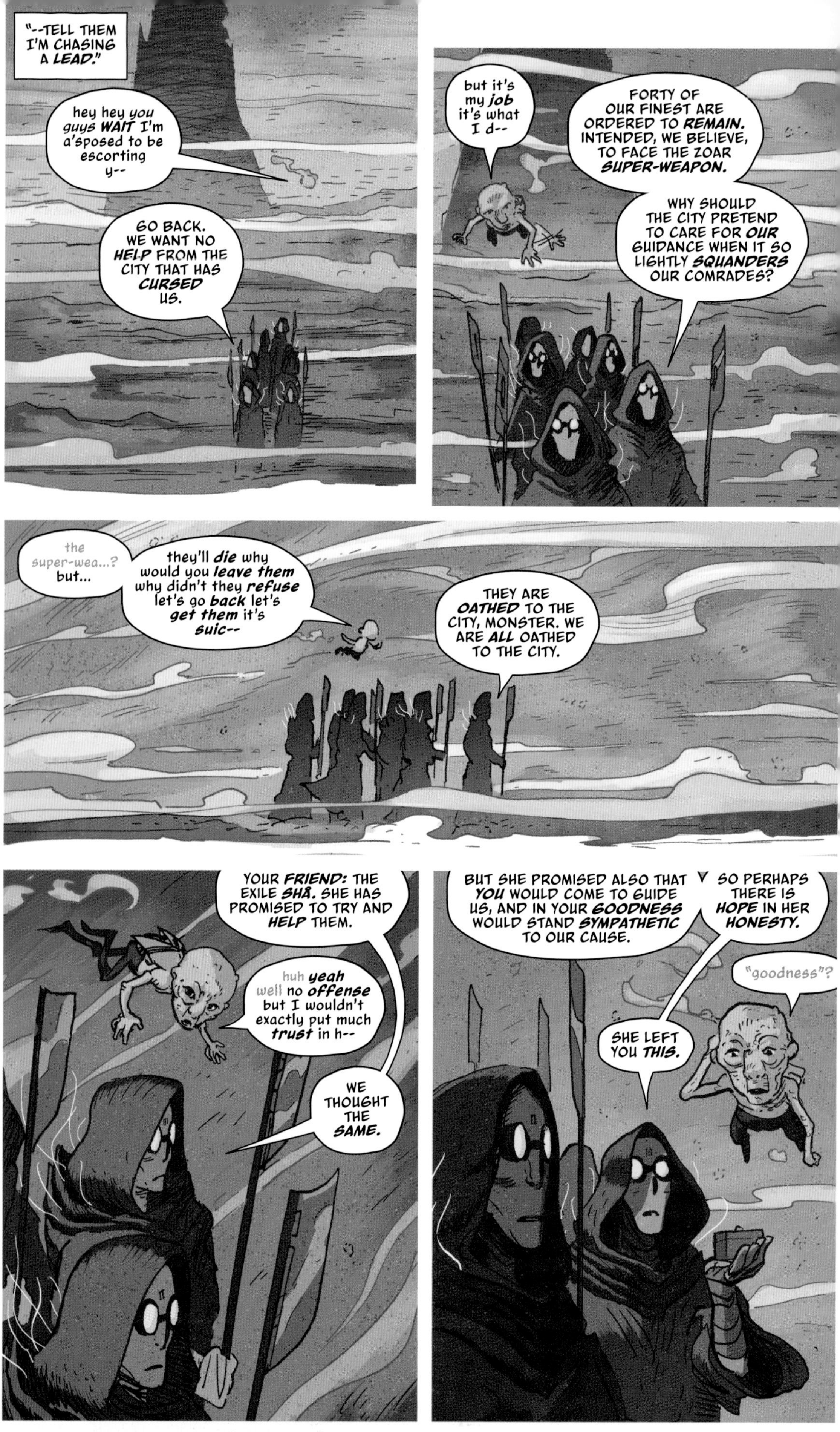

"--TELL THEM I'M CHASING A LEAD."
hey hey you guys WAIT I'm a'sposed to be escorting y--
GO BACK. WE WANT NO HELP FROM THE CITY THAT HAS CURSED US.
but it's my job it's what I d--
FORTY OF OUR FINEST ARE ORDERED TO REMAIN. INTENDED, WE BELIEVE, TO FACE THE ZOAR SUPER-WEAPON.
WHY SHOULD THE CITY PRETEND TO CARE FOR OUR GUIDANCE WHEN IT SO LIGHTLY SQUANDERS OUR COMRADES?
the super-wea...? but...
they'll die why would you leave them why didn't they refuse let's go back let's get them it's suic--
THEY ARE OATHED TO THE CITY, MONSTER. WE ARE ALL OATHED TO THE CITY.
YOUR FRIEND: THE EXILE SHÅ. SHE HAS PROMISED TO TRY AND HELP THEM.
huh yeah well no offense but I wouldn't exactly put much trust in h--
WE THOUGHT THE SAME.
BUT SHE PROMISED ALSO THAT YOU WOULD COME TO GUIDE US, AND IN YOUR GOODNESS WOULD STAND SYMPATHETIC TO OUR CAUSE.
SO PERHAPS THERE IS HOPE IN HER HONESTY.
"goodness"?
SHE LEFT YOU THIS.

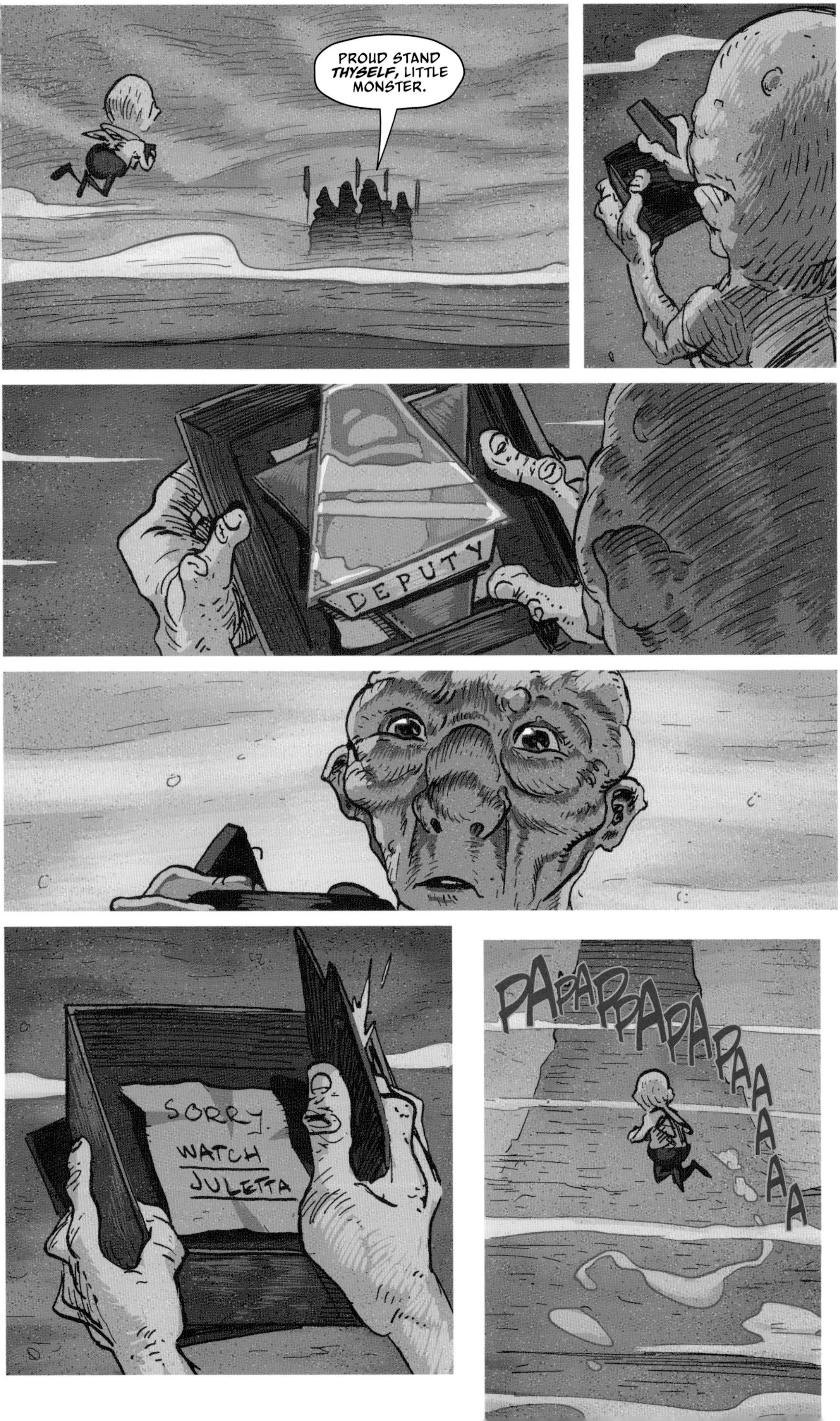
PROUD STAND *THYSELF*, LITTLE MONSTER.
DEPUTY
SORRY
WATCH
JULETTA
PAPAPAPAPAPAPAAAAAA

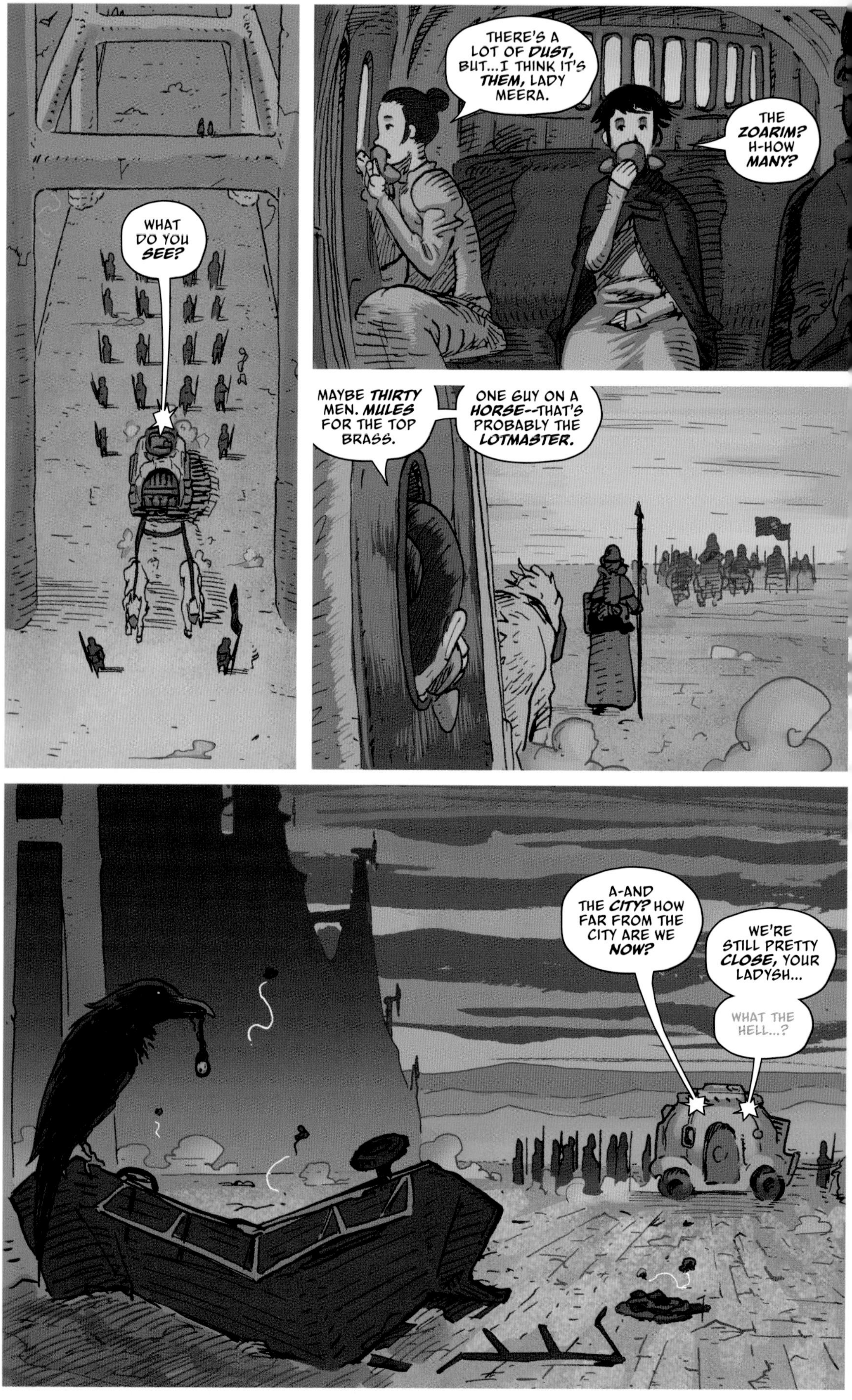
WHAT DO YOU SEE?
THERE'S A LOT OF DUST, BUT...I THINK IT'S THEM, LADY MEERA.
THE ZOARIM? H-HOW MANY?
MAYBE THIRTY MEN. MULES FOR THE TOP BRASS.
ONE GUY ON A HORSE--THAT'S PROBABLY THE LOTMASTER.
A-AND THE CITY? HOW FAR FROM THE CITY ARE WE NOW?
WE'RE STILL PRETTY CLOSE, YOUR LADYSH...
WHAT THE HELL...?

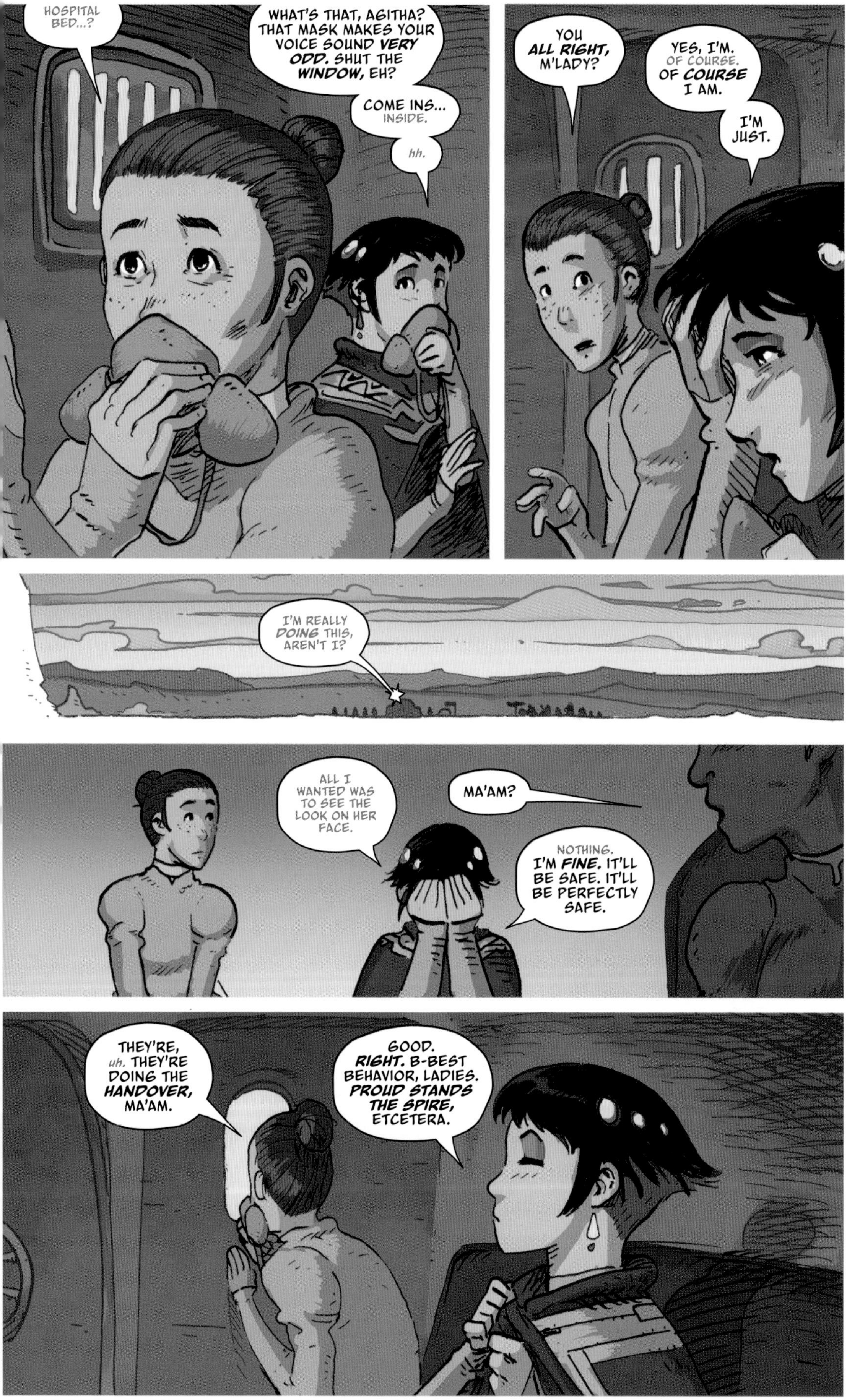
HOSPITAL BED...?
WHAT'S THAT, AGITHA? THAT MASK MAKES YOUR VOICE SOUND VERY ODD. SHUT THE WINDOW, EH?
COME INS... INSIDE.
hh.
YOU ALL RIGHT, M'LADY?
YES, I'M. OF COURSE. OF COURSE I AM.
I'M JUST.
I'M REALLY DOING THIS, AREN'T I?
ALL I WANTED WAS TO SEE THE LOOK ON HER FACE.
MA'AM?
NOTHING. I'M FINE. IT'LL BE SAFE. IT'LL BE PERFECTLY SAFE.
THEY'RE, uh. THEY'RE DOING THE HANDOVER, MA'AM.
GOOD. RIGHT. B-BEST BEHAVIOR, LADIES. PROUD STANDS THE SPIRE, ETCETERA.

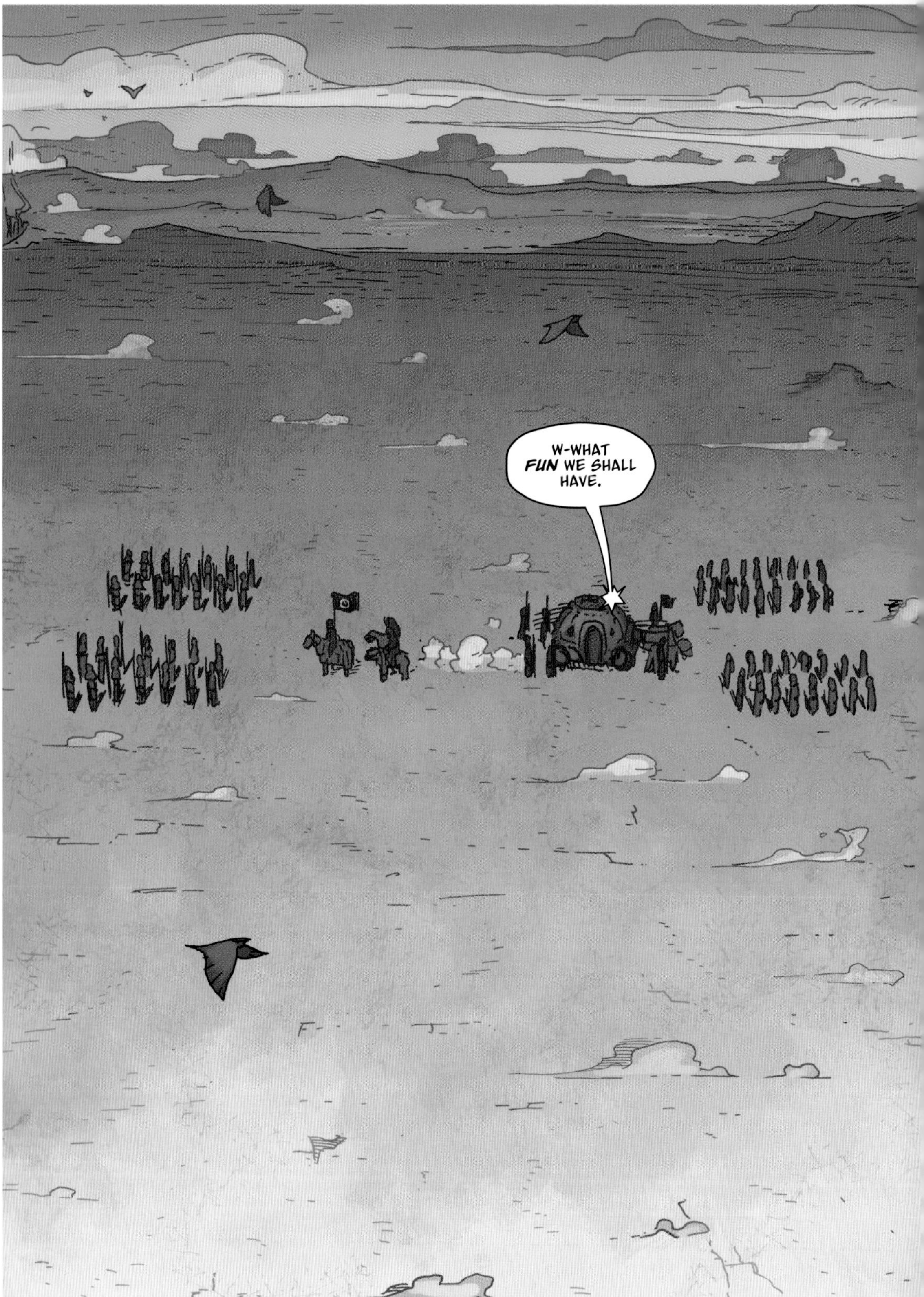
W-WHAT *FUN* WE SHALL HAVE.

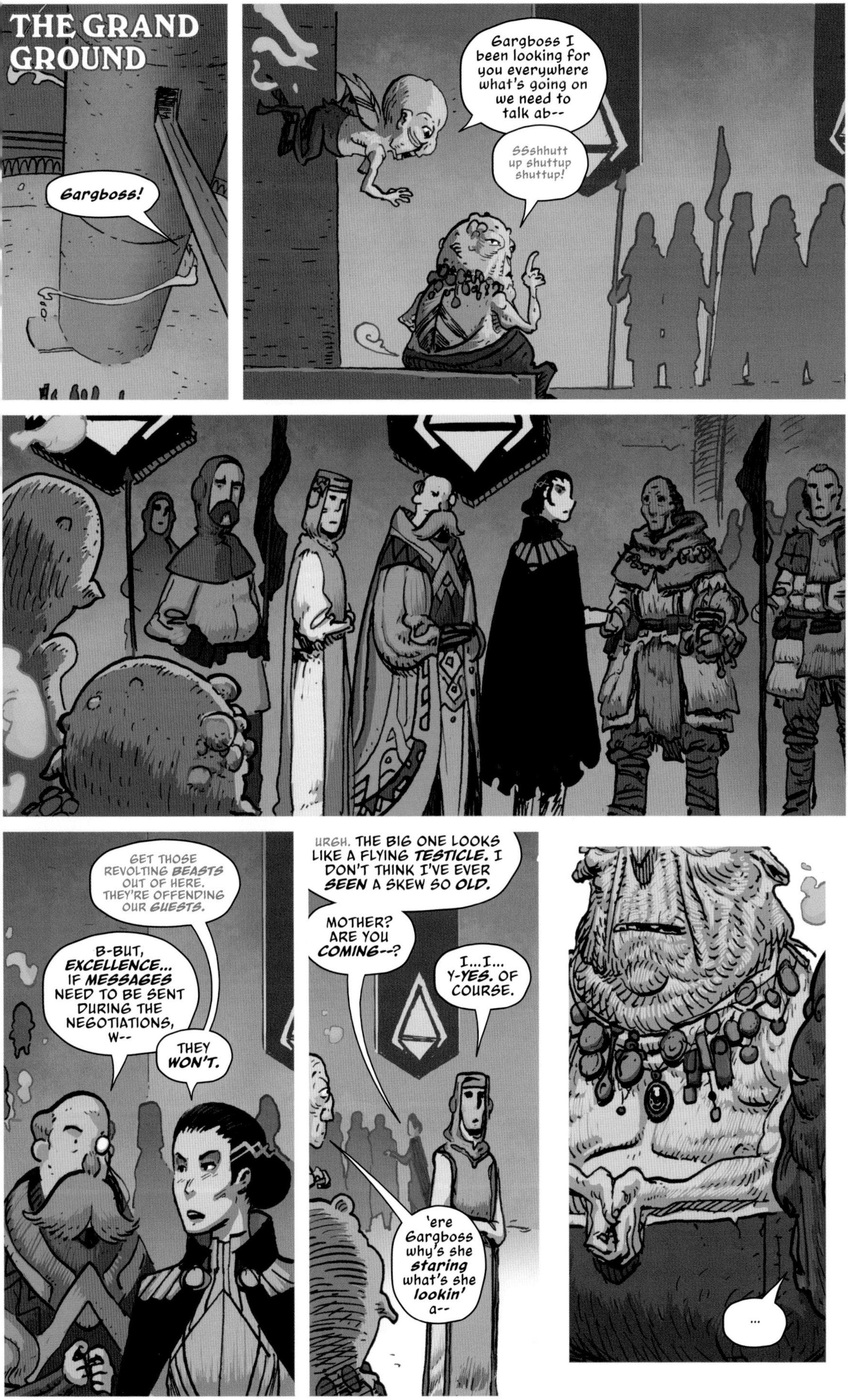
THE GRAND GROUND
Gargboss!
Gargboss I been looking for you everywhere what's going on we need to talk ab--
SSshhutt up shuttup shuttup!
GET THOSE REVOLTING BEASTS OUT OF HERE. THEY'RE OFFENDING OUR GUESTS.
B-BUT, EXCELLENCE... IF MESSAGES NEED TO BE SENT DURING THE NEGOTIATIONS, W--
THEY WON'T.
URGH. THE BIG ONE LOOKS LIKE A FLYING TESTICLE. I DON'T THINK I'VE EVER SEEN A SKEW SO OLD.
MOTHER? ARE YOU COMING--?
I...I... Y-YES. OF COURSE.
'ere Gargboss why's she staring what's she lookin' a--
...

ZOARIM CAMP

WE PRAY THE *PURE-TENT* IS TO YOUR SATISFACTION, LADYSHIP?

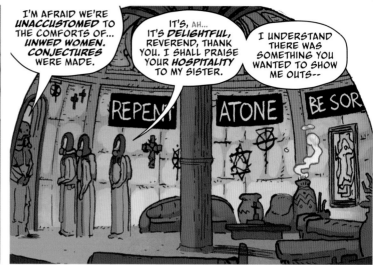

I'M AFRAID WE'RE *UNACCUSTOMED* TO THE COMFORTS OF... *UNWED WOMEN. CONJECTURES* WERE MADE.

IT'S, AH... IT'S *DELIGHTFUL,* REVEREND, THANK YOU. I SHALL PRAISE YOUR *HOSPITALITY* TO MY SISTER.

I UNDERSTAND THERE WAS SOMETHING YOU WANTED TO SHOW ME OUTS--

REPENT   ATONE   BE SOR

PRISONERS SEIZED FROM THE *NOTHINGLANDS,* GOD BE PRAISED, UPON OUR PILGRIMS' PATH.

WE THOUGHT YOU MIGHT BE *INTERESTED.* A CULTURAL *INSIGHT,* AS IT WERE.

MANY OF THE *ABOMINABLE* WILL BE *FAMILIAR* TO YOU, OF COURSE.

THE *MOLLUSC FACES,* FOR INSTANCE, WE USE FOR *SADDLES* AND *BEDPANS.*

"USE"...? Y-YOU MEAN...?

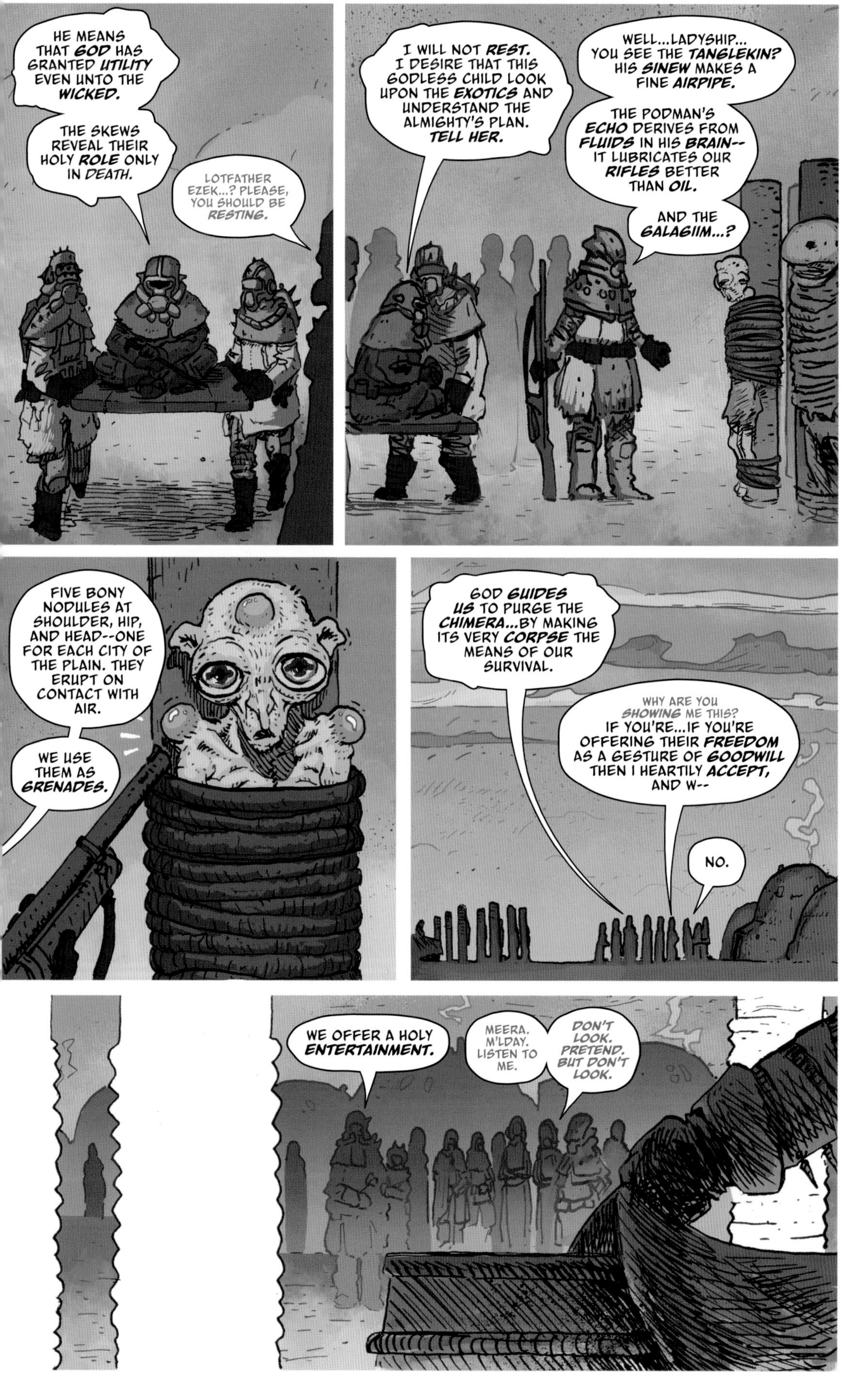
HE MEANS THAT GOD HAS GRANTED UTILITY EVEN UNTO THE WICKED.
THE SKEWS REVEAL THEIR HOLY ROLE ONLY IN DEATH.
LOTFATHER EZEK...? PLEASE, YOU SHOULD BE RESTING.
I WILL NOT REST. I DESIRE THAT THIS GODLESS CHILD LOOK UPON THE EXOTICS AND UNDERSTAND THE ALMIGHTY'S PLAN. TELL HER.
WELL...LADYSHIP... YOU SEE THE TANGLEKIN? HIS SINEW MAKES A FINE AIRPIPE.
THE PODMAN'S ECHO DERIVES FROM FLUIDS IN HIS BRAIN--IT LUBRICATES OUR RIFLES BETTER THAN OIL.
AND THE GALAGIIM...?
FIVE BONY NODULES AT SHOULDER, HIP, AND HEAD--ONE FOR EACH CITY OF THE PLAIN. THEY ERUPT ON CONTACT WITH AIR.
WE USE THEM AS GRENADES.
GOD GUIDES US TO PURGE THE CHIMERA...BY MAKING ITS VERY CORPSE THE MEANS OF OUR SURVIVAL.
WHY ARE YOU SHOWING ME THIS? IF YOU'RE...IF YOU'RE OFFERING THEIR FREEDOM AS A GESTURE OF GOODWILL THEN I HEARTILY ACCEPT, AND W--
NO.
WE OFFER A HOLY ENTERTAINMENT.
MEERA. M'LDAY. LISTEN TO ME.
DON'T LOOK. PRETEND. BUT DON'T LOOK.

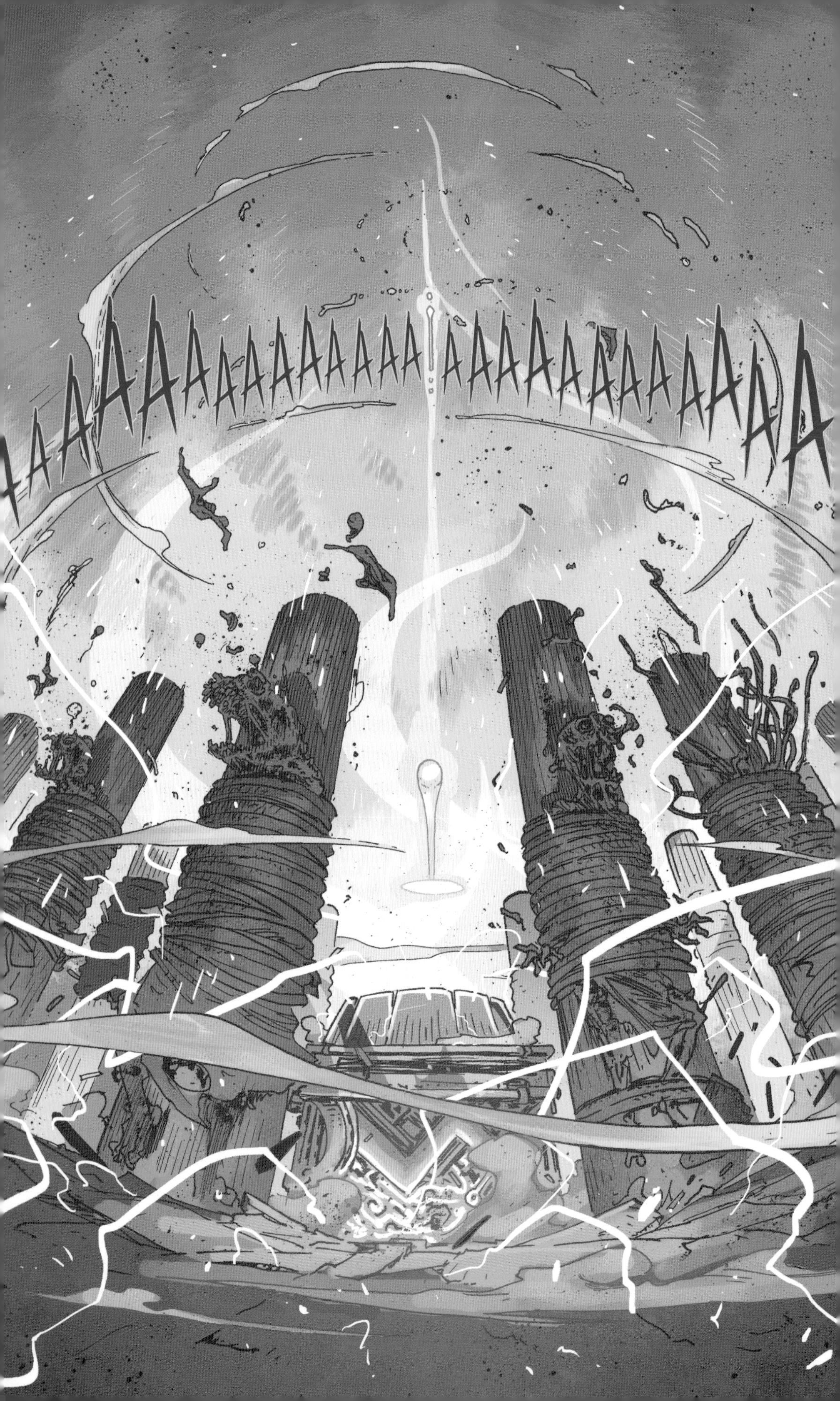
AAAAAAAAAAAAAAAAAAAAAAAAAAA

DO NOT REACT.

DO NOT REACT.

DO NOT REACT.

NN.

IT'S. IT'S *CALCULATED.* OFFEND AND INTIMIDATE.

DON'T GIVE THEM THE £$%&ING *SATISFACTION,* M'LADY.

DO. *NOT.* REACT.

I'M.

I'M A LITTLE *TIRED,* FATHERS. ALL THIS *SILLINESS* HAS WORN ME OUT.

DO EXCUSE US.

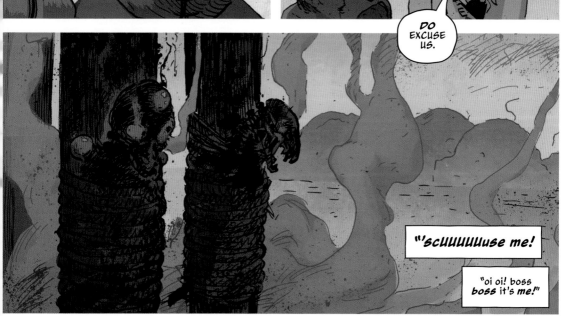

"scuuuuuuse me!

"oi oi! boss boss it's me!"

GO AWAY!
...milky Milk that you in there
CAPTAIN'S BUSY! DEEP THOUGHT! HEAVY PONDERING! NO VISITORS!
THE PRESUNK
NO, NOT YOU, DARLING, HAHA, AS IF I'D EVER TELL YOU TO GO AWAY--
MIDDLE OF AN INVESTIGATION! COME BACK LATER!
CITY-WATCH HQ
LOOK, SWEETIE, I'M SORRY YOUR INMATE'S ACTING UP AGAIN, BUT IT'S NOT LIKE I COULD EVEN HELP MUCH WHEN I CAME LAST TIME.
CAPTAIN'S LEFT ME IN CHARGE AND... AND I DON'T KNOW WHEN SHE'LL BE BACK OR EVEN IF SHE WILL AND I'M PANICKING ENOUGH AS IT IS WITHOUT Y--
HUH?
NO, NO, I DON'T CARE IF YOUR NUTCASE HAS BEEN RANTING ABOUT MARCHIONESS JULETTA, IT'S NOTHING TO DO WITH M--
'ere
who's been rantin' about Juletta

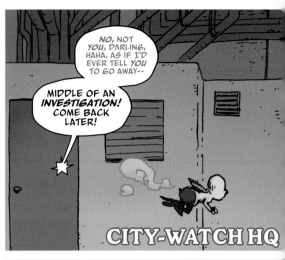

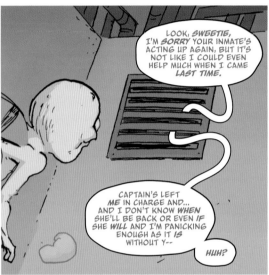

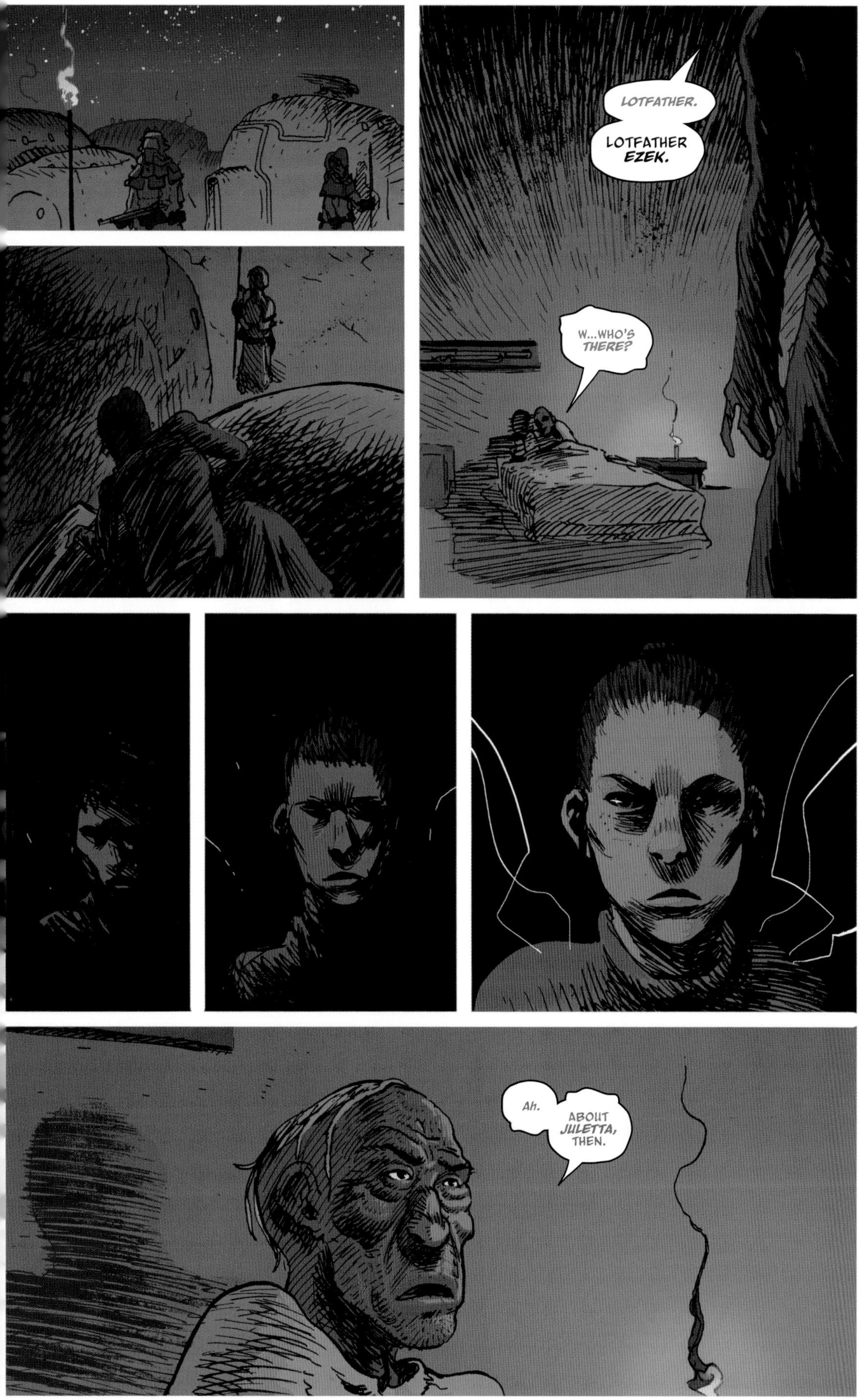
LOTFATHER.
LOTFATHER EZEK.
W...WHO'S THERE?
Ah.
ABOUT JULETTA, THEN.

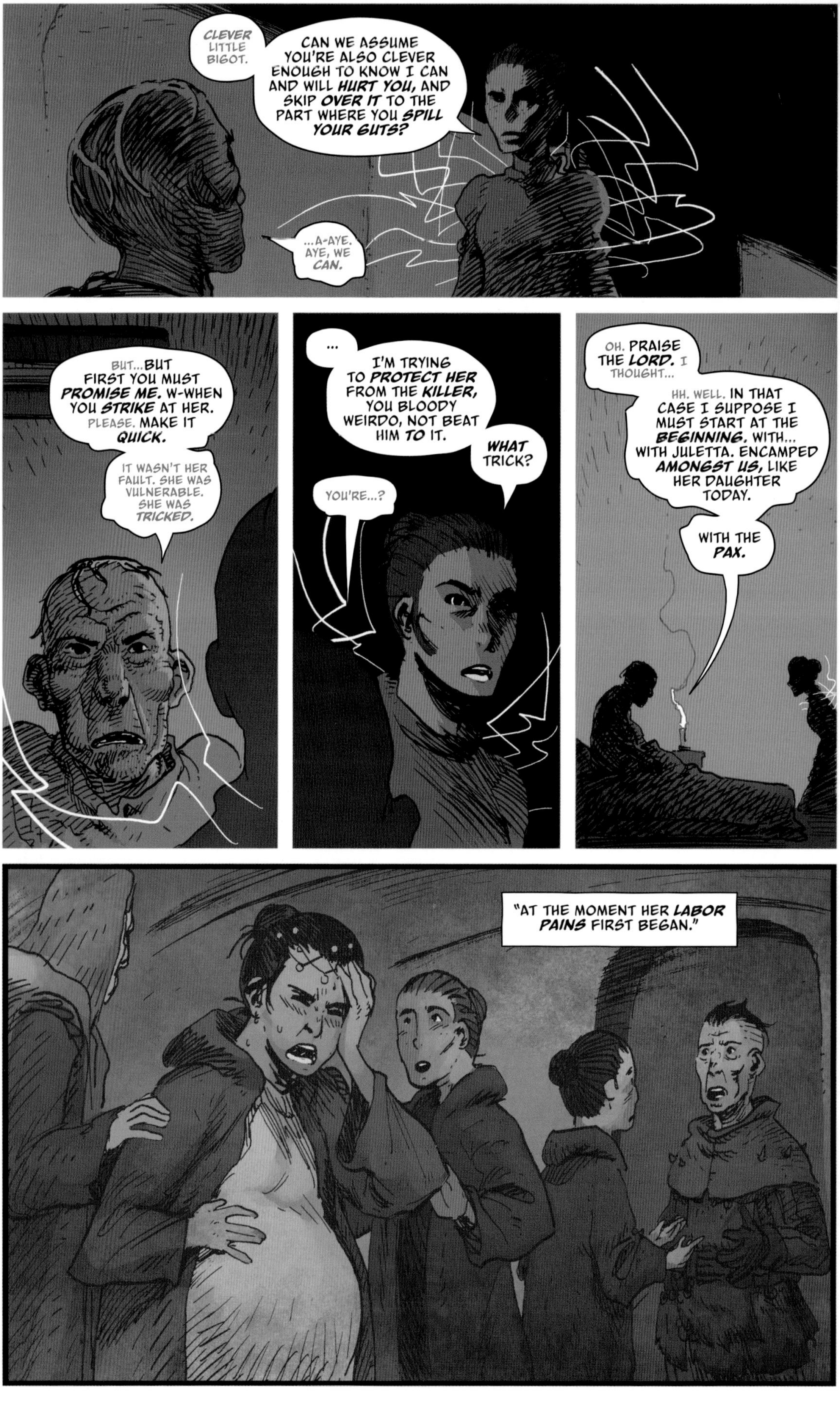
CLEVER LITTLE BIGOT.
CAN WE ASSUME YOU'RE ALSO CLEVER ENOUGH TO KNOW I CAN AND WILL HURT YOU, AND SKIP OVER IT TO THE PART WHERE YOU SPILL YOUR GUTS?
...A-AYE. AYE, WE CAN.
BUT...BUT FIRST YOU MUST PROMISE ME. W-WHEN YOU STRIKE AT HER. PLEASE. MAKE IT QUICK.
IT WASN'T HER FAULT. SHE WAS VULNERABLE. SHE WAS TRICKED.
...
I'M TRYING TO PROTECT HER FROM THE KILLER, YOU BLOODY WEIRDO, NOT BEAT HIM TO IT.
WHAT TRICK?
YOU'RE...?
OH. PRAISE THE LORD. I THOUGHT...
HH. WELL. IN THAT CASE I SUPPOSE I MUST START AT THE BEGINNING. WITH... WITH JULETTA. ENCAMPED AMONGST US, LIKE HER DAUGHTER TODAY.
WITH THE PAX.
"AT THE MOMENT HER LABOR PAINS FIRST BEGAN."

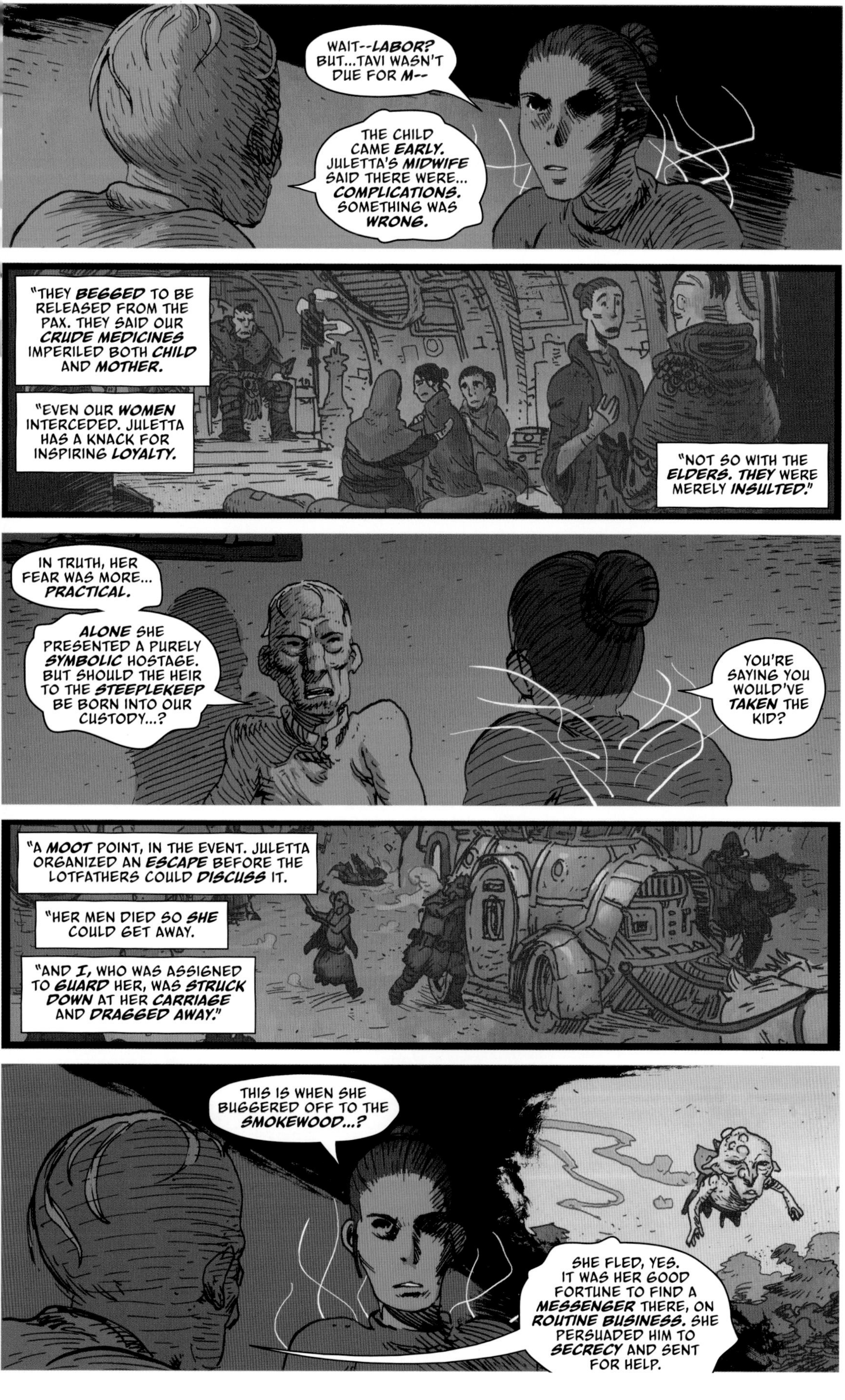
WAIT--LABOR? BUT...TAVI WASN'T DUE FOR M--
THE CHILD CAME EARLY. JULETTA'S MIDWIFE SAID THERE WERE... COMPLICATIONS. SOMETHING WAS WRONG.
"THEY BEGGED TO BE RELEASED FROM THE PAX. THEY SAID OUR CRUDE MEDICINES IMPERILED BOTH CHILD AND MOTHER.
"EVEN OUR WOMEN INTERCEDED. JULETTA HAS A KNACK FOR INSPIRING LOYALTY.
"NOT SO WITH THE ELDERS. THEY WERE MERELY INSULTED."
IN TRUTH, HER FEAR WAS MORE... PRACTICAL.
ALONE SHE PRESENTED A PURELY SYMBOLIC HOSTAGE. BUT SHOULD THE HEIR TO THE STEEPLEKEEP BE BORN INTO OUR CUSTODY...?
YOU'RE SAYING YOU WOULD'VE TAKEN THE KID?
"A MOOT POINT, IN THE EVENT. JULETTA ORGANIZED AN ESCAPE BEFORE THE LOTFATHERS COULD DISCUSS IT.
"HER MEN DIED SO SHE COULD GET AWAY.
"AND I, WHO WAS ASSIGNED TO GUARD HER, WAS STRUCK DOWN AT HER CARRIAGE AND DRAGGED AWAY."
THIS IS WHEN SHE BUGGERED OFF TO THE SMOKEWOOD...?
SHE FLED, YES. IT WAS HER GOOD FORTUNE TO FIND A MESSENGER THERE, ON ROUTINE BUSINESS. SHE PERSUADED HIM TO SECRECY AND SENT FOR HELP.

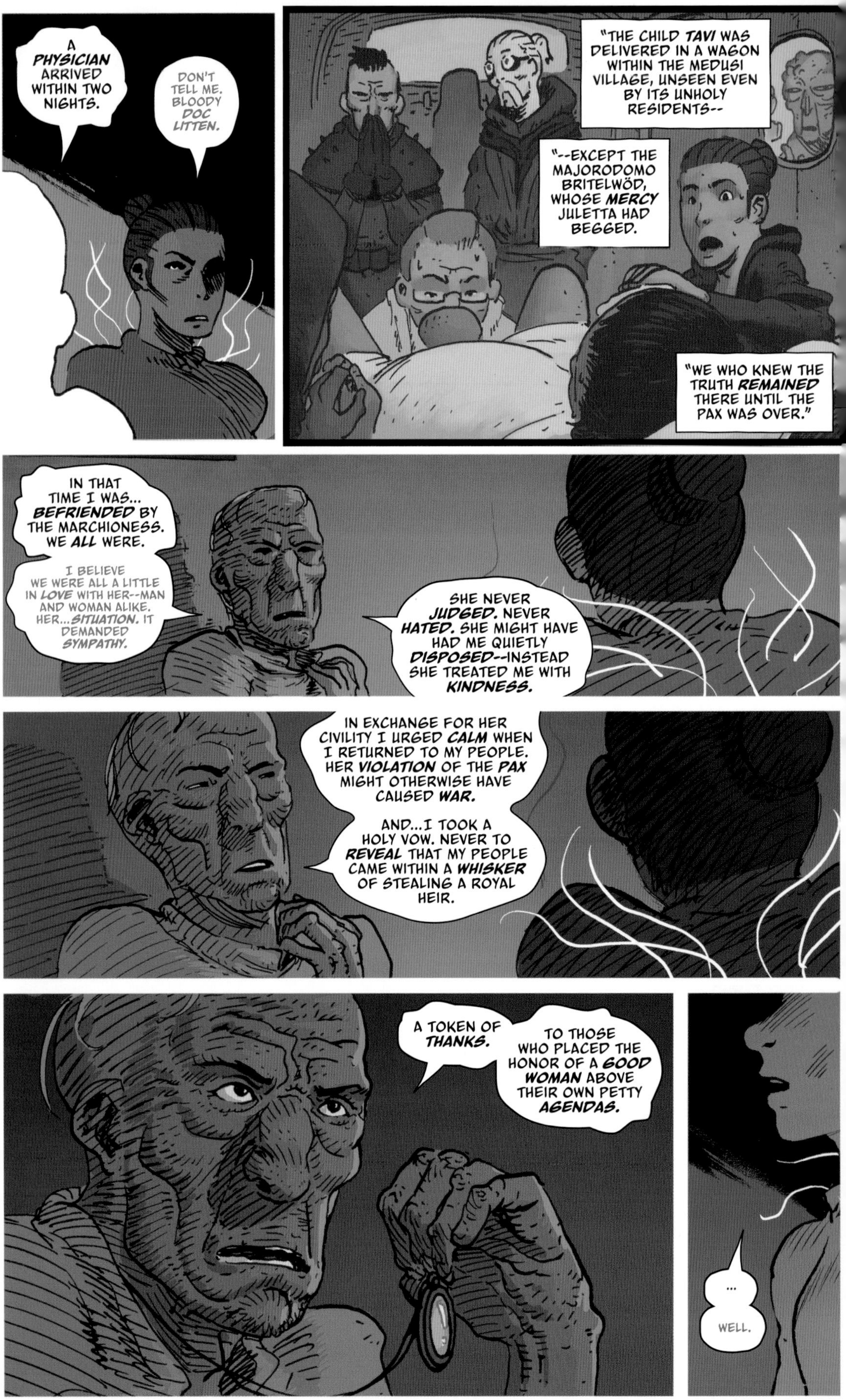
A PHYSICIAN ARRIVED WITHIN TWO NIGHTS.
DON'T TELL ME. BLOODY DOC LITTEN.
"THE CHILD TAVI WAS DELIVERED IN A WAGON WITHIN THE MEDUSI VILLAGE, UNSEEN EVEN BY ITS UNHOLY RESIDENTS--
"--EXCEPT THE MAJORODOMO BRITELWÖD, WHOSE MERCY JULETTA HAD BEGGED.
"WE WHO KNEW THE TRUTH REMAINED THERE UNTIL THE PAX WAS OVER."
IN THAT TIME I WAS... BEFRIENDED BY THE MARCHIONESS. WE ALL WERE.
I BELIEVE WE WERE ALL A LITTLE IN LOVE WITH HER--MAN AND WOMAN ALIKE. HER...SITUATION. IT DEMANDED SYMPATHY.
SHE NEVER JUDGED. NEVER HATED. SHE MIGHT HAVE HAD ME QUIETLY DISPOSED--INSTEAD SHE TREATED ME WITH KINDNESS.
IN EXCHANGE FOR HER CIVILITY I URGED CALM WHEN I RETURNED TO MY PEOPLE. HER VIOLATION OF THE PAX MIGHT OTHERWISE HAVE CAUSED WAR.
AND...I TOOK A HOLY VOW. NEVER TO REVEAL THAT MY PEOPLE CAME WITHIN A WHISKER OF STEALING A ROYAL HEIR.
A TOKEN OF THANKS.
TO THOSE WHO PLACED THE HONOR OF A GOOD WOMAN ABOVE THEIR OWN PETTY AGENDAS.
...
WELL.

RECKON I'LL START *CUTTING* YOU NOW.

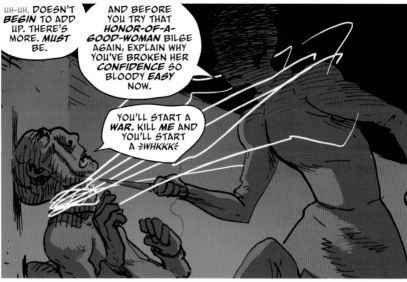

UH-UH. DOESN'T *BEGIN* TO ADD UP. THERE'S MORE. *MUST* BE.

AND BEFORE YOU TRY THAT *HONOR-OF-A-GOOD-WOMAN* BILGE AGAIN, EXPLAIN WHY YOU'VE BROKEN HER *CONFIDENCE* SO BLOODY *EASY* NOW.

YOU'LL START A *WAR.* KILL *ME* AND YOU'LL START A ⸘WHKKK⸘

WHAT? B-BUT I TOLD YOU THE *TRUTH!*

LONG WAY TO GO BEFORE *THAT,* NUMPTY.

"*RACIST FANATIC @#$HOLES ALMOST GRABBED THE ROYAL HEIR...BUT IN THE END THEY DIDN'T.*" NOT WORTH HALF A DOZEN MURDERS, AS CONSPIRACIES GO.

WHAT HAPPENED TO THE *MIDWIFE?* JULETTA NEVER MENTIONED *HER.*

G-*GREPP.* MRS. *GREPP.* SHE SUCCUMBED TO THE AIR POISON AND WALKED INTO THE WILDERN--

MORE.

WHY DID THE *KID* COME EARLY? WHY DID JULETTA RUN TO THE *FOREST?* WHAT DID YOU *MEAN* "SHE WAS *TRICKED*"? WHAT CAUSED A HATEFUL OLD £$%& LIKE YOU TO *SYMPATHIZE* WITH *HER?*

WHAT AREN'T YOU *SAYING,* MAN OF GOD?

CALM C-C-ALM LET ME *TALK* LET ME T-T-T

...HH. *HK.* HH. W-WE PRETEND.

WE *PRETEND* TO FIND NOBILITY IN THE SKEWS. THEIR *DEATHS.* THEIR *USEFUL CORPSES.* WE INVOKE *HOLINESS* EVEN IN *ABOMINATION.*

IT IS A *POLITE FICTION.*

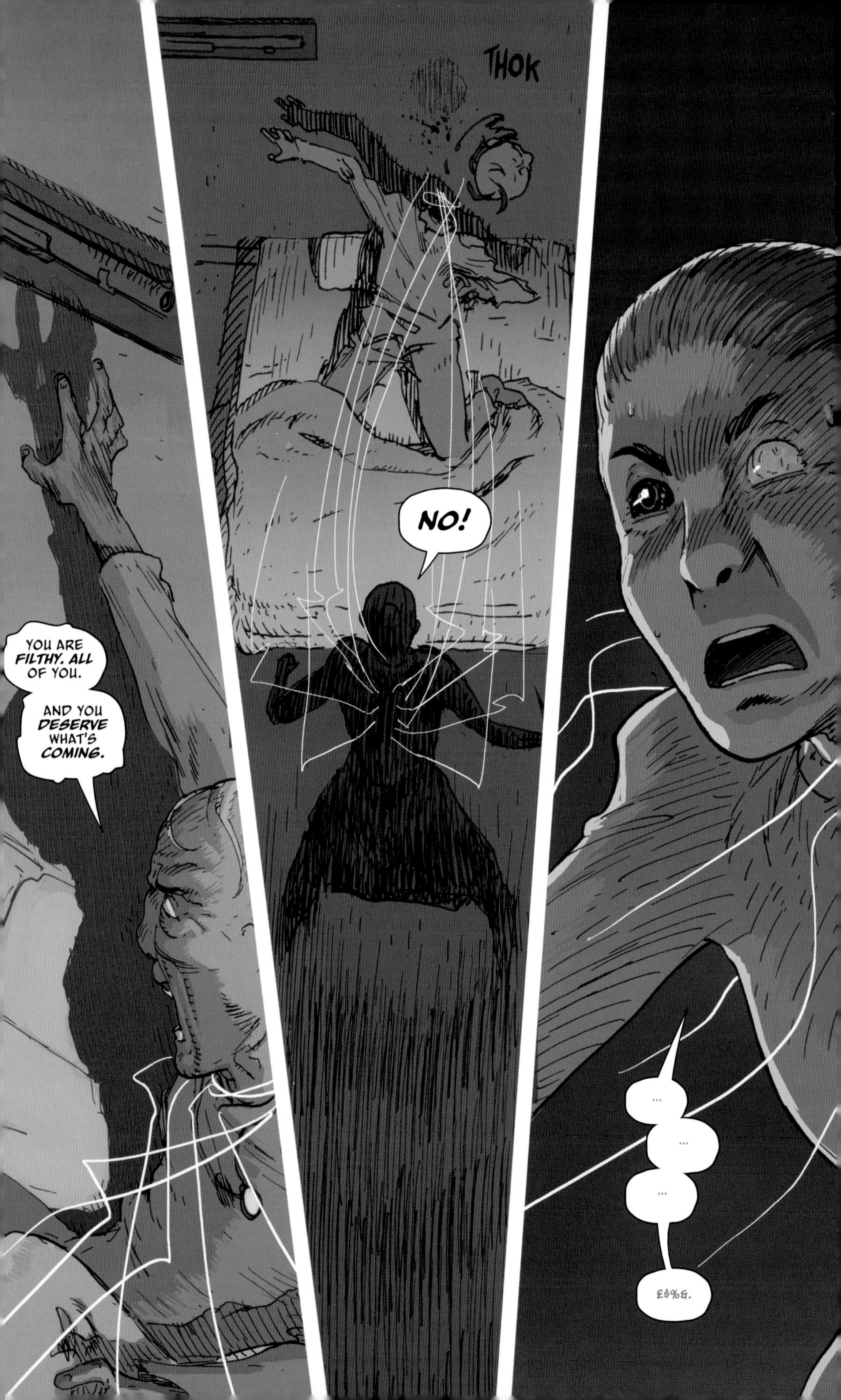
YOU ARE FILTHY. ALL OF YOU.
AND YOU DESERVE WHAT'S COMING.
THOK
NO!
...
...
...
£$%&.

ISSUE #6 COVER BY **JEFF STOKELY**
WITH COLORS BY **TAMRA BONVILLAIN**

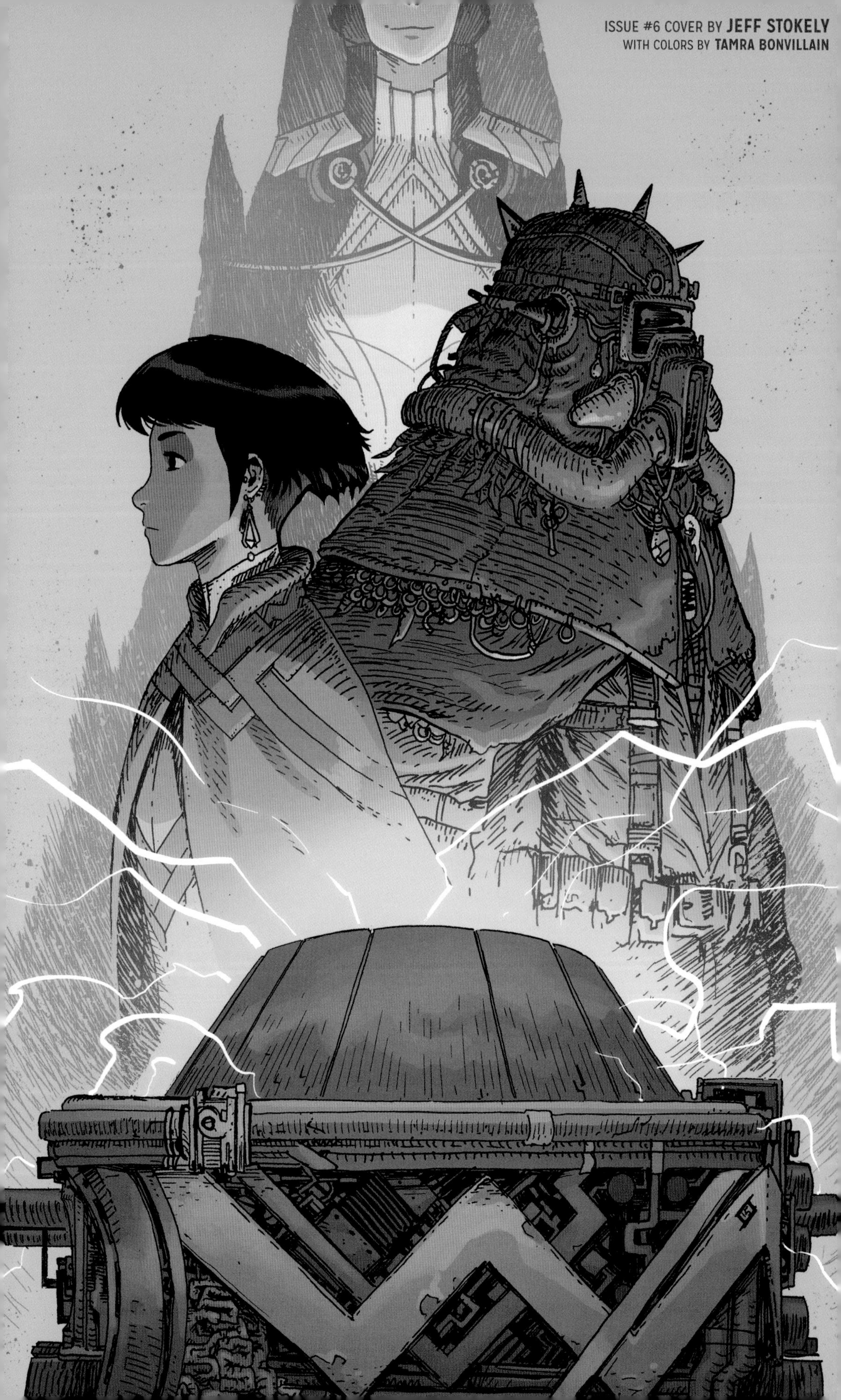

CHAPTER
SEVEN

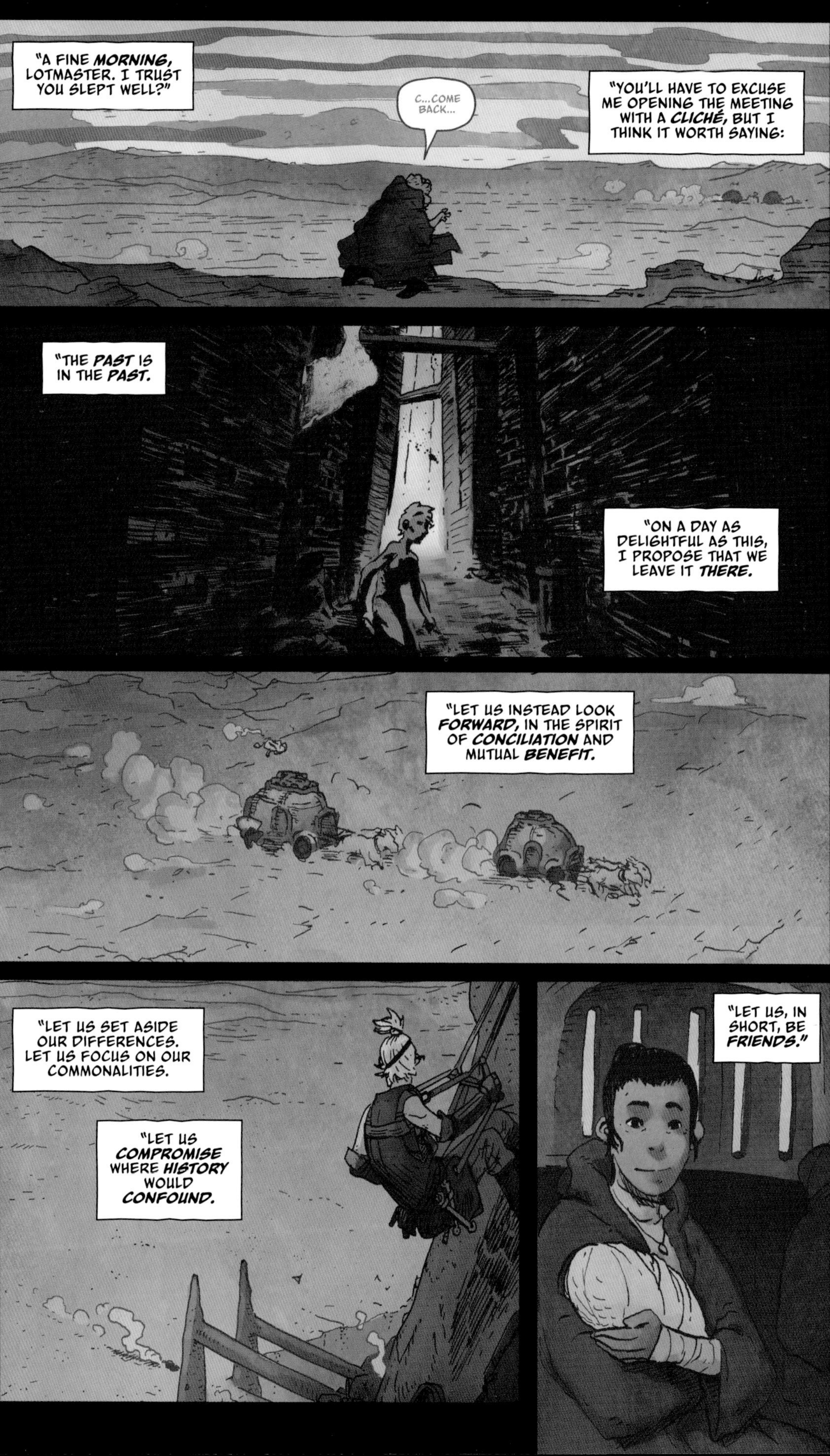
"A FINE MORNING, LOTMASTER. I TRUST YOU SLEPT WELL?"
C...COME BACK...
"YOU'LL HAVE TO EXCUSE ME OPENING THE MEETING WITH A CLICHÉ, BUT I THINK IT WORTH SAYING:
"THE PAST IS IN THE PAST.
"ON A DAY AS DELIGHTFUL AS THIS, I PROPOSE THAT WE LEAVE IT THERE.
"LET US INSTEAD LOOK FORWARD, IN THE SPIRIT OF CONCILIATION AND MUTUAL BENEFIT.
"LET US SET ASIDE OUR DIFFERENCES. LET US FOCUS ON OUR COMMONALITIES.
"LET US COMPROMISE WHERE HISTORY WOULD CONFOUND.
"LET US, IN SHORT, BE FRIENDS."

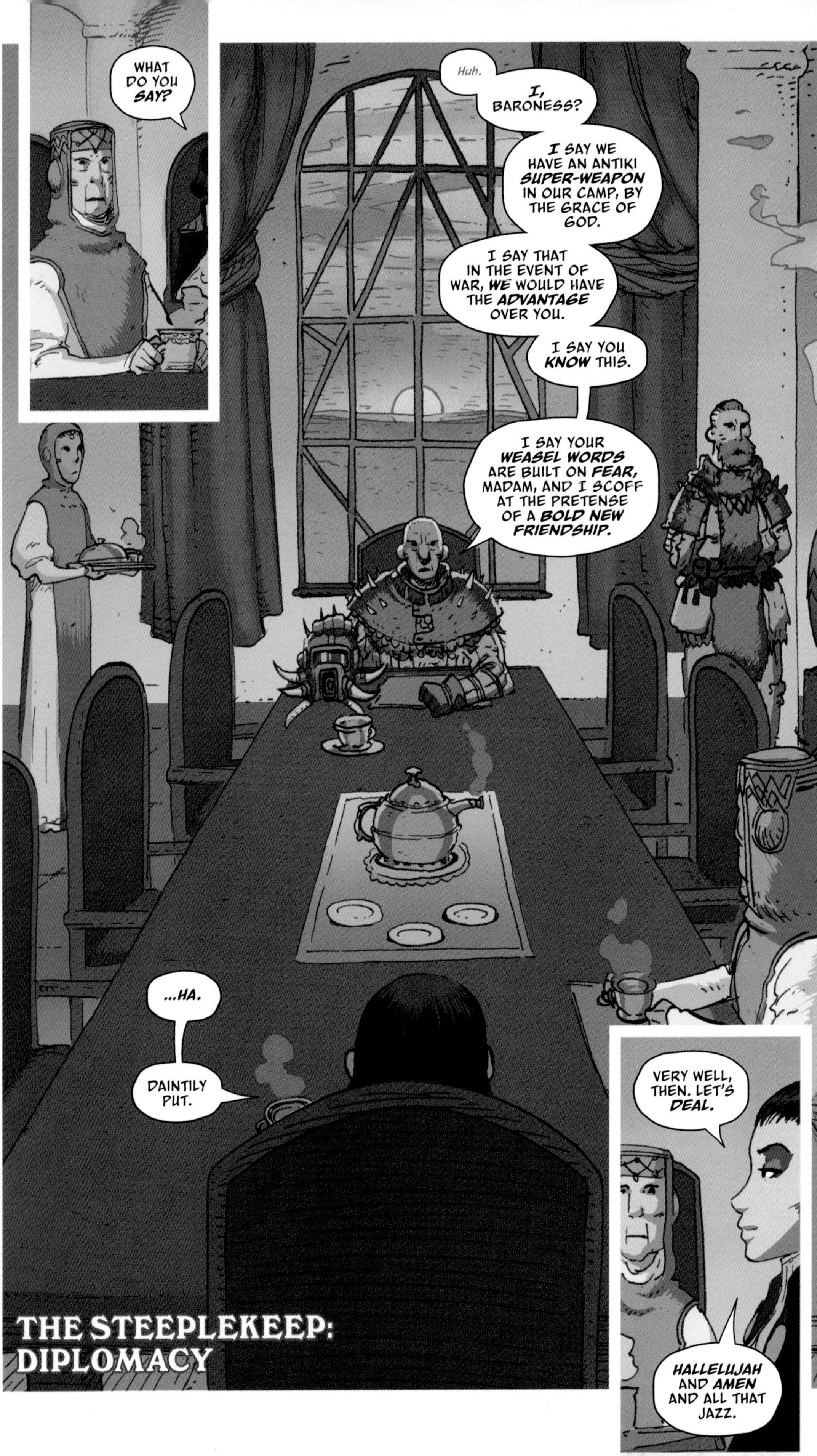
WHAT DO YOU *SAY?*
Huh.
I, BARONESS?
I SAY WE HAVE AN ANTIKI *SUPER-WEAPON* IN OUR CAMP, BY THE GRACE OF GOD.
I SAY THAT IN THE EVENT OF WAR, *WE* WOULD HAVE THE *ADVANTAGE* OVER YOU.
I SAY YOU *KNOW* THIS.
I SAY YOUR *WEASEL WORDS* ARE BUILT ON *FEAR,* MADAM, AND I SCOFF AT THE PRETENSE OF A *BOLD NEW FRIENDSHIP.*
...HA.
DAINTILY PUT.
THE STEEPLEKEEP: DIPLOMACY
VERY WELL, THEN. LET'S *DEAL.*
HALLELUJAH AND *AMEN* AND ALL THAT JAZZ.

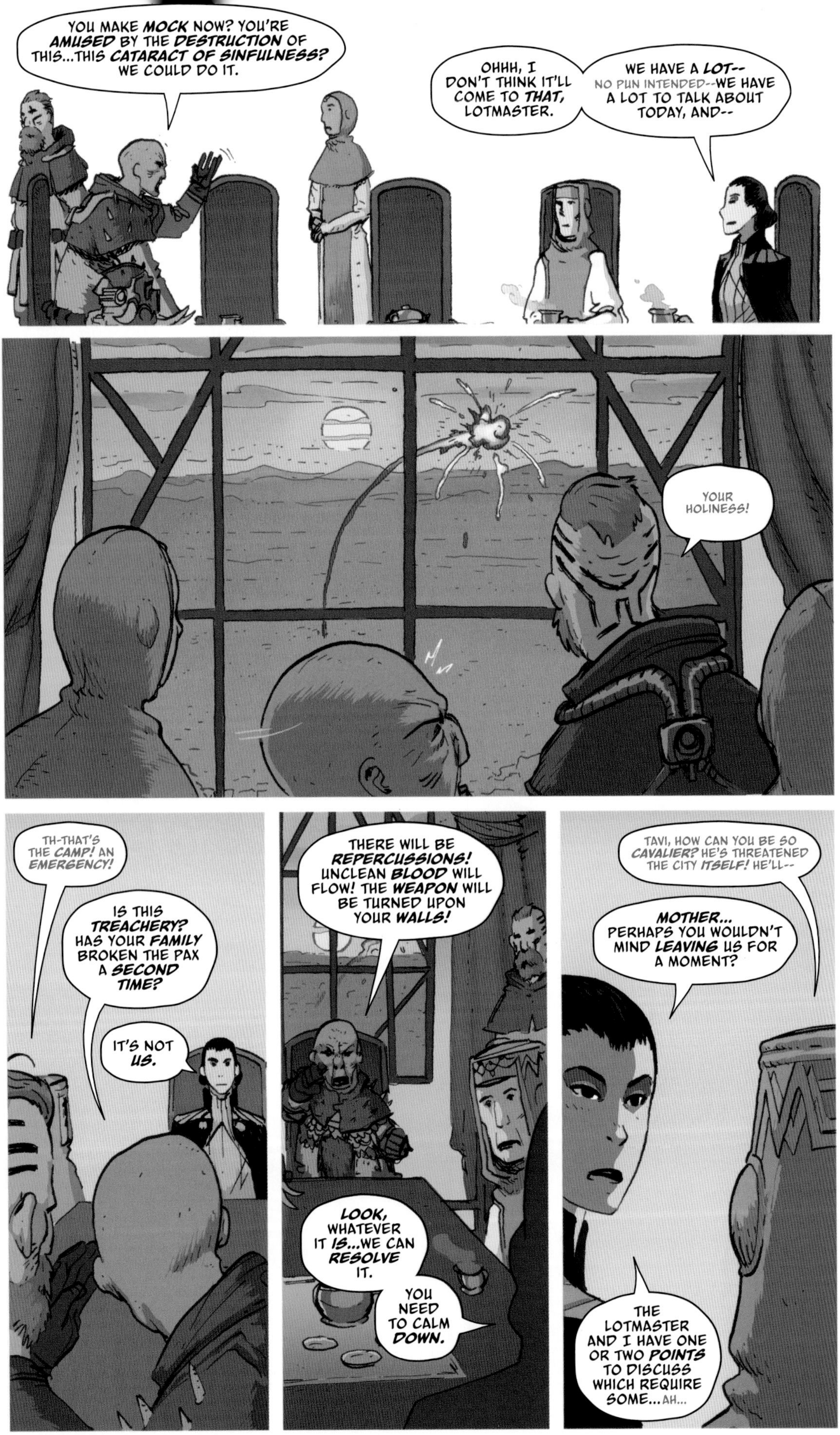
YOU MAKE MOCK NOW? YOU'RE AMUSED BY THE DESTRUCTION OF THIS...THIS CATARACT OF SINFULNESS? WE COULD DO IT.
OHHH, I DON'T THINK IT'LL COME TO THAT, LOTMASTER.
WE HAVE A LOT-- NO PUN INTENDED--WE HAVE A LOT TO TALK ABOUT TODAY, AND--
YOUR HOLINESS!
TH-THAT'S THE CAMP! AN EMERGENCY!
IS THIS TREACHERY? HAS YOUR FAMILY BROKEN THE PAX A SECOND TIME?
IT'S NOT US.
THERE WILL BE REPERCUSSIONS! UNCLEAN BLOOD WILL FLOW! THE WEAPON WILL BE TURNED UPON YOUR WALLS!
LOOK, WHATEVER IT IS...WE CAN RESOLVE IT.
YOU NEED TO CALM DOWN.
TAVI, HOW CAN YOU BE SO CAVALIER? HE'S THREATENED THE CITY ITSELF! HE'LL--
MOTHER... PERHAPS YOU WOULDN'T MIND LEAVING US FOR A MOMENT?
THE LOTMASTER AND I HAVE ONE OR TWO POINTS TO DISCUSS WHICH REQUIRE SOME...AH...

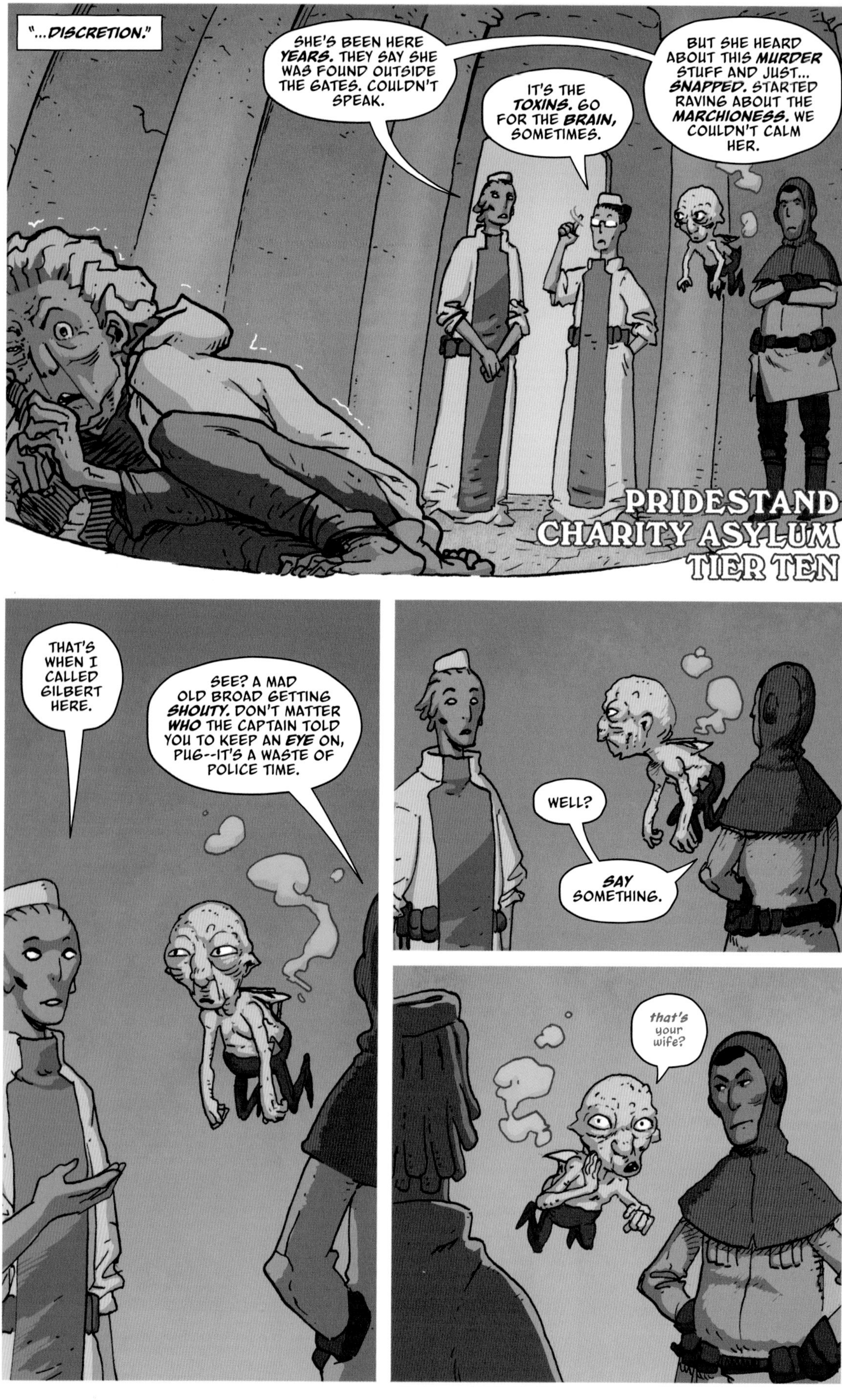
"...DISCRETION."
SHE'S BEEN HERE YEARS. THEY SAY SHE WAS FOUND OUTSIDE THE GATES. COULDN'T SPEAK.
BUT SHE HEARD ABOUT THIS MURDER STUFF AND JUST... SNAPPED. STARTED RAVING ABOUT THE MARCHIONESS. WE COULDN'T CALM HER.
IT'S THE TOXINS. GO FOR THE BRAIN, SOMETIMES.
PRIDESTAND CHARITY ASYLUM TIER TEN
THAT'S WHEN I CALLED GILBERT HERE.
SEE? A MAD OLD BROAD GETTING SHOUTY. DON'T MATTER WHO THE CAPTAIN TOLD YOU TO KEEP AN EYE ON, PUG--IT'S A WASTE OF POLICE TIME.
WELL?
SAY SOMETHING.
that's your wife?

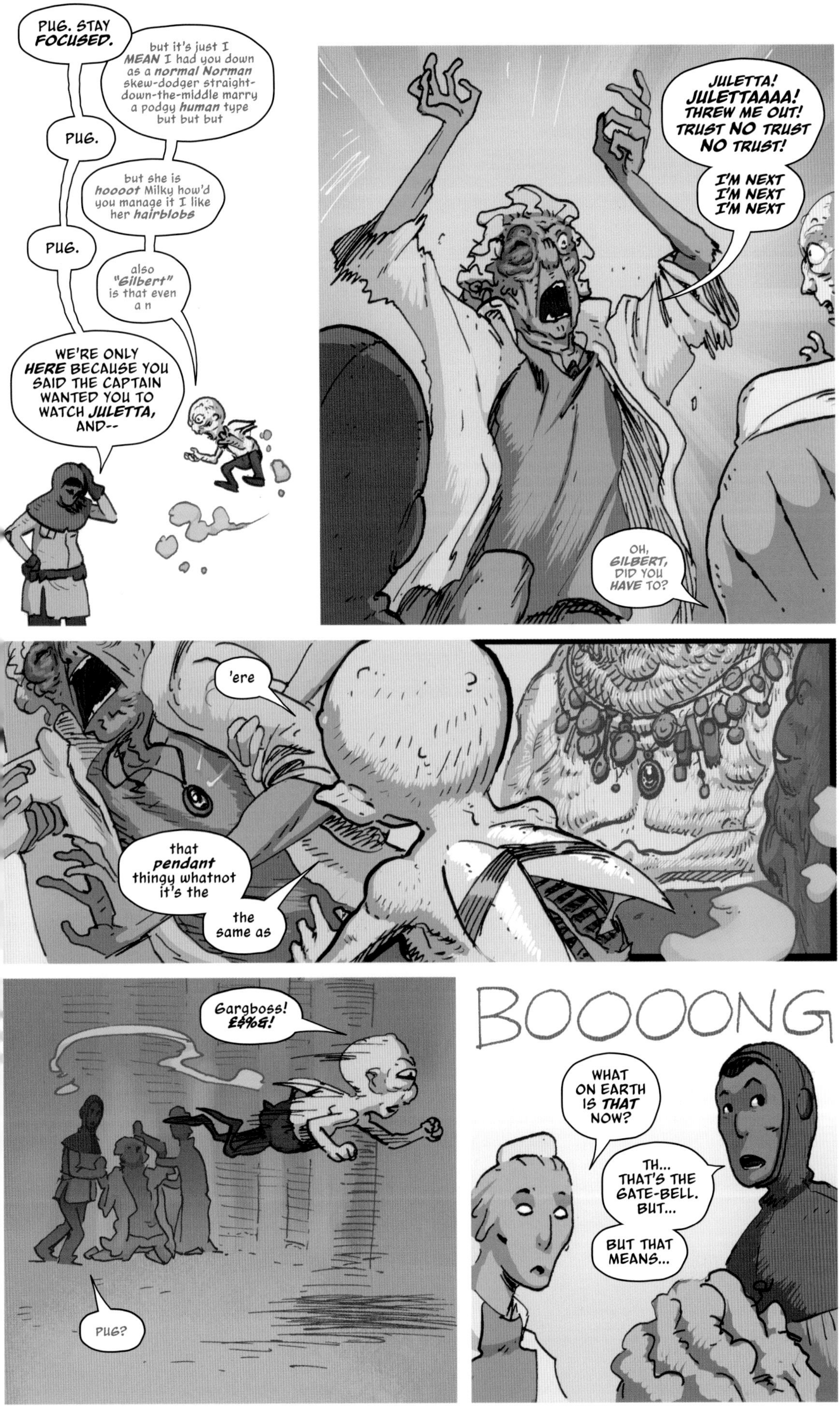
PUG. STAY FOCUSED.
but it's just I MEAN I had you down as a normal Norman skew-dodger straight-down-the-middle marry a podgy human type but but but
PUG.
but she is hoooot Milky how'd you manage it I like her hairblobs
PUG.
also "Gilbert" is that even a n
WE'RE ONLY HERE BECAUSE YOU SAID THE CAPTAIN WANTED YOU TO WATCH JULETTA, AND--
JULETTA! JULETTAAAA! THREW ME OUT! TRUST NO TRUST NO TRUST!
I'M NEXT I'M NEXT I'M NEXT
OH, GILBERT, DID YOU HAVE TO?
'ere
that pendant thingy whatnot it's the
the same as
Gargboss! £$%G!
PUG?
BOOOONG
WHAT ON EARTH IS THAT NOW?
TH... THAT'S THE GATE-BELL. BUT...
BUT THAT MEANS...

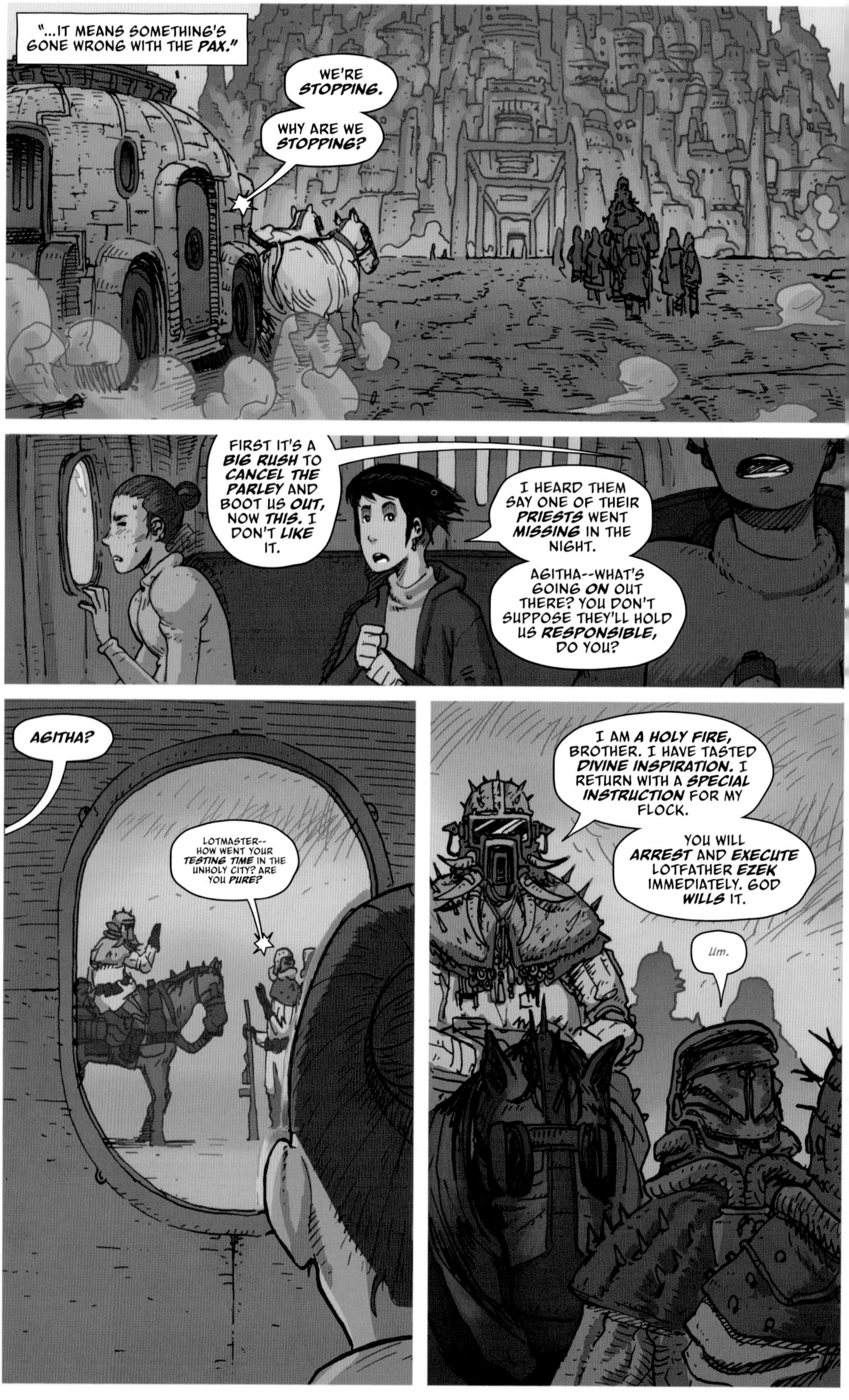
"...IT MEANS SOMETHING'S GONE WRONG WITH THE PAX."
WE'RE STOPPING.
WHY ARE WE STOPPING?
FIRST IT'S A BIG RUSH TO CANCEL THE PARLEY AND BOOT US OUT, NOW THIS. I DON'T LIKE IT.
I HEARD THEM SAY ONE OF THEIR PRIESTS WENT MISSING IN THE NIGHT.
AGITHA--WHAT'S GOING ON OUT THERE? YOU DON'T SUPPOSE THEY'LL HOLD US RESPONSIBLE, DO YOU?
AGITHA?
LOTMASTER--HOW WENT YOUR TESTING TIME IN THE UNHOLY CITY? ARE YOU PURE?
I AM A HOLY FIRE, BROTHER. I HAVE TASTED DIVINE INSPIRATION. I RETURN WITH A SPECIAL INSTRUCTION FOR MY FLOCK.
YOU WILL ARREST AND EXECUTE LOTFATHER EZEK IMMEDIATELY. GOD WILLS IT.
Um.

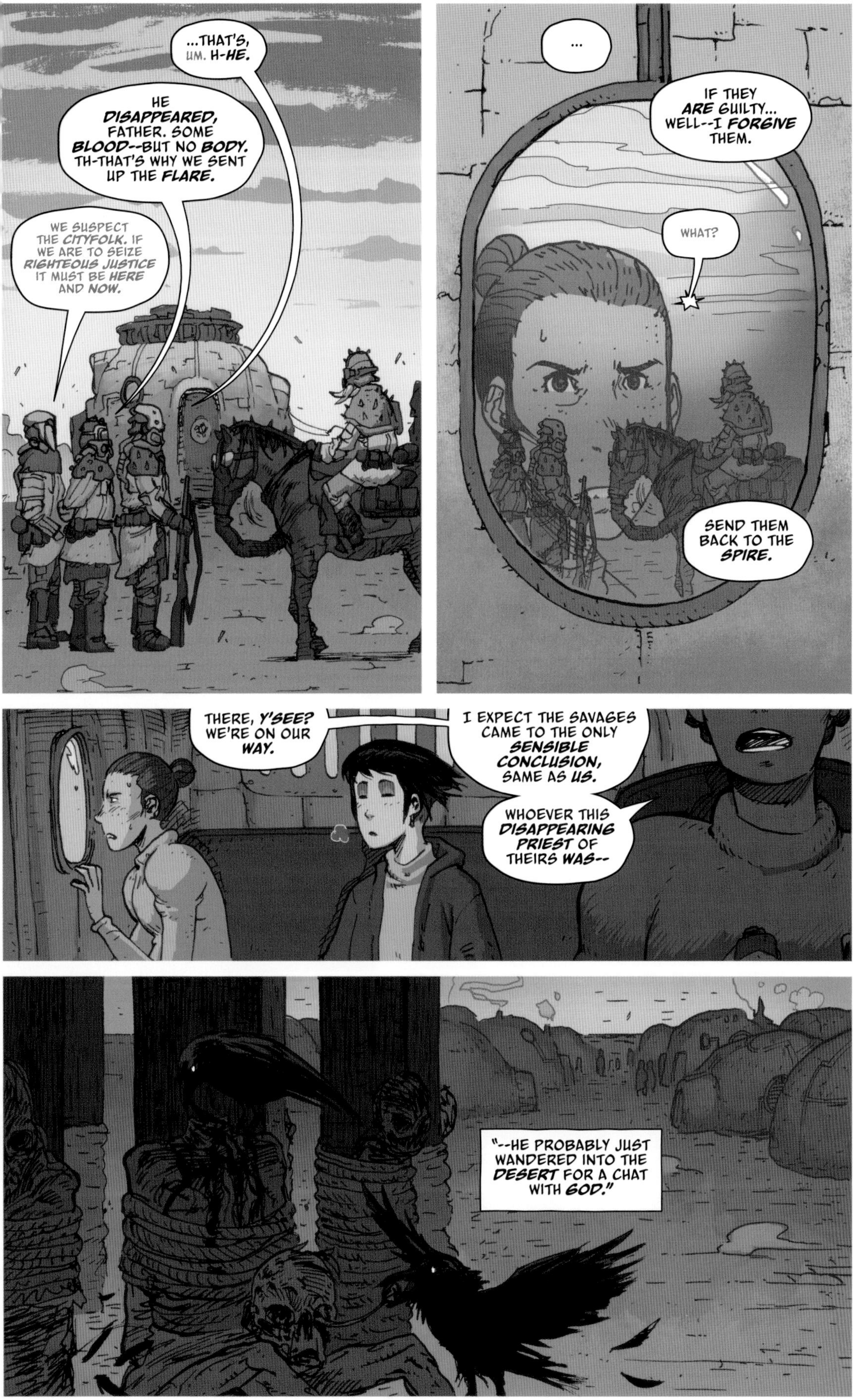
...THAT'S, UM. H-HE.
HE DISAPPEARED, FATHER. SOME BLOOD--BUT NO BODY. TH-THAT'S WHY WE SENT UP THE FLARE.
WE SUSPECT THE CITYFOLK. IF WE ARE TO SEIZE RIGHTEOUS JUSTICE IT MUST BE HERE AND NOW.
...
IF THEY ARE GUILTY... WELL--I FORGIVE THEM.
WHAT?
SEND THEM BACK TO THE SPIRE.
THERE, Y'SEE? WE'RE ON OUR WAY.
I EXPECT THE SAVAGES CAME TO THE ONLY SENSIBLE CONCLUSION, SAME AS US.
WHOEVER THIS DISAPPEARING PRIEST OF THEIRS WAS--
"--HE PROBABLY JUST WANDERED INTO THE DESERT FOR A CHAT WITH GOD."

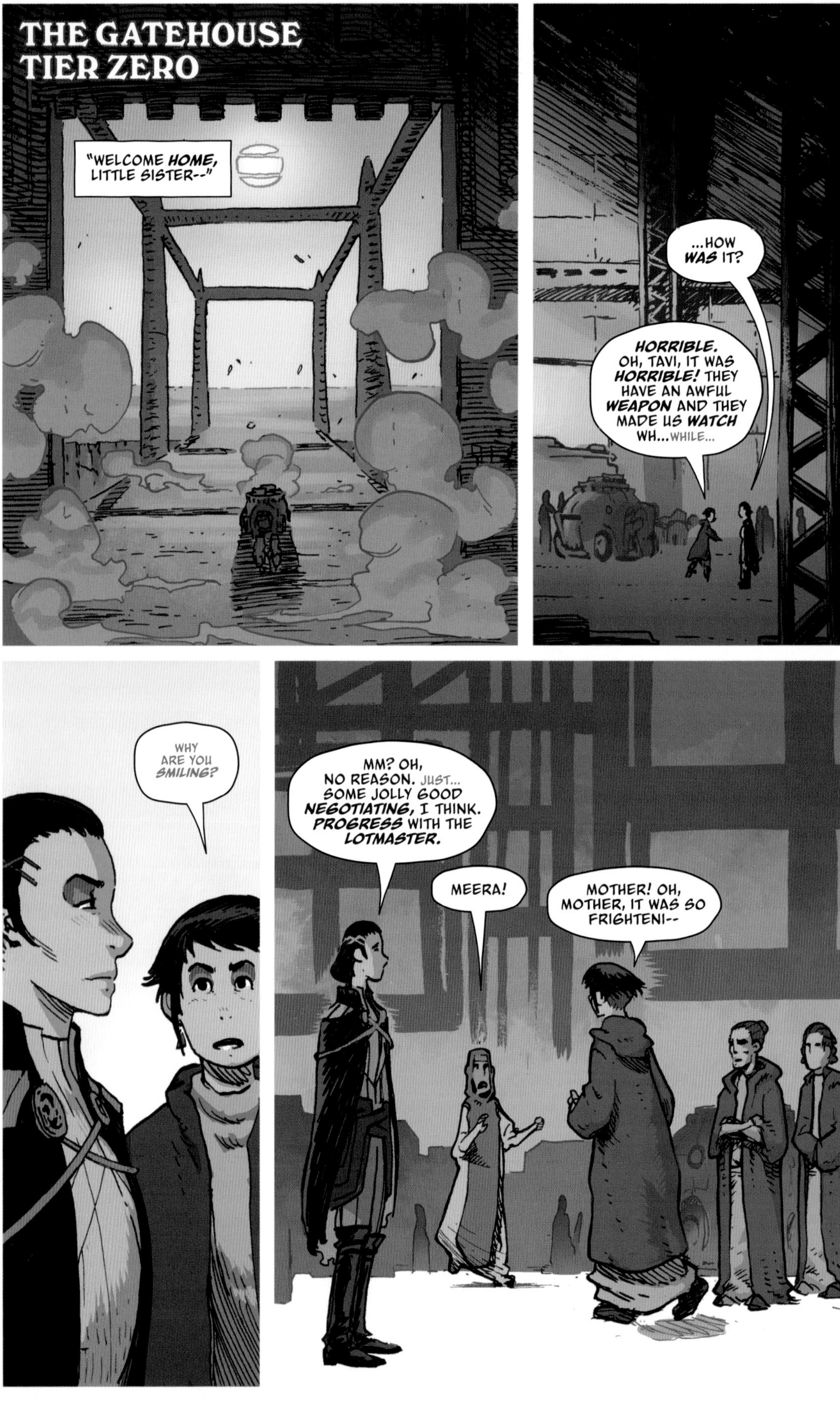
THE GATEHOUSE
TIER ZERO
"WELCOME HOME, LITTLE SISTER--"
...HOW WAS IT?
HORRIBLE. OH, TAVI, IT WAS HORRIBLE! THEY HAVE AN AWFUL WEAPON AND THEY MADE US WATCH WH...WHILE...
WHY ARE YOU SMILING?
MM? OH, NO REASON. JUST... SOME JOLLY GOOD NEGOTIATING, I THINK. PROGRESS WITH THE LOTMASTER.
MEERA!
MOTHER! OH, MOTHER, IT WAS SO FRIGHTENI--

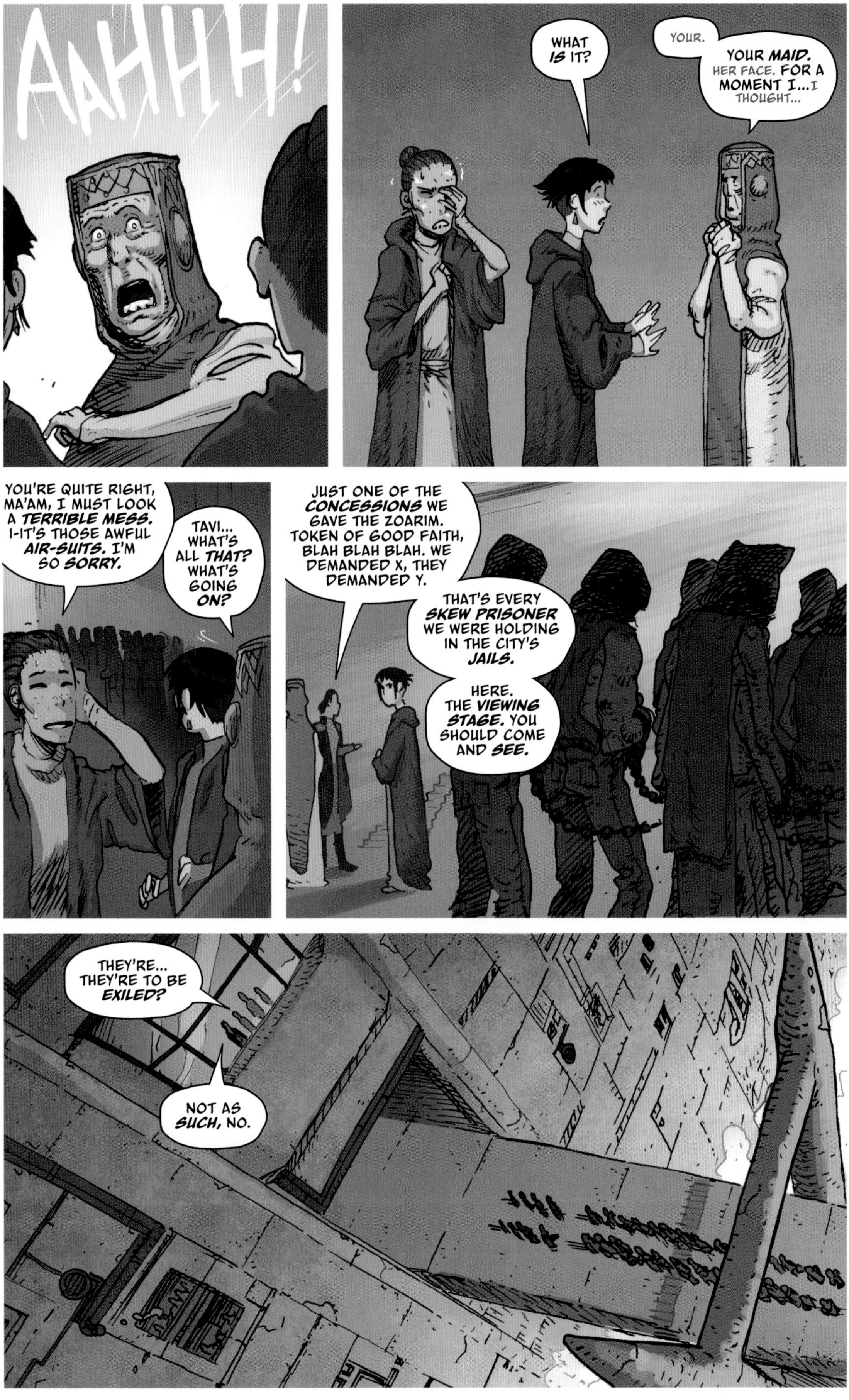
AAHHH!
WHAT IS IT?
YOUR.
YOUR MAID. HER FACE. FOR A MOMENT I...I THOUGHT...
YOU'RE QUITE RIGHT, MA'AM, I MUST LOOK A TERRIBLE MESS. I-IT'S THOSE AWFUL AIR-SUITS. I'M SO SORRY.
TAVI... WHAT'S ALL THAT? WHAT'S GOING ON?
JUST ONE OF THE CONCESSIONS WE GAVE THE ZOARIM. TOKEN OF GOOD FAITH, BLAH BLAH BLAH. WE DEMANDED X, THEY DEMANDED Y.
THAT'S EVERY SKEW PRISONER WE WERE HOLDING IN THE CITY'S JAILS.
HERE. THE VIEWING STAGE. YOU SHOULD COME AND SEE.
THEY'RE... THEY'RE TO BE EXILED?
NOT AS SUCH, NO.

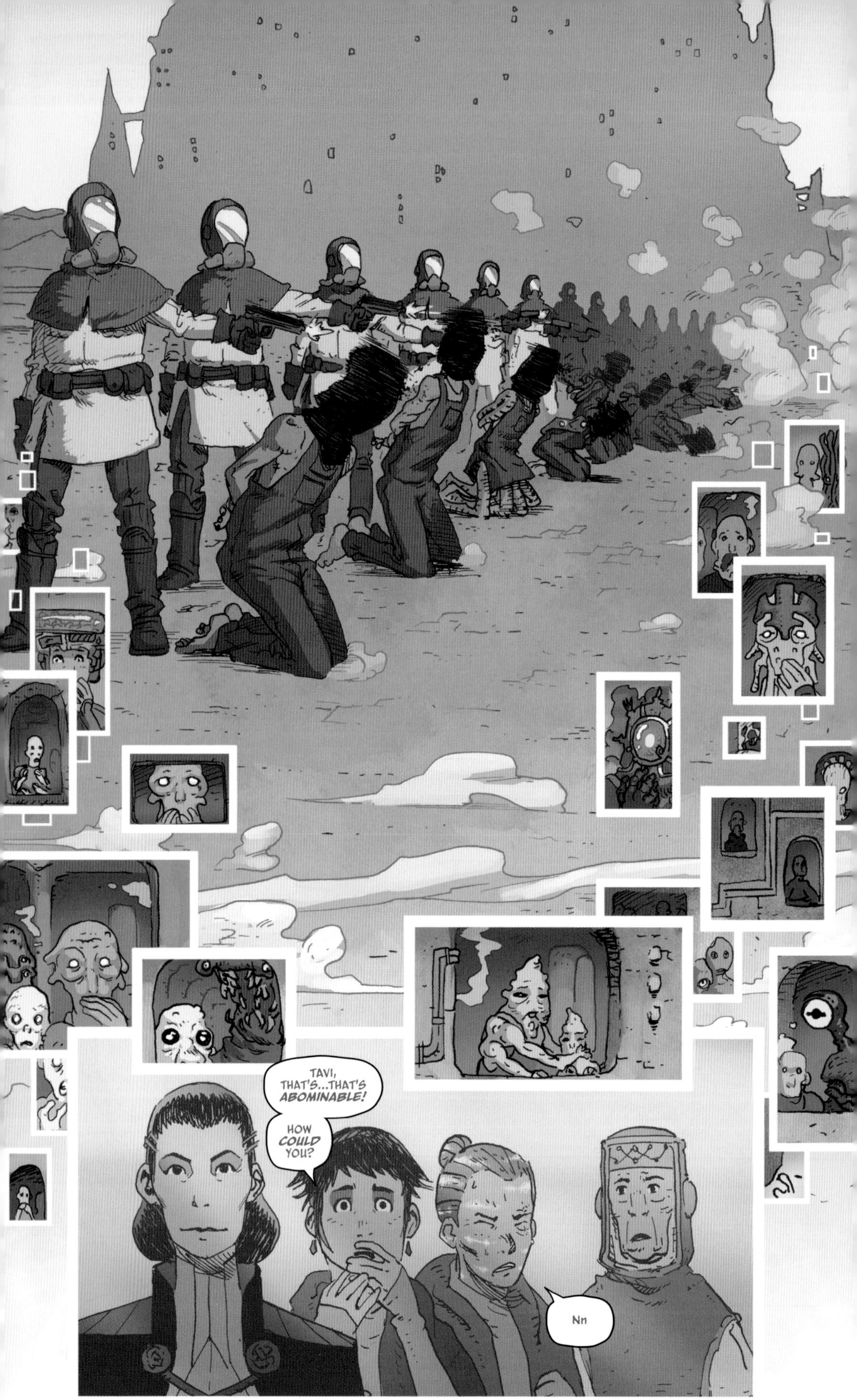
TAVI, THAT'S...THAT'S ABOMINABLE!
HOW COULD YOU?
Nn

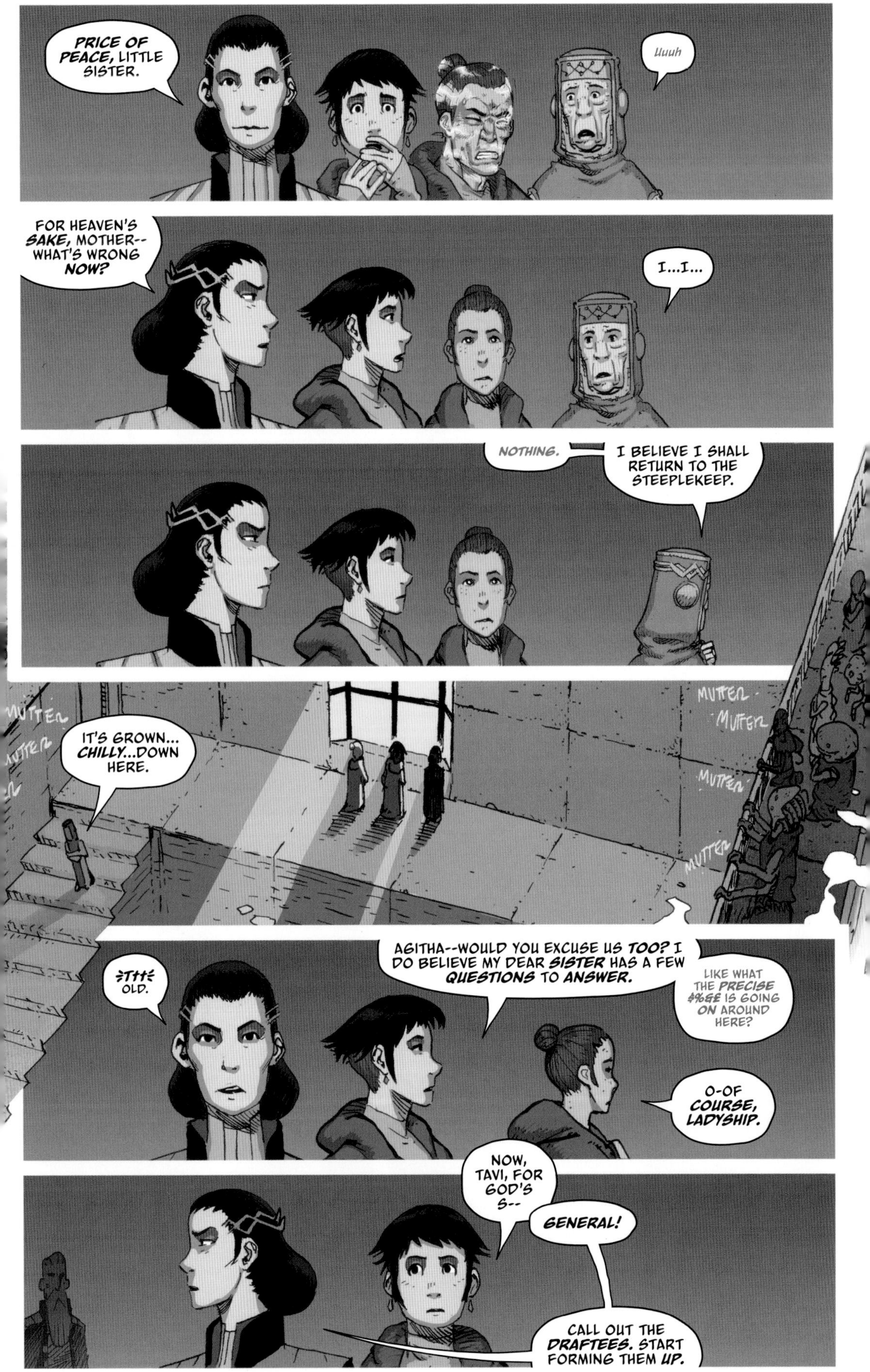
PRICE OF PEACE, LITTLE SISTER.
Uuuh
FOR HEAVEN'S SAKE, MOTHER--WHAT'S WRONG NOW?
I...I...
NOTHING.
I BELIEVE I SHALL RETURN TO THE STEEPLEKEEP.
MUTTER
MUTTER
IT'S GROWN... CHILLY...DOWN HERE.
MUTTER
MUTTER
MUTTER
MUTTER
TTT OLD.
AGITHA--WOULD YOU EXCUSE US TOO? I DO BELIEVE MY DEAR SISTER HAS A FEW QUESTIONS TO ANSWER.
LIKE WHAT THE PRECISE $%G£ IS GOING ON AROUND HERE?
O-OF COURSE, LADYSHIP.
NOW, TAVI, FOR GOD'S S--
GENERAL!
CALL OUT THE DRAFTEES. START FORMING THEM UP.

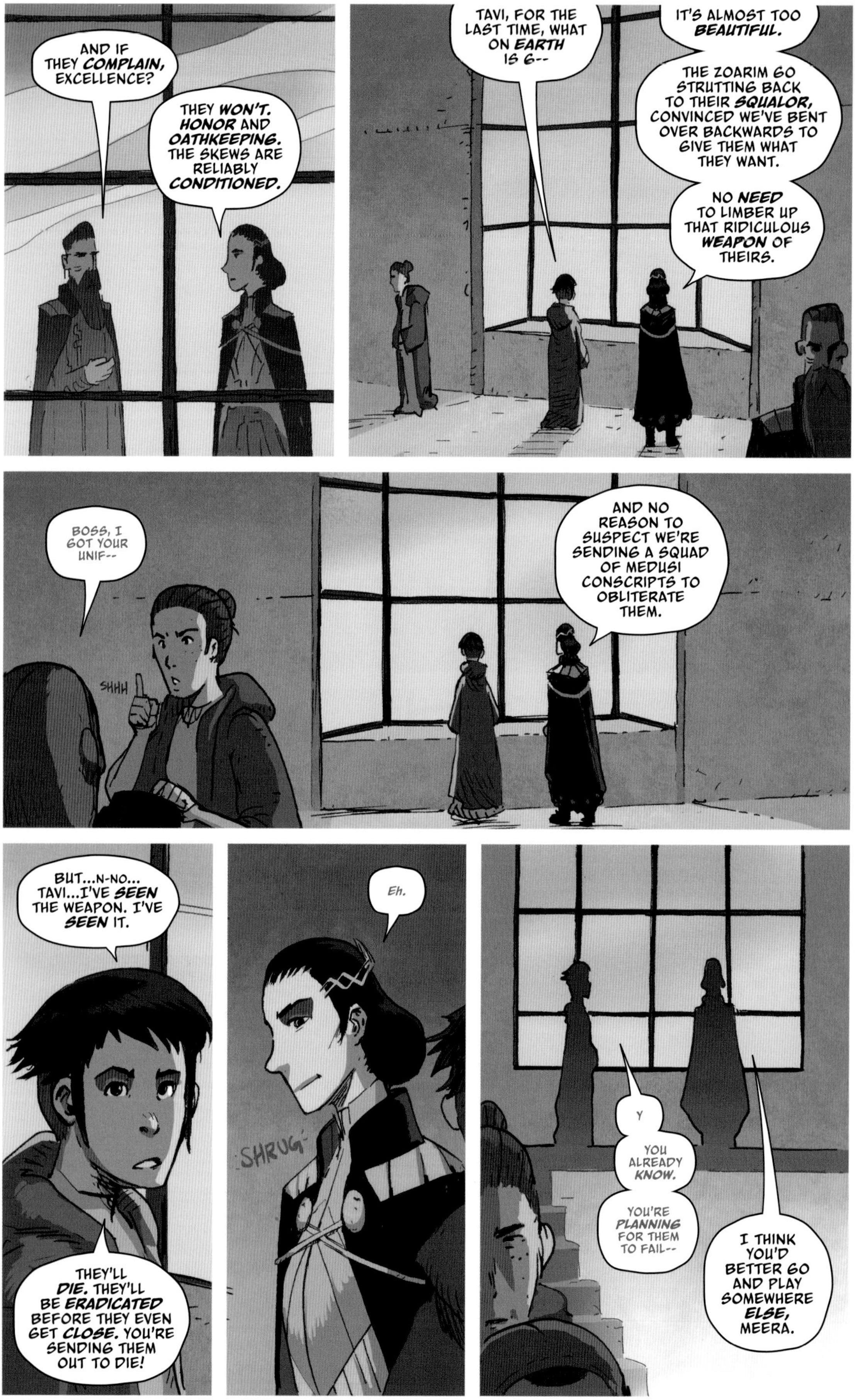
AND IF THEY COMPLAIN, EXCELLENCE?
THEY WON'T. HONOR AND OATHKEEPING. THE SKEWS ARE RELIABLY CONDITIONED.
TAVI, FOR THE LAST TIME, WHAT ON EARTH IS G--
IT'S ALMOST TOO BEAUTIFUL.
THE ZOARIM GO STRUTTING BACK TO THEIR SQUALOR, CONVINCED WE'VE BENT OVER BACKWARDS TO GIVE THEM WHAT THEY WANT.
NO NEED TO LIMBER UP THAT RIDICULOUS WEAPON OF THEIRS.
BOSS, I GOT YOUR UNIF--
SHHH
AND NO REASON TO SUSPECT WE'RE SENDING A SQUAD OF MEDUSI CONSCRIPTS TO OBLITERATE THEM.
BUT...N-NO... TAVI...I'VE SEEN THE WEAPON. I'VE SEEN IT.
THEY'LL DIE. THEY'LL BE ERADICATED BEFORE THEY EVEN GET CLOSE. YOU'RE SENDING THEM OUT TO DIE!
Eh.
SHRUG
Y
YOU ALREADY KNOW.
YOU'RE PLANNING FOR THEM TO FAIL--
I THINK YOU'D BETTER GO AND PLAY SOMEWHERE ELSE, MEERA.

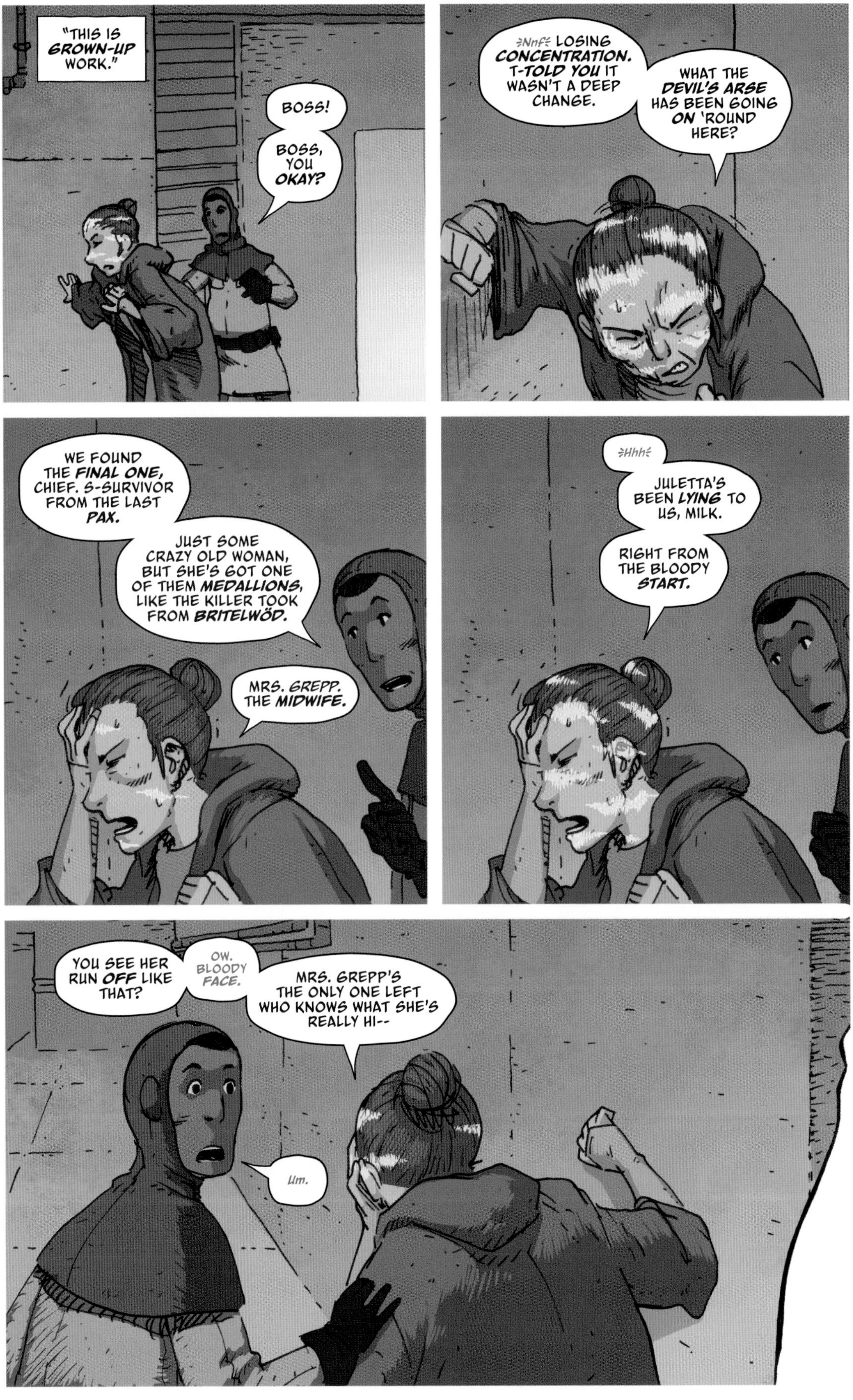
"THIS IS GROWN-UP WORK."
BOSS!
BOSS, YOU OKAY?
≠Nnf≠ LOSING CONCENTRATION. T-TOLD YOU IT WASN'T A DEEP CHANGE.
WHAT THE DEVIL'S ARSE HAS BEEN GOING ON 'ROUND HERE?
WE FOUND THE FINAL ONE, CHIEF. S-SURVIVOR FROM THE LAST PAX.
JUST SOME CRAZY OLD WOMAN, BUT SHE'S GOT ONE OF THEM MEDALLIONS, LIKE THE KILLER TOOK FROM BRITELWÖD.
MRS. GREPP. THE MIDWIFE.
≠Hhh≠
JULETTA'S BEEN LYING TO US, MILK.
RIGHT FROM THE BLOODY START.
YOU SEE HER RUN OFF LIKE THAT?
OW. BLOODY FACE.
MRS. GREPP'S THE ONLY ONE LEFT WHO KNOWS WHAT SHE'S REALLY HI--
Um.

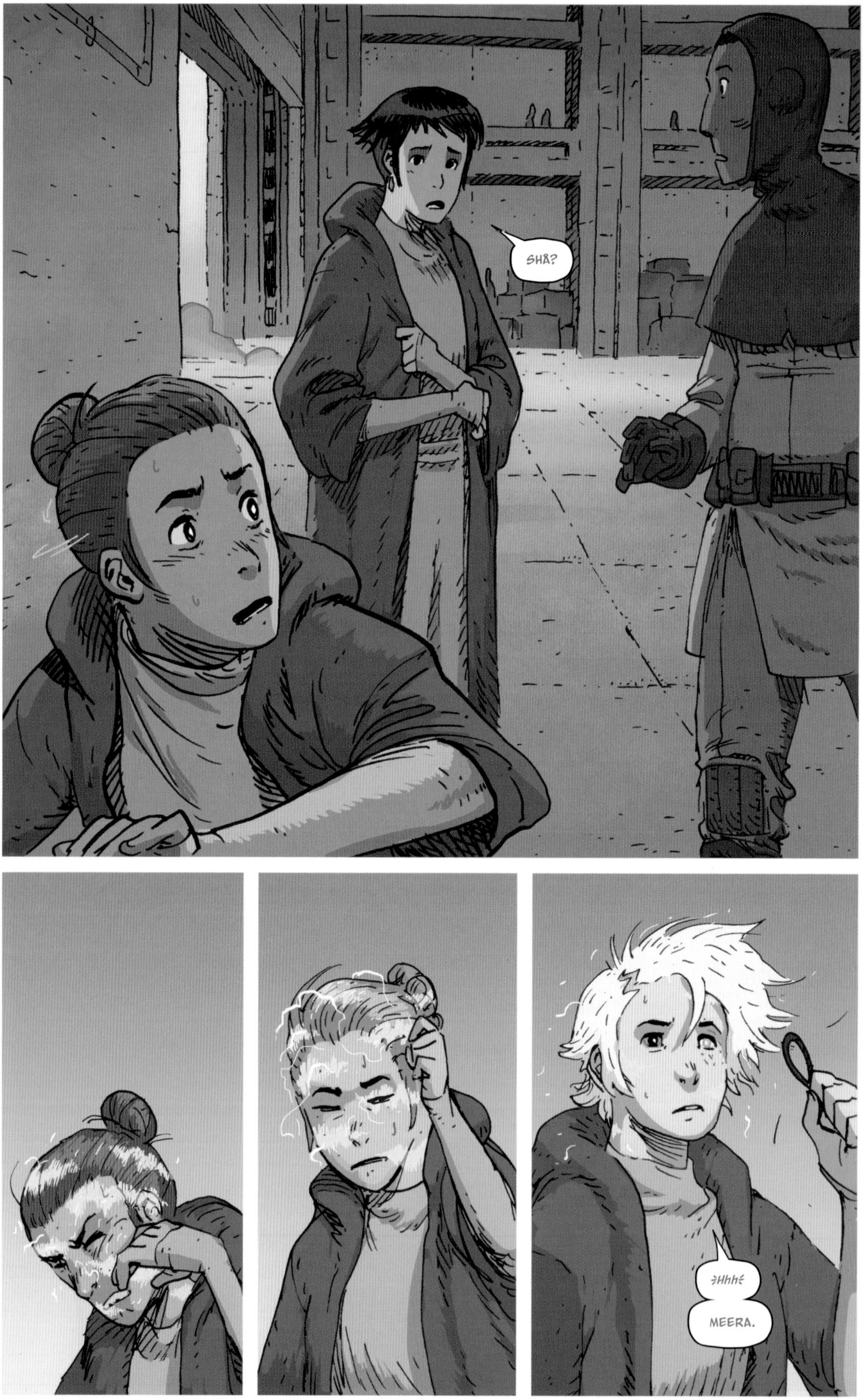
SHÅ?
Hhh
MEERA.

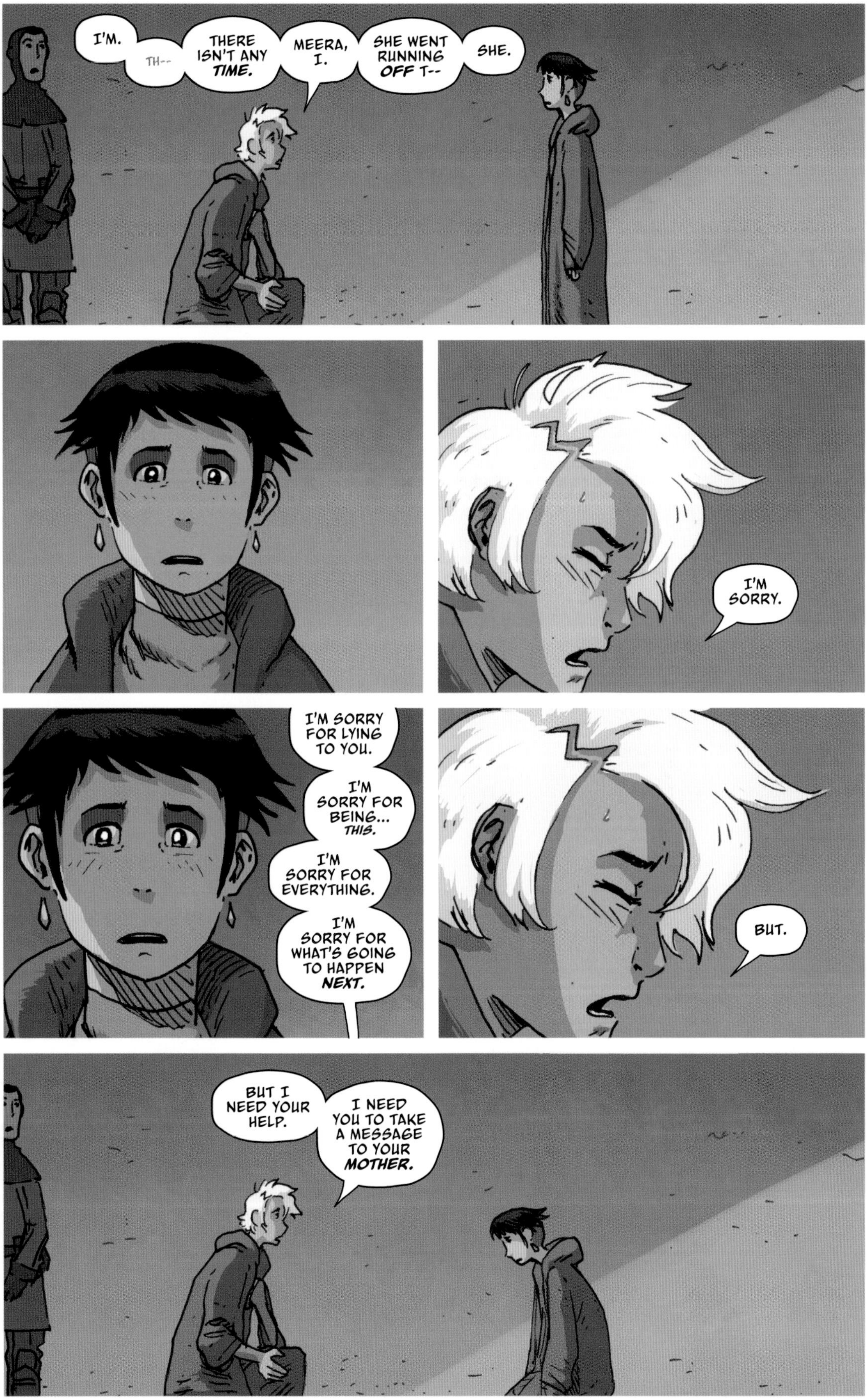
I'M.
TH--
THERE ISN'T ANY *TIME.*
MEERA, I.
SHE WENT RUNNING *OFF* T--
SHE.
I'M SORRY.
I'M SORRY FOR LYING TO YOU.
I'M SORRY FOR BEING... *THIS.*
I'M SORRY FOR EVERYTHING.
I'M SORRY FOR WHAT'S GOING TO HAPPEN *NEXT.*
BUT.
BUT I NEED YOUR HELP.
I NEED YOU TO TAKE A MESSAGE TO YOUR *MOTHER.*

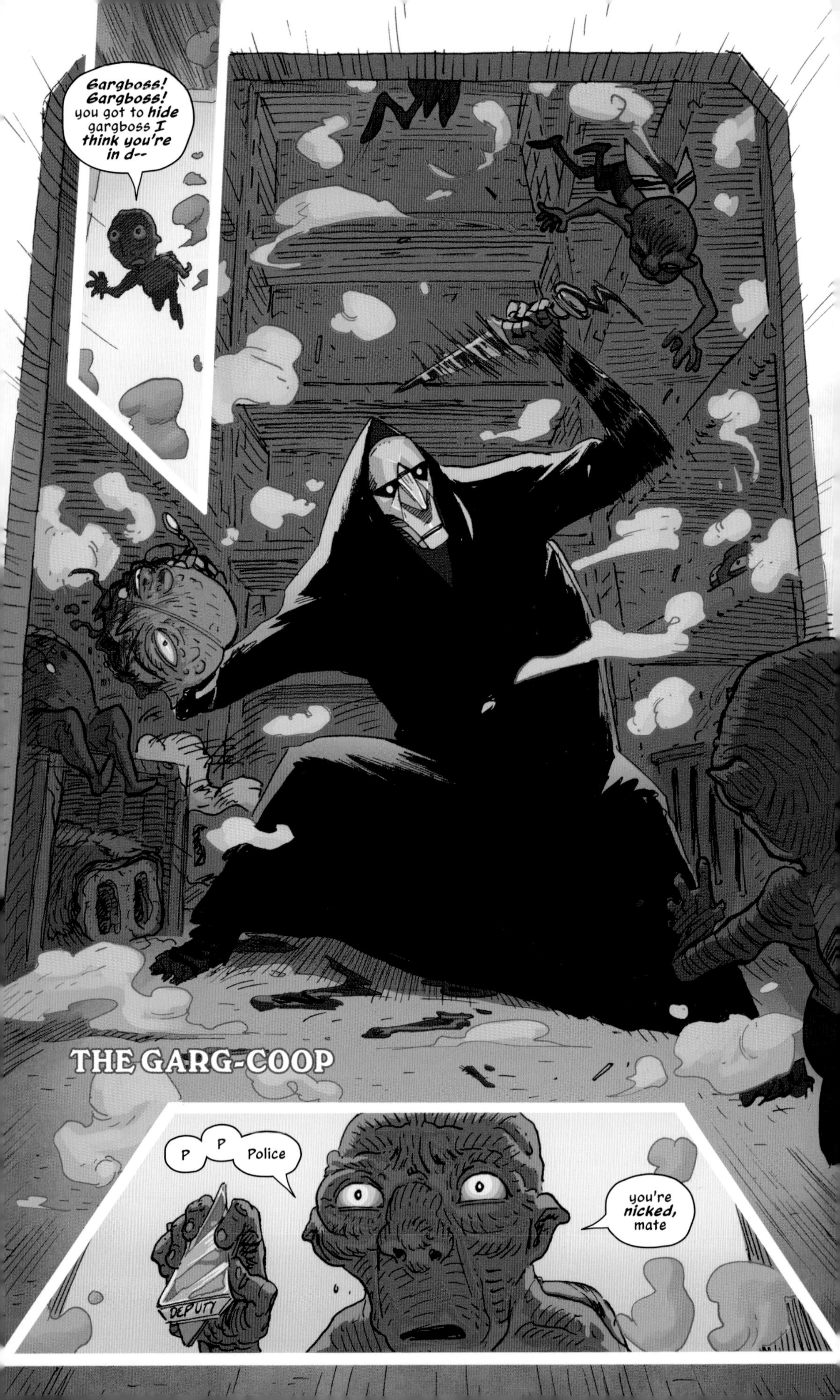
Gargboss! Gargboss! you got to *hide* gargboss *I think you're in d--*
THE GARG-COOP
P
P
Police
you're *nicked,* mate
DEPUTY

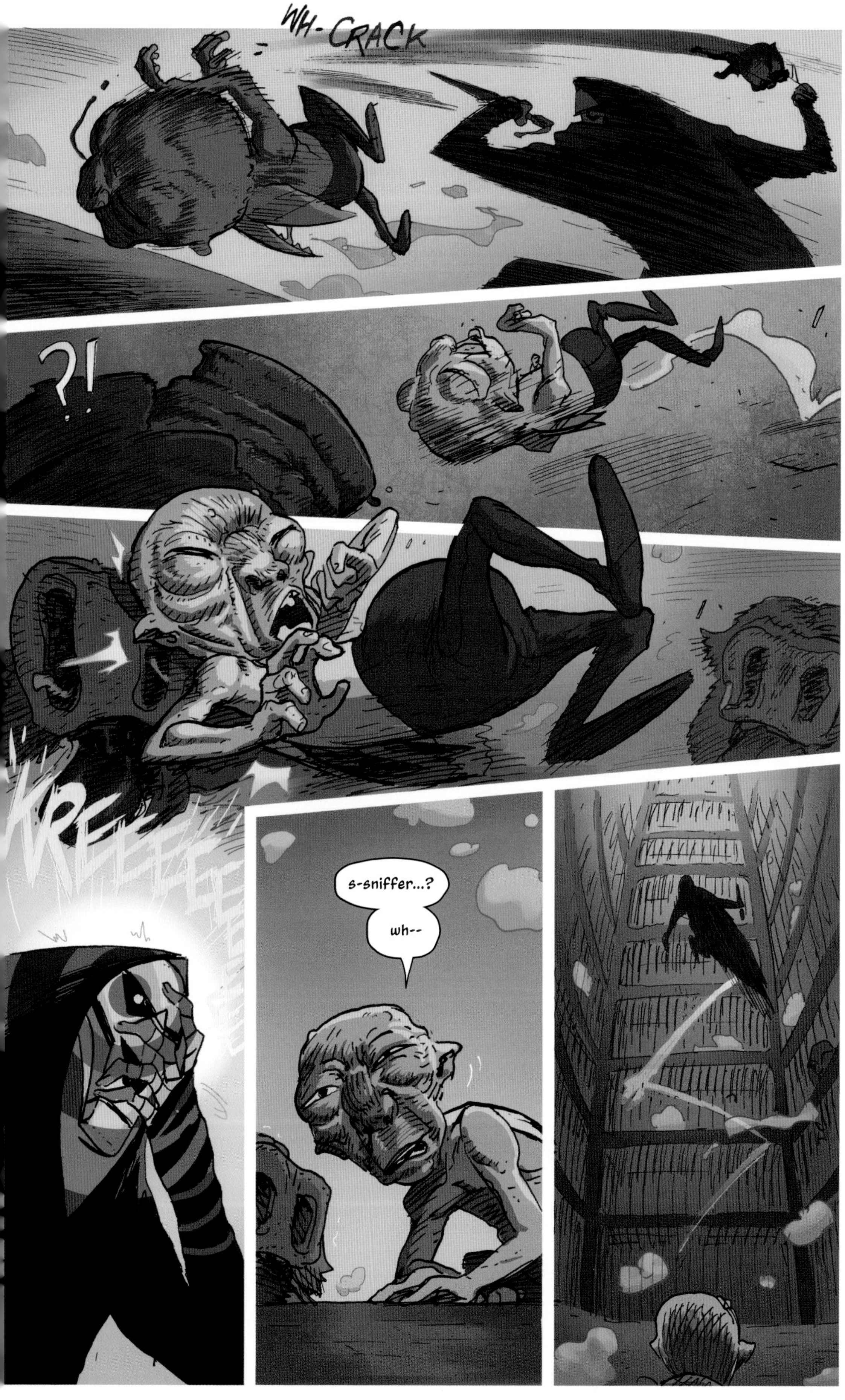
WH-CRACK
?!
KREEEEEEE
s-sniffer...?
wh--

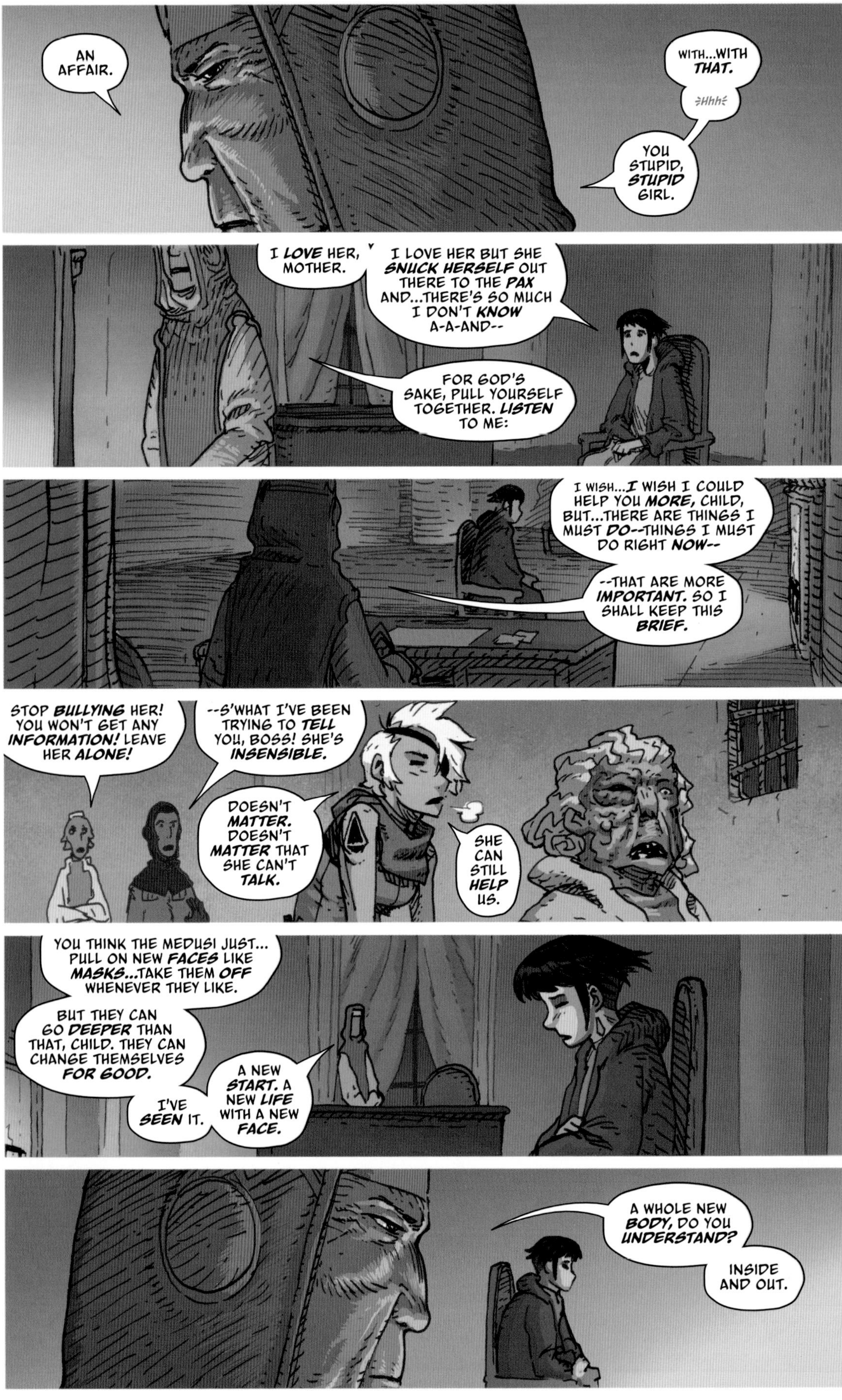
AN AFFAIR.
WITH...WITH THAT.
HHH
YOU STUPID, STUPID GIRL.
I LOVE HER, MOTHER.
I LOVE HER BUT SHE SNUCK HERSELF OUT THERE TO THE PAX AND...THERE'S SO MUCH I DON'T KNOW A-A-AND--
FOR GOD'S SAKE, PULL YOURSELF TOGETHER. LISTEN TO ME:
I WISH...I WISH I COULD HELP YOU MORE, CHILD, BUT...THERE ARE THINGS I MUST DO--THINGS I MUST DO RIGHT NOW--
--THAT ARE MORE IMPORTANT. SO I SHALL KEEP THIS BRIEF.
STOP BULLYING HER! YOU WON'T GET ANY INFORMATION! LEAVE HER ALONE!
--S'WHAT I'VE BEEN TRYING TO TELL YOU, BOSS! SHE'S INSENSIBLE.
DOESN'T MATTER. DOESN'T MATTER THAT SHE CAN'T TALK.
SHE CAN STILL HELP US.
YOU THINK THE MEDUSI JUST... PULL ON NEW FACES LIKE MASKS...TAKE THEM OFF WHENEVER THEY LIKE.
BUT THEY CAN GO DEEPER THAN THAT, CHILD. THEY CAN CHANGE THEMSELVES FOR GOOD.
I'VE SEEN IT.
A NEW START. A NEW LIFE WITH A NEW FACE.
A WHOLE NEW BODY, DO YOU UNDERSTAND?
INSIDE AND OUT.

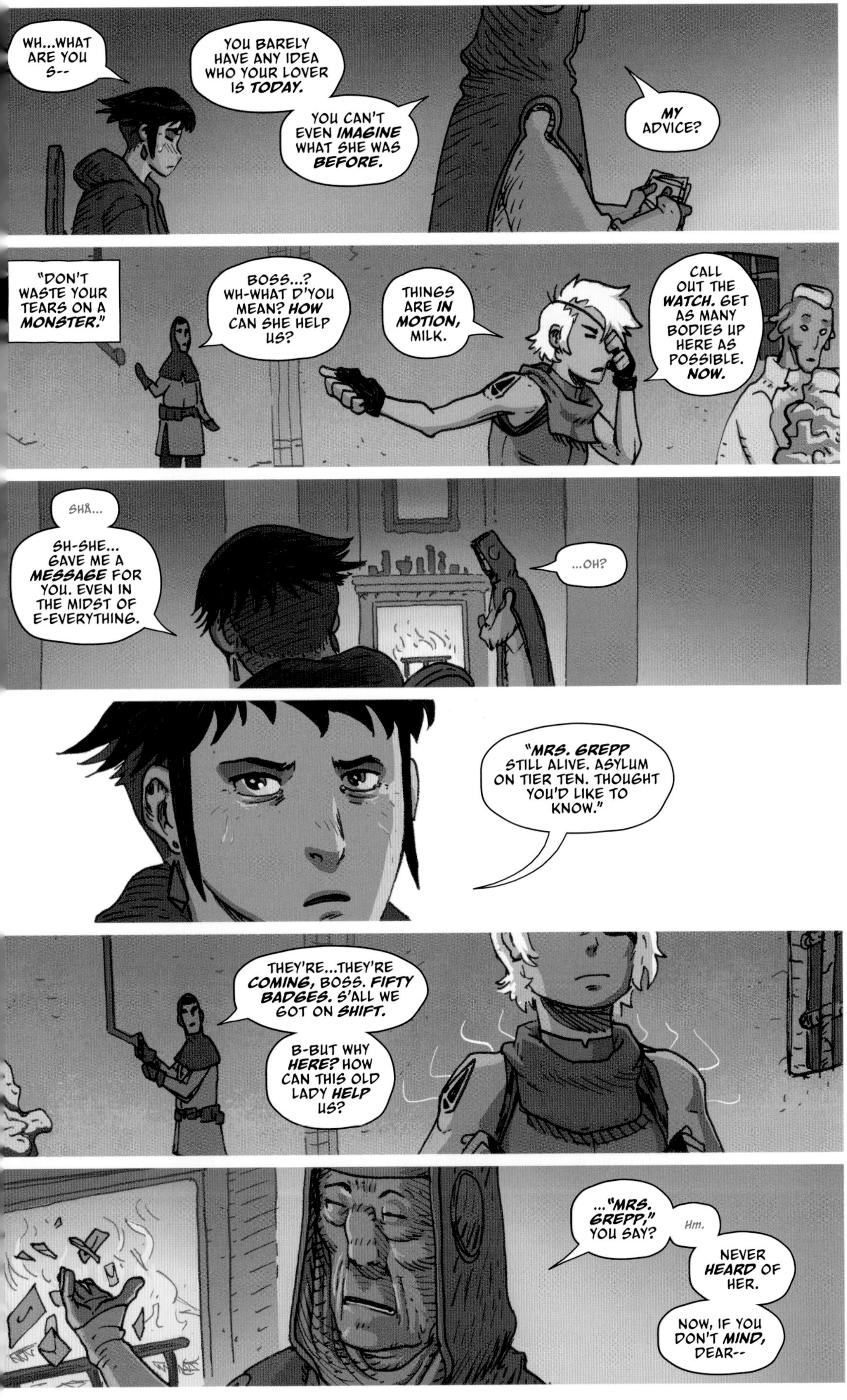
WH...WHAT ARE YOU S--
YOU BARELY HAVE ANY IDEA WHO YOUR LOVER IS TODAY.
YOU CAN'T EVEN IMAGINE WHAT SHE WAS BEFORE.
MY ADVICE?
"DON'T WASTE YOUR TEARS ON A MONSTER."
BOSS...? WH-WHAT D'YOU MEAN? HOW CAN SHE HELP US?
THINGS ARE IN MOTION, MILK.
CALL OUT THE WATCH. GET AS MANY BODIES UP HERE AS POSSIBLE. NOW.
SHH...
SH-SHE... GAVE ME A MESSAGE FOR YOU. EVEN IN THE MIDST OF E-EVERYTHING.
...OH?
"MRS. GREPP STILL ALIVE. ASYLUM ON TIER TEN. THOUGHT YOU'D LIKE TO KNOW."
THEY'RE...THEY'RE COMING, BOSS. FIFTY BADGES. S'ALL WE GOT ON SHIFT.
B-BUT WHY HERE? HOW CAN THIS OLD LADY HELP US?
..."MRS. GREPP," YOU SAY?
Hm.
NEVER HEARD OF HER.
NOW, IF YOU DON'T MIND, DEAR--

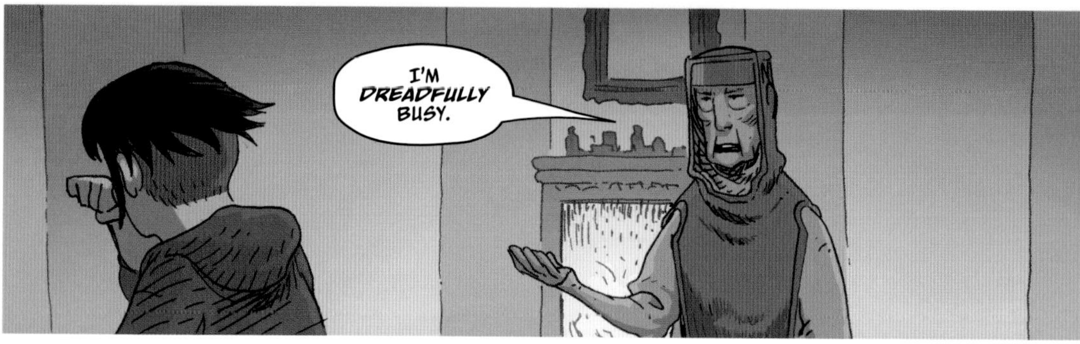
I'M *DREADFULLY* BUSY.

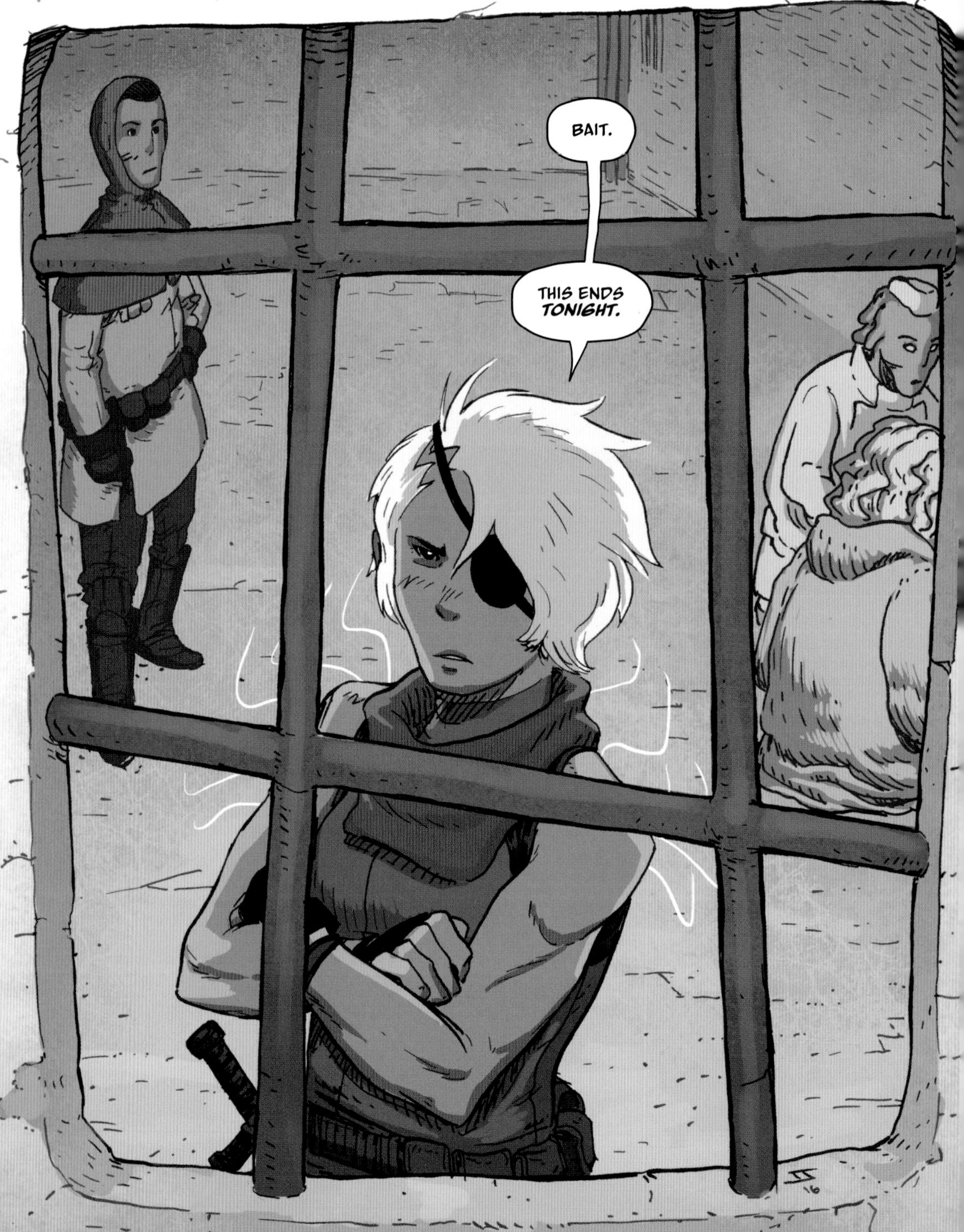
BAIT.
THIS ENDS *TONIGHT.*

ISSUE #7 COVER BY **JEFF STOKELY**
WITH COLORS BY **TAMRA BONVILLAIN**

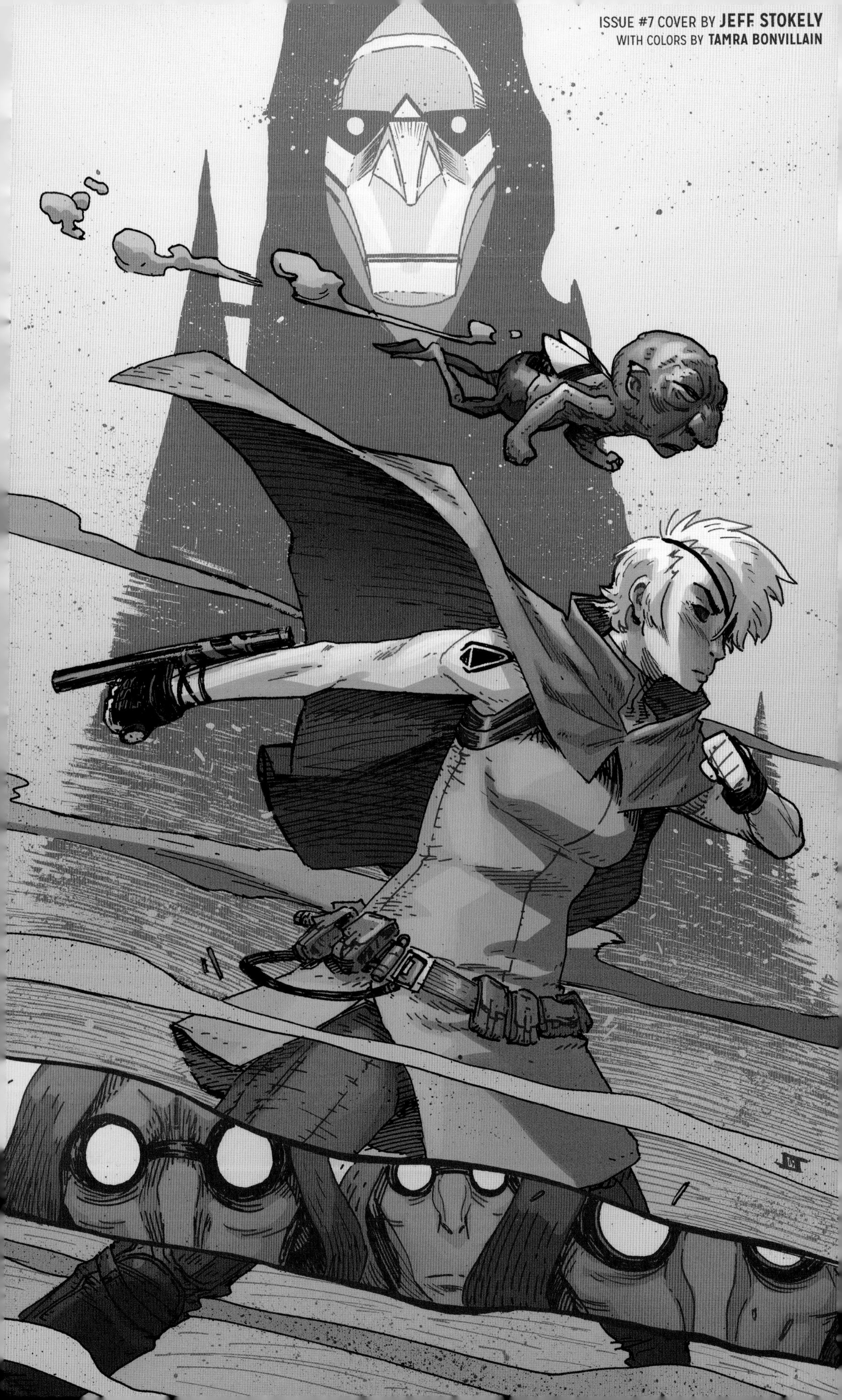

CHAPTER
EIGHT

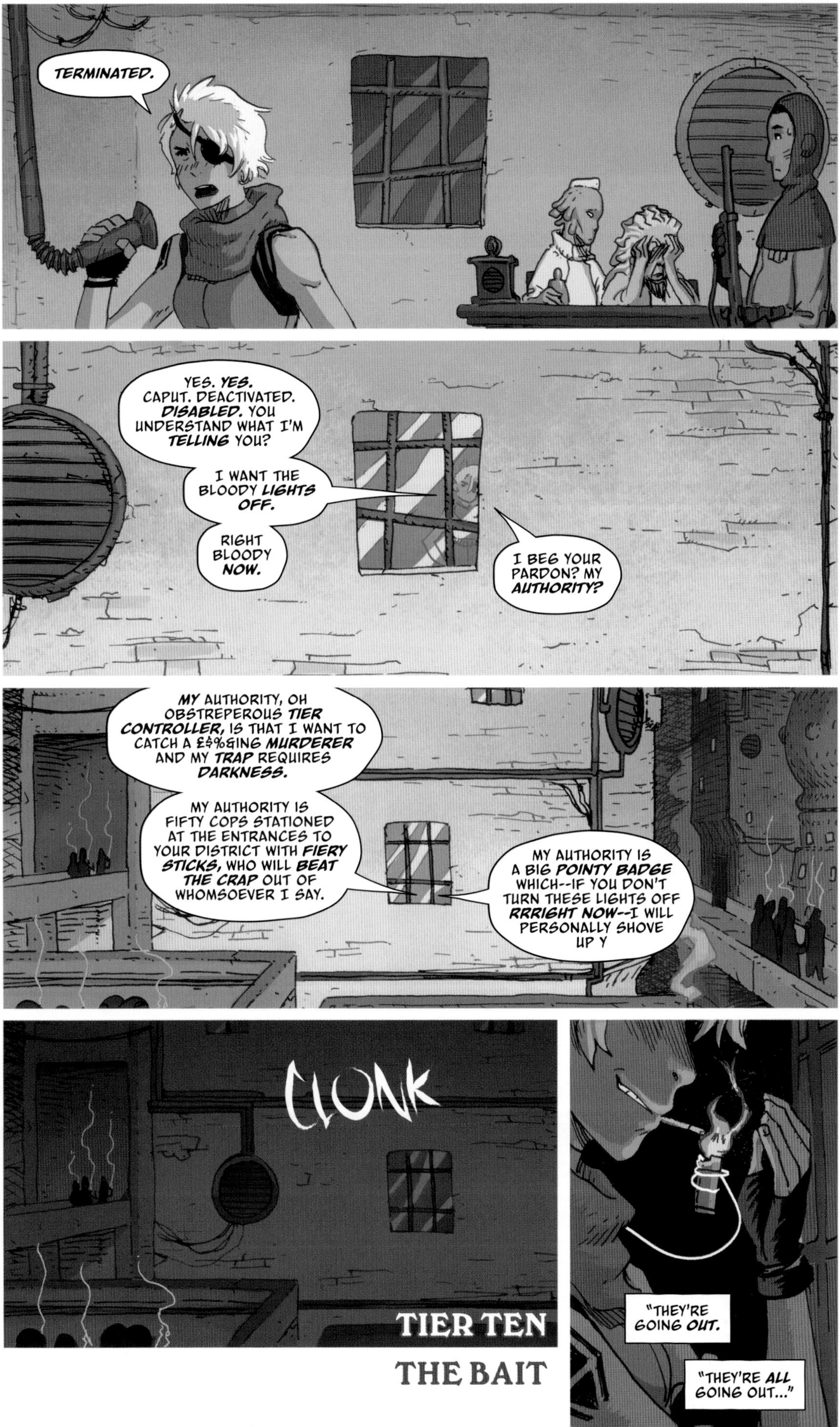
TERMINATED.
YES. YES. CAPUT. DEACTIVATED. DISABLED. YOU UNDERSTAND WHAT I'M TELLING YOU?
I WANT THE BLOODY LIGHTS OFF.
RIGHT BLOODY NOW.
I BEG YOUR PARDON? MY AUTHORITY?
MY AUTHORITY, OH OBSTREPEROUS TIER CONTROLLER, IS THAT I WANT TO CATCH A £$%&ING MURDERER AND MY TRAP REQUIRES DARKNESS.
MY AUTHORITY IS FIFTY COPS STATIONED AT THE ENTRANCES TO YOUR DISTRICT WITH FIERY STICKS, WHO WILL BEAT THE CRAP OUT OF WHOMSOEVER I SAY.
MY AUTHORITY IS A BIG POINTY BADGE WHICH--IF YOU DON'T TURN THESE LIGHTS OFF RRRIGHT NOW--I WILL PERSONALLY SHOVE UP Y
CLONK
TIER TEN
THE BAIT
"THEY'RE GOING OUT.
"THEY'RE ALL GOING OUT..."

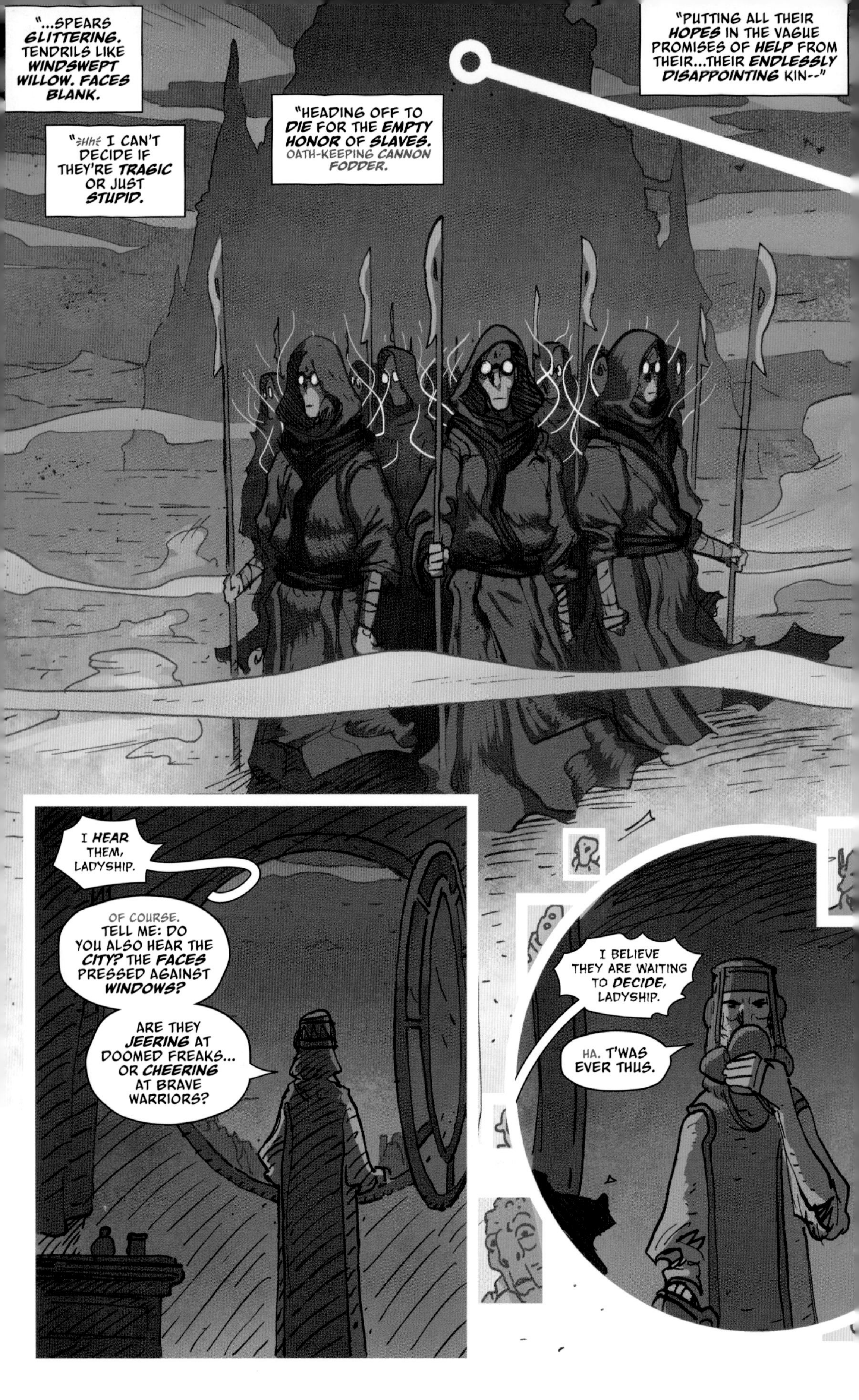
"...SPEARS GLITTERING. TENDRILS LIKE WINDSWEPT WILLOW. FACES BLANK.
"HHH I CAN'T DECIDE IF THEY'RE TRAGIC OR JUST STUPID.
"HEADING OFF TO DIE FOR THE EMPTY HONOR OF SLAVES. OATH-KEEPING CANNON FODDER.
"PUTTING ALL THEIR HOPES IN THE VAGUE PROMISES OF HELP FROM THEIR...THEIR ENDLESSLY DISAPPOINTING KIN--"
I HEAR THEM, LADYSHIP.
OF COURSE. TELL ME: DO YOU ALSO HEAR THE CITY? THE FACES PRESSED AGAINST WINDOWS?
ARE THEY JEERING AT DOOMED FREAKS... OR CHEERING AT BRAVE WARRIORS?
I BELIEVE THEY ARE WAITING TO DECIDE, LADYSHIP.
HA. T'WAS EVER THUS.

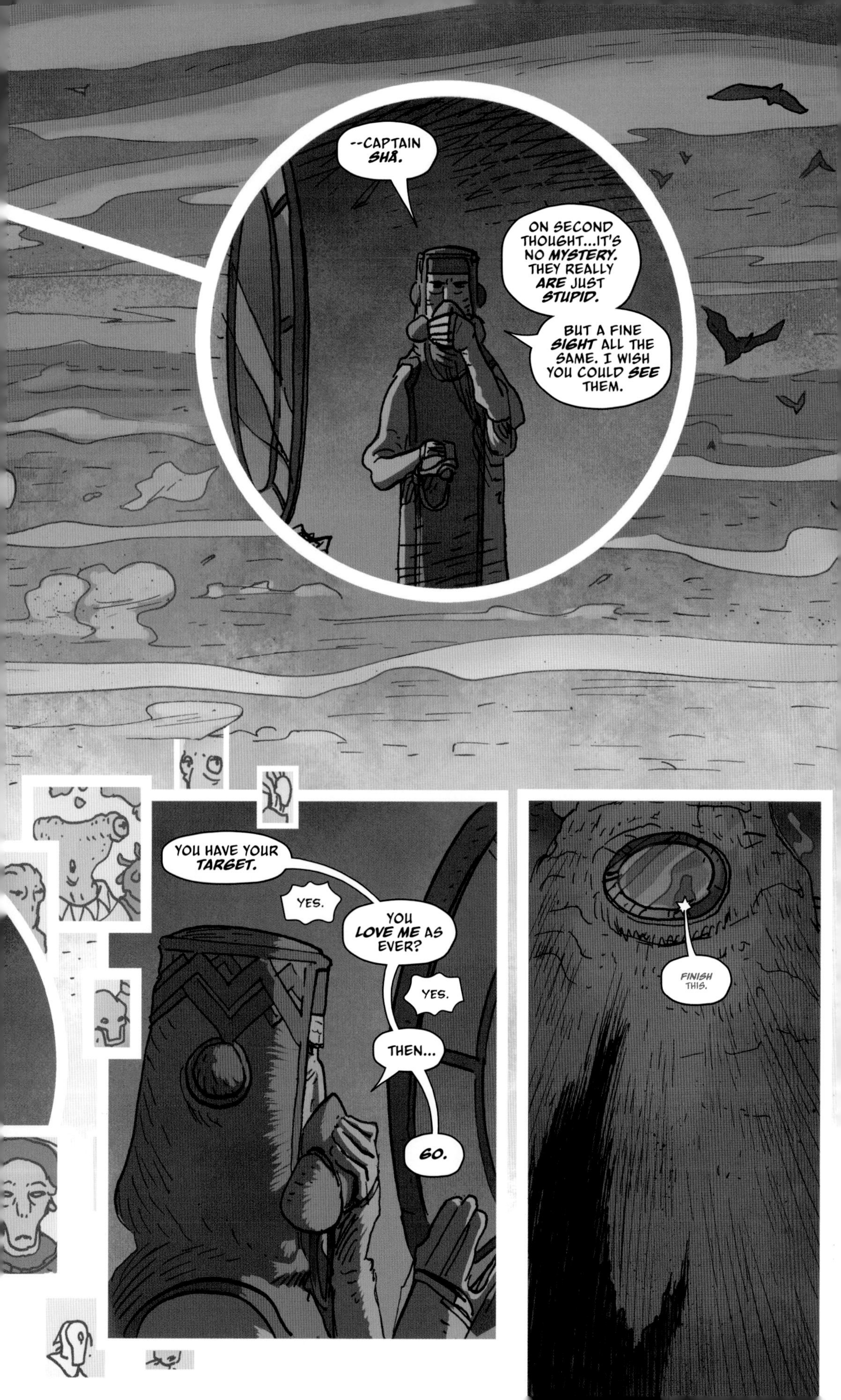
--CAPTAIN SHĀ.
ON SECOND THOUGHT...IT'S NO MYSTERY. THEY REALLY ARE JUST STUPID.
BUT A FINE SIGHT ALL THE SAME. I WISH YOU COULD SEE THEM.
YOU HAVE YOUR TARGET.
YES.
YOU LOVE ME AS EVER?
YES.
THEN...
GO.
FINISH THIS.

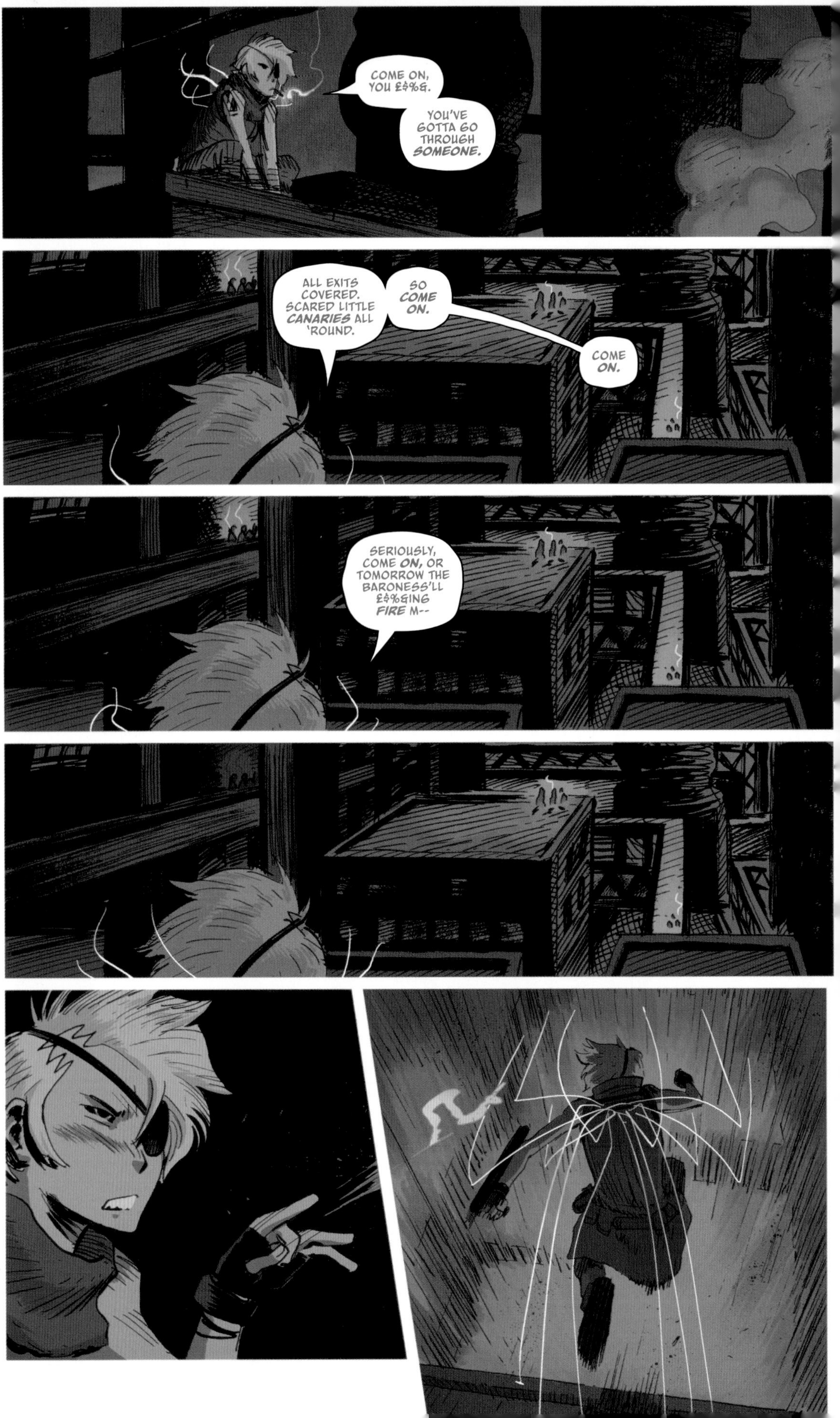
COME ON, YOU £$%&.
YOU'VE GOTTA GO THROUGH SOMEONE.
ALL EXITS COVERED. SCARED LITTLE CANARIES ALL 'ROUND.
SO COME ON.
COME ON.
SERIOUSLY, COME ON, OR TOMORROW THE BARONESS'LL £$%&ING FIRE M--

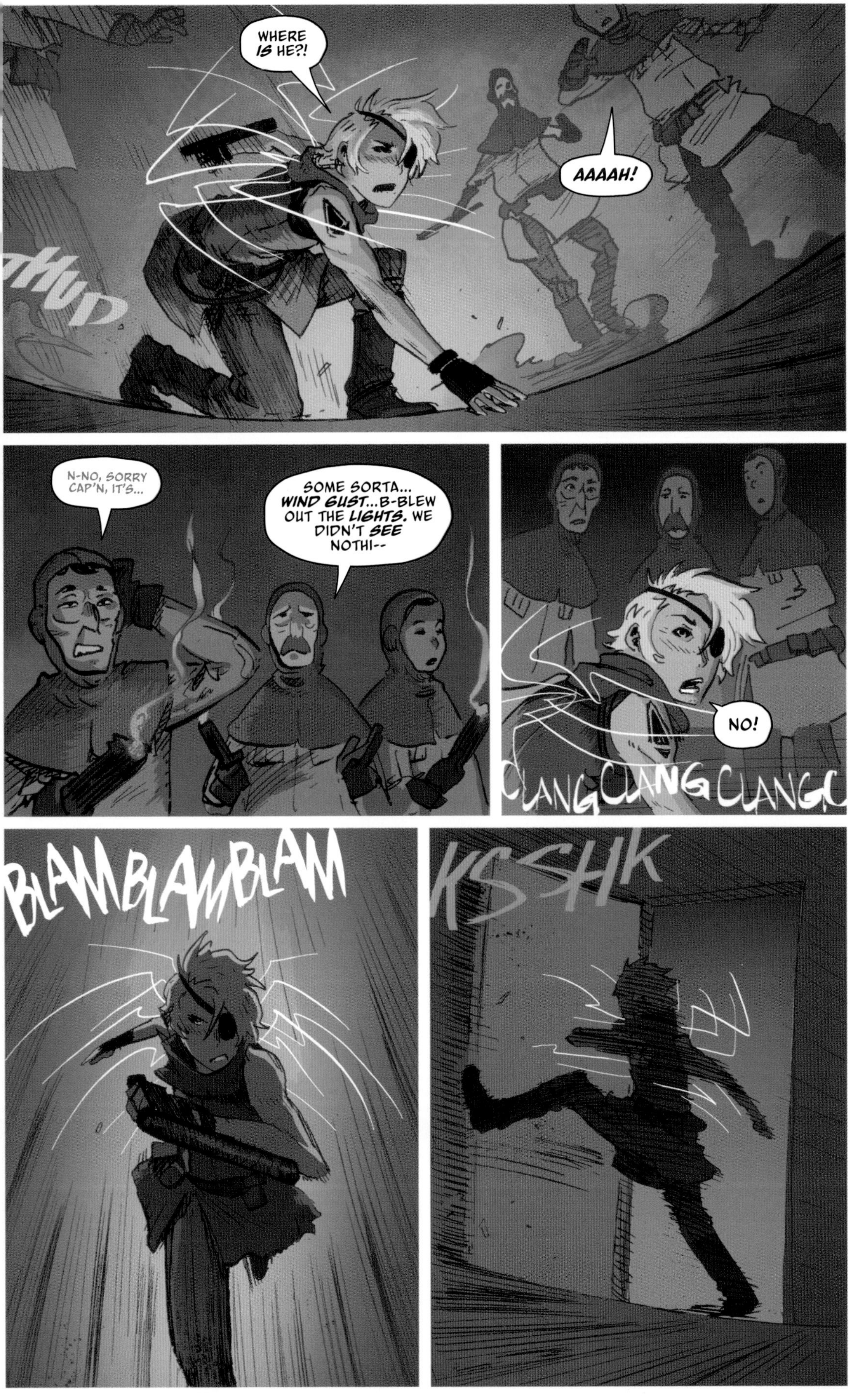
WHERE IS HE?!
AAAAH!
THUD
N-NO, SORRY CAP'N, IT'S...
SOME SORTA... WIND GUST...B-BLEW OUT THE LIGHTS. WE DIDN'T SEE NOTHI--
NO!
CLANG CLANG CLANG
BLAMBLAMBLAM
KSSHK

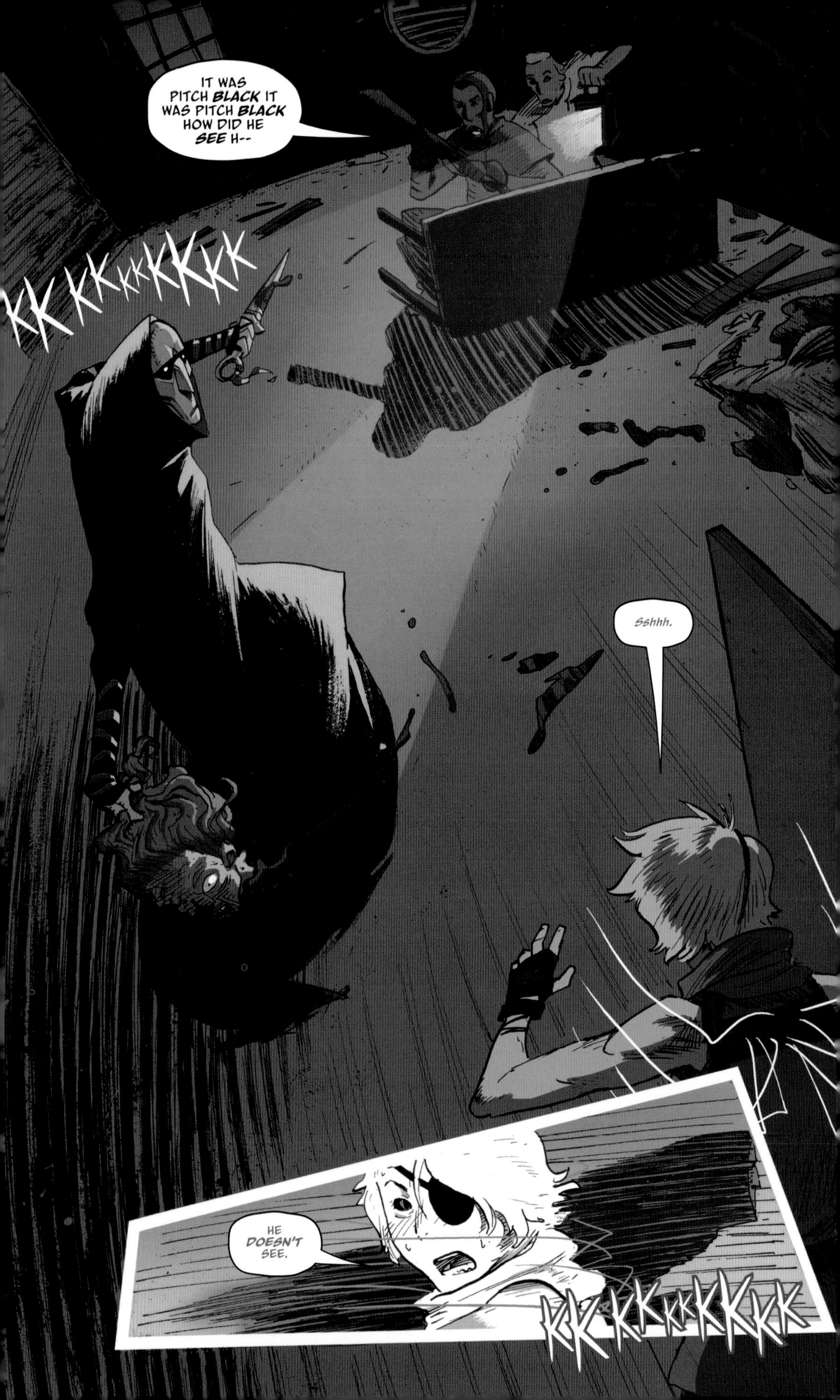
IT WAS PITCH BLACK IT WAS PITCH BLACK HOW DID HE SEE H--
KKKKKKKKKKK
Sshhh.
HE DOESN'T SEE.
KKKKKKKKKKK

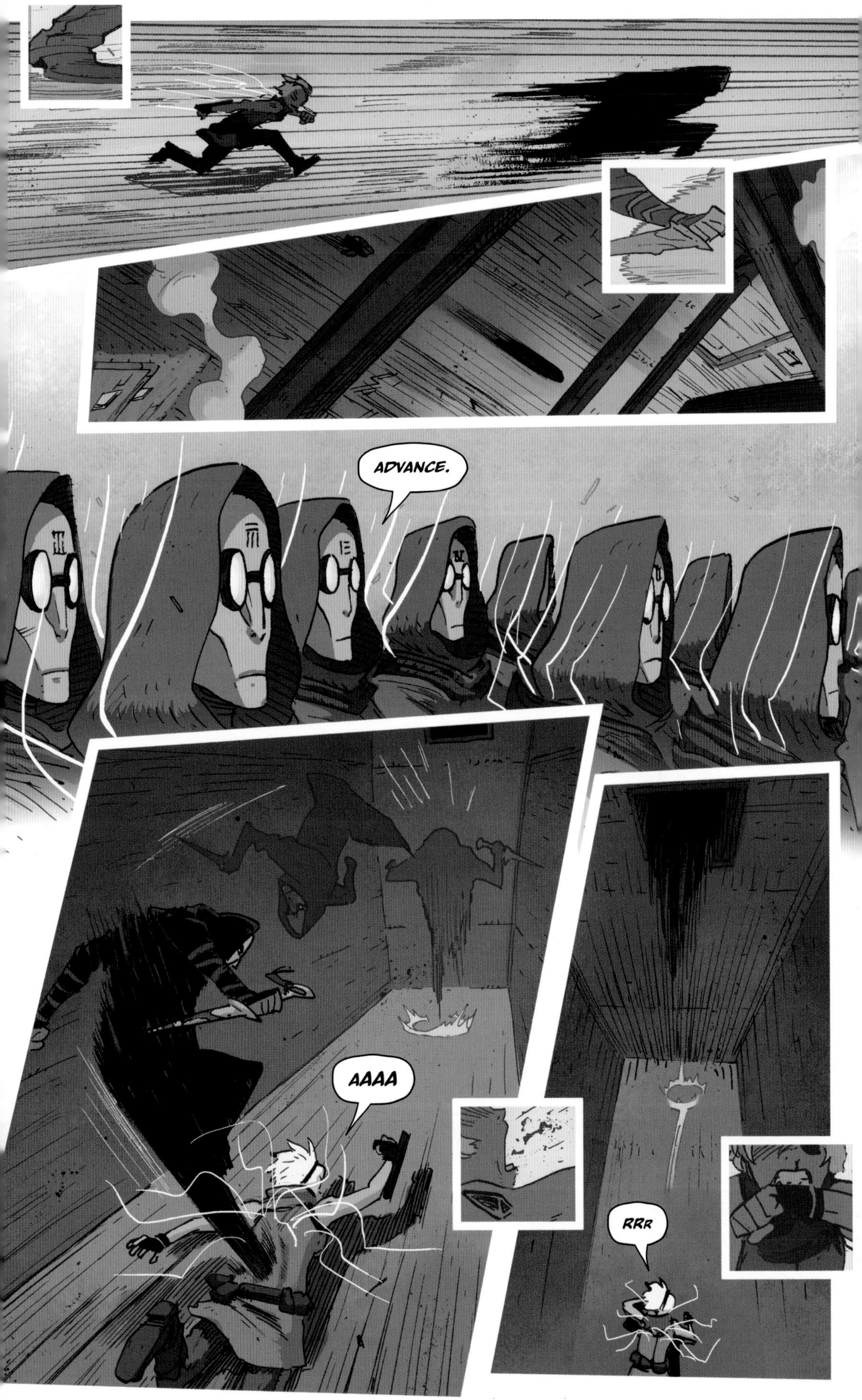
ADVANCE.
AAAA
RRR

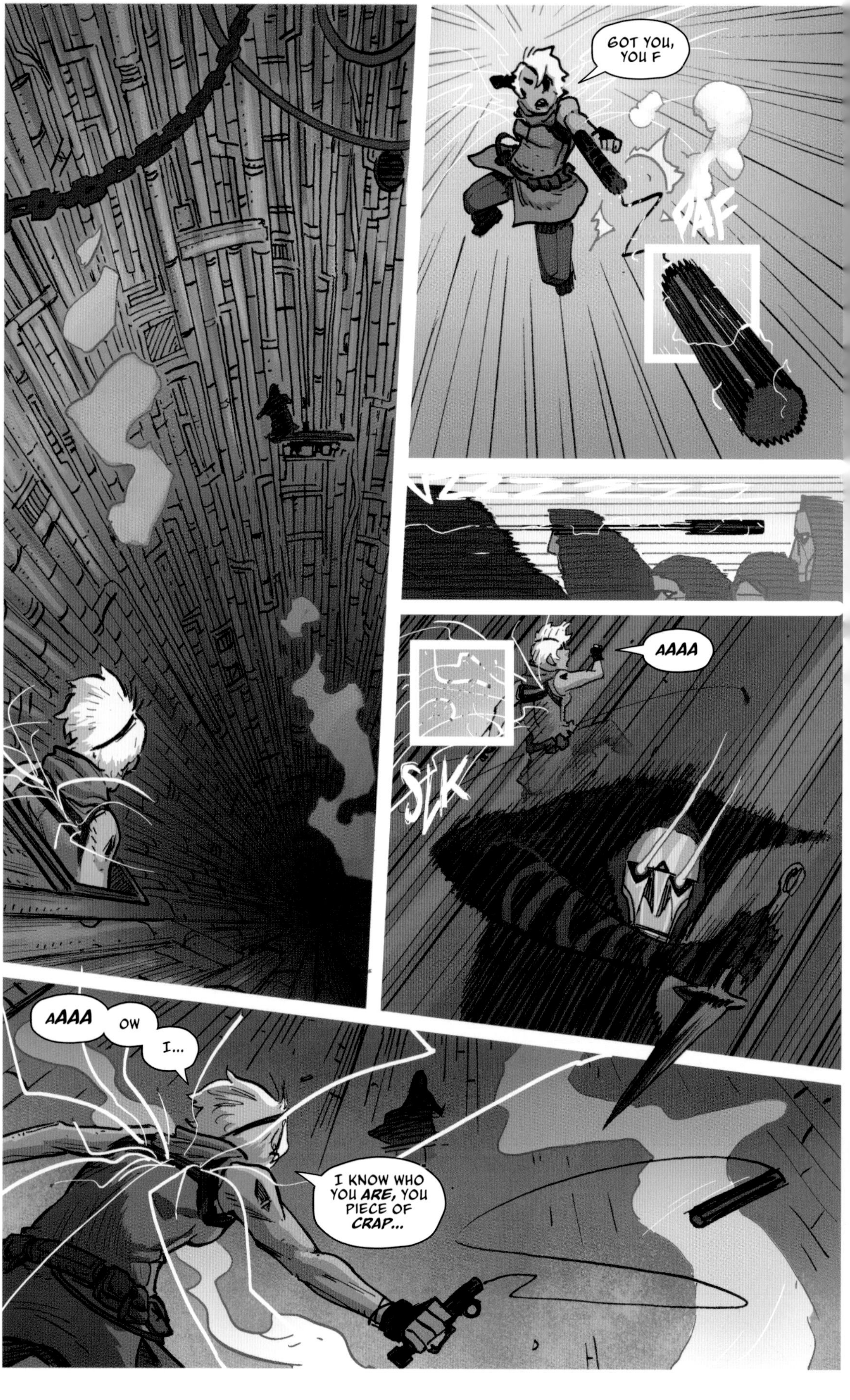
GOT YOU, YOU F
DAF
AAAA
SLK
AAAA
OW
I...
I KNOW WHO YOU ARE, YOU PIECE OF CRAP...

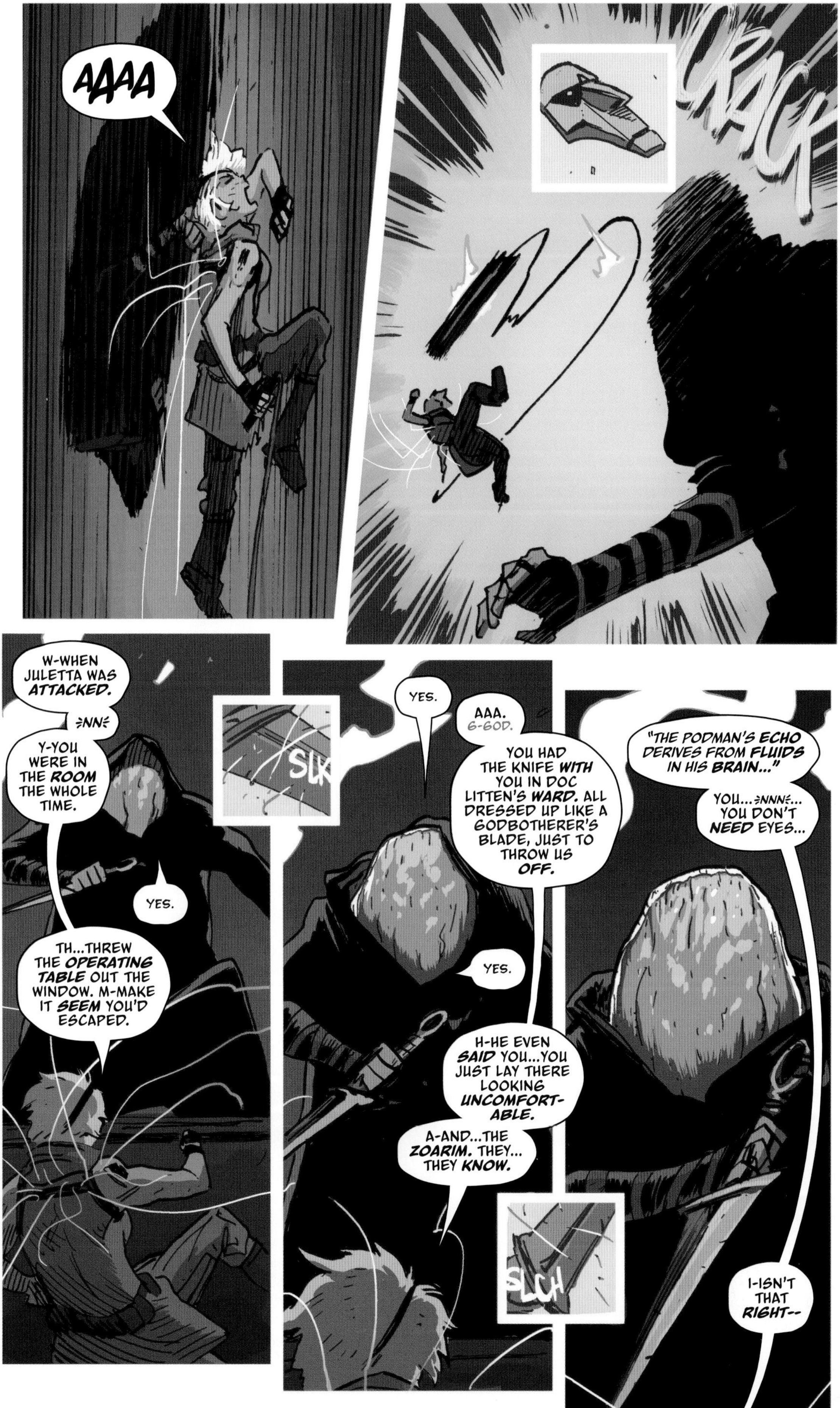

AAAA
CRACK
W-WHEN JULETTA WAS ATTACKED.
NN
Y-YOU WERE IN THE ROOM THE WHOLE TIME.
YES.
TH...THREW THE OPERATING TABLE OUT THE WINDOW. M-MAKE IT SEEM YOU'D ESCAPED.
SLK
YES.
AAA. G-GOD.
YOU HAD THE KNIFE WITH YOU IN DOC LITTEN'S WARD. ALL DRESSED UP LIKE A GODBOTHERER'S BLADE, JUST TO THROW US OFF.
YES.
H-HE EVEN SAID YOU...YOU JUST LAY THERE LOOKING UNCOMFORT-ABLE.
A-AND...THE ZOARIM. THEY... THEY KNOW.
SLCH
"THE PODMAN'S ECHO DERIVES FROM FLUIDS IN HIS BRAIN..."
YOU...NNN... YOU DON'T NEED EYES...
I-ISN'T THAT RIGHT--

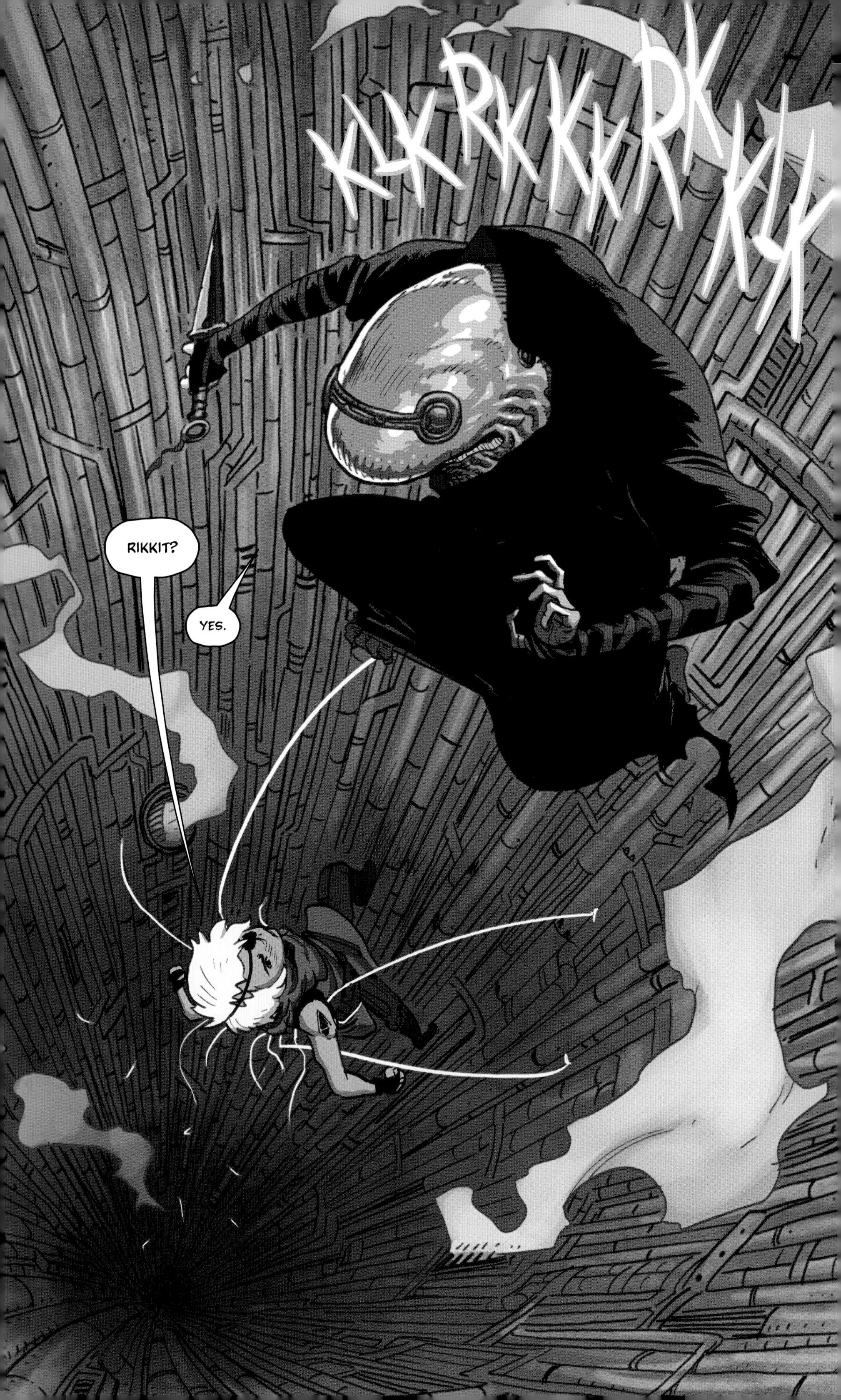
KLK RK KK RK KLK
RIKKIT?
YES.

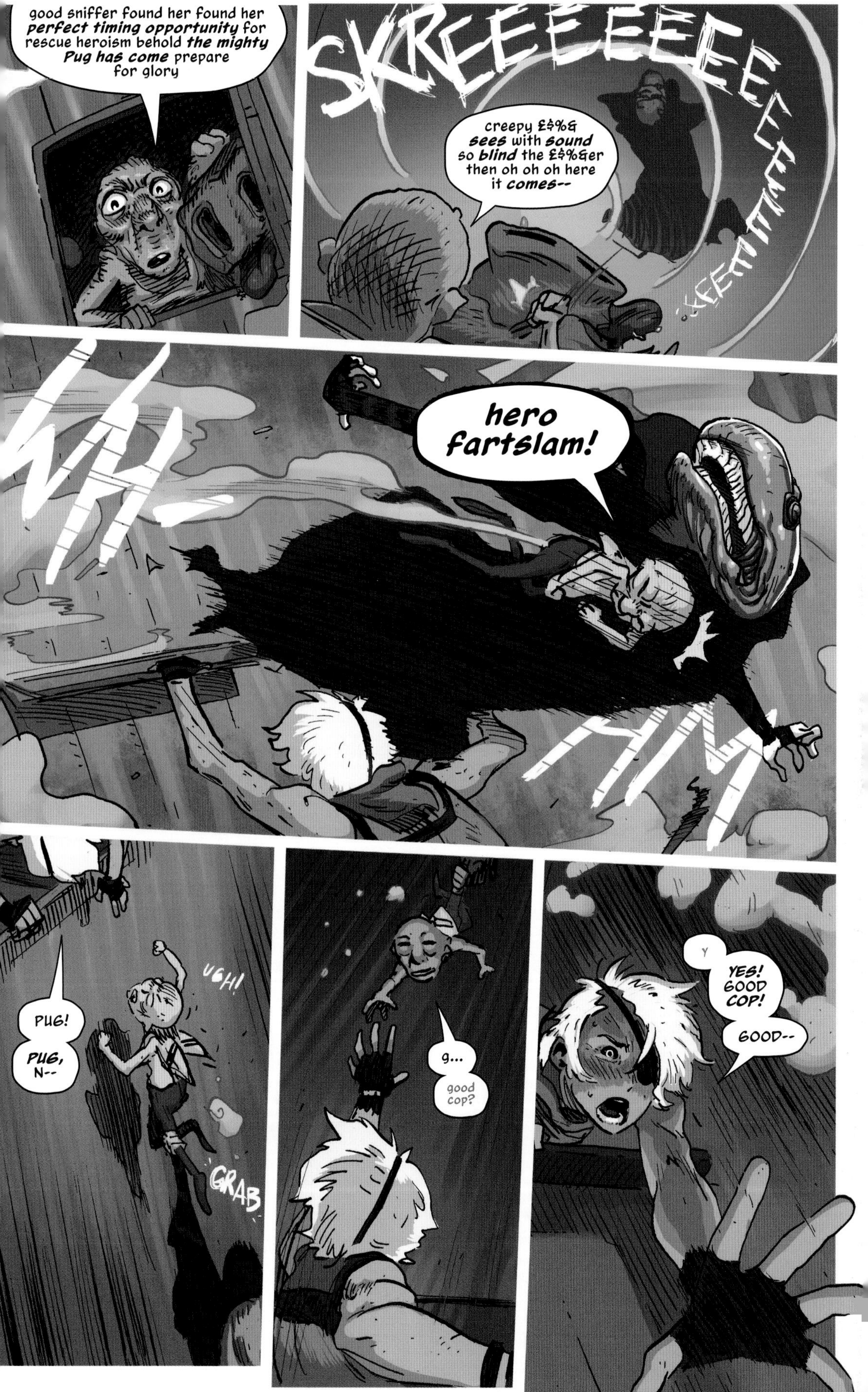
good sniffer found her found her *perfect timing opportunity* for rescue heroism behold *the mighty Pug has come* prepare for glory
creepy £$%& *sees* with *sound* so *blind* the £$%&er then oh oh oh here it *comes--*
hero fartslam!
PUG!
PUG, N--
UGH!
GRAB
g...
good cop?
Y
YES! GOOD COP!
GOOD--

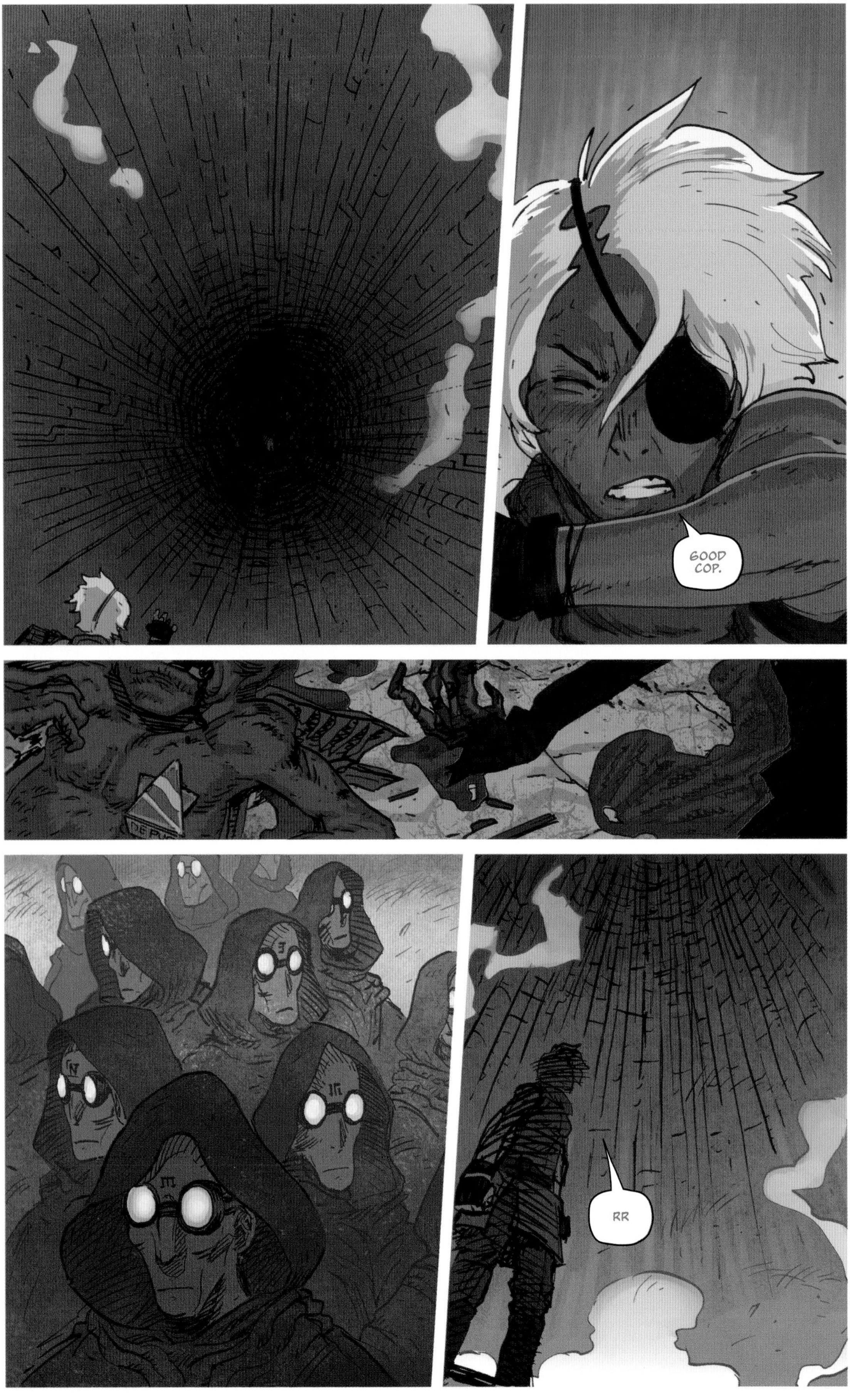
GOOD COP.
RR

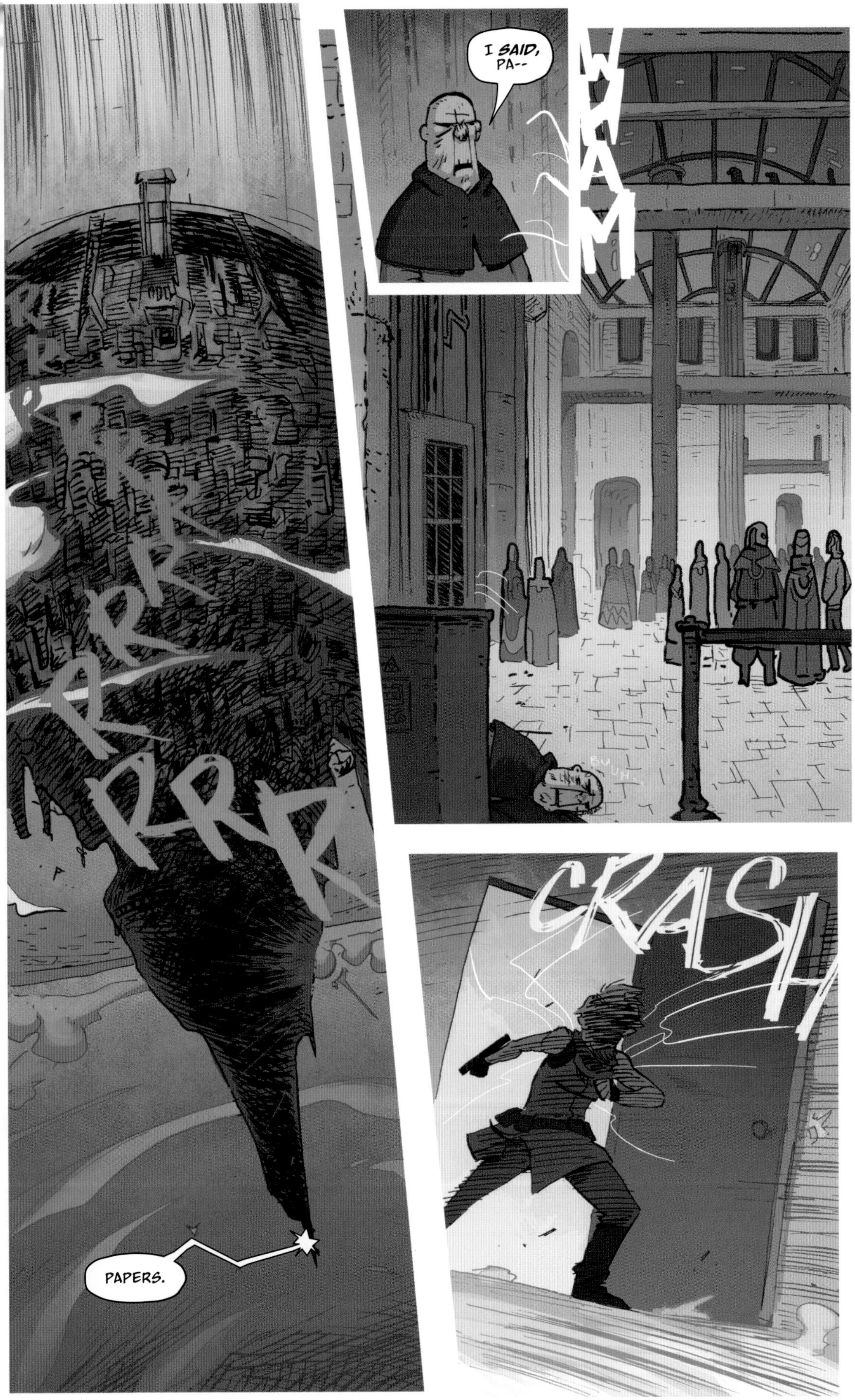

KRRRRRRR
PAPERS.
I SAID, PA--
WHAM
BUUH--
CRASH

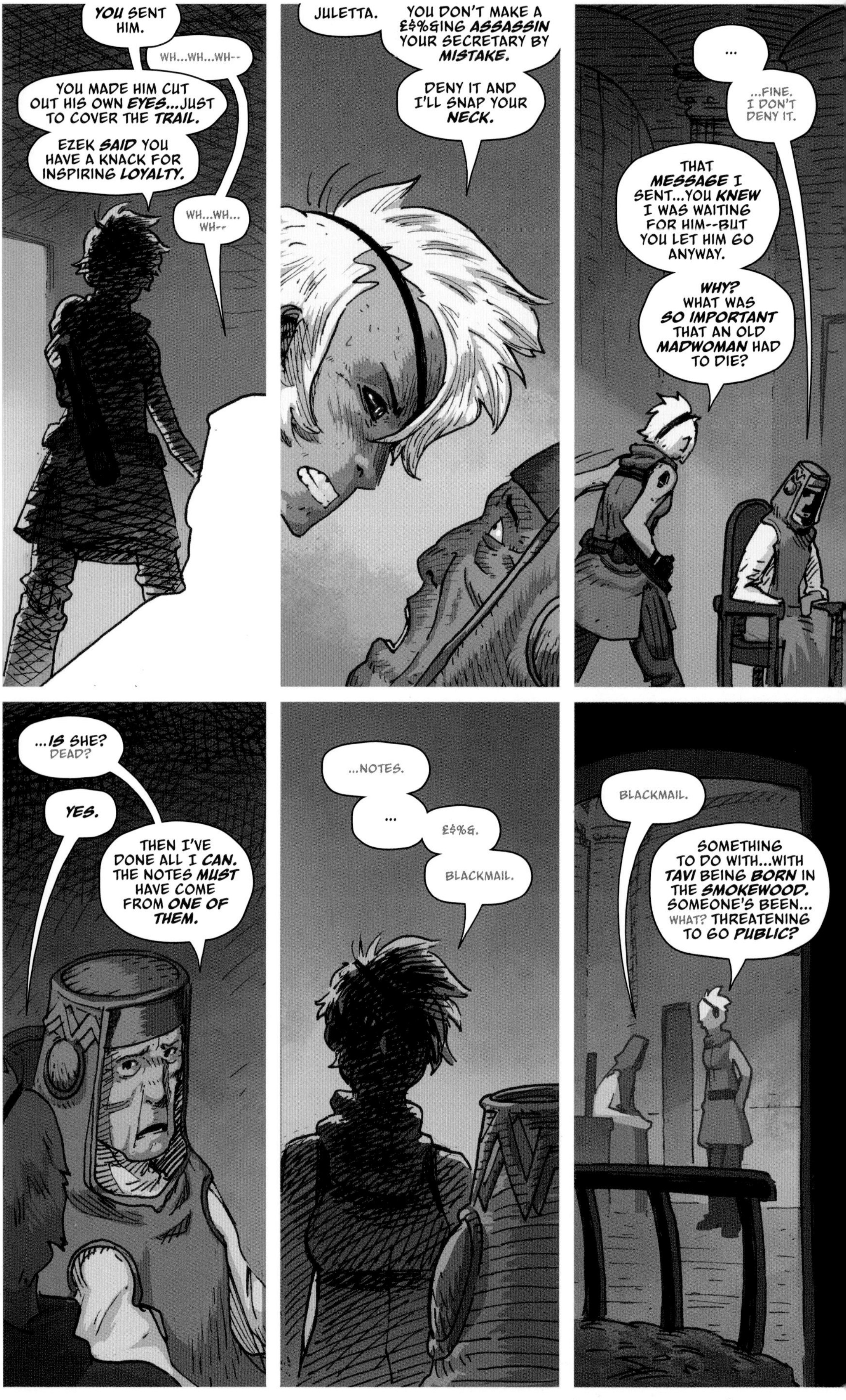
YOU SENT HIM.
WH...WH...WH--
YOU MADE HIM CUT OUT HIS OWN EYES...JUST TO COVER THE TRAIL.
EZEK SAID YOU HAVE A KNACK FOR INSPIRING LOYALTY.
WH...WH... WH--
JULETTA.
YOU DON'T MAKE A £$%&ING ASSASSIN YOUR SECRETARY BY MISTAKE.
DENY IT AND I'LL SNAP YOUR NECK.
...
...FINE. I DON'T DENY IT.
THAT MESSAGE I SENT...YOU KNEW I WAS WAITING FOR HIM--BUT YOU LET HIM GO ANYWAY.
WHY? WHAT WAS SO IMPORTANT THAT AN OLD MADWOMAN HAD TO DIE?
...IS SHE? DEAD?
YES.
THEN I'VE DONE ALL I CAN. THE NOTES MUST HAVE COME FROM ONE OF THEM.
...NOTES.
...
£$%&.
BLACKMAIL.
BLACKMAIL.
SOMETHING TO DO WITH...WITH TAVI BEING BORN IN THE SMOKEWOOD. SOMEONE'S BEEN... WHAT? THREATENING TO GO PUBLIC?

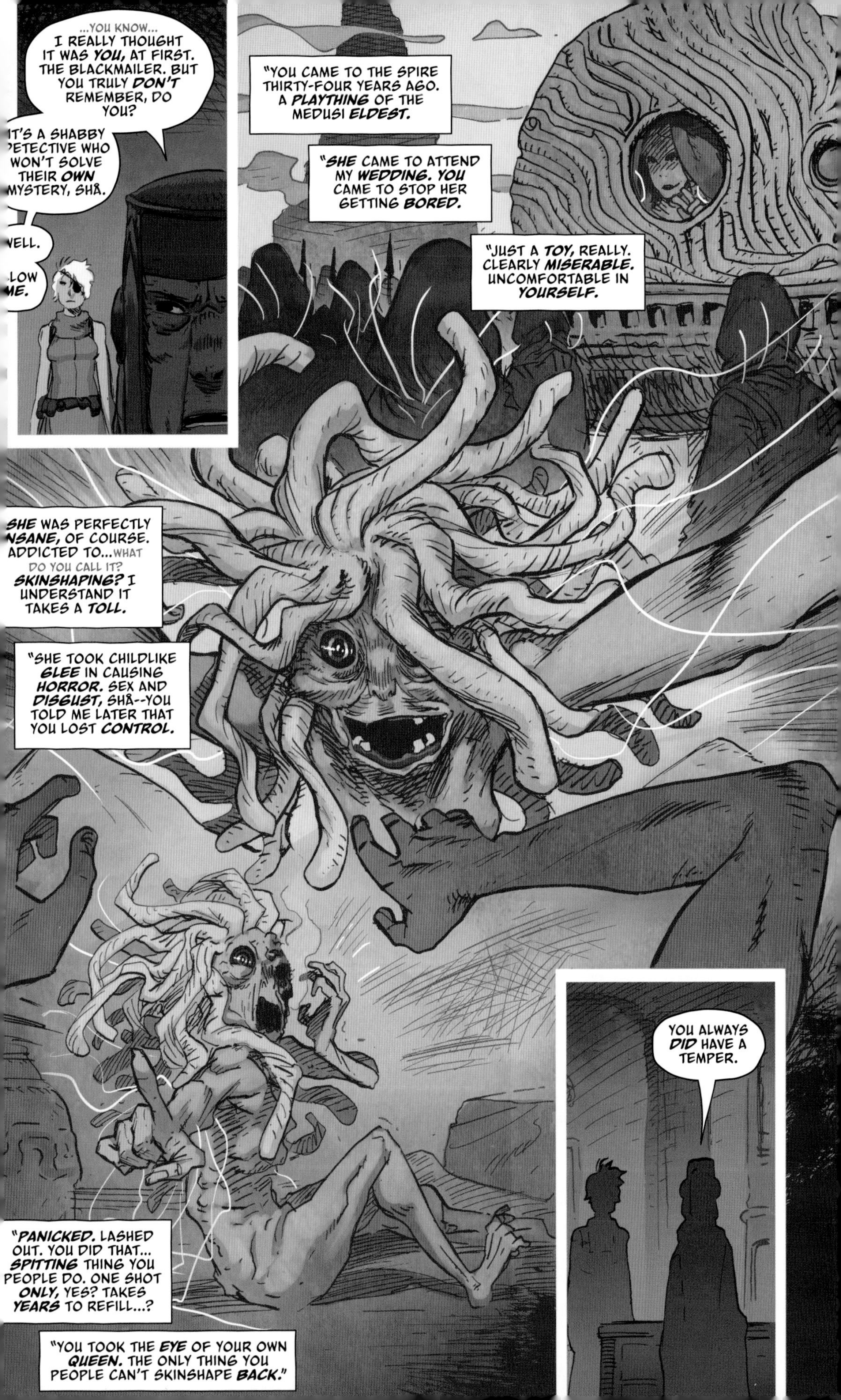

...YOU KNOW... I REALLY THOUGHT IT WAS *YOU*, AT FIRST. THE BLACKMAILER. BUT YOU TRULY *DON'T* REMEMBER, DO YOU?
IT'S A SHABBY ETECTIVE WHO WON'T SOLVE THEIR *OWN* MYSTERY, SHÅ.
VELL.
LOW *ME.*
"YOU CAME TO THE SPIRE THIRTY-FOUR YEARS AGO. A *PLAYTHING* OF THE MEDUSI *ELDEST*.
"*SHE* CAME TO ATTEND MY *WEDDING*. *YOU* CAME TO STOP HER GETTING *BORED*.
"JUST A *TOY*, REALLY. CLEARLY *MISERABLE*. UNCOMFORTABLE IN *YOURSELF*.
SHE WAS PERFECTLY NSANE, OF COURSE. ADDICTED TO...WHAT DO YOU CALL IT? *SKINSHAPING?* I UNDERSTAND IT TAKES A *TOLL*.
"SHE TOOK CHILDLIKE *GLEE* IN CAUSING *HORROR*. SEX AND *DISGUST*, SHÅ--YOU TOLD ME LATER THAT YOU LOST *CONTROL*.
"*PANICKED*. LASHED OUT. YOU DID THAT... *SPITTING* THING YOU PEOPLE DO. ONE SHOT *ONLY*, YES? TAKES *YEARS* TO REFILL...?
"YOU TOOK THE *EYE* OF YOUR OWN *QUEEN*. THE ONLY THING YOU PEOPLE CAN'T SKINSHAPE *BACK*."
YOU ALWAYS *DID* HAVE A TEMPER.

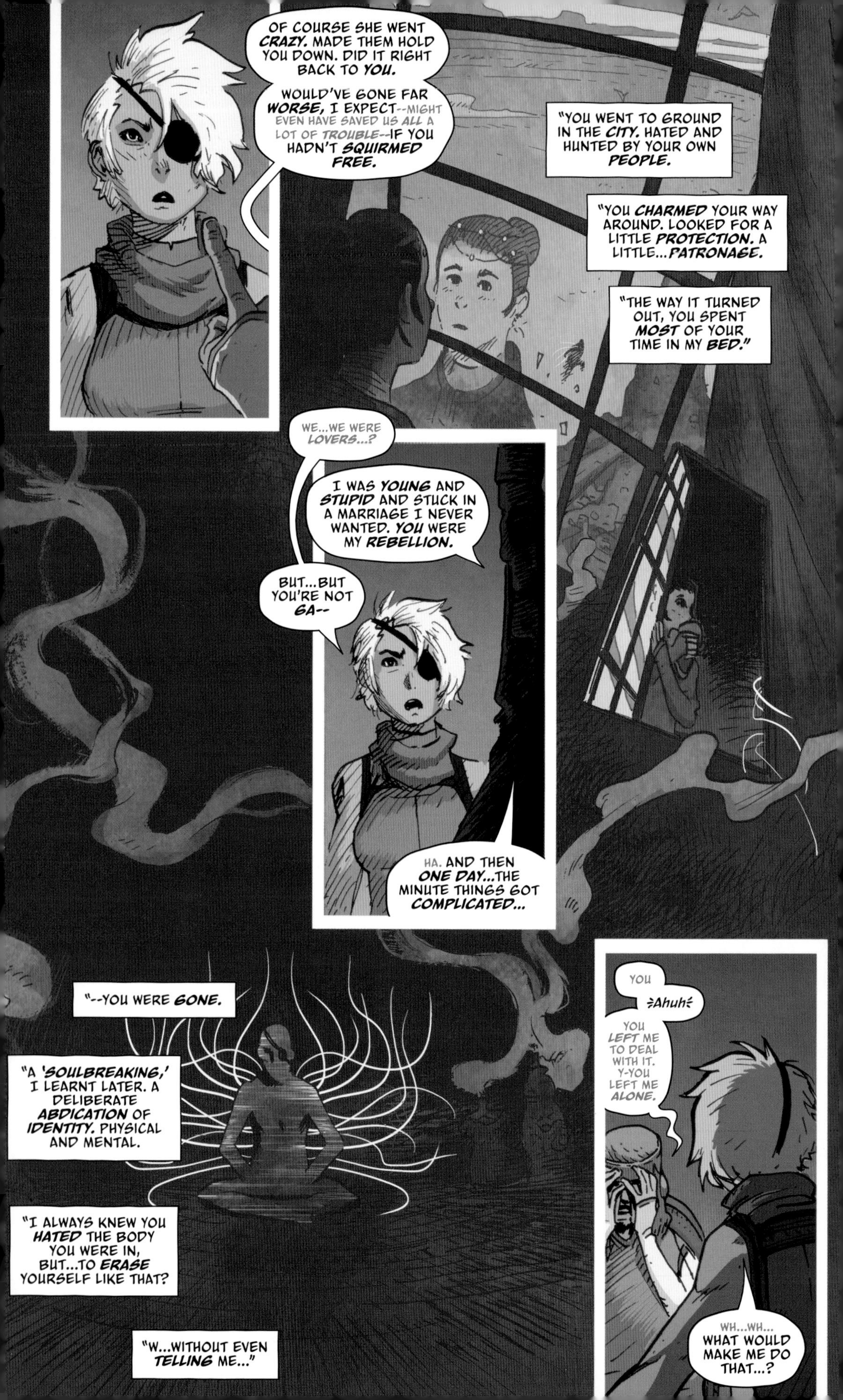
OF COURSE SHE WENT CRAZY. MADE THEM HOLD YOU DOWN. DID IT RIGHT BACK TO YOU.
WOULD'VE GONE FAR WORSE, I EXPECT--MIGHT EVEN HAVE SAVED US ALL A LOT OF TROUBLE--IF YOU HADN'T SQUIRMED FREE.
"YOU WENT TO GROUND IN THE CITY. HATED AND HUNTED BY YOUR OWN PEOPLE.
"YOU CHARMED YOUR WAY AROUND. LOOKED FOR A LITTLE PROTECTION. A LITTLE...PATRONAGE.
"THE WAY IT TURNED OUT, YOU SPENT MOST OF YOUR TIME IN MY BED."
WE...WE WERE LOVERS...?
I WAS YOUNG AND STUPID AND STUCK IN A MARRIAGE I NEVER WANTED. YOU WERE MY REBELLION.
BUT...BUT YOU'RE NOT GA--
HA. AND THEN ONE DAY...THE MINUTE THINGS GOT COMPLICATED...
"--YOU WERE GONE.
"A 'SOULBREAKING,' I LEARNT LATER. A DELIBERATE ABDICATION OF IDENTITY. PHYSICAL AND MENTAL.
"I ALWAYS KNEW YOU HATED THE BODY YOU WERE IN, BUT...TO ERASE YOURSELF LIKE THAT?
"W...WITHOUT EVEN TELLING ME..."
YOU
Ahuh
YOU LEFT ME TO DEAL WITH IT. Y-YOU LEFT ME ALONE.
WH...WH... WHAT WOULD MAKE ME DO THAT...?

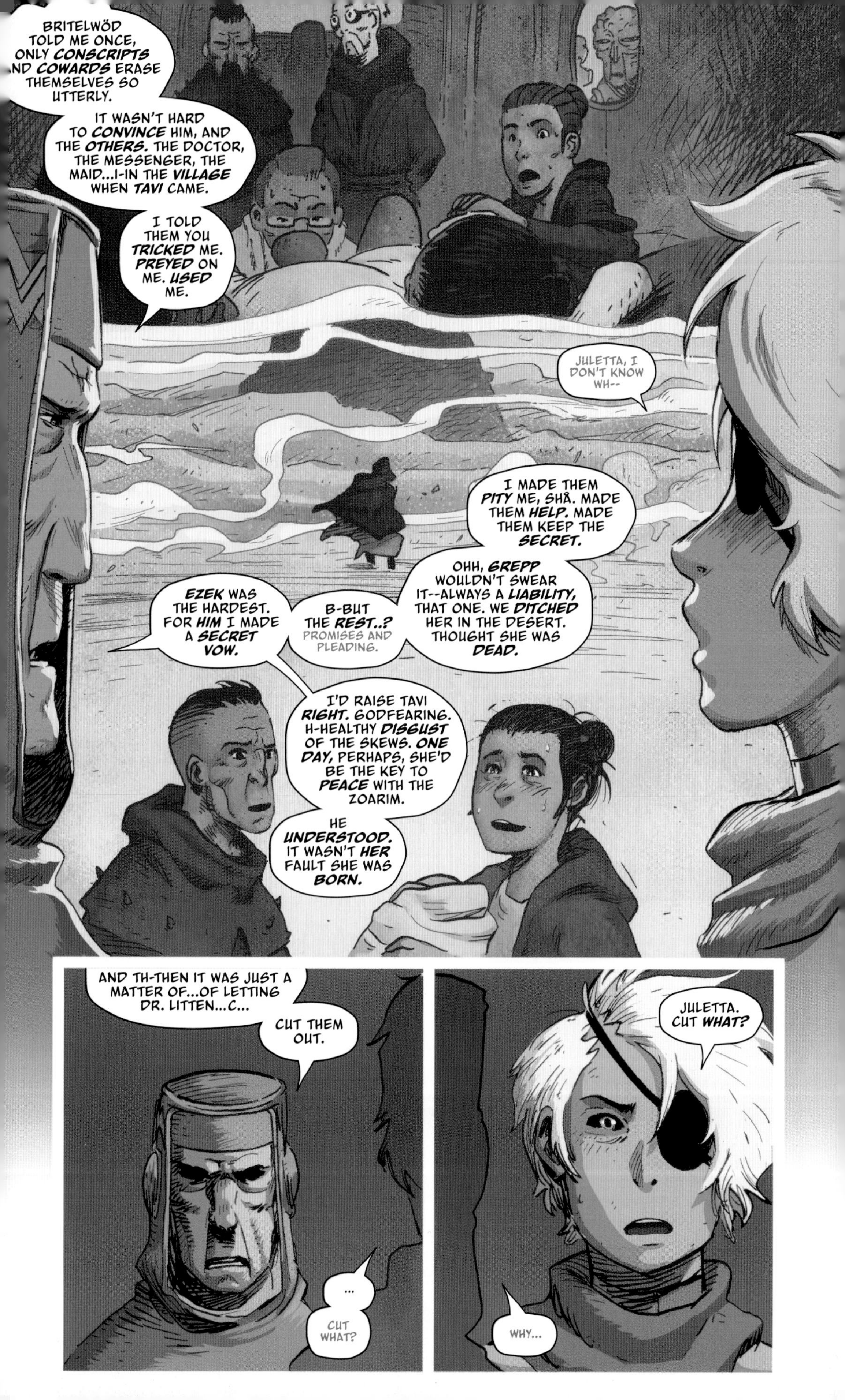
BRITELWÖD TOLD ME ONCE, ONLY CONSCRIPTS AND COWARDS ERASE THEMSELVES SO UTTERLY.
IT WASN'T HARD TO CONVINCE HIM, AND THE OTHERS. THE DOCTOR, THE MESSENGER, THE MAID...I-IN THE VILLAGE WHEN TAVI CAME.
I TOLD THEM YOU TRICKED ME. PREYED ON ME. USED ME.
JULETTA, I DON'T KNOW WH--
I MADE THEM PITY ME, SHÅ. MADE THEM HELP. MADE THEM KEEP THE SECRET.
OHH, GREPP WOULDN'T SWEAR IT--ALWAYS A LIABILITY, THAT ONE. WE DITCHED HER IN THE DESERT. THOUGHT SHE WAS DEAD.
B-BUT THE REST..? PROMISES AND PLEADING.
EZEK WAS THE HARDEST. FOR HIM I MADE A SECRET VOW.
I'D RAISE TAVI RIGHT. GODFEARING. H-HEALTHY DISGUST OF THE SKEWS. ONE DAY, PERHAPS, SHE'D BE THE KEY TO PEACE WITH THE ZOARIM.
HE UNDERSTOOD. IT WASN'T HER FAULT SHE WAS BORN.
AND TH-THEN IT WAS JUST A MATTER OF...OF LETTING DR. LITTEN...C...
CUT THEM OUT.
...
CUT WHAT?
JULETTA. CUT WHAT?
WHY...

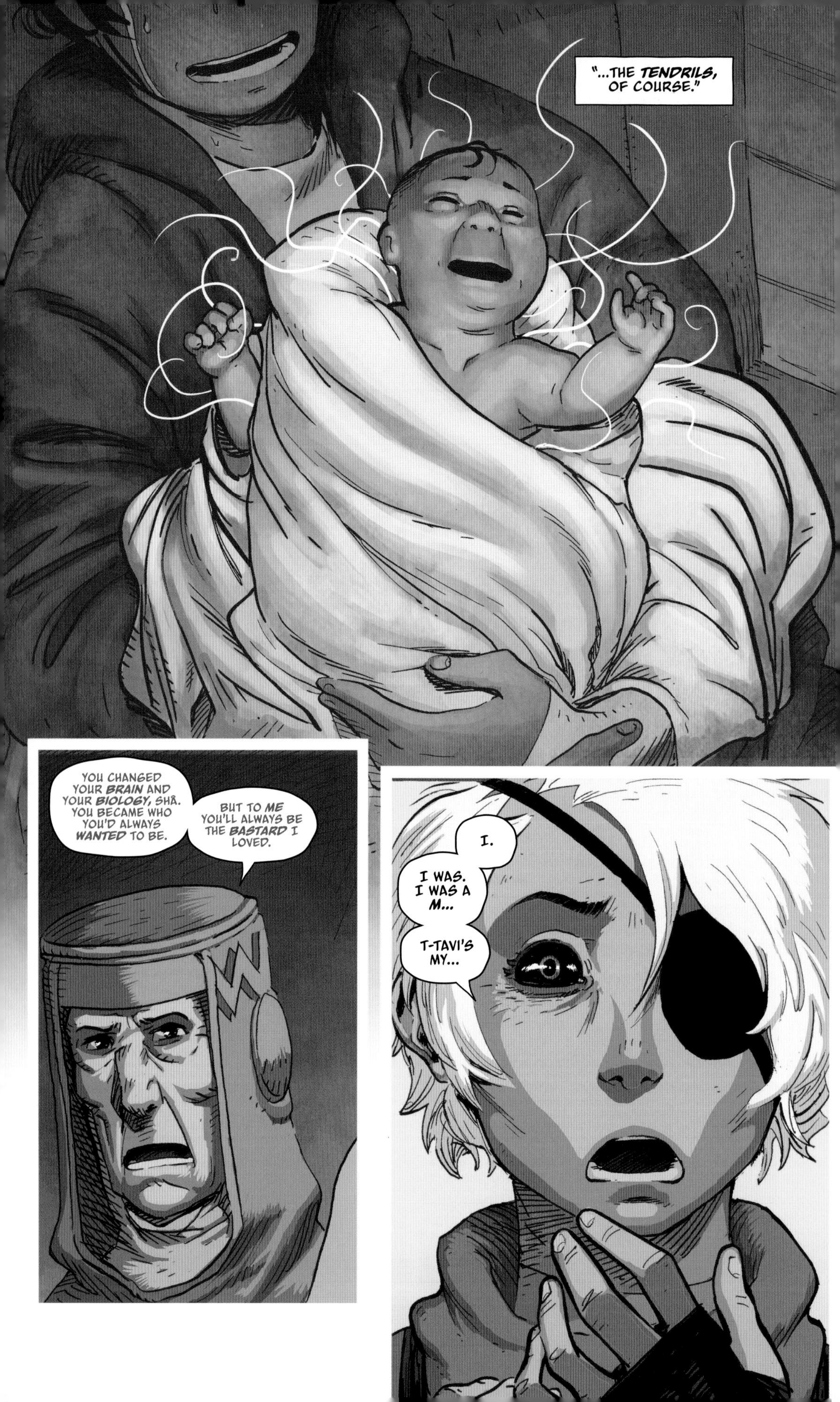

"...THE TENDRILS, OF COURSE."
YOU CHANGED YOUR BRAIN AND YOUR BIOLOGY, SHĀ. YOU BECAME WHO YOU'D ALWAYS WANTED TO BE.
BUT TO ME YOU'LL ALWAYS BE THE BASTARD I LOVED.
I.
I WAS. I WAS A M...
T-TAVI'S MY...

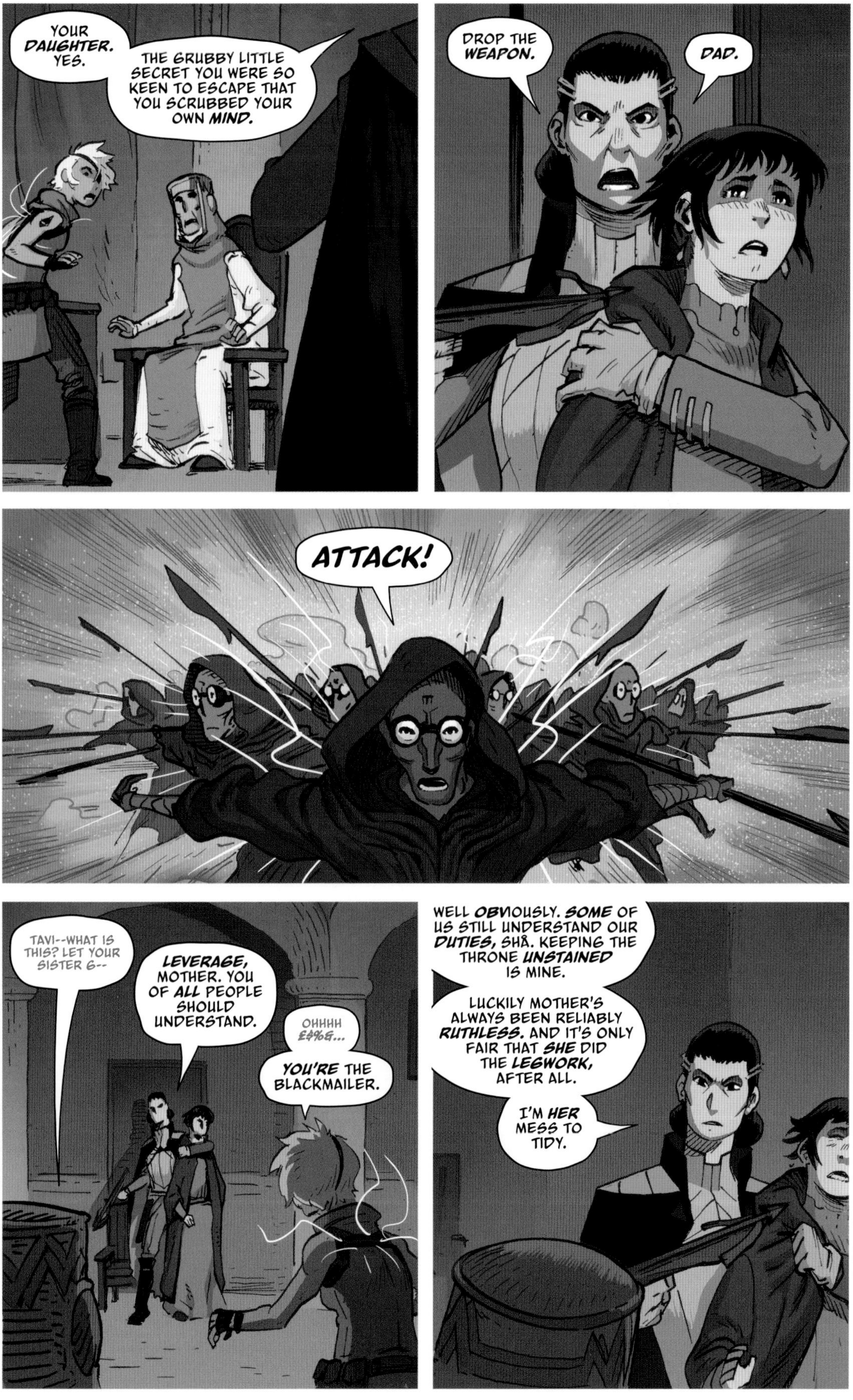
YOUR DAUGHTER. YES.
THE GRUBBY LITTLE SECRET YOU WERE SO KEEN TO ESCAPE THAT YOU SCRUBBED YOUR OWN MIND.
DROP THE WEAPON.
DAD.
ATTACK!
TAVI--WHAT IS THIS? LET YOUR SISTER G--
LEVERAGE, MOTHER. YOU OF ALL PEOPLE SHOULD UNDERSTAND.
OHHHH £$%&...
YOU'RE THE BLACKMAILER.
WELL OBVIOUSLY. SOME OF US STILL UNDERSTAND OUR DUTIES, SHÅ. KEEPING THE THRONE UNSTAINED IS MINE.
LUCKILY MOTHER'S ALWAYS BEEN RELIABLY RUTHLESS. AND IT'S ONLY FAIR THAT SHE DID THE LEGWORK, AFTER ALL.
I'M HER MESS TO TIDY.

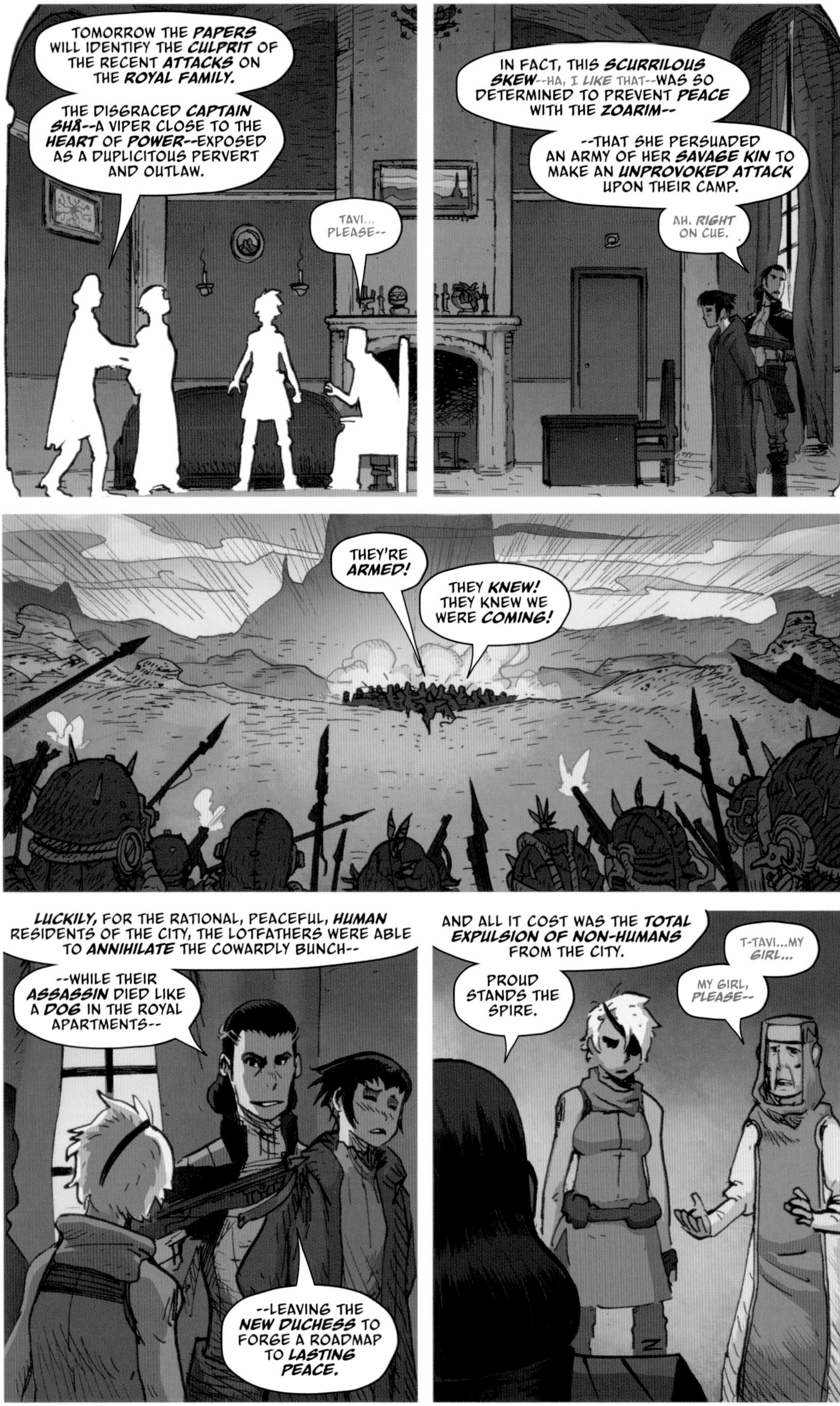
TOMORROW THE PAPERS WILL IDENTIFY THE CULPRIT OF THE RECENT ATTACKS ON THE ROYAL FAMILY.
THE DISGRACED CAPTAIN SHÂ--A VIPER CLOSE TO THE HEART OF POWER--EXPOSED AS A DUPLICITOUS PERVERT AND OUTLAW.
TAVI... PLEASE--
IN FACT, THIS SCURRILOUS SKEW--HA, I LIKE THAT--WAS SO DETERMINED TO PREVENT PEACE WITH THE ZOARIM--
--THAT SHE PERSUADED AN ARMY OF HER SAVAGE KIN TO MAKE AN UNPROVOKED ATTACK UPON THEIR CAMP.
AH. RIGHT ON CUE.
THEY'RE ARMED!
THEY KNEW! THEY KNEW WE WERE COMING!
LUCKILY, FOR THE RATIONAL, PEACEFUL, HUMAN RESIDENTS OF THE CITY, THE LOTFATHERS WERE ABLE TO ANNIHILATE THE COWARDLY BUNCH--
--WHILE THEIR ASSASSIN DIED LIKE A DOG IN THE ROYAL APARTMENTS--
--LEAVING THE NEW DUCHESS TO FORGE A ROADMAP TO LASTING PEACE.
AND ALL IT COST WAS THE TOTAL EXPULSION OF NON-HUMANS FROM THE CITY.
PROUD STANDS THE SPIRE.
T-TAVI...MY GIRL...
MY GIRL, PLEASE--

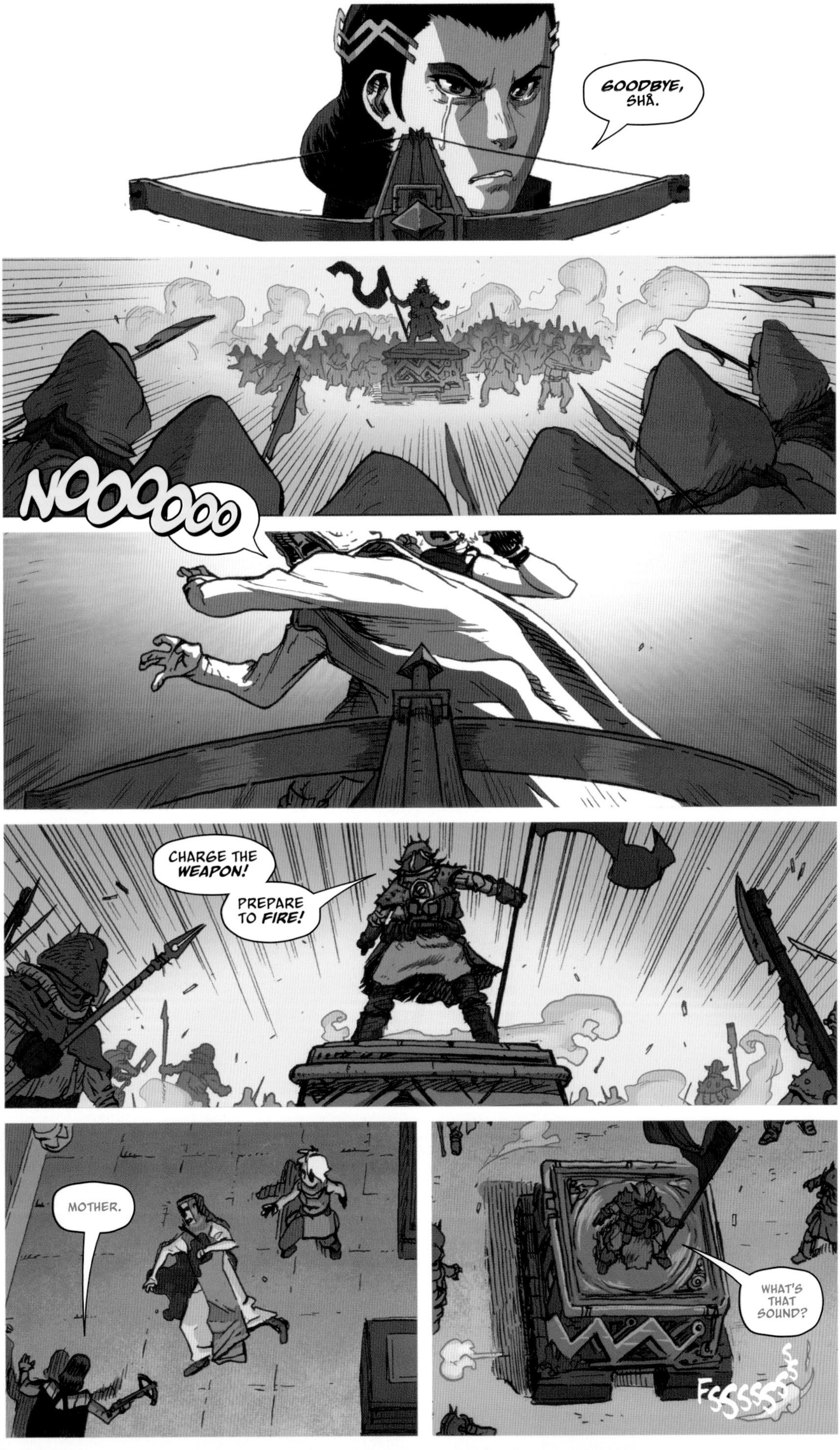
GOODBYE, SHÅ.
NOOOOOOO
CHARGE THE WEAPON!
PREPARE TO FIRE!
MOTHER.
WHAT'S THAT SOUND?
FSSSSSSSSSS

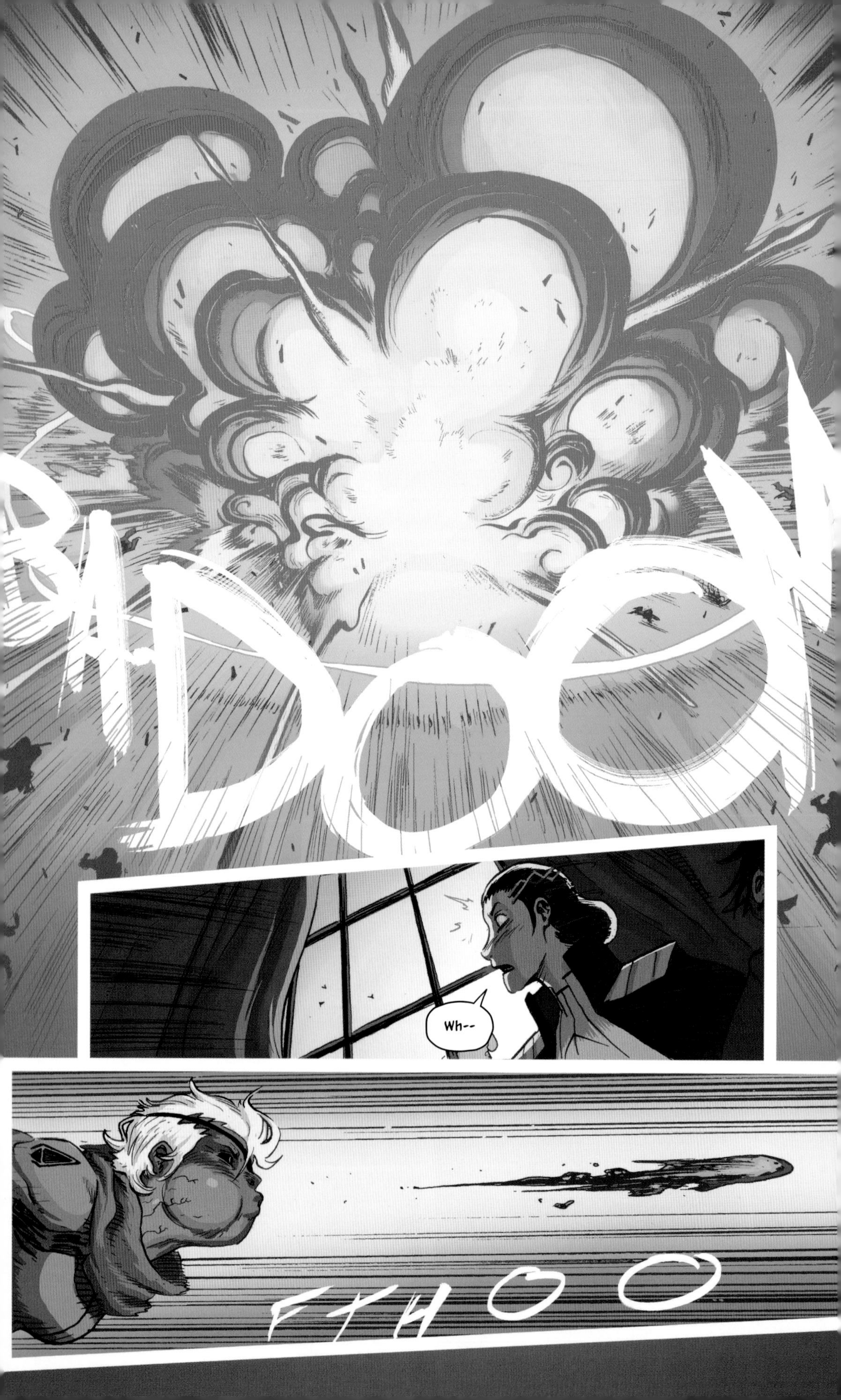
BADOO
Wh--
FTHOO

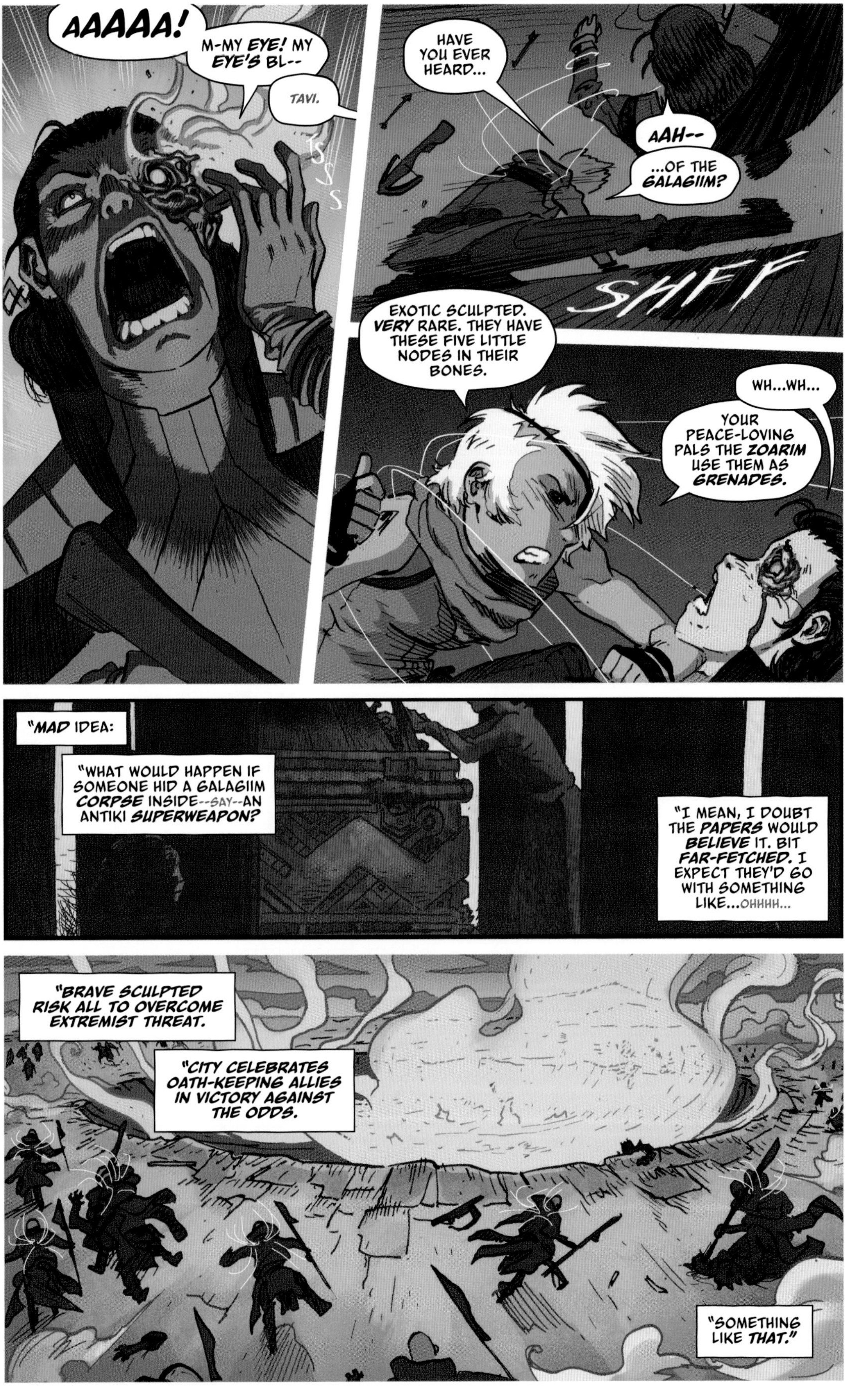
AAAAA!
M-MY EYE! MY EYE'S BL--
TAVI.
TSSS
HAVE YOU EVER HEARD...
AAH--
...OF THE GALAGIIM?
SHFF
EXOTIC SCULPTED. VERY RARE. THEY HAVE THESE FIVE LITTLE NODES IN THEIR BONES.
WH...WH...
YOUR PEACE-LOVING PALS THE ZOARIM USE THEM AS GRENADES.
"MAD IDEA:
"WHAT WOULD HAPPEN IF SOMEONE HID A GALAGIIM CORPSE INSIDE--SAY--AN ANTIKI SUPERWEAPON?
"I MEAN, I DOUBT THE PAPERS WOULD BELIEVE IT. BIT FAR-FETCHED. I EXPECT THEY'D GO WITH SOMETHING LIKE...OHHHH...
"BRAVE SCULPTED RISK ALL TO OVERCOME EXTREMIST THREAT.
"CITY CELEBRATES OATH-KEEPING ALLIES IN VICTORY AGAINST THE ODDS.
"SOMETHING LIKE THAT."

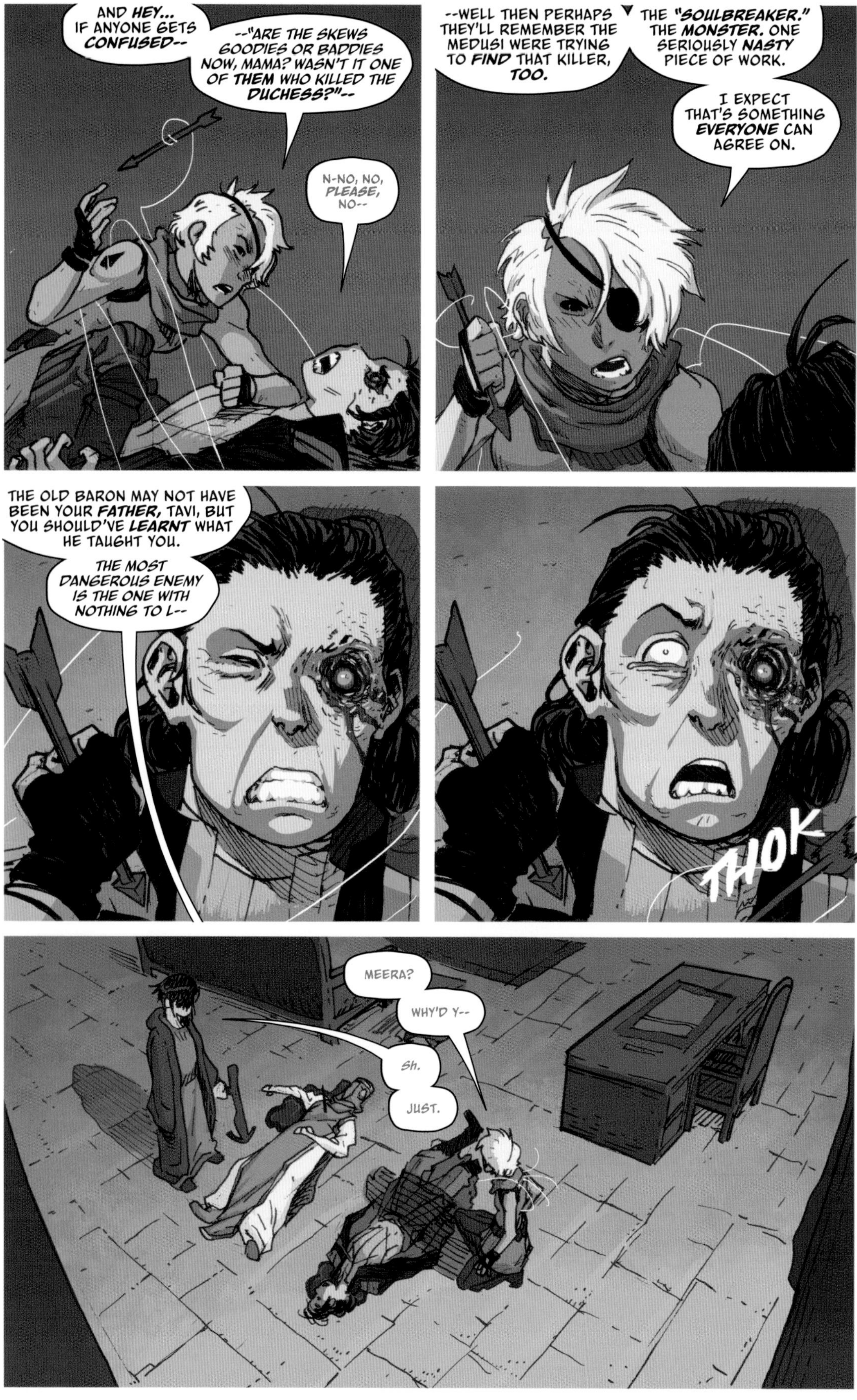
AND HEY... IF ANYONE GETS CONFUSED--
--"ARE THE SKEWS GOODIES OR BADDIES NOW, MAMA? WASN'T IT ONE OF THEM WHO KILLED THE DUCHESS?"--
N-NO, NO, PLEASE, NO--
--WELL THEN PERHAPS THEY'LL REMEMBER THE MEDUSI WERE TRYING TO FIND THAT KILLER, TOO.
THE "SOULBREAKER." THE MONSTER. ONE SERIOUSLY NASTY PIECE OF WORK.
I EXPECT THAT'S SOMETHING EVERYONE CAN AGREE ON.
THE OLD BARON MAY NOT HAVE BEEN YOUR FATHER, TAVI, BUT YOU SHOULD'VE LEARNT WHAT HE TAUGHT YOU.
THE MOST DANGEROUS ENEMY IS THE ONE WITH NOTHING TO L--
THOK
MEERA?
WHY'D Y--
Sh.
JUST.

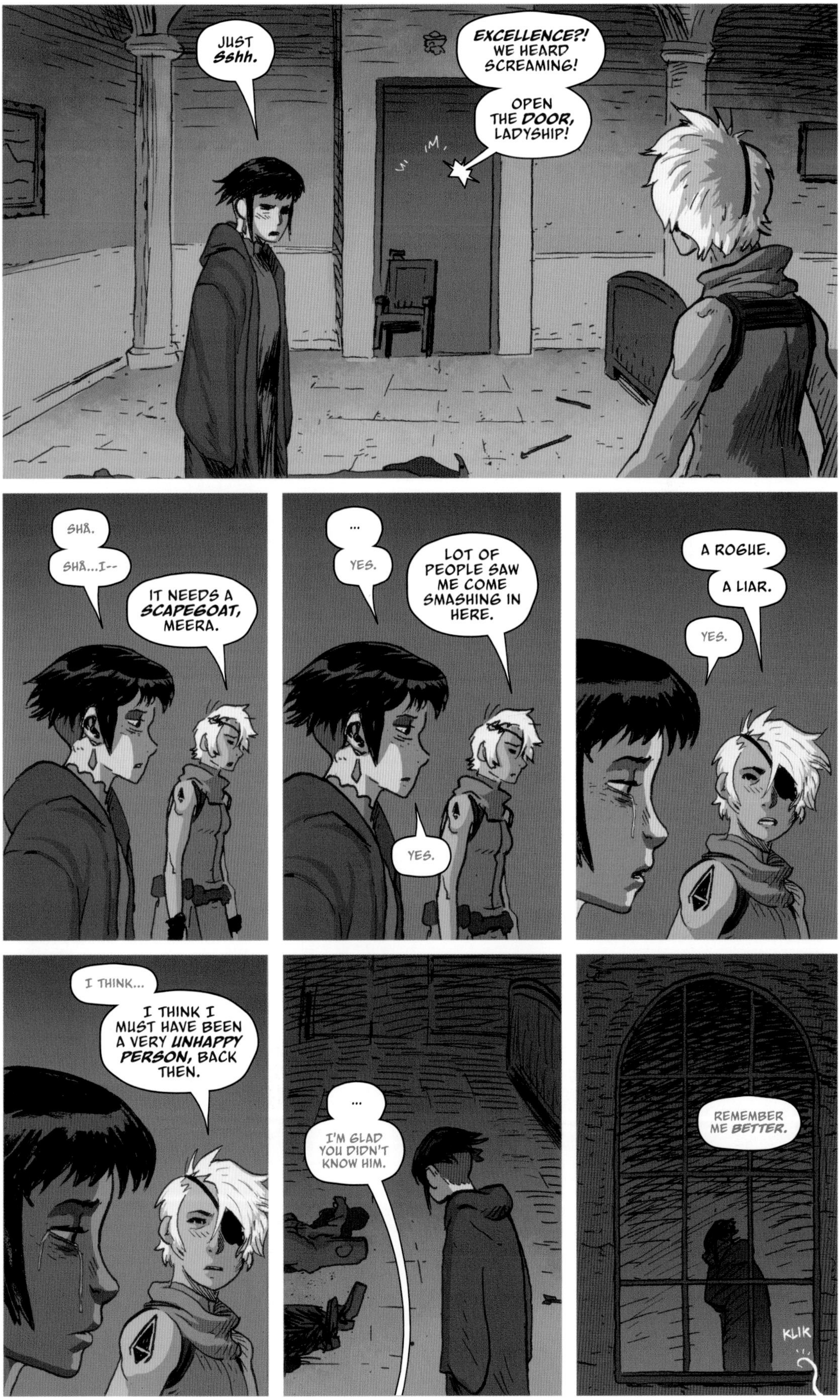
JUST *Sshh.*
EXCELLENCE?! WE HEARD SCREAMING!
OPEN THE *DOOR,* LADYSHIP!
SHÅ.
SHÅ...I--
IT NEEDS A *SCAPEGOAT,* MEERA.
...
YES.
LOT OF PEOPLE SAW ME COME SMASHING IN HERE.
YES.
A ROGUE.
A LIAR.
YES.
I THINK...
I THINK I MUST HAVE BEEN A VERY *UNHAPPY PERSON,* BACK THEN.
...
I'M GLAD YOU DIDN'T KNOW HIM.
REMEMBER ME *BETTER.*
KLIK

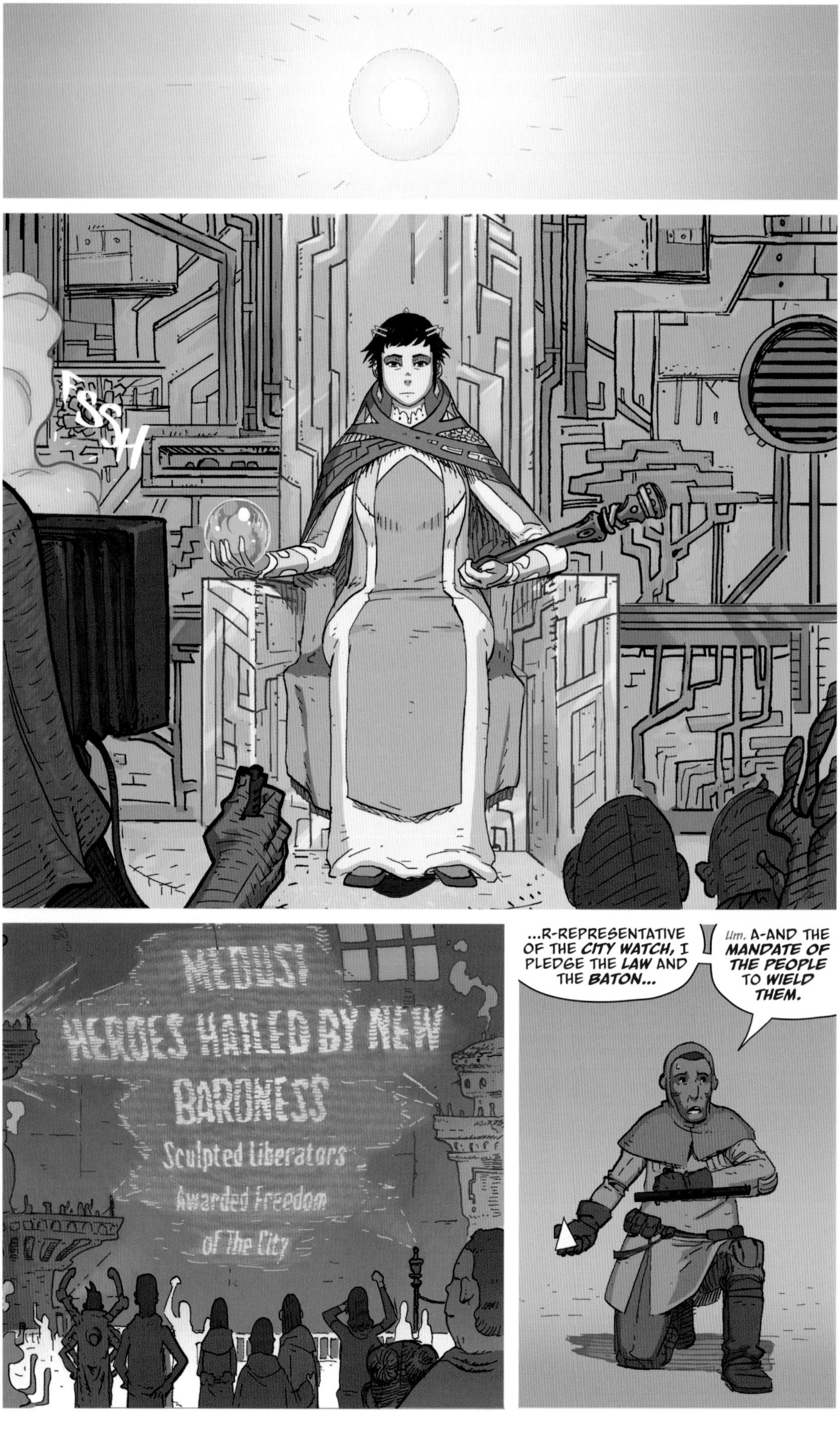
FSSH
HEROES HAILED BY NEW BARONESS
Sculpted Liberators Awarded Freedom of The City
...R-REPRESENTATIVE OF THE CITY WATCH, I PLEDGE THE LAW AND THE BATON...
Um. A-AND THE MANDATE OF THE PEOPLE TO WIELD THEM.

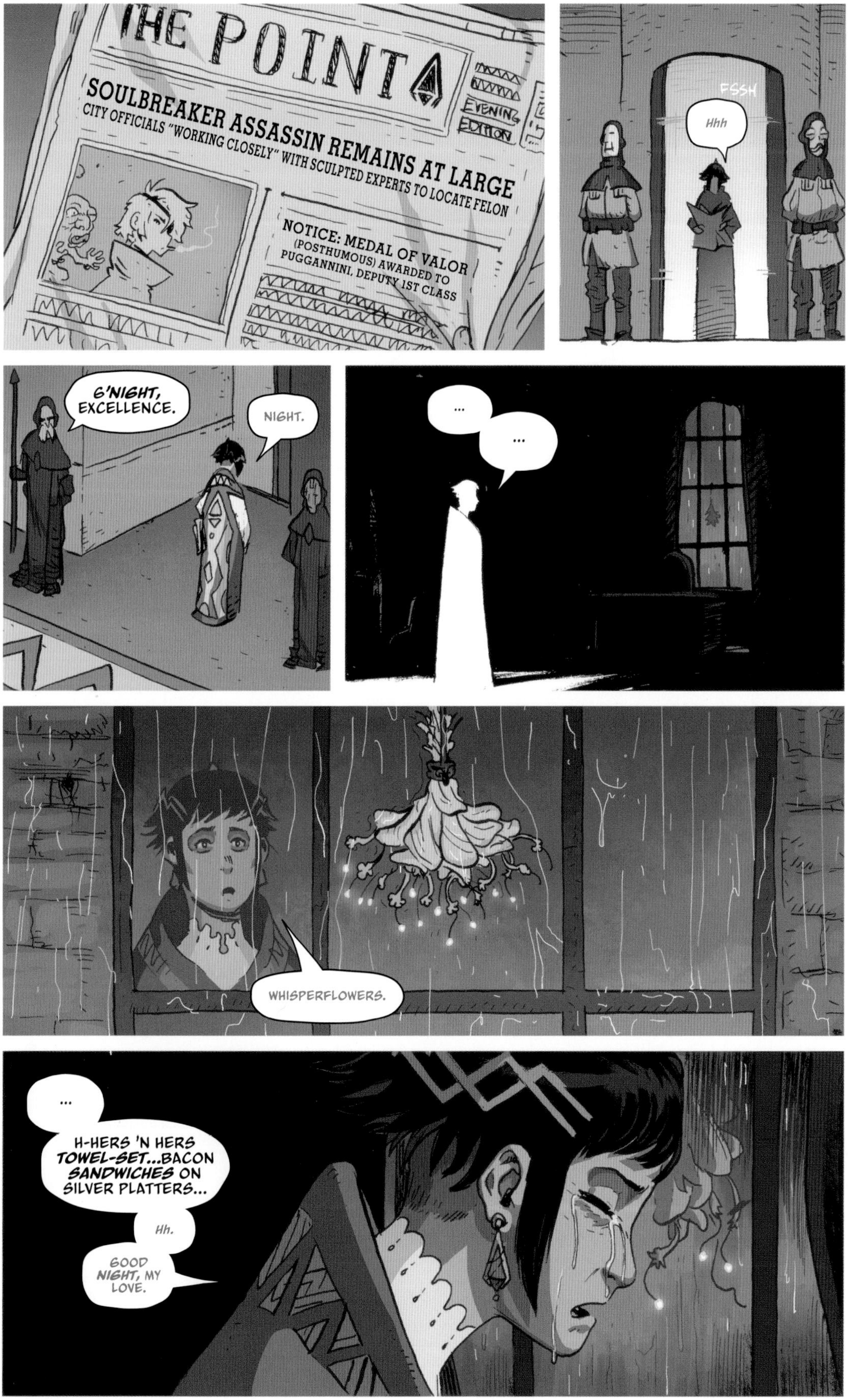
THE POINT
SOULBREAKER ASSASSIN REMAINS AT LARGE
CITY OFFICIALS "WORKING CLOSELY" WITH SCULPTED EXPERTS TO LOCATE FELON
EVENING EDITION
NOTICE: MEDAL OF VALOR (POSTHUMOUS) AWARDED TO PUGGANNINI, DEPUTY 1ST CLASS
FSSH
Hhh
G'NIGHT, EXCELLENCE.
NIGHT.
...
...
WHISPERFLOWERS.
...
H-HERS 'N HERS TOWEL-SET...BACON SANDWICHES ON SILVER PLATTERS...
Hh.
GOOD NIGHT, MY LOVE.

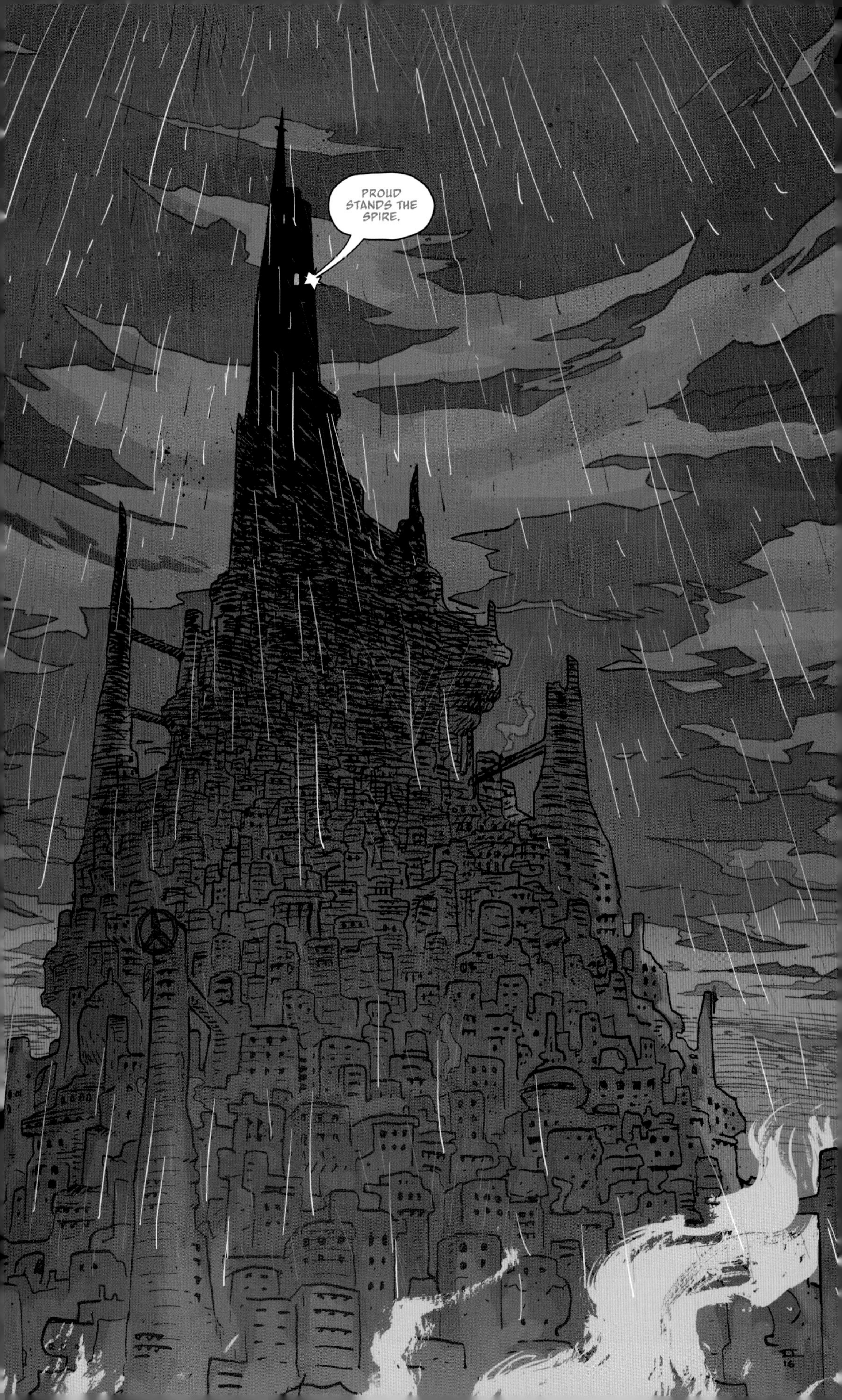
PROUD STANDS THE SPIRE.

ISSUE #8 COVER BY **JEFF STOKELY**
WITH COLORS BY **TAMRA BONVILLAIN**

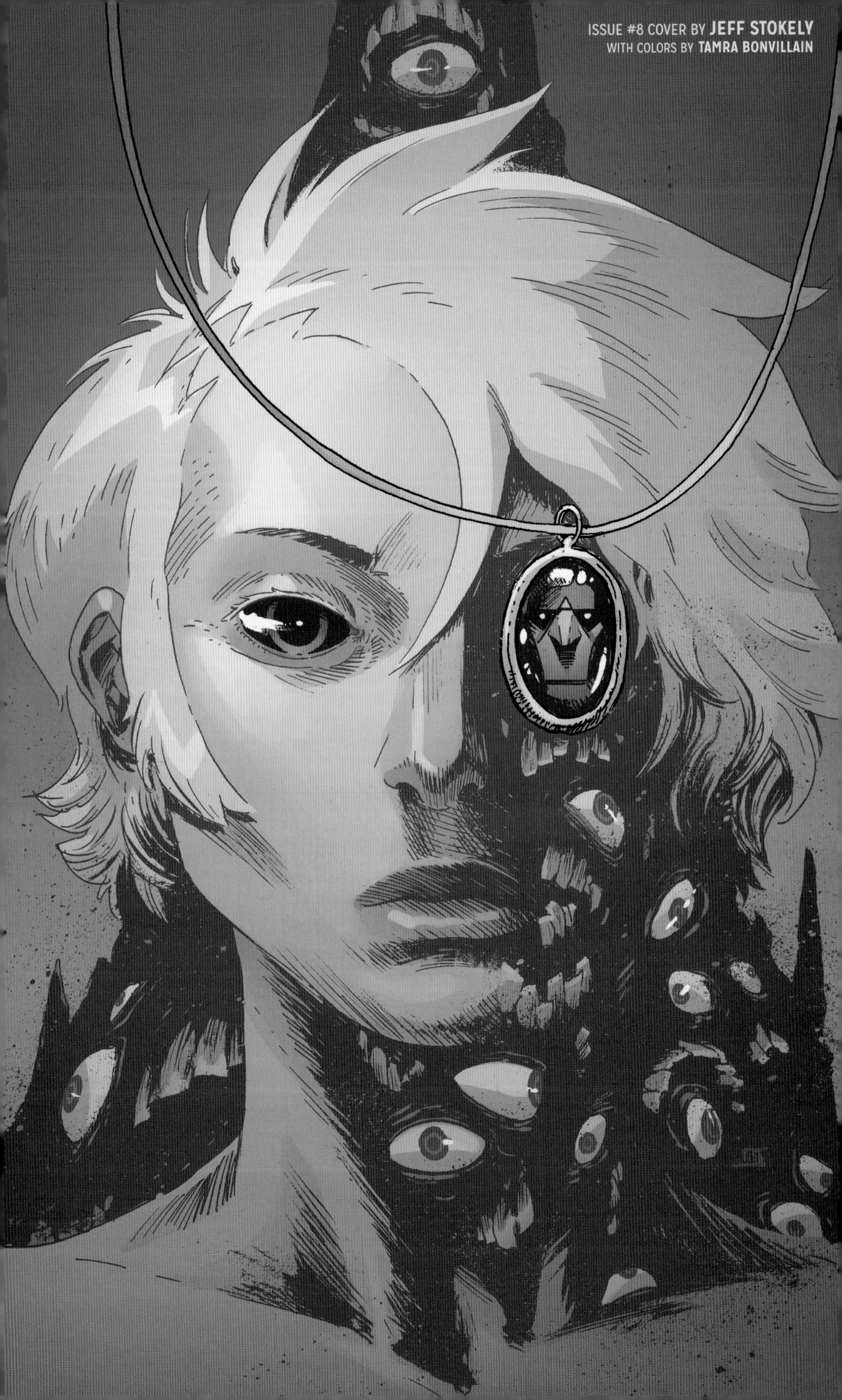

ISSUE #1 SECOND PRINT COVER BY
JEFF STOKELY

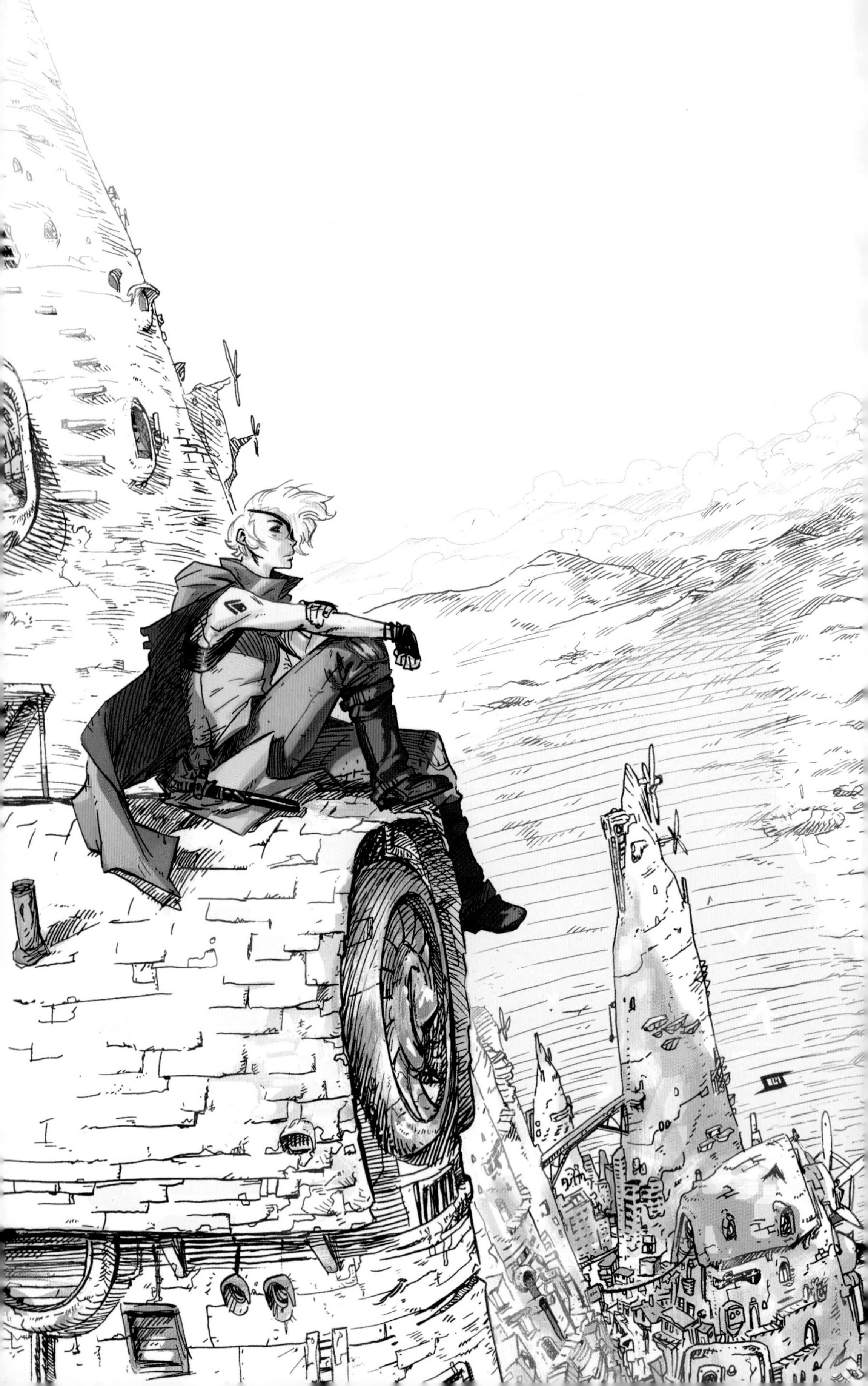

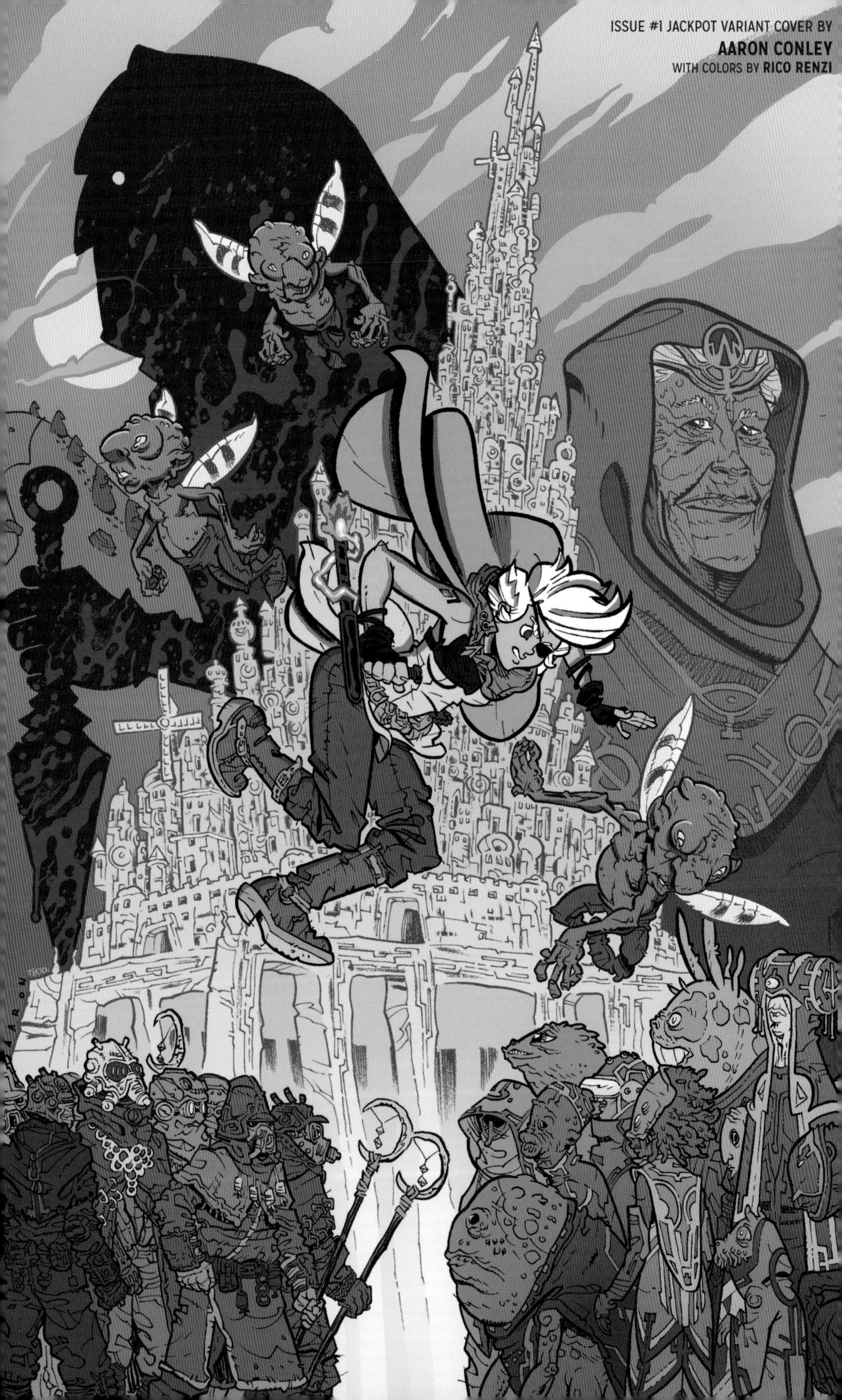

ISSUE #1 JACKPOT VARIANT COVER BY
AARON CONLEY
WITH COLORS BY **RICO RENZI**

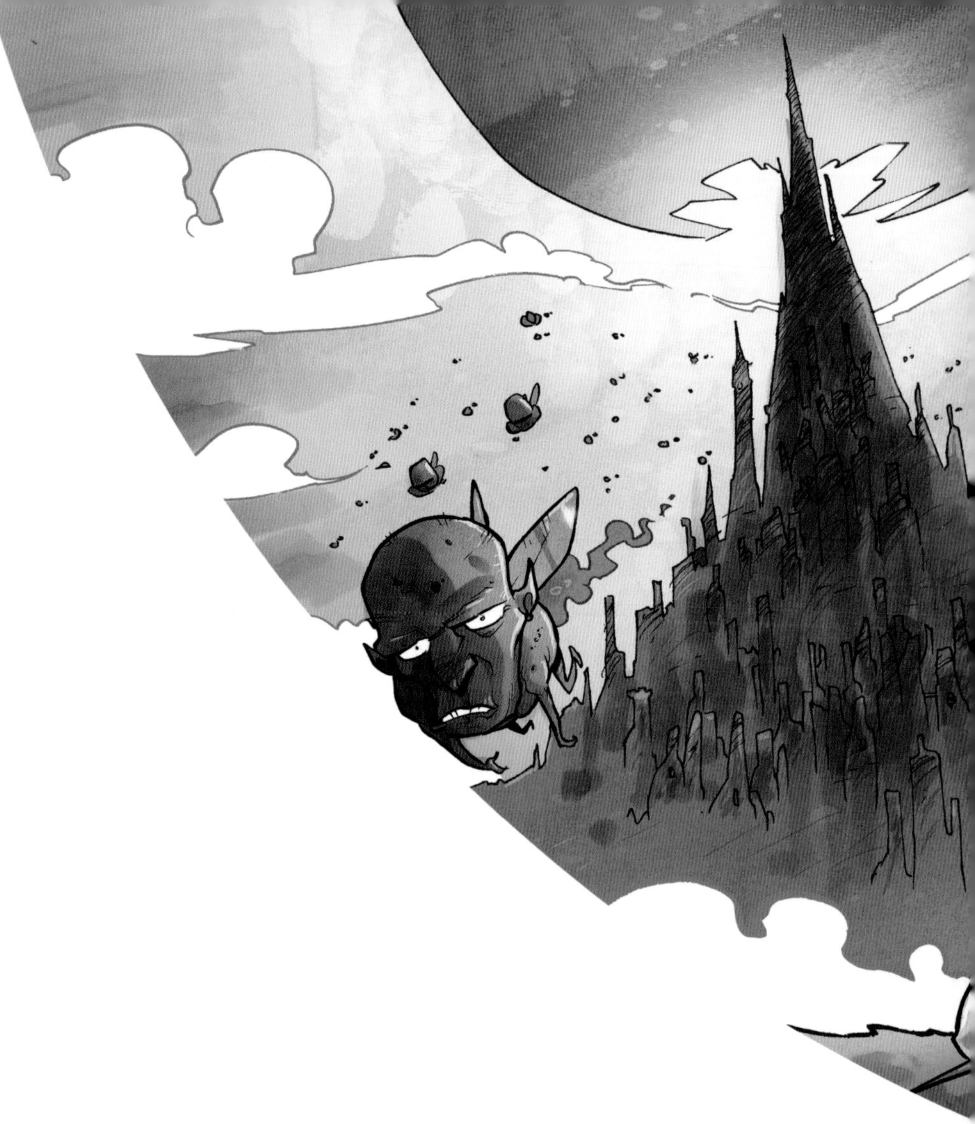

ISSUE #1 BOOM! TEN YEARS VARIANT COVER BY
ROB GUILLORY

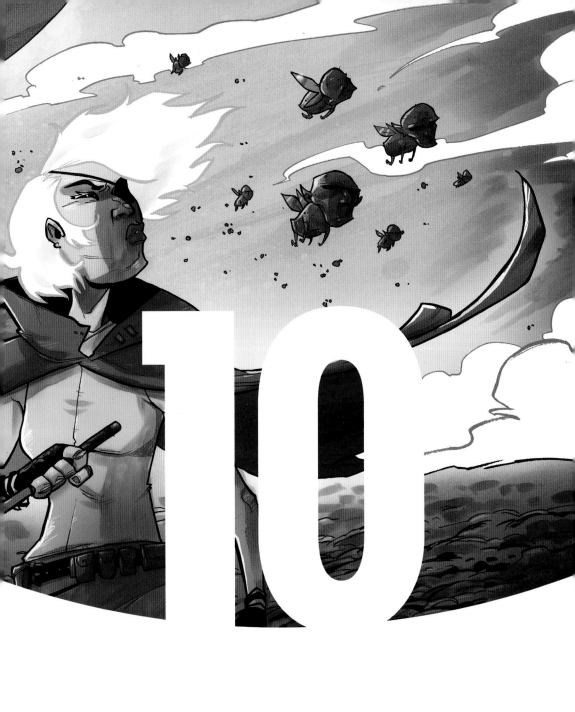

ISSUE #1 VARIANT COVER BY

DAVID LAFUENTE

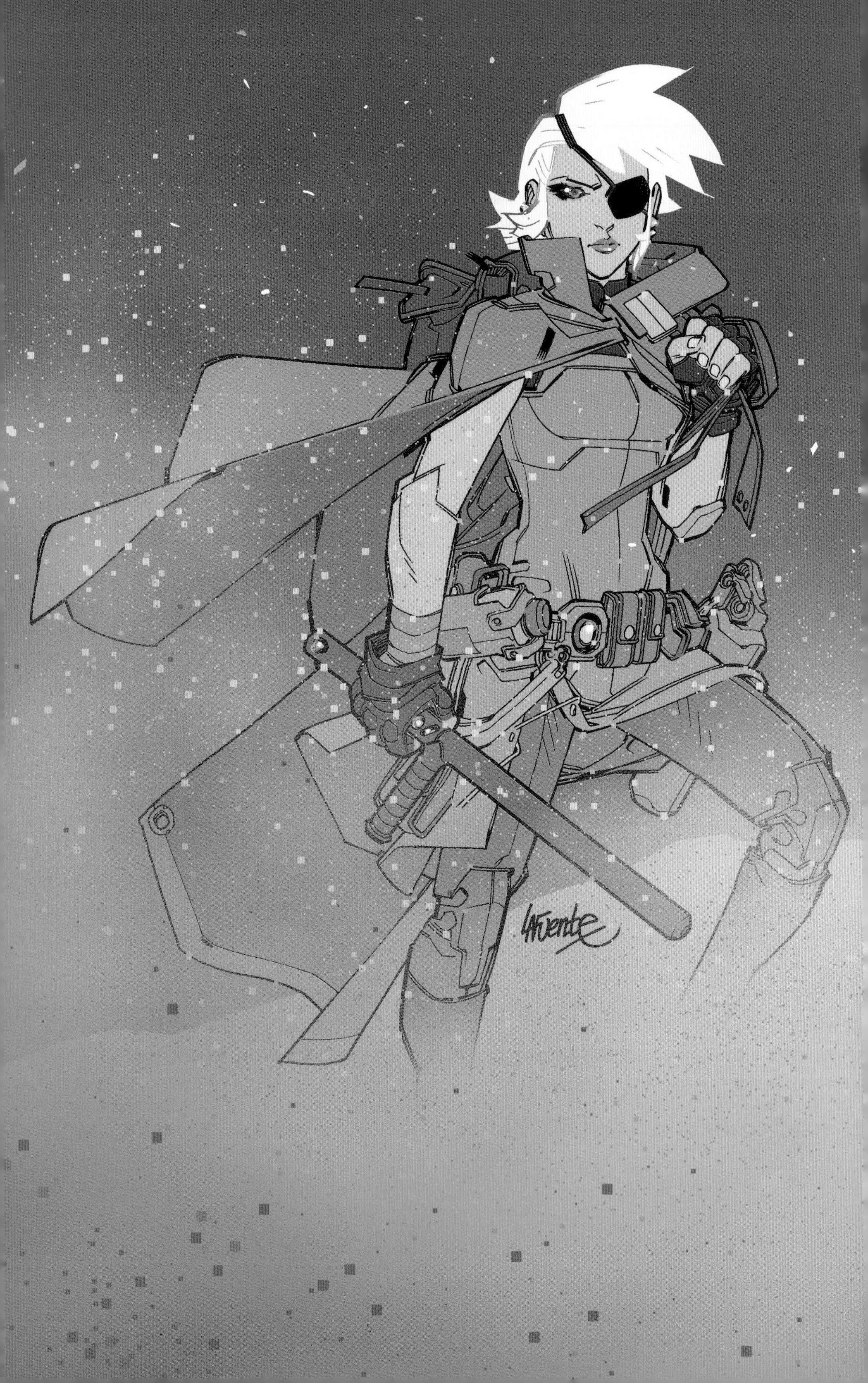

LAFUENTE

ISSUE #1 MIDTOWN COMICS EXCLUSIVE
NYCC 2015 VARIANT COVER BY
JAMIE McKELVIE

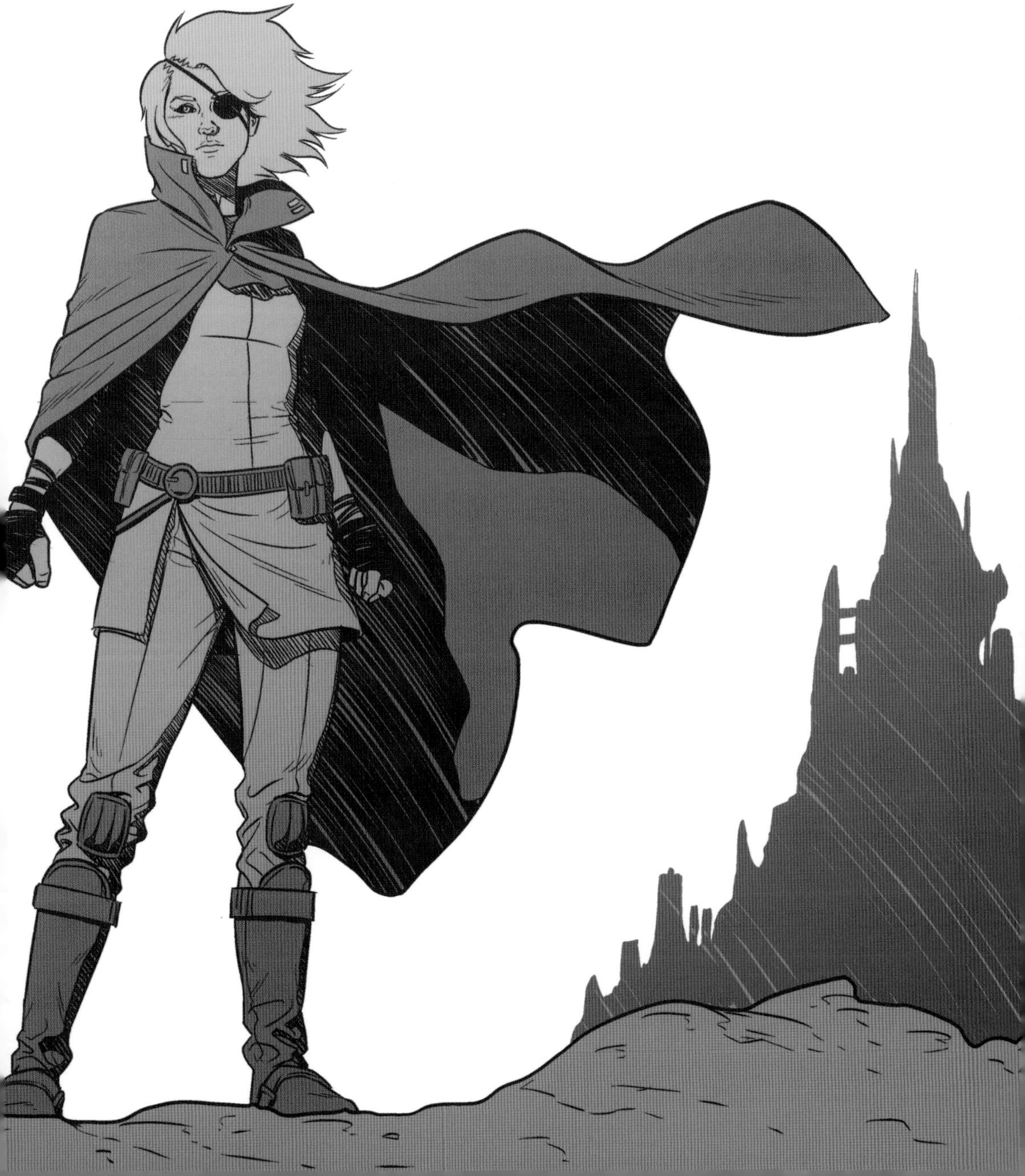

Not Controlling the Outcome:
Si Spurrier and Jeff Stokely Talk *The Spire*

Interview by Keith Silva for ComicsBulletin.com, originally published April 29, 2015

What made the two of you decide *The Spire* would be the next Spurrier-Stokely joint?

Si Spurrier: For me—and I hate to admit this while the beardy upstart is listening (it never pays to let an artist learn his or her importance, it bungs up their creative circuitry)—but yes, it arose from the powerful desire to work with Jeff again.

Six-Gun Gorilla was one of those projects I sat down to build before I even knew who'd be drawing it, so the writing process was a very personal thing. I think that's reflected in some of the more contemplative and metafictional elements which bubbled out of the mix from that particular comic. When Jeff started turning in pages I had the privilege of witnessing an alchemy unique to our medium, in which something I'd considered **solely mine** suddenly manifested a whole new creative spirit, and became greater than the sum of its parts. All, somehow, without lessening my sense of an authorial connection to the work. Magical stuff.

So, yes, I wanted more. And I wanted to do it more organically this time 'round: bringing in Jeff at the very top, insisting that he and I share all creator rights, and letting things develop symbiotically rather than retrospectively.

Generally speaking I detest elevator pitches, loglines and similar reductive story short-selling, but I'm also a horribly manipulative bastard, so to get Jeff's attention I started with something I knew he could never possibly refuse. "It's *Blade Runner* meets *Dark Crystal* by way of *Mad Max*." To an artist of the genus Stokely, that's like sex made of chocolate.

Jeff Stokely: It's a rare and truly awesome thing for a publisher to put together a creative team and have something like *Six-Gun Gorilla* come out of that. I don't think BOOM! or any of us could tell how much that book would mean to us all by the time it was done. It was like a magical comic-making blind date. Since then I've told Si on several slovenly drunken occasions that I'd work with him again in

a heartbeat. And it's true. So when he told me he wanted to make *Dark Crystal*-y *Blade Runner* sex chocolate with *Mad Max* sprinkles, I was quite helpless to resist. Those are literally all of the things I cherish most in the world lumped into one steaming pile.

How do each of you leave the world-building so as not to make it cumbersome let alone stall the process of telling the story?

Spurrier: My sense is readers put far more emotional investment into a world which feels like it's functional and continuous, rather than one which defines itself according to big events or big plot-points. People respond to worlds dotted with relatable stories and characters; worlds of which they're given small glimpses, rather than onerous descriptions and backstories, or genealogies and maps.

Why should I give a toss about a reality whose only interesting feature is that Doomlord Graglathox (or who-the-bollocks-ever) wants to burn it to cinders in the unpronounceable name of his crappy Chthonic hell-god? Or a galaxy which sits On! The! Cusp! Of! Annihilation! Or a world so shamefully ill-conceived that it needs bucketloads of magic macguffins, secret wizard-passwords or mother@#$%ing dragons to make actual stories occur within it. In other words, with *The Spire* we wanted to create a world which doesn't feel as though it disappears the moment the story's over. The key, very simply, is to give way more of a damn about the characters.

With *The Spire* I wanted to work with Jeff to create a huge, mysterious, strange, unforgettable world—and then to somewhat ignore that in favor of the tight, razor-sharp story unfolding in the midst of it. I wanted the world of the Spire to be extraordinary…but to feel ordinary to the people who live there. I wanted the world to impinge upon the narrative *only* in as much as events become more fascinating or more bizarre than if our story were set in the real world, but then to maintain an internal logic which doesn't rely on contrivance or macguffin. I wanted our characters' reactions to be human and sympathetic, no matter how strange or inhuman they themselves may seem.

In practical terms what this meant was setting out the rough edges of the world and deliberately leaving gaping holes for Jeff to work his magic. Technologies, inhuman races, even the architecture of the city itself: they all play very prominent roles in the story or its subtext, and they've all been built by Jeff from scratch, rather than described by me. That was a scary relinquishment of responsibility, at first, but for one thing I never doubted Jeff could deliver, and for another it's a weirdly honest application of fantasy thought. Real people don't live in worlds which have been perfectly designed to accommodate them and their stories, after all. People *don't* spend their time walking around, blurting exposition about how their TVs or cellphones work, what their moral code is based upon, why they've chosen to wear *that* hat instead of *that* one, etc. Genre stories—especially sci-fi and fantasy—are frequently guilty of all the above, when in fact I suspect readers get a lot more involved in stories where things aren't laboriously explained. Hence it felt *right* to be inventing a world where half of it—the stuff coming out of Jeff's brain—was a mystery to me.

Stokely: This is a great question because it took me months to get the look of this world how I wanted it, and it still evolves from page to page. To peg back to what Si said, part of the creative process on my end is very much me thinking to myself, "How can I convey exactly what Si wants out of this character? But also, how can I push that idea's design on the page and add in my own spice?" And then sometimes I'll do something that I just think is dumb and fun and Si will end up loving it. Not to simplify Si's taste, but we share a lot of common interests and I know that chances are if it's off the wall and makes me laugh, it'll make him laugh.

I've done plenty of concept sketches, just getting the right feel for the various inhabitants and cultures. Most of which are great and bizarre, but oddly enough a lot of choices have boiled down to fashion for me. The Spire is a singular structure with dozens of cultures and races, but they all fall at the whim of its societal hierarchy. This was important from day one, the design had to reflect these undertones that run throughout the story. Which brings us back to inhabiting a believable world with believable problems. It's world-building 101.

Interestingly enough, for the look of the world I haven't used any photo reference regarding settings or structures, I've tried to pull all of that from my own imagination and logic it out. Doing that, I hope, will breathe a sense of mystery into the Spire and its subset societies. It also keeps me on my toes.

Readers are going to see references to *Heavy Metal* and manga (specifically Miyazaki). Was this a conscious choice as creators or do you see *The Spire* as a chance to write a chapter in that tradition?

Spurrier: Not an act of conscious homage, I think, but those are certainly some of the texts we've each internalized over the years, which quite conspicuously influenced *The Spire*. For me it's a ragged pulp-up of *2000AD's* "@#$% you" to the Rules Of Genre, China Mieville's elaborately febrile imagination, and *Nausicaä*-era Miyazaki's attention to detail, with a dusting of *Gormenghast* and *Dune* over the top. But comics are at their best when neither artist nor writer has a controlling interest in the outcome, and the work winds up being greater than the sum of its collective schizophrenic influences.

Ultimately, I see *The Spire* as a twisty, funny, blood-drenched thriller led by an extraordinary woman—quite possibly the snarkiest and kickass-iest she-cop in comics—which just happens to take place in one of the most fascinating worlds ever created. The latter part is possibly the feature people will talk about most, but it's the former parts which do the heavy lifting.

Stokely: I like to think there's a bit of *Heavy Metal* and manga in everything I do. At least I hope so, it's what I read the most during my impressionable years. Miyazaki and Moebius are certainly huge influences to me and just about every living artist I know, and they're quite shamelessly present here. They'll most definitely be the ones people reference most with this book.

I've been wanting to steer away from my brush work for a while now (not permanently) because I always find the sketches in my sketchbook to be closer to that loose scratchy line art style that Miyazaki uses in *Nausicaä*, or even the look of his overall design. So this has been the perfect chance for me to try and hone that style, which is oddly both natural and foreign for me on the finished page. So to put it more simply, while they are influences they aren't controlling influences.

I do think once people see the book in full color, it will really live on its own merit. One of the beautiful things about André's colors is he's incredibly versatile and has changed his style a bit to match mine. It's like we're all stepping out of our comfort zones while not trying to hide our influences. After all, there's really no point in this day and age to hiding them.

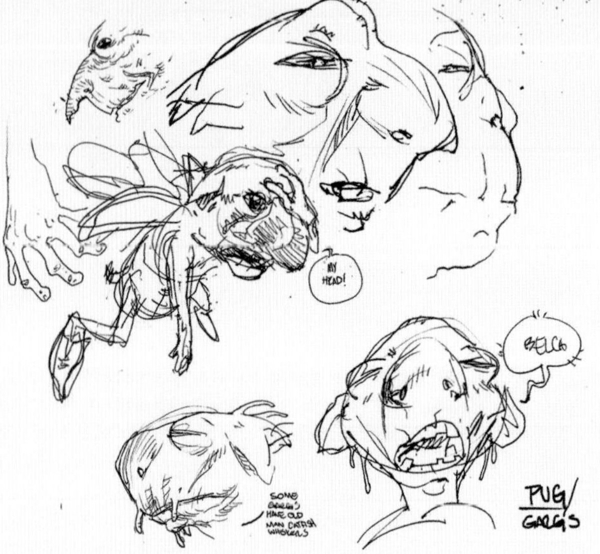
MY HEAD!
BELCH
PUG/
GARGS

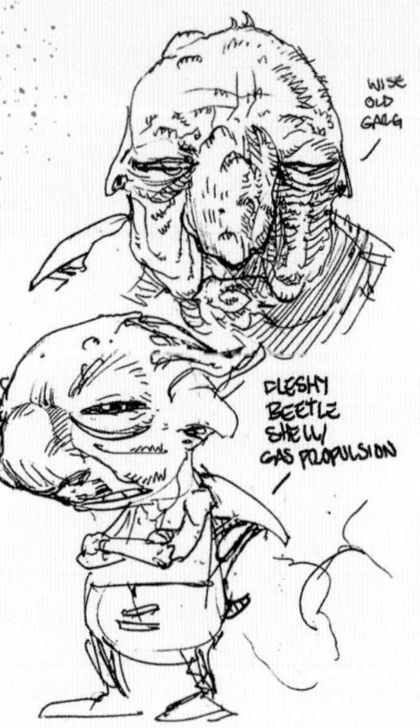
WISE
OLD
GARG
FLESHY
BEETLE
SHELL/
GAS PROPULSION

Who's Shå and why the ring diacritic over the "a"—got a thing for Swedes?

Spurrier: Shå is…incredible. Funny, warm, sharper than a lightsaber lobotomy. For those who've enjoyed my take on Doctor Nemesis, she's cut from a similarly snarky cloth. But she's also riddled with secrets and doesn't understand herself nearly as well as she'd like. This is the sort of comic where the mystery of the external always mirrors the mystery of the internal.

She's the Captain of the City Watch, which is the dysfunctional civilian organization—dreadfully overstretched—which polices the majority of the titular "Spire": a mega-structural city which juts from the desert like an inconceivably vast termite hill. In the Spire, status and social class are indelibly linked to altitude: the higher one lives in the city the more affluent and cultured one probably is. Hence the aristocrats, oligarchs, and media-wankers live in the uppermost portions, while the dregs sink to the bottom. That is: Shå's beat.

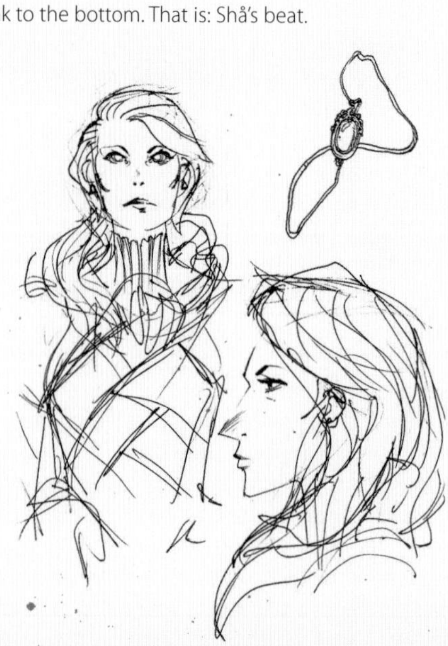

The Spire is a weird—but also weirdly recognizable—melting pot of social pressures. Its people pride themselves on being inclusive, progressive and non-prejudiced, but of course ideals are never quite as shiny as they seem when you look at them in dim light. In the Spire's case it's the immigrant classes which get the crappiest deal: members of strange hybrid-races whose origins are unrecorded, who come to the city for work and sanctuary. They're called "skews," or "the sculpted" if you're feeling polite. In public the city's ideological culture calls for their integration and equality; in private people mutter and resent.

It has been fascinating to play with a very specific breed of social commentary here. In a lot of ways the Spire represents a society we'd all like to see—Shå doesn't get any @#$% for being a gay woman in a powerful position, for instance—but like a worm that has to wriggle out somewhere, people always find someone to blame. In the Spire's case that's the skews. And, like a bird waiting for the worms, there's *always* someone looking to exploit that blame.

Regarding that diacritic ring over the "a," that's one of those daft little details which has gathered some unexpected significance as the boulder rolls downhill. For reasons I can't adequately explain, presumably to do with some second-level abstract onomatopoeia, the syllable "Shah" was one of the first bits of flotsam which tangled itself around the seed of this idea. I couldn't write the word just-so—too many real-world connotations—and the obvious umlaut (Shä) made my beloved protagonist look like a reject from a Tolkien-inspired metal band. The diacritic ring feels more right—there's enough ambiguity and regional variance in its meaning that people can cheerfully call her "Shaugh" or "Shau" or "Shae" if they prefer—and in a (frankly invisible) sort of way it's informed some of my thoughts and decisions about Shå's own people.

Jeff, who's the character you most wanted to draw as you and Si were developing the story?

Stokely: There are so many! Hard to pin just one down. Developing all of the skews and non-humans was so much fun. Probably too much fun, as it cut into my actual page-drawing time. They're challenging, though; Si and I both knew they couldn't be "too alien" or "too fantasy" yet had to still be something people didn't look at and go, "Oh, a mutant." So, trying to hit a look that makes people question its origin rather than jump to the conclusion.

I really love drawing Shå, it's been incredibly fun but also challenging just trying to get her to emote with one eye and I think it's actually working better than I'd hoped. Her expressions become really unique in that regard and I think it only helps serve her singularity in the story. I did about two or three sheets of various designs of her before settling on the current one which came more naturally as a doodle in my sketchbook. Which oddly enough brings me back to the point of trying to hone my finished art to be closer to my sketches (I know, it sounds quite backwards). There's another character who I think Si and I love, who's started as a background character with this huge brain tank thing on the top of his head. I love that guy. Brain-tank guy.

Though the character I really, truly, wholly enjoy drawing the most is probably the killer.

Comics have been experiencing a science fiction and fantasy renaissance of late—why and what's going to make The Spire stand out?

Spurrier: Urgh. Horribly unfair question.

Okay, well…I'll gloss over the "why" part—if only because I have some deeply entrenched and frankly rather ranty views about the whole concept of genre classification, specifically the fact that it's a pitiful, unhealthy, and totally-unfit-for-purpose system designed to accommodate administrators while forcing everyone else into reductive cliché-defined little holes which actively punish originality and fusion—yes indeed, I'll gloss over that and instead pirouette gracefully into the part about what will make *The Spire* stand out.

Firstly and most obviously, the art is scintillatingly good and totally unique. In Jeff I've found a collaborator who eschews conventional design and intuits storytelling solutions like an artist twice his age. He's destined for the big time, but not in some dismal bloody House Style sort of way. He's already a favorite of a lot of the biggest names out there—though that's possibly just because of his delicious beard—and *The Spire* is his first major creator-owned project. Very worth a look.

For those of you whose interest isn't adequately piqued by beautiful art or attractively hirsute artists, *The Spire* is a totally unique tale from a world unlike any other, full of the intimate and the epic in equal measure, coiled around layers of mystery and led by the world's grumpiest inhuman detective.

If you absolutely must use genre terminologies, then it's an apocalyptic fantasy murder-mystery comedy sci-fi conspiracy thriller, but we'd far rather you kept things sibilant and went for "strange, singular, startling, sinister, sexy, secretive."

Stokely: Plus, how many sci-fi fantasy-whatevers out there have beetle-winged, fart-propulsion cherub goblins? JUST ONE!

ROSS RICHIE CEO & Founder
MATT GAGNON Editor-in-Chief
FILIP SABLIK President of Publishing & Marketing
STEPHEN CHRISTY President of Development
LANCE KREITER VP of Licensing & Merchandising
PHIL BARBARO VP of Finance
BRYCE CARLSON Managing Editor
MEL CAYLO Marketing Manager
SCOTT NEWMAN Production Design Manager
IRENE BRADISH Operations Manager
SIERRA HAHN Senior Editor
DAFNA PLEBAN Editor, Talent Development
SHANNON WATTERS Editor
ERIC HARBURN Editor
WHITNEY LEOPARD Associate Editor
JASMINE AMIRI Associate Editor
CHRIS ROSA Associate Editor
ALEX GALER Associate Editor
CAMERON CHITTOCK Associate Editor
MARY GUMPORT Assistant Editor
MATTHEW LEVINE Assistant Editor
KELSEY DIETERICH Production Designer
JILLIAN CRAB Production Designer
MICHELLE ANKLEY Production Designer
GRACE PARK Production Design Assistant
AARON FERRARA Operations Coordinator
ELIZABETH LOUGHRIDGE Accounting Coordinator
STEPHANIE HOCUTT Social Media Coordinator
JOSÉ MEZA Sales Assistant
JAMES ARRIOLA Mailroom Assistant
HOLLY AITCHISON Operations Assistant
SAM KUSEK Direct Market Representative
AMBER PARKER Administrative Assistant

THE
SPIRE
™

SIMON **SPURRIER**
JEFF **STOKELY**
ANDRÉ **MAY**